Guarding Neutral Ireland

Guarding Neutral Ireland

The Coast Watching Service and
Military Intelligence, 1939–1945

MICHAEL KENNEDY

FOUR COURTS PRESS

Typeset in 10.5 pt on 12.5 pt Ehrhardt by
Carrigboy Typesetting Services
FOUR COURTS PRESS LTD
7 Malpas Street, Dublin 8, Ireland
e-mail: info@fourcourtspress.ie
and in North America for
FOUR COURTS PRESS
c/o ISBS, 920 NE 58th Avenue, Suite 300, Portland, OR 97213.

A catalogue record for this title is available
from the British Library.

ISBN 978–1–84682–097–7

SPECIAL ACKNOWLEDGMENT

This publication has received support from the Heritage Council
under the 2008 Publications Grant Scheme.

AN
CHOMHAIRLE
OIDHREACHTA

THE
HERITAGE
COUNCIL

Printed in England
by Cromwell Press, Trowbridge, Wiltshire.

Contents

'A little study of Irish history ... ought to convince anyone of the exceptional importance of Ireland in relation to questions of maritime and naval power and having arrived at this state the natural sequel ought to be an examination of Ireland's relation to these mighty problems and how they are likely to affect the Saorstát in peace and more particularly in war.'

Captain Dan Bryan, G2,
September 1927

'National defence problems are primarily affected by geography.'

Commandant Dan Bryan, G2,
'Fundamental Factors Affecting Saorstát Defence Problem',
May 1936

'Geography itself was a decisive factor in the character of the planes which overflew our territory.'

Joseph Walshe, Secretary, Department of External Affairs,
December 1943

Abbreviations and conventions

All times are in 24-hour clock.

'Army' refers to the army of the Irish Defence Forces.

'Ireland' refers to the twenty-six county state established under the 1921 Anglo-Irish Treaty.

'Éire' is used when it appears in direct quotations and to refer to navigation signs constructed in 1943 and 1944 along the Irish coast; the E is accented even if no accent was used.

AA	Anti-Aircraft
ADC	Air Defence Command
AMI	Air and Marine Intelligence
ARP	Air Raid Protection
ASDIC	Allied Submarine Detection Investigation Committee
ASV	Air-to-Surface-Vessel (Radar)
ATFERO	Atlantic Ferry Organization
BOAC	British Overseas Airways Corporation
BDST	British Double Summer Time
C3	Garda Crime and Security Branch
CIC	Combined Intelligence Committee (Britain)
CIO	Command Intelligence Officer
DNI	Director of Naval Intelligence (Admiralty)
DRS	Daily Reports Summary
FAW7	Fleet Air Wing 7 (United States Navy)
G2	Intelligence Branch of the Irish Defence Forces
GHQ	General Headquarters
GOC	General Officer Commanding
IO	Intelligence Officer
IRA	Irish Republican Army
IST	Irish Summer Time
LDF	Local Defence Force
LOP	Look Out Post
LSF	Local Security Force
M&CWS	Marine and Coast Watching Service
MI5	Military Intelligence Section 5, correctly, the Security Service

MI6	Military Intelligence Section 6, correctly, SIS, the Secret Intelligence Service
NCO	Non-Commissioned Officer
NID	Naval Intelligence Department (Admiralty)
OC	Officer Commanding
OIC	Operational Intelligence Centre (Admiralty)
OPW	Office of Public Works
OSS	Office of Strategic Services (USA)
RAF	Royal Air Force
RCAF	Royal Canadian Air Force
RDF	Radio Direction Finding
RUC	Royal Ulster Constabulary
SHAEF	Supreme Headquarters Allied Expeditionary Force
SIS	Secret Intelligence Service (MI6)
SSF	Security Segregated Files
USAAF	United States Army Air Force
VLR	Very Long Range

Acknowledgments

A VISIT TO A RUINED Coast Watching Service Look Out Post (LOP) on a headland in north Mayo in April 2003 began my curiosity with the soldiers who manned these LOPs during the Second World War, known as 'The Emergency' in neutral Ireland. It led me to investigate the conflict they recorded in the skies and seas along the Irish coast. The story of the Coast Watching Service, unarmed observers who became Ireland's front line defence force during the Second World War, is told below. Their tale shows that Ireland, though a neutral, could not escape the global conflict and how geography placed Ireland on the frontline of the war in the Atlantic. Neutrality precluded overt Irish involvement in the Second World War as a belligerent, but the history of the Coast Watching Service shows that the war came to Irish seas and skies notwithstanding. It shows that the Irish government and its military forces could not and did not retreat and ignore the war in Europe, but rather that they sought a full understanding of the conflict and responded to threats and opportunities as far as Ireland's limited military resources allowed.

Between 2003 and 2007 I visited as many of the surviving ruined LOPs as possible. These trips were made more pleasant by the company of friends and I would like to thank them: Dairin Evers-Nolan, Dr Marnie Hay, Dr Ivar McGrath, Alan Kennedy, Dr David Lee, Gillian Murphy, Simon Nolan, Dr Susannah Riordan, Neville Scarlett and Dee Smyth.

Research into the operations of the Coast Watching Service involved much archival work, primarily at Military Archives, Cathal Brugha Barracks, in Rathmines in Dublin. I would like to thank the Director of Military Archives, Commandant Victor Laing, and his colleagues Commandant Pat Brennan, Commandant Billy Campbell, Captain Stephen McEoin, Sergeant Chris Donovan and Private Alan Manning. They were unfailingly generous with their time as I pieced together the history of the Coast Watching Service from the records in their care. When it came to viewing examples of the equipment mentioned below – from aircraft to anti-aircraft guns – my thanks to Airman Michael Whelan, Curator of the Air Corps Museum at Casement Aerodrome, Baldonnell, an expert guide through the collection in his care. My thanks also to Billy Galligan at the Defence Forces Press Office for permission to use photographs in his care.

The coastwatchers operated locally within the national military structure but the information they gathered had a national and international audience. Examining the wider role of the Coast Watching Service brought me to a number of archives. I would particularly like to thank Dr David Craig and his staff at the National Archives of Ireland; Seamus Helferty and his colleagues at the University College Dublin Archives; the staff of the archives of An Garda Síochána; the staff of the National Archives and Records Administration, College Park, Maryland, especially Michael Hussey and Bob Chadduck, and the staff of the National Archives, Kew, London especially Hugh Alexander.

Sandra McDermott at the National Library of Ireland and Sara Smyth at the National Photographic Archive were immensely helpful in my last minute search for illustrations. So too was Kirsten Beasty at ITN Source who tracked down the newsreel footage which is included in the cover illustration.

I was uniquely lucky to have Simon Nolan's assistance and advice while researching and writing this book. Simon put at my disposal his own encyclopaedic knowledge of legal, military, air and marine affairs and his extensive library. He answered many of my queries about military matters and cast a critical eye over the text. Any errors or omissions below are my own but a great deal fewer of them remain thanks to Simon.

Michael Adams, Martin Healy, Martin Fanning and their colleagues at Four Courts Press showed an immediate interest in this work when I first discussed its publication with them. I was delighted when they accepted this work for publication and I thank them for their support and help in seeing the work through to publication.

I also thank General Bill Callaghan, Professor Louis Cullen, Professor Fergus d'Arcy, Dr Anne Dolan, Bob Donaldson, John Donnelly, Colonel E.D. Doyle, Alan Kennedy, Anthony Kennedy, Catherine Kennedy, Dr John Logan, Dr Deirdre MacMahon, Conor Galvin, Dr Till Geiger, Sheelagh Hawkins, Colonel Richard Heaslip, Colonel Tom Kelly, Tony Kinsella, Mary Layden, James McBride, Niall McCarthy, Sanchia O'Connor, Professor Eunan O'Halpin, Dr Kate O'Malley, Colonel Dr Terry O'Neill, Finbarr O'Shea, Maura O'Shea, Professor Hilary Owen, James Sharkey, Pat Sweeney, Joe Varley, Dr Bernadette Whelan, Captain Richard N. White and Professor Clair Wills. Between them, they lent or directed me to source material, spoke to me about the Coast Watching Service, commented on the text, sent me pictures of Coast Watching Service LOPs, gave me a place to write and on occasion a bed for the night during my travels. I must thank the many people I met as I traipsed the Irish coastline who provided information on the location of LOPs. In particular, I am grateful, where a post was on private property, to landowners who let me cross their lands to see the post in question. Finally, as always, I thank Susannah, who, though she expressed very early on in the research for this book a 'finite interest' in scrambling along barren hillsides and bleak headlands to visit abandoned LOPs, was always supportive of my research and writing and displayed her characteristic tolerance when our trips to various parts of Ireland were reorganized enroute to include a diversion to yet another LOP.

Eros at Errarooey Strand

O N 14 JUNE 1940, the day Paris fell to the Wehrmacht, Volunteers McFadden and Greer of the Coast Watching Service were on duty at Horn Head LOP. From the 700-foot summit of this isolated headland on the north Donegal coast they had a panoramic view over the Atlantic Ocean. At 2130 that summer evening they sighted an 'armed cruiser' of unknown nationality four miles to the north-east steaming west towards a stationary vessel of the Irish Marine Service. The two coastwatchers recorded that the armed cruiser 'came alongside [the] Eire patrol vessel and brought five men on board and proceeded west'.[1] Their report is sparse, though it and other sources show that the Irish craft was the deep-sea trawler *Fort Rannoch*, converted for military use, and the 'armed cruiser' was a British vessel.[2] While the coastwatchers did not identify the nationality of the five men, reading the Horn Head LOP logbook in the context of local naval activity suggests that they were British seamen.

The Horn Head logbook reveals more about this unusual episode and why an Irish Marine Service patrol vessel, a vessel from a neutral state, was rendez-vousing with a Royal Navy ship, a vessel from a belligerent power. Earlier on 14 June *Fort Rannoch* had sailed from nearby Port na Blagh and patrolled north through Sheep Haven, around Horn Head and west towards Errarooey Strand, where on 8 June a British cargo ship, *Eros* (5,888 tons), had beached.[3] En-route from Montreal to Liverpool without escort, *Eros* had been less than one hundred miles off north-west Donegal when, at 0322 on 7 June, she was torpedoed by the German submarine U-48.[4] There were no fatalities among *Eros*' sixty-two crew but the attack damaged the ship's propulsion system. The British rescue tug *Bandit* met the crippled *Eros* and, in calm seas and clear skies, *Bandit* – escorted by the Hunt Class destroyer HMS *Berkeley* – towed the crippled merchant vessel stern first towards Lough Swilly in Donegal. By the afternoon of 7 June *Eros* had become 'much deeper by the head' and was unlikely to make Lough Swilly.[5] Reports received by the Irish Defence Forces suggested that the vessel

1 Military Archives, Cathal Brugha Barracks, Dublin (hereafter MA), LOP 77, 14 June 1940.
2 The Marine Service's second patrol vessel *Muirchú* was patrolling off the south coast while *Eros* was at Errarooey. Motor torpedo boat *M1* was expected off Errarooey on 11 June, but no mention of her arriving appeared in any of the documents consulted for this section. The logbook for St John's Point (LOP 70) shows that *M1* was operating in the Killybegs area from 13 to 17 June 1940.   3 By 2100 on 8 June Horn Head LOP had identified the ship as the *Eros*.
4 At 55°33′N, 8°26′W.   5 MA LOP 77, 8 June 1940 and the National Archives, Kew, London (hereafter TNA) ADM 1/20419, Johnson to Commander in Chief, Rosyth, 27 July

had in fact sunk. *Berkeley* gave orders for the small convoy to proceed to Tramore Bay where, at Errarooey Strand, about four miles west of Horn Head, and in view of the coastwatchers on the headland, *Eros* was run aground on neutral Irish territory 'stern on about six cables distant from a sandy beach with her deck forward from the bridge submerged'.[6] From this point, Horn Head LOP recorded continuous military activity near the stricken vessel. Irish police and soldiers picketed on the beach guarded *Eros*, while two British 'battleships', as the coastwatchers incorrectly called them, stood by; HMS *Berkeley* having been joined by the Halcyon class minesweeper HMS *Gleaner*. Irish Air Corps aircraft patrolled over these vessels. The two ships kept watch on *Eros* from outside the three-mile limit of Irish territorial waters, though they came within half a mile of the shore when escorting a coaster removing cargo from the damaged vessel. The district Defence Forces officer Commandant Ryan, accompanied by Garda Superintendent Murphy, visited *Gleaner* to inquire about the work of *Bandit*; afterwards 'Bandit did not fly an ensign for the remainder of the time she was in Irish waters'.[7] This is not to suggest undue pressure from the Irish authorities: the Chief Salvage Officer for the operation wrote that Ryan was 'most helpful and gave us every assistance'.[8] Indeed so helpful that, with *Eros* beached within Irish waters, 'an armed guard of British Marines was placed on the "EROS"' with the full knowledge of the Irish authorities and in clear breach of Ireland's wartime neutrality.[9]

The Defence Forces and the Gardaí continually updated senior officials in Dublin at the Department of Justice and the Department of External Affairs by telephone on developments in north Donegal.[10] Ensuring the safety of *Eros* became a British-Irish security operation. British armed forces operating in neutral Irish territory pushed the limits of Irish neutrality, showing the close level of wartime co-operation between neutral and belligerent. The explanation lies in the cargo carried by the ship. In addition to 301 tons of copper and 108 tons of ferrochrome, raw materials vital for the British war effort, *Eros* held a more lethal cargo: 200 tons of small arms and ammunition which the British and Irish authorities did not want to fall into hostile hands. Destined for the British army *Eros*' cargo was now even more valuable given the 'staggering' losses of arms and equipment by the British at Dunkirk.[11] In June 1940 Britain stood alone. With the campaign in Norway lost and France on the brink of surrender,

1940.   6 TNA ADM 1/20419, report by I.J. Kay, Chief Salvage Officer, 15 Aug. 1941. Six cables is just over a kilometre.   7 Ibid., Johnson to Commander in Chief, Rosyth, 27 July 1940.   8 Ibid., report by Chief Salvage Officer, 15 Aug. 1941.   9 MA DRS 230, 10 June 1940.   10 Rough notes by the Legal Adviser at the Department of External Affairs, Michael Rynne contain precise references to the progress of the operation in Donegal such as '6.22 *Eros* being towed into L.[ough] Swilly' (National Archives of Ireland (hereafter NAI), Department of Foreign Affairs (hereafter DFA), Legal Adviser's Papers, Box 42).   11 NAI DFA Secretary's Files P12/14(1), Dulanty to Walshe, quoting Sir Eric Machtig, Permanent Under-Secretary, Dominions Office, 24 July 1940.

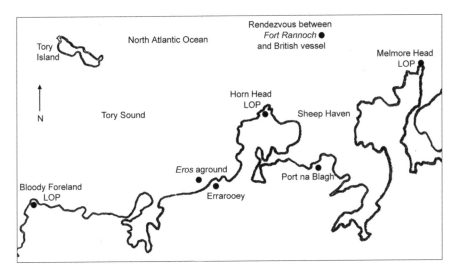

1.1 Horn Head LOP and environs

the British military could not afford to lose these weapons. After the successful IRA raid on the Defence Forces' main ammunition dump at the Magazine Fort in the Phoenix Park in Dublin on 23 December 1939, neither could the Irish authorities afford to leave this cargo of arms unguarded. *Eros* also carried four Hurricane fighters, 'urgently required' aircraft that played a vital role in the battle of Britain during the summer of 1940, and a considerable tonnage of food, which required guarding against looters.[12] Defence Forces intelligence reports indicated that *Eros* also carried an unknown amount of gold bullion.[13] It was essential for both neutral and belligerent to guard the cargo carried by *Eros*.

Under the 1907 Hague Convention, which governed neutrality during the Second World War, neutral Ireland could not support the belligerents in a conflict and was to deny them use of its territory. Belligerents were forbidden to move troops, munitions and supplies across neutral territory. However, in the case of *Eros* a belligerent placed its armed forces on Irish territory and was moving munitions and supplies across that territory. The Irish forces in close proximity to the ship could easily be interpreted as a sign of support for Britain. Ultimately, the operation to protect and re-float *Eros*, which included the transfer of the men from *Fort Rannoch* to the British vessel, fell into a grey area in the operation of neutrality. Making no reference to the ship's cargo or to the armed British military forces within Irish territory during the salvage operation, Dublin could maintain it was simply helping a stranded merchant vessel, a casualty of war. The events following the beaching of *Eros* vividly illustrate how

12 TNA ADM 1/20419, 'Eros', Statement of Facts. The cargo included twenty-five tons of Rice Krispies.   13 MA DRS 230, 10 June 1940.

Ireland's neutrality was favourably disposed towards Britain and her allies during the Second World War. The Irish military facilitated and assisted the guarding of the stricken ship while her cargo was off-loaded and repairs carried out. At 1500 on 17 June coastwatchers sighted the refloated *Eros*, accompanied by three vessels, one of which was an Irish patrol vessel, being towed north-east around Horn Head and towards Lough Swilly.[14]

The episode at Errarooey, crisply captured by the coastwatchers at Horn Head with all the immediacy of the time retained, reveals a forgotten event along the Irish coast during the summer of 1940.[15] From it the complex nature of wartime British-Irish relations and the intricacies of Irish neutrality are apparent at local and international level. The history of the Coast Watching Service has much to reveal about wartime British-Irish relations, Ireland's wartime neutrality and how that neutrality was flexibly interpreted to give support to the Allies. It also illustrates the course of the Second World War and the battle of the Atlantic in Irish seas and skies – a conflict in which the beaching of *Eros* at Errarooey Strand was one small part.

The LOP on Horn Head was one of eighty-three established by the Defence Forces from September 1939 at commanding locations at regular intervals along the Irish coastline. Initially intended as 'a land improvisation for the coastal protection of a country that had no naval force of any kind', the Coast Watching Service ensured that no vulnerable stretch of Ireland's coast remained unobserved by the Defence Forces during the Emergency.[16] The coastwatchers were members of a part-time local military force. At their core were former members of the Army reserve Volunteer Force who lived in coastal districts and who transferred into the newly formed Coast Watching Service on the outbreak of hostilities. The Volunteer Force had its origins in a government initiative from the mid-1930s; many who joined were former members of the IRA and old soldiers with service between 1916 and 1923. With this background, allegations were often made of low-grade local favouritism in the recruitment of coastwatchers. Coastwatchers were recruited locally and with some urgency, so brothers, relations and friends served together. It is easy to see how allegations of

---

14 At Lough Swilly *Eros* was again beached on Irish territory, at Saltpans Bay, near Buncrana, on the eastern side of the Lough. *Eros* eventually arrived in Belfast Lough on 6 July.   15 The treatment afforded to *Eros* was not unique. After German aircraft attacked *Panthion* eighty miles north-west of Aranmore on 28 Jan. 1941 the ship ran aground off Fanad Head. An Irish shore guard was placed at the vessel to prevent looting. The guard fired on a British boarding party from the salvage tug *Salvonia* when they failed to obey an Irish order to withdraw. On boarding the vessel the British party found it 'impossible to get on to the fore deck owing to the sniping from the shore' and they abandoned their work on board (TNA ADM 1/11104, message from *Salvonia* to Flag Officer Greenock, 1 Feb. 1941). G2 Western Command reported that 'an amicable agreement ... was arrived at regarding the disposal of the vessel' (MA G2/X/315 Pt II, Western Command Monthly Report, Jan. 1941).   16 MA EDP 20/5, untitled memorandum, 1 Oct. 1940.

favouritism arose. The force expanded by recruiting volunteers from coastal districts, men for whom seafaring was a way of life. Coastwatchers, serving locally, knew their districts, they knew what conditions to expect around their posts, what was normal and what was unusual. There was no high-technology equipment available to these men. Their eyes and ears and years of accumulated local knowledge were augmented only by telescopes and binoculars in the hunt for enemy forces seeking to invade Ireland, spies landing in the dead of night, overflights of belligerent aircraft, unexploded mines, and bodies washed ashore following sinkings beyond the horizon.

Lieutenant Commander Eric Feldt, who organized the Australian Coast Watching Service, described his force's task as being 'to sit circumspectly and unobtrusively and gather information'; it was the same for their Irish counterparts.[17] Feldt codenamed his service 'FERDINAND', after the eponymous hero in Walt Disney's 1938 cartoon 'Ferdinand the Bull'. Ferdinand did not fight, instead sitting quietly under a tree smelling flowers.[18] The Irish coastwatchers were nicknamed 'the Saygulls'. They, like seagulls, sat perched on remote headlands and cliff tops surveying the seas below and the skies above. They kept a six-year unbroken watch on the seas and skies around Ireland and were on active service for the duration of the Emergency. In all weather they responded to wartime conditions on the frontline of the battle of the Atlantic. Louis Cullen of Trinity College Dublin remembered seeing the men on duty at Forlorn Point LOP on the south Wexford coast as a boy. It was a post described as 'one of our busy LOPs' by Colonel Dan Bryan,[19] Director of Military Intelligence from July 1941 and an important supporter of the work of the Coast Watching Service.[20] Professor Cullen recalled how even though all was peaceful the coastwatchers at Forlorn Point constantly scanned the horizon through binoculars, one of them singing the wartime favourite 'Lili Marlene' as he watched for passing shipping and aircraft, reports of which would be phoned through to the Curragh Command IO and to ADC in Dublin.[21]

As a force built from scratch, the quality of Coast Watching Service operations was at first amateur; indeed early in their existence they were castigated in the Seanad as 'farcical' and a 'scandalous waste of public money', being 'planted like palm trees on the tops of hills overlooking the sea'.[22] In Dáil Éireann they fared

---

17 Quoted in I.C.B. Dear, and M.R.D. Foot, *The Oxford companion to World War II* (Oxford, 2005 edition), p. 190. **18** The Australian coastwatchers' task was to watch Japanese shipping movements and work behind enemy lines in preparation for United States landings on the Solomon Islands and at Guadalcanal. **19** Dan Bryan (1900–85), Deputy Director of Military Intelligence (1938–41), Chief Staff Officer and Director of Military Intelligence (July 1941–52), Commandant of the Military College (1952–5). **20** NAI DFA Secretary's Files A44, Bryan to Boland, 19 Jan. 1942. **21** Comment by Professor Louis Cullen, following Michael Kennedy, 'G2, the Coast Watching Service and the battle of the Atlantic', paper to the Trinity College Dublin Centre for Contemporary Irish History weekly seminar, 13 Oct. 2004. **22** Senator MacLoughlin, *Seanad deb.*, vol. 24; col. 12, 6 Dec. 1939.

little better, Fine Gael Deputy Sir John Esmonde remarking that 'all over the coast of Wexford there are people who have been put there to watch the waves like King Canute in the days of old'.[23] However, under the guiding hand of successive Directors of Military Intelligence and through intensive training at local level, the coastwatchers developed into a well-run observation and information gathering force. While no reconnaissance could 'be relied upon to obtain all the information required and to attain complete accuracy', the information gathered by the coastwatchers was generally up-to-date, and after the introduction of telephones to LOPs during the summer of 1940, normally never more than fifteen minutes old when it reached intelligence officers at command headquarters.[24]

Unlike its civilian counterpart in Britain, the Coast Watching Service was a military force from the outset and subject to military rules and discipline. It was administered from 1939 to 1942 by the naval wing of the Defence Forces, the Marine Service, and from 1942 to 1945 by the Army. It operated in tandem with the Military Intelligence branch of the Defence Forces, G2,[25] which was solely 'concerned with the results' of the coastwatchers' work.[26] In 1939, on Taoiseach Éamon de Valera's instructions, G2 had assumed responsibility for 'duties in relation to a number of questions affecting the security of the state, especially its external aspects'.[27] Accordingly, it sought 'all information regarding the probable movements and intentions of the enemy, and the investigation of all factors conducive towards a proper organization of defence'.[28] A military intelligence organization depends on good sources of information and the work of the Coast Watching Service shows the importance of personnel on the ground gathering that information. By communicating situation reports from around the coastline to G2 the coastwatchers became an essential source of intelligence information for the Defence Forces. Good intelligence being the key to good decision-making, Coast Watching Service reports assisted the Defence Forces in taking tactical operational decisions. Information from LOPs was thus initially for 'immediate action' and, as Commandant W.P. Delamere, OC ADC, put it: 'When Immediate Action has been taken, it is then, that the real intelligence work begins.'[29] Following standard procedures, observations from LOPs were

---

23 *Dáil deb.*, vol. 77; col. 1446, 15 Nov. 1939.　**24** TNA WO 287/84, *Manual of coast defence* (London, 1939), chapter II, p. 11.　**25** According to Dan Bryan, 'G2 Section was the whole Directorate of Military, Air and Marine Intelligence and [had] thirty-six officers. The security section comprised about a third of them but also employed civil servants, including ladies and other ranks. It also had officers in commands and detachments in other departments who provided services' (University College Dublin Archives Department (hereafter UCDA) P71/97). G2 also had a signals section that detected illicit radio transmissions emanating from within Irish territory.　**26** MA EDP 20/5, Bryan to McKenna, 11 June 1945.　**27** NAI DFA Secretary's Files A8 (1), Defence Security Intelligence, undated 1946 memo by Bryan.　**28** TNA WO 287/84, *Manual of coast defence* (London, 1939), chapter II, p.1.　**29** MA G2/X/318, Air Defence Command, 18 Oct. 1940.

transmitted as raw information to intelligence officers at regional command level. They collated the material, provided basic interpretation and relayed it for detailed analysis by the Air and Marine Intelligence section of G2 at GHQ in Dublin. An article in *An Cosantóir*, the Defence Forces journal, summarized this process:

> Data concerning enemy activity is not intelligence, it is merely information and remains so until separate items illustrate and confirm each other and so, one becoming the logical sequel to the other, at last some fragments of the enemy's plan become visible.[30]

Adding further sources – what Colonel Liam Archer,[31] Director of Military Intelligence and head of G2 to July 1941, termed 'negative information which could only be compiled over a period', in other words information on what was not happening at any particular location – G2 officers pieced together and analysed reports from the Coast Watching Service to assess belligerent strategies and capabilities near Ireland.[32] Were flights over Ireland of aircraft en-route to attack convoys in the North Atlantic or were they on reconnaissance missions over strategic areas in Ireland such as the Shannon estuary, Dublin port or Rosslare harbour? Did the patterns or the frequency of such flights change over time, indicating an increased interest in Ireland, perhaps hinting at preparations for an invasion, or did they herald changed tactics in the battle of the Atlantic? British-Irish intelligence and security co-operation developed greatly during the Second World War but when it came to interpreting the course of the war near Ireland, the state's small defence forces had first to look to their own resources for information; they looked in particular to the Coast Watching Service.[33]

Such defensive use of intelligence allowed G2 to make decisions on how it perceived the warring nations regarded Irish neutrality, these perceptions were then channelled to wartime policy-makers. Reports from LOPs thus became part of what later writers would call the 'intelligence product': the content of briefings to ministers, senior military officers and civilian officials on the military situation around Ireland.[34] 'Daily Report Summaries' from coastwatchers were circulated every twenty-four hours by the Director of Military Intelligence to the Minister for the Co-ordination of Defensive Measures, the Minister for Defence, the Chief of Staff and the Assistant Chief of Staff of the Defence Forces, and the

30 'How information is treated: the work of the Intelligence Officer', *An Cosantóir*, 1:38 (27 Sept. 1941), 9–11, at 9.   **31** Liam Archer (1892–1969), Chief Staff Officer, Military Intelligence (1932–41), Assistant Chief of Staff (1941–9), Chief of Staff (1949–52).   **32** MA G2/X/318, Archer to Lawlor, 29 Sept. 1939.   **33** Intelligence information came from a wide variety of other sources such as fishermen, lighthouse keepers, the Gardaí, shipwrecked sailors and downed pilots. G2 officers were also stationed at Foynes seaplane terminal and Rineanna (Shannon) airport.   **34** See Abram N. Shulsky and Gary J. Schmitt, *Silent warfare: understanding the world of intelligence* (Washington, 3rd edition, 2002), p. 41.

Secretaries of the Department of External Affairs and the Department of Defence. It is notable that de Valera did not directly receive these briefings; instead he received oral briefings on their contents from senior officials at the Department of External Affairs.

Many regular soldiers viewed the coastwatchers with a barely hidden scorn. They knew it would be the regular army and not these part-time soldiers that would take a stand against any force invading Ireland. These regulars forgot that they would rely on the Coast Watching Service to report the first sightings of an invasion force in the seas and skies off Ireland. When senior Defence Forces officers met with their British counterparts in March 1941 and discussed the possibility of German landings on the west coast of Ireland, the 'tough, rough [and] forceful'[35] Chief of Staff of the Defence Forces, Lieutenant General Dan McKenna, described such a possibility as 'a serious problem'.[36] He continued, 'the earliest information we could get would be from our LOPs and it would be our endeavour to get speedy and accurate information'. This simple and effective use of the Coast Watching Service amply illustrates a British intelligence service description of McKenna as 'a hardworking keen soldier with a practical mind'.[37] He used the coastwatchers to assist wider defence planning; 'Immediate Action' reports from LOPs of imminent threats would give the regular army extra time to mobilize to meet the invader. If Ireland was invaded – and by 1941 it was a German invasion that seemed most likely – no matter how ill-equipped the Defence Forces were to meet the invader, every hour gained was vital to allow Irish forces to group to make a token response before a call for assistance from Britain was made. The regular forces relied on the volunteer coastwatchers more than they realized: the first step in defending Ireland was to mount a constant watch along the coastline. It would be up to the Coast Watching Service to take local tactical decisions on which the strategic defence of independent Ireland might ultimately rest.

Reports from LOPs and their analysis by intelligence officers did have limitations. From May 1940 'accurate information about foreign armies' was 'difficult to obtain' in Ireland.[38] G2 often lacked an understanding of the specifics of Allied and Axis equipment and were slow to incorporate new weapons systems and equipment into their analysis, often relying on pre-war publications and out of date manuals. This led to inaccurate analyses of events and

35 UCDA P71/98, manuscript notes by Bryan.   36 UCDA, P150/2836, Notes of a discussion which took place on 10.3.'41 between Brig. Gen Gregson Ellis, Lt. Col. Pryce, the Chief of Staff, and Colonel Archer. General Daniel McKenna (1893–1975), born in Maghera, Derry; Second Derry Battalion, Irish Volunteers; Deputy OC 2nd Northern Division; Adjutant of the Waterford and Claremorris Commands, 1922–4; Adjutant Southern Command, 1924–30; Deputy QMG, 1930–33; Director, Cavalry Corps, 1933–6; Deputy Quartermaster General, 1936–9; Chief of Staff and GOC of the Defence Forces, 1940–9. 37 TNA AIR 10/3990, Air Intelligence Notes, p. 42. 38 UCDA P71/29, Military Information and General Section.

misunderstanding and misidentification of new weapons and equipment seen in action off the Irish coast. Coastwatchers were fallible; they made errors and were on occasion negligent. LOPs could miss actions seen by neighbouring posts, perhaps because of local variations in weather or because personnel were not alert. The desire not to be caught being negligent of duty meant that coast-watchers were hardly likely to record their more serious lapses. Despite such failings, the record in LOP logbooks stands up to scrutiny as an accurate account of the Second World War around Ireland. As the fields of vision covered by LOPs overlapped, neighbouring posts often saw and reported the same incident or series of incidents. Colonel James O'Hanrahan, OC Southern Command, defined the 'creditable reporting' of incidents as cases where they were 'corroborated by more than one LOP in every case'.[39] He felt that corroborated reports were 'evidence of the keenness of the personnel of LOPs to collect the greatest possible amount of relevant data whenever the opportunity presents itself'. Since more than one LOP often observed incidents, the Coast Watching Service had its own internal check on the accuracy of reporting. Cross-refer-enced reports allowed G2 to see the same incident from different viewpoints. After German seaplanes attacked a trawler off the Old Head of Kinsale, reports from nearby LOPs revealed that

> shortly before the time of the attack three seaplanes were observed going east by both Power Head LOP (17.22 hrs) and Knockadoon LOP (17.29 hrs) and by Ram Head LOP (17.31 hrs) going south-east. This group of planes could have returned to the vicinity of the Old Head and the direction of flight as observed by Ram Head LOP indicates that they were actually turning.[40]

Using such reports, rumours could be quickly verified or discounted by the correlation of information from neighbouring posts and, if need be, nerves calmed.

These agitated nerves were often in London and not Dublin. Through G2, Coast Watching Service operations linked into wartime British-Irish diplomatic and security relations. At External Affairs, Secretary of the Department Joseph Walshe had a close working relationship with Archer and Bryan of G2. Bryan, Archer's 'very active'[41] deputy to July 1941, described G2's operations with External Affairs as taking place at 'the point at which military policy and political affairs met'.[42] He later wrote that though he worked with External Affairs 'in a possibly unorthodox fashion',[43] he included in Walshe's 'wide

39 MA G2/X/315 Pt II, Southern Command, Monthly Report on Coastal Intelligence – November 1942. 40 NAI DFA Secretary's Files A44, Bryan to Boland, 19 Jan. 1942. 41 UCDA P71/102, manuscript notes by Bryan. 42 Ibid. 43 NAI DFA Secretary's Files P168, Bryan to Nunan, 5 Oct. 1950.

responsibilities' the definition of wartime policy for G2 'in their external relations'.[44] Walshe agreed with Bryan on the closeness of their working relationship, in his opinion 'security questions' could

> not be divorced from foreign policy. It would be impossible to imagine a Security service which had no relation with the foreign service … it is, therefore, of the highest importance that the Department of Foreign Affairs and the Security Department should be closely linked together … in our country at any rate, the liaison between Security officials and the Foreign Affairs officials is so close, so interwoven, as to form almost one Department.[45]

Walshe, Archer and Bryan co-operated closely on the operational use of intelligence and its incorporation into government policy on neutrality and Ireland's relations with the belligerent powers. G2 provided External Affairs with reports from the Coast Watching Service and, as it felt the need arose External Affairs released portions of this material, generally on German activities close to Ireland, in a slow trickle to Britain. Archer and Bryan had formal but highly secret links with MI5 and with the Admiralty's Naval Intelligence Department (NID).[46] Information from the coastwatchers found its way into the British intelligence community through these channels. The British authorities and security services frequently scoffed at the Irish coastwatchers but they were eager to have access to the information the service provided not least because they were initially convinced, through flawed intelligence and rumours circulating in London, that there were German submarines operating out of Irish bays.[47] Ultimately, thanks to reports from the coastwatchers, there was found to be no such submarine activity and British opinion of the Coast Watching Service improved. After the war, Admiral John Godfrey, Director of Naval Intelligence (DNI) from 1939 to 1942, wrote that 'as we know now from German records, no naval activities favourable to the Germans took place in Eirean [*sic*] waters, and there is no evidence of the Eirean coast being used for U-boat, or supply bases'.[48]

Information received from LOPs did much to stabilize British-Irish relations in the early years of the war when the battle of the Atlantic was at its most severe and the likelihood of a British invasion of Ireland to secure naval facilities at its greatest. Coastwatchers' reports calmed some of the wilder opinions in London –

44 UCDA P71/102, manuscript notes by Bryan.   **45** NAI DFA Secretary's Files A60, secret memorandum by Walshe, 23 June 1944.   **46** See Eunan O'Halpin, *Defending Ireland* (Oxford, 1999) and Eunan O'Halpin (ed.), *MI5 and Ireland: the official history* (Dublin, 2002). **47** Midge Gillies, *Waiting for Hitler: voices from Britain on the brink of invasion* (London, 2006), while not mentioning the rumours on U-boats operating from Irish waters, places these wartime rumours in a wider context.   **48** TNA ADM 223/486, Eire, memorandum by

many of them held by Winston Churchill – on the need to reoccupy the three former treaty ports, Cobh, Berehaven and Lough Swilly, which had been returned by Britain to Irish control in 1938. The diary of Guy Liddell, MI5's Director of Counter-Intelligence, shows just how high reports from the Coast Watching Service circulated in the British intelligence establishment. On 10 November 1941 Liddell recorded a meeting with Bryan concerning the German spy Herman Görtz. In the course of that meeting Liddell questioned whether Görtz had 'been picked up either by a ship plying between Eire and the Iberian Peninsula or by seaplane'. Bryan was able to assert that 'there has been no seaplane in the vicinity of Brittas Bay, neither have there been any submarines in the Irish Channel'.[49] The information came from the LOPs in the Brittas Bay area.[50]

Beyond British-Irish relations the coastwatchers' work had a significant impact on wartime Irish foreign policy. Coastwatchers logged the passage of flights through Irish airspace and naval activity off the Irish coast. External Affairs used this information when making protests to belligerent governments when their armed forces violated Irish territory. Information from the coast-watchers fed into the complex manoeuvres undertaken by the Irish diplomatic and intelligence services in their contacts with Britain, Germany and, from December 1941, the United States. After an unidentified aircraft dropped a bomb on Campile creamery in Wexford on 26 August 1940, killing three young women, it was the definite identification of the aircraft as German by Volunteers Green and Goodall of Greenore LOP that provided the essential evidence enabling the Irish government to obtain compensation from Germany for the attack.[51] The OC Curragh Command, Colonel Thomas J. McNally, personally commended both men for their actions.[52] Coastwatchers also logged the approach of the Luftwaffe aircraft that were to bomb Dublin on the early morning of 31 May 1941. Reports from LOPs to ADC gave advance warning to the Dublin anti-aircraft artillery batteries to prepare to engage the aircraft. When Dublin successfully sought compensation from Berlin for the raid, which left thirty-four dead, the most accurate picture of the bombing came from the coastwatchers.

As the threat of invasion declined after the summer of 1941, the role of the coastwatchers changed from keeping watch for invading forces and monitoring infringements of neutrality to observing the course of the war around Ireland. Coastwatchers in Donegal and Sligo reported the operations of the British rescue vessel *Robert Hastie* from Killybegs harbour and the flights through the 'Donegal air corridor' of British seaplanes from Castle Archdale on Lough Erne. On the early morning of 26 May 1941 LOPs along the south Donegal and north Mayo coast logged the passage of two seaplanes from Castle Archdale which

Godfrey, Aug. 1947. **49** Nigel West (ed.), *The Guy Liddell diaries, vol. 1: 1939–1942* (Abingdon, 2005), p. 190. **50** These posts were Wicklow Head, Kilmichael Point and Cahore Point. **51** NAI DFA 221/147, Archer to Walshe, 11 Sept. 1940. **52** Owen Quinn, 'The

(though the coastwatchers and G2 did not know this at the time) were in search of, and would later locate the German battleship *Bismarck*, enabling the sinking of *Bismarck* by British naval forces. On the Inishowen peninsula in north Donegal coastwatchers logged traffic from the naval base at Derry and Coastal Command flights from Eglington, Ballykelly and Limavady aerodromes. Coastwatchers also kept a look out for aircraft on delivery flights from North America in the final hours of their transatlantic crossing as they headed for airfields in Northern Ireland and Scotland and were among the first contacted if the Allies reported to the Irish that a flight was missing.

These are only a handful of examples of the varied work undertaken by the Coast Watching Service and the character of the information they provided. As the outposts of the country's defences the coastwatchers helped ensure that the intelligence service of the under-resourced Irish Defence Forces maintained an understanding of the changing intentions of the belligerents on the borders of Irish territory. As these examples – and that of the *Eros* – illustrate, the coastwatchers recorded the Second World War from a day-to-day perspective in Irish coastal waters and skies. The vast body of information they collected is contained in the logbooks of each LOP. Until the 1970s these logbooks were thought lost, but they were discovered when the Defence Forces' archives were re-organized. The surviving 501 logbooks, held at Military Archives at Cathal Brugha Barracks in Dublin, are a war diary of Ireland's involvement as a neutral or non-belligerent in the Second World War. Commandant Owen Quinn, a former District Officer with the Coast Watching Service who began studying the work of the service in the late 1980s, considered that 'a conservative estimate of the number of reports logged, overall, would be one-and-a-half million'.[53] The logbooks provide an unrivalled account of the Second World War around Ireland and enable the course of the conflict from an Irish perspective to be analyzed in hitherto unknown detail. Chronicling one branch of the Defence Forces on active service in the defence of Ireland during the Second World War, they show how close the conflict was to the lives of Irish men and women. They record dogfights in Irish skies, heavily escorted convoys passing the Irish coast, bodies of the victims of war washed up on Irish shores, mines exploding on the seashore and the events which led to deaths and injuries from aerial bombing.

Strung out along Ireland's shores, the coastwatchers performed a valuable role, one that was largely unknown and unappreciated, in defending Ireland during the Second World War. Wartime Dáil debates suggest that the government deliberately refused to inform the Dáil about the work of the Coast Watching Service. This secrecy led many deputies to infer incorrectly that the coastwatchers did little other than stare at empty sea. In reality, the coastwatchers saw the war

---

Coast Watching Service', *Irish Sword*, 19:75–8 (1993–5), p. 92. Quinn states that Colonel Seán Collins-Powell commanded Curragh Command, but he did not take command until Nov. 1944.   53 MA LOP 82, note by Quinn on the last page of the last logbook for LOP 82, 2 Dec.

in the Atlantic unfold before them and they recorded it as it happened in their post logbooks. Together, the coastwatchers guarding Ireland's wartime frontline and the G2 officers who analysed their reports provided the air and marine intelligence that underpinned the defence of neutral Ireland during the Second World War. General McKenna wrote to Minister for Defence Oscar Traynor as the war in Europe was drawing to a close that Ireland 'stood at the edge of this mighty conflict'.[54] The mighty conflict in the seas and skies off Ireland's coasts was 'the western arm of the great pincer movement by which the German Third Reich was crushed, complementing the Red Army's war on the eastern front'.[55] Through the combined operations of the Coast Watching Service and G2, the chapters below bear out McKenna's judgment and show just how close neutral Ireland was to the war that crushed the Third Reich.

1989. **54** MA General report on the Army 1944–1945. **55** Richard Woodman, *The real cruel sea* (London, 2004), p. 1.

CHAPTER ONE

The origins of the Coast Watching Service

GEOPOLITICS AND IRELAND – THE NEED TO DEFEND
THE COASTLINE

A S ASSISTANT DIRECTOR AND then Director of Military Intelligence
Colonel Dan Bryan had a defining influence on the shape and work of the
Coast Watching Service. That influence stemmed from his keen understanding
of the inter-relationship between military strategy, geography and international
relations. What particularly interested Bryan was its application to contemporary
Irish circumstances in the 1920s and the 1930s. He had for at least a decade-and-
a-half before taking command of G2 in 1941 maintained that for geographic,
military and international relations reasons a coastguard was necessary for the
defence of Ireland in time of war in order to keep 'the whole Coast line and
adjoining waters under continuous observation'.[1] He had come to this conclusion after applying to Ireland the works of American geostrategist Alfred
Mahan on naval strategy and geopolitics. Bryan's writings, including a draft
article 'Why we need a Defence Force' submitted to the Defence Forces journal
An t-Óglach, show the direct influence of Mahan on his thinking. In one section
Bryan began by directly quoting Mahan: "'Ireland by geographical position lies
across and controls the communications of Great Britain with all the outside
world save only that considerable but far more preponderant portion which
borders the North Sea and Baltic.'" Additionally, Bryan continued,

> it is impossible to fly from America to any, except the Mediterranean
> countries of Europe without touching or passing close to Ireland, and a
> very short examination of a map indicating the trade routes of the world
> will satisfy those interested that Mahan's description can also be applied to
> Ireland's relation to the trade routes of all other European countries.[2]

Bryan argued that 'sight has been lost in the Saorstát of its geographical and
historical relations to Europe' because of the concentration in Ireland on internal
affairs during the First World War. This created a situation where Ireland 'lost
sight of the very considerable extent to which the submarine war was fought off
the Irish coast'. Since independence proper coastal defences for the state had not
developed. The coastguard had been disbanded and Ireland had no navy.

1 UCDA P71/5, 'Why we need a Defence Force'.   2 Ibid.

14

Coastal defence was a thorny subject for the Irish authorities following the failure of the 1926–7 review of the defence articles of the 1921 Anglo-Irish treaty. In this abortive review Ireland sought the return of the treaty ports – the defended anchorages of Cobh, Berehaven and Lough Swilly retained by Britain under articles six and seven of the treaty. Britain refused and the negotiations collapsed with British forces still in place. Britain planned to use the ports in any future Atlantic naval war. This would leave Ireland, since independence seeking to follow a policy of military neutrality, in a very difficult position with her nearest neighbour. The realist might argue that the British navy defended independent Ireland and that Britain would not let any invading force land in Ireland without first launching a pre-emptive strike to deny Ireland to the invaders.[3] In addition to the maritime superiority of the Royal Navy in the seas around Ireland the Royal Air Force, as air power developed, gained air superiority over southern Irish coastal regions. A surprise seaborne invasion of Ireland would be very difficult without the hostile power first gaining air superiority and command of the seas off the south coasts of Britain and Ireland. This state of affairs, while perhaps comforting to the Irish government, did not do away with the need to keep a watch on, if not actually defend, the Irish coastline from the landward side.

By the 1930s the security and defence of the Irish coastline had not improved. Bryan held that 'beyond vague general ideas no one in the Department [of Defence] knows anything about most of these subjects'. Colonel A.J. 'Tony' Lawlor, later head of the Marine and Coast Watching Service (M&CWS), added to Bryan's bleak analysis that there was 'no one capable of advising our government on the detail of naval or coastal positions'.[4] As Ireland held a critical strategic position on Britain's western flank and on the sea-lanes off the west coast of Europe this situation was distressing but it was not surprising given the low priority afforded by successive governments since independence to the defence of Ireland from external attack. Between the wars the Defence Forces planned for operations in Northern Ireland and the border region but it took little imagination to realize that the state's coastline would also be Ireland's frontline in a European conflict. There was little academic awareness in Ireland of the island's significant geopolitical position. Irish university syllabi put no emphasis on the teaching of geopolitics, then a fashionable area of study in

3 During an after-lunch conversation at the American legation in Dublin on 6 November 1940 Joseph Walshe seems to have made this very point to the American Minister to Ireland, David Gray. Walshe later retracted the comment suggesting that, though their conversation was frank, his having 'imbibed over-freely of the excellent wines which you gave us at lunch' may have influenced his views (NAI DFA Secretary's Files P48A, Walshe to Gray, 12 Nov. 1940). Gray replied that he was 'sure' that Walshe had 'never said that the majority of the Irish people were grateful for the protection of the British Fleet; undoubtedly, it was "recognised" or some similar word' (ibid., Gray to Walshe, 13 Nov. 1940). 4 UCDA P71/27, Present Commitments – Future Policy and Programme, annotation on memorandum.

British, German, Italian and Japanese universities.[5] In the mid-1930s, when he was a junior officer in military intelligence, Bryan was alone in arguing that Ireland needed 'fixed and mobile coastal defences', a coastguard and 'a Marine or Naval Service'.[6] Except for Bryan, and later Lawlor, there is no evidence to suggest that the importance of Ireland's geopolitical position was appreciated in the Irish military. With the exception of the treaty ports, the Irish coastline remained undefended.

In the seminal May 1936 memorandum 'Fundamental factors affecting Saorstát defence problem' which built upon and developed ideas he had first expressed in the 1920s, Bryan returned to examine Ireland's geopolitical position in the North Atlantic. He focussed on the factors underlying Ireland's strategic location vis-à-vis Britain stressing how the development of submarine warfare 'increased rather than lessened Ireland's strategic importance'.[7] Bryan reasoned that as Britain by her geographic location controlled access by sea to Germany, so Ireland controlled access to Britain. A foreign naval power at war with Britain could paralyse Britain by first gaining control of Ireland. Conversely, Britain could deny control of Ireland to a foreign power by first invading and occupying Ireland. Either way Ireland could suffer from invasion should Britain be at war. With this in mind Bryan highlighted Ireland's lack of military power to defend herself 'against any Great Power'.[8]

When the Irish government finally took over the treaty ports in 1938 the facilities were run-down. Without a coastguard and despite the return of the ports the Irish coast remained undefended as war loomed in Europe. As one former Irish Navy officer observed:

> A maritime nation must also establish itself as such by exercising control and jurisdiction over the waters off its coasts. If it does not do this then its very existence, apart from its independence, is threatened. Some of these fundamental facts were missed by the founders of the new Irish state, and their neglect was to prove costly and dangerous in due course.[9]

Bryan had warned that 'the need for a close watch on the North and South Irish Coast, with its constant stream of shipping traffic during a period of submarine warfare, is obvious'.[10] Examining the experience of the First World War, he argued that a land-based sentry force based in static look out posts and working in co-operation with air and marine patrols would be necessary to monitor

5 Making this point, Bryan referred to the only relevant Irish source being *Ireland in the European system* (London, 1920) by Professor James Hogan of University College Cork. 6 UCDA P71/27, Present Commitments – Future Policy and Programme. 7 O'Halpin, *Ireland*, p. 137. 8 UCDA P71/8, Fundamental factors affecting Saorstát defence problem, May 1936. 9 Daire Bruincairdi, *The Seahound: the story of an Irish ship* (Cork, 2001), p.1. 10 UCDA P71/8, Fundamental Factors Affecting Saorstát Defence Problem, May 1936.

Ireland's coastline in time of war. Through the 1920s and 1930s Bryan's had remained a lone voice, but with Second World War on the horizon the

> realisation dawned in Ireland that the country was surrounded by water and that the sea was of vital importance to her. Neutrality was declared with just nothing whatever to defend it with in the internationally vital area of the territorial sea.[11]

THE ESTABLISHMENT OF THE COAST WATCHING SERVICE, SEPTEMBER 1938–AUGUST 1939

The initial decision to establish a coast watching service was taken with great haste during the Munich crisis of September 1938. De Valera emphasized the need for Ireland to re-arm and the Department of Defence planned to call up the Reserve of the Defence Forces and begin the requisitioning of supplies and equipment and the compulsory billeting of troops.[12] Walshe, recently returned from London where he had been discussing British-Irish security co-operation in time of war, wrote to the Irish Minister to Spain that the international situation was 'extremely grave ... [A]t the moment we are afraid that a general European war is very near ... [W]e are taking it for granted that preparations must be made for an immediate war.'[13] The Department of Defence panicked and began hurried internal discussions 'in view of the present circumstances' to ensure that the Irish coast would be under observation if conflict broke out.[14] Minister for Defence Frank Aiken wrote frantically to Minister for Finance Seán MacEntee that 'arrangements should be made immediately for an effective system of Coast Watching' and that 'urgent action' was required for the appointment of a military head and a civilian deputy head of the proposed coast watching service.[15] Aiken suggested Mr J. Dunphy, Assistant District Engineer of the Electricity Supply Board in Waterford, who had served as a Lieutenant Commander in the British Navy during the First World War, as deputy head of the Coast Watching Service. No name emerged for the head of the new service.

Before Finance considered the merits of Dunphy's appointment the Department of Defence submitted in 'an atmosphere of red hot haste' a plan for a volunteer peacetime coast watching force of 1,000 watchers manning 200 posts.[16] The 200 posts were based loosely on the locations of the pre-1922

---

11 Captain Tony McKenna, quote in Bernard Share, *The Emergency* (Dublin, 1978), p. 94.
12 A rough note in Bryan's papers in his own hand reads: 'What got de V going on Army in 1938–39? – Was it my Fundamental Factors' (UCDA P71/89).   13 NAI DFA Secretary's Files S92, Walshe to Kerney, 9 Sept. 1938.   14 MA 2/55390, draft letter, MacMahon to McElligott, 20 Sept. 1938.   15 NAI DF S4/84/38, MacMahon to McElligott, 22 Sept. 1938.
16 Ibid., Doolin to MacEntee, 22 Sept. 1938.

coastguard and the coastal watchtowers built during the Napoleonic Wars. The coastwatchers would be men over the age of military service. An officer at the rank of major would head the service with a civilian as its temporary deputy head. The force would be activated in the event of an international emergency. Considered by the Department of Finance to be 'half-baked … an illustration of the way in which [the Department of Defence] is tending to rush its fences',[17] the scheme envisaged only the monitoring of 'shipping and their communication with other shipping or land' and, with attempts to land arms for subversives in mind, the monitoring of 'the movement of individuals on the coast line'.[18] No mention was made of the observation of aircraft and submarines, the recovery of bodies and flotsam, the monitoring of attacks on air and naval craft or the reporting of drifting mines, all of which were to become primary duties of the Coast Watching Service as eventually constituted in April 1939. Assistant Secretary at Finance Walter Doolin treated Defence's tentative scheme with disdain: 'when they have observed, what then?'[19] Doolin scornfully told his minister that the proposal was 'a futile waste of effort'.[20]

The Department of Defence had a more complex scheme in mind but inexplicably the Secretary of the department, General Peadar MacMahon, only communicated it orally to the Department of Finance. This scheme made a much stronger case and had at its core the protection of Ireland's neutrality. It worked from the theories of early twentieth century British geographer, and one of the fathers of geopolitics, Halford Mackinder, that in time of war Britain would defend the port of Liverpool by restricting access to the Irish Sea from the Northern Channel and St George's Channel.[21] Irish military planners reasoned that with the seas on the east coast likely to be well protected by Britain, a watch could be kept on the exposed north, west and south coasts of Ireland facing out onto the four 'cones of approach' through which shipping bound for Britain converged from the North Atlantic through the Western Approaches.[22] Perhaps with memories of the sinking of *Lusitania* by a U-boat off the Old Head of Kinsale during World War One and with possible contacts between submarines and subversives in mind, the plan emphasized the detection of submarines, in particular countering 'the suspected establishment of a base for submarines as a source of supply or as a means of communicating or receiving messages'.[23] This fear was particularly strongly held in London and rumours of German U-boat bases on remote sections of the Irish coast gravely destabilized British-Irish relations for the first years of the Second World War.

To answer Doolin's question of 'what then?', coastwatchers would use the telephones in the four hundred Garda barracks along the coast to communicate

17 Ibid.   18 Ibid., MacMahon to McElligott, 22 Sept. 1938.   19 Ibid., minute by Doolin, 22 Sept. 1938.   20 Ibid., Doolin to MacEntee, 22 Sept. 1938.   21 H.J. Mackinder, *Britain and the British seas* (Oxford, 1907), p. 21.   22 See John Terraine, *Business in great waters: the U-boat wars 1916–1945* (London, 1989), pp 41–3.   23 NAI DF S4/84/38, minute by Doolin,

incident reports to a central location. Coastwatchers were thus not to be a deterrent to any invasion of Ireland. The service was simply to be an observation force. Any belligerent craft that entered Irish coastal waters or any aircraft that flew through Irish airspace would be tracked and the details transmitted to the headquarters of military districts, military commands and to Defence Forces GHQ in Dublin for analysis. Vessels and aircraft attempting to make contact with persons within Irish territorial limits would also be monitored. It would be for the regular army to meet any invader with an armed response. Underlying the scheme was the worry that 'if an efficient counter-service is not established by the Irish Government, the danger is that it may be imposed on it to the prejudice of the principle of neutrality'.[24] It was a very real fear and beside this sentence a Department of Finance official carefully noted de Valera's 'repeated declarations that "we will not allow Ireland to be used as a base for an attack on Great Britain by its enemies"'.

MacEntee's response to this revised Department of Defence plan was founded on Doolin's scepticism. He considered a land-based watching service 'ineffective and fruitless unless supported by close and rapid cooperation with a system of coast patrols operating at sea'. Accordingly, his attitude was 'one of reserve'. However, MacEntee showed no desire to establish naval patrols and argued that the problem needed to 'be examined in its technical aspects', which suggested that he wished to kill the scheme by endless discussion of detail.[25] He told Defence that they should give 'further consideration [to] the tentative scheme submitted but agreed that Dunphy's services be utilized to assist planning'.[26]

MacEntee and his officials remained sceptical on the need to establish a coast watching service but powerful forces outside the Irish administration saw its establishment as an urgent requirement. The Dominions Office in London had lamented in March 1938 that when it came to emergency planning

> in the case of the Irish Free State (now Eire) it has not so far been possible to make so much progress with pre-concerted arrangements as in the case of the other Dominions ... [T]he position generally with regard to co-operation with or by that country at any rate in a war not arising directly out of a League [of Nations] issue is uncertain.[27]

Exploratory moves in developing British-Irish security co-operation to counter the actions of possible German agents in Ireland commenced in the summer of 1938. In the autumn John Dulanty, the Irish High Commissioner in London,

undated. **24** Ibid. **25** Ibid., Doolin to MacMahon, 23 Sept. 1938. **26** Ibid., Doolin to MacMahon, 1 Oct. 1938. Dunphy was seconded from the ESB to Defence from Sept. to Nov. 1938 and again in early 1939 as the Defence Forces considered the purchase of trawlers, mines, depth charges and torpedoes. **27** TNA CAB 21/2576, Batterbee to Whiskard and

met with senior British military figures and members of the Committee of Imperial Defence. In particular, he met the DNI, Admiral James Troup, to discuss how Ireland could institute a coastal watch. Dulanty, 'anxious' to develop British–Irish co-operation in the area, was given by the Admiralty 'a complete scheme of the Coast Watching and intelligence organisation, such as existed during the First World War'.[28] Bryan had already suggested that 'in view of the greater nature of the threat' any Irish coast watching organisation 'would have to be on an even more extensive scale and provided with better communication and other facilities' than the First World War vintage service.[29] Throughout the year the Admiralty, working in conjunction with the Dominions Office, pushed for the establishment by Dublin of a coastal watch. Little immediately resulted from these moves but Dulanty's contacts established a vital link. Following from Dulanty's talks Major A.J. Maher and his assistant, Mr Hyland, of the Department of Defence, met with Admiralty officials to discuss the acquisition of minesweepers, anti-submarine vessels and 'naval defence matters in general'.[30]

In the autumn of 1938, on the decision of General MacMahon, Colonel Archer, the head of G2, became involved in the establishment of the Coast Watching Service and this move also brought Bryan directly into the planning process.[31] Bryan later wrote how in the Intelligence Branch 'in 1938 problems arising from a submarine war in the Atlantic were anticipated and plans for a Coast Watching Service were made'.[32] Archer and Bryan explained to the Department of Defence that from the initial planning stage G2 attached the highest level of importance to the Coast Watching Service. G2 knew the value of a chain of coastal observation posts in monitoring belligerent operations close to Ireland. Each post would provide pieces in a larger puzzle that G2 could piece together and interpret to build an overall picture of the conflict around Ireland. Archer and Bryan regarded the Coast Watching Service as vital to Ireland's security. Without regular reports from Coast Watching Service LOPs, G2 would be blind to belligerent activities around the Irish coastline.

By late 1938, with G2 involved at a high-level in establishing the Coast Watching Service, the Department of External Affairs and G2 developing intelligence links with London, and the Admiralty eager – perhaps too eager – to assist the Irish military in their plans, the players in the story of the Coast Watching Service, the key actors throughout its history, had all made their first moves. However, with the fear of an immediate European war receding after Munich, the Department of Defence slowed the pace of planning for the establishment of the Coast Watching Service as the focus moved to local level

others, 3 Mar. 1938.   **28** TNA ADM 223/486, Eire, memorandum by Godfrey, Aug. 1947. During the First World War seventeen officers and 776 petty officers were employed on coast watching duty in Ireland.   **29** UCDA P71/8, Fundamental Factors Affecting Saorstát Defence Problem, May 1936.   **30** TNA DO 35/894/10, Snelling to Stephenson, 24 Sept. 1938.   **31** MA 2/55390, minute on file, 19 Sept. 1938.   **32** UCDA P71/171, rough notes by

along the Irish coastline. Working in conjunction with the Office of Public Works (OPW), the Defence Forces picked suitable sites for look out posts. The figure of 200 posts was reconsidered and reduced to eighty-eight permanent structures 'necessary for the complete supervision of the coastline'.[33] Each would have heating and cooking facilities and, in some remote areas, sleeping quarters. The plan was a considerable development on the coastguard of the First World War which employed continuous patrols along the coastline. By 1939 it was considered 'by most maritime countries that fixed watching points, sited as much to seaward as possible and giving at the same time as wide a range of vision as practicable have many advantages over a patrol system'.[34] Following Bryan's thinking, the Department of Defence adopted this system for the Coast Watching Service. Later in the war, the fixed positions of the coastwatchers were augmented by coastal patrols undertaken by the Garda-run Local Security Force (LSF) and the military-run Local Defence Force (LDF). Garda patrols in remote coastal districts also became part of the wider wartime watch on the Irish coastline.

The Army Reorganization Scheme adopted by the government in January 1939 approved in principle the establishment of the Coast Watching Service. By February the Department of Defence had revised their plan for this new wing of the Defence Forces. The vague figure of 1,000 personnel fell to a precise peacetime establishment of 386, of which 374 would serve on the coastline. These numbers would double in time of emergency to approximately 800 all ranks.[35] The Department of Defence would run the service through an officer at the rank of Commandant assisted by a civilian specialist in nautical matters. Aiken announced the creation of the Coast Watching Service in the context of general defence preparations during the Army Vote in the Dáil in February 1939 but, as a number of deputies pointed out, the Minister was rather vague on the details of the new service.[36] In April, having been told grudgingly by his officials that the Coast Watching Service 'seems essential',[37] MacEntee approved expenditure from £7,000 to £8,000 to construct look out posts, establish the force and keep it operational. This suited Aiken who instructed his officials that the establishment of the Coast Watching Service was 'to be pursued urgently'.[38] In April 1939 the Coast Watching Service was officially established. Later in the month Aiken approved posters calling for 800 volunteers to join the new force. Volunteers were to be between 17 years old and 50 years old and reside in 'Maritime Districts'.[39] It was hoped they would be fishermen, boatmen, those with farms by the seashore, members of yacht clubs, in short, anyone who as

Bryan, Military Sections.   33 NAI DF S4/84/38, memorandum by the Department of Defence, Coast Watching Service.   34 MA G2/X/318, Memorandum on Coastal Observation, no date.   35 In practice actual all ranks strength was closer to 700.   36 *Dáil deb.*, vol. 74; col. 525, 15 Feb. 1939.   37 NAI DF S4/84/38, minute on file.   38 MA 2/55390, minute to Assistant Secretary, 19 Apr. 1939.   39 Ibid., draft recruiting notice

part of their day-to-day business or their leisure activities was involved in seafaring. The eventual personnel of the Coast Watching Service did not always fit this profile either in background or in age. Most recruits were younger men, between 17 and 30 years old. Of the eight men who later operated Bray Head LOP in Wicklow, three were fishermen, two were bookkeepers, one was a labourer, one an apprentice and the final member was an electrician who also worked as an insurance agent.[40] But it was generally men with seafaring experience who knew the waters and the coast in the vicinity of their LOP who were recruited; men 'who were born, and reside with their families, within a couple of miles from the LOP'.[41]

Tom Kelly, later a Colonel in the Defence Forces, joined the Coast Watching Service in September 1939 at Whitegate Garda Station in Cork with a couple of other local men. Kelly had considered joining the British navy, a route taken by many in the area, but following family pressure he changed his plans. He opted for service closer to home and became a coastwatcher because it was, as he bluntly put it, 'a job'.[42] Coastwatchers were paid at army rates: two shillings a day for a Fourth Class Private, two shillings and six pence a day for a First Class Private, and four shillings a day for a Corporal. The men also received an allowance of three shillings a day in lieu of army rations because they lived at home.[43] All men were paid by cheque and in more poverty stricken areas coastwatchers were regarded as having a relatively comfortable regular income. There were few promotions in the Coast Watching Service. Except for those promoted to Corporal, men who joined as Volunteers remained Volunteers; they were the cheapest troops in the Defence Forces.

The careers of the eleven coastwatchers known to have served at Dalkey LOP on the south side of Dublin Bay show the stability of the teams at LOPs. When records began being kept at Dalkey in June 1940 seven Volunteers manned the post, suggesting that one coastwatcher, perhaps the NCO in charge of the post, had recently left. The seven were Volunteers Samuel Williams (201757), Thomas Smiles (206911), James Dalton (207445), Alfred Hill (207839), Vincent Delaney (207840), John Mooney (207843) and Nicholas Kinsella (207844). Volunteer Charles Craney (207842) joined in late June 1940, having transferred to Dalkey from Bray Head LOP, the next post to the south. His arrival brought the post back to full strength. Delaney, Craney, Mooney and Kinsella had almost sequential Volunteer numbers, suggesting they joined or transferred into the Coast Watching Service at the same time. Dalton was promoted to Corporal in

'approved by Minister', no date.   **40** NAI DFA Secretary's Files A8, memorandum attached to MacMahon to Walshe, 24 Mar. 1942.   **41** NAI DFA Secretary's Files P94, Memorandum on Coastal Observation, undated, but attached to Guilfoyle to Walshe, 20 Feb. 1943.   **42** Author's correspondence with Colonel Kelly, Oct. 2005.   **43** An allowance was also available for fuel if it could not be provided locally from Army stocks. Medical care was also available at public expense if no military doctor was available. From 1943 coastwatchers were

June 1940 and he remained in charge until October 1941, seeing the LOP
through the invasion scares of the summer of 1940 and the German bombings
along the east coast which culminated in the North Strand bombing of May
1941. Craney then succeeded Dalton as Corporal and Volunteer John Larkin
(211587) joined the post, replacing Dalton, in November 1941. Hill left in
December 1942 and Volunteer Henry Mullen (211631) replaced him. From 1942
to mid-1944 Dalkey LOP was run by Williams, Smiles, Delaney, Mooney,
Kinsella, Larkin and Mullen, with Craney NCO in charge. Williams left in May
1944 and was replaced by the last newcomer to the LOP, Volunteer James Smith
(211650). On Craney's departure in December 1944 he was not replaced as the
Coast Watching Service was by then being run down as the war in Europe drew
to a close. Mullen became Corporal and with Smiles, Delaney, Mooney, Kinsella,
Larkin and Smith manned the LOP until its closure in June 1945. Smiles,
Delaney, Mooney and Kinsella served at Dalkey LOP for the duration of the
war and Craney, with four-and-a-half years service was not long behind them.
Stability of personnel built up experience and comradeship as men who joined
the service together often served together for the duration of the 'Emergency'.

Recruitment of coastwatchers did lead to high-level interdepartmental rivalry.
When the Department of Defence proposed that members of the Coast Life
Saving Service run by the Department of Industry and Commerce would make
ideal coastwatchers, it did not meet with the approval of the Secretary of the
Department of Industry and Commerce, John Leydon. Leydon wrote to
MacMahon that Defence should 'take steps which will ensure that you do not
take all our Coast Life Saving Crews ... we naturally do not want to have the
Coast Life Saving Service crippled'.[44] MacMahon consulted Archer who
commented that 'the trouble is that the two Departments are looking for the
same type of man and our terms will be more attractive'.[45] On Archer's
suggestion, Leydon was diplomatically informed that 'the Officer responsible for
the formation of the Coast Watching Service is aware of your views and will take
all possible steps to ensure that the interests of the Coast Life Saving Service are
safeguarded'.[46] Further calming words were that 'of the 49 Coast Life Saving
Stations in existence only 13 are situated at places convenient to our proposed
look out posts', and since fifteen men crewed each station 'we would not, even if
we drew solely on these crews, take them all'.[47] The two services would remain
separate, though arrangements were made to enable the Coast Life Saving
Service co-operate with the Coast Watching Service in reporting suspicious
movements by sea and air and members of the Coast Life Saving Service also
served as coastwatchers and vice versa.

paid marriage allowances, children's allowances and an allowance for boot repairs.   **44** MA
2/55390, Leydon to MacMahon, 2 May 1939.   **45** Ibid., Archer to MacMahon, 4 May 1939.
46 Ibid., MacMahon to Leydon, 8 May 1939.   **47** Ibid.

In May 1939 Commandant Joseph Barrett was appointed to head the Coast Watching Service. Barrett had been promoted from Captain to Commandant in March and was posted to G2 specifically because he was to head the Coast Watching Service.[48] The move showed the continuing connection between Military Intelligence and the coastwatchers. A training depot was established at Fort Westmoreland in Cork harbour and the military began preparing a training syllabus and establishing sub-depots in each Command area. In the meantime, the British-Irish dimension to the Coast Watching Service re-emerged.

BRITISH-IRISH CO-OPERATION ON COAST WATCHING

Through late 1938, as British-Irish intelligence co-operation developed, the Admiralty discussed the establishment of the Coast Watching Service with the Irish authorities. Dublin and London agreed that the exchange of intelligence 'might well be organized in peacetime with a view to our mutual benefit in war time' and that passing information to London was on a different plane to British forces taking action against enemy forces in Irish waters, this latter being deemed politically undesirable.[49] In reality 'little progress' was made as the discussions stalled when the immediate crisis over Czechoslovakia passed following the Munich agreement. By the summer of 1939 the British were anxious to 'secure progress' with Ireland on 'the organisation of a coast watching and intelligence service'.[50] Dulanty confessed to the Admiralty that 'the machinery in Dublin for dealing with Naval Intelligence was still rather behind-hand'.[51]

In June 1939 London judged de Valera's political objections to naval intelligence co-operation with Britain to be 'too strong to enable a start to be made'.[52] The Admiralty felt that there was 'deadlock', and as 'the need of intelligence in this vitally important area is paramount', considered patrolling off the Irish coast with a fleet of yachts, though they realized that this would achieve 'very little'.[53] To resolve matters Percivale Liesching, Assistant Secretary at the Dominions Office, who had just taken over responsibility for matters relating to Ireland, visited Dublin in the first days of July 'to get to know the Eire officials there and establish contact with them'.[54] Liesching 'was not charged with any special mission' but he was briefed in advance of his trip on the development of the Irish Coast Watching Service by the DNI. He had important and sensitive high-level work to undertake.

London hoped that the Irish would organize their peacetime coast watching service speedily so that it could be operational quickly in the event of an

48 MA Council of Defence Minutes, vol. ix, minutes, 14 Mar. 1939.   49 TNA ADM 223/486, Eire, memorandum by Godfrey, Aug. 1947.   50 TNA DO 35/894/1 X11/316, Coast watching and the exchange of Naval Intelligence, 5 July 1939.   51 TNA ADM 223/486, Discussions as to the possibility of establishing Coast Watching and Intelligence Organisations in Eire, June 1939.   52 Ibid.   53 Ibid., Godfrey(?) to Sinclair, 11 May 1939. 54 TNA DO 35/548/25 E70/06, Harding to Campbell, 19 July 1939.

international emergency. When Liesching met with Walshe he found him favouring the faster organization of the service to help develop the reciprocal exchange of intelligence information between the two states. London already knew that Walshe 'was strongly in favour of the fullest co-operation with the British Government';[55] it was no surprise that he 'personally welcomed the renewed initiative' from the British, remarking that after the autumn 1938 attempt at establishing the Coast Watching Service there had been 'an unfortunate tendency for interest to be lost as tension relaxed'.[56] Liesching hoped to kick-start the stalled process and he discussed the establishment of the Coast Watching Service with Walshe and Leydon. He did not meet with officials from the Department of Defence. London was worried that the Irish had not realized how much prior organization was needed, in particular 'in linking up the Eire organisation with the Postal, Customs and Police authorities ... this could not be done overnight, the sooner progress was made the better'.[57] Walshe agreed and discussed this with MacMahon and Archer. It was arranged that Captain John Fitzgerald of the Admiralty, who was about to take leave in Ireland, meet with officials from the Department of Defence as 'a lever for accelerating consideration of the scheme by the Defence authorities'.[58] Fitzgerald was an interesting choice; as Director of Torpedoes and Mining at the Admiralty he would be in a prime position to advise Dublin on coastal defence and would report to the Admiralty on the conclusion of his Irish trip.

Liesching's report on his visit suggests that External Affairs wished to move much faster than Defence in establishing the Coast Watching Service. Walshe's encouragement of Fitzgerald's visit was deliberate as it 'would also help Mr Walshe in bringing the Defence authorities to the point'.[59] The groundwork had been set to allow an unpublicized visit for 'a purely technical consultation' to take place between the British and Irish authorities on the establishment of the Coast Watching Service. When Liesching returned to London, he told Godfrey that an understanding had been reached allowing a visit by one of his intelligence officers to Dublin. It was the result the Admiralty and the Dominions Office had wanted. Permanent Under-Secretary at the Dominions Office, Sir Edward Harding minuted that Liesching should be 'congratulated on a very successful visit – which produced the "contacts" which we were specially anxious that he should make'.[60] These contacts would become extremely important once war broke out.

---

55 TNA KV 4/279, memorandum by Guy Liddell on meeting with Walshe and Dulanty, 1 Sept. 1938.   56 TNA DO 35/894/1 X11/316, Coast watching and the exchange of Naval Intelligence, 5 July 1939.   57 Ibid.   58 Ibid.   59 Ibid.   60 Ibid., minute by Harding, 6 July 1939. Liesching also met de Valera, and senior cabinet members Lemass, MacEntee and O'Ceallaigh as well as Walshe, to whom he gave a copy of the British War Book, Leydon and Boland. Liesching also met the Papal Nuncio and officials from the French and American

CONCLUSION

It had been a slow and hesitating start for the Coast Watching Service. By the late summer of 1939 a rough plan was in place for the new service, a handful of personnel had been identified and top-level posts were being filled. There was a difficulty filling these posts due to 'the comparatively limited number of people in [Ireland] who possess the requisite qualifications and experience'.[61] Some recruits had come forward and some training had taken place. 'Progress', Dulanty optimistically considered, 'is being made', but it was slow.[62] Locations for LOPs existed on paper, though the sites had yet to be acquired. Slowly too, agreement on what the coastwatchers would look out for had been reached, but little attention had been paid to how they would communicate that information to Dublin. The proposed use of telephones in Garda stations and communication by bicycle couriers suggested a response to a slower form of warfare more suited to the age of the supremacy of naval power than the fast moving warfare of the mid-twentieth century. There certainly remained problems to iron out.

Liesching and his colleagues were right to be worried that the Irish had left it late in their planning. As the following chapters will show, a co-ordinated watch on the Irish coast could not be established overnight. There would be teething problems. But the British diplomat missed or perhaps underestimated the importance of his own achievement. The contacts that he made in Dublin were central to the foundation of the wartime relationship between Dublin and London. Liesching's mission linked the 1938 intelligence discussions and Sir John Maffey's appointment in September 1939 as British Representative to Ireland. It reinvigorated British-Irish security and defence co-operation. But it remained to be seen whether the Coast Watching Service could be built up from the bare minimum and function in practice. Perhaps above all else it remained to be seen how Britain and Germany would react to an Irish declaration of neutrality and what would happen off the Irish coast in the first days of a European war.

legations.   **61** TNA ADM 1/10214, Dulanty to Godfrey, 29 June 1939.   **62** Ibid.

CHAPTER TWO

Mobilizing and training coastwatchers and building LOPs

MOBILIZATION

IN THE WEEKS LEADING to the outbreak of the Second World Ireland began the transition from peacetime to wartime government. During this period the Coast Watching Service mobilized. On 25 August, 'pending the completion of the organisation of the service' and before the coastwatchers finally took up positions, An Garda Síochána was instructed by the Cabinet to 'immediately' stand in for the coastwatchers should hostilities break out.[1] A high-level meeting that day laid the foundations. Present were Minister for Justice, P.J. Ruttledge; Minister for Defence, Frank Aiken; Michael Kinnane, the Garda Commissioner, who was accompanied by the head of the Crime and Security Branch of the Garda, Assistant Commissioner General William Murphy; General Michael Brennan, Chief of Staff of the Defence Forces; Colonel Archer of G2; and two other officers representing the military. They agreed that in the event of war Gardaí in coastal regions would keep increased vigilance along the shoreline and assist in recruiting 'suitable men' for the Coast Watching Service. At Garda stations in coastal regions the Barrack Orderly would include coastal observation in his regular duties and report the movements of naval vessels and aircraft and all unusual activity along the coast to the nearest military post. At remote locations 'a special effort' would be made 'to secure the co-operation of persons living near such portions of the coast' with the Gardaí in reporting suspicious activity.[2]

A further provisional decision of the Cabinet of 25 August built on Liesching's visit in July and empowered the Minister for Defence to 'arrange through the Department of External Affairs to send an Officer to London to discuss arrangements' to establish a coast watching service.[3] The following day Archer headed a military and civil service mission to London to see the DNI, Admiral John Godfrey and representatives of the Admiralty and the Board of Trade. They provided 'more particulars of what was needed to establish a Coast Watching system'.[4] Archer explained that permanent personnel for the Coast

1 NAI JUS 8/756, Moynihan to Ruttledge, 26 Aug. 1939.   2 Ibid., Emergency Order No. 1 Coast Watching Service, 29 Aug. 1939.   3 Ibid., Moynihan to Ruttledge, 26 Aug. 1939.
4 TNA ADM 223/486, Eire, memorandum by Godfrey, Aug. 1947.

Watching Service could not be recruited until October and that in the interim
Gardaí were standing in as temporary coastwatchers. To improve the quality of
the information obtained by Gardaí, the services of 'a British Naval Officer to
work in conjunction with Colonel Archer' were offered by the Admiralty and
Godfrey 'indicated' that the Admiralty would place great value on the
information secured by the coastwatchers, suggesting possible channels of
communication to London.[5] The Irish would report air and naval activity to the
Admiralty, who by way of trade would communicate to G2 advance information
on 'German intentions to land arms, etc., on the Eire coast'. This, the British
maintained, would be 'to the advantage of both Governments' and, conscious of
the views of Archer's political superiors, the British added 'that the passing and
reception of intelligence was on a different plane to the taking of action, which
might be politically undesirable'.

As Archer met with Godfrey in London the Cabinet in Dublin agreed that
'members of the Volunteer Force to man the harbour fortifications ... should be
called up on the outbreak of war'.[6] Three days later the Minister for Defence
was instructed to make all necessary provisions for calling up the Volunteer
Force and the regular Reserve including the Coast Watching Service.[7] A
Government Information Bureau broadcast warned that these men 'should hold
themselves in readiness'; the Volunteer Force finally received call-up notices on
8 September.[8] Given the poor state of the Army reserves this had little impact
except possibly the psychological one of giving the appearance that Ireland was
preparing to defend itself. The role the Volunteer Force would play in coastal
defence was nevertheless apparent from the days leading to the outbreak of the
Second World War. On 1 September Volunteers in coastal areas were summarily
transferred into the Coast Watching Service, greatly augmenting the paltry
figure of thirty-four men already recruited.[9] To assist them Gardaí were
instructed on 1 September to begin coast watching duties. As the Second World
War began a mixed force of coastwatchers and Gardaí began a twenty-four hour
watch along the Irish coastline. By the night of 2 September thirteen LOPs had
opened, mostly along the south-west coast. A further twenty, mainly in Donegal,
opened on 3 September. Sixteen posts along the south coast were established on
4 September and seventeen LOPs covering the coast from Dublin to Waterford
came into being on 5 September. The posts opened on 4 and 5 September gave
extended coverage to the Rosslare to Dungarvan coastline, the most likely
location for a seaborne invasion of Ireland and the landfall point for any airborne
force from the continent seeking to attack Dublin. Remembering the experience

5 TNA KV 4/279, The situation in regard to coastwatching in Eire, 4 Dec. 1939.   6 NAI DT
CAB 2/2, G.C. 2/90B, 26 Aug. 1939.   7 NAI DT S10869A, extract from minutes of a
meeting of the Cabinet (G.C. 2/91A), 29 Aug. 1939.   8 Ibid., Broadcast, 3 Sept. 1939.
9 Tony McKenna, '"Thank God We're Surrounded by Water"', *An Cosantóir* 33:4 (Apr.
1973), 103–24, at 108.

of the First World War, these posts also covered the zone in which submarine and anti-submarine warfare was expected to commence. Volunteer William Whelan, based on the Western end of the likely invasion zone at LOP 20 at Ram Head, Ardmore, Waterford, recalled that

> the war started on Sunday and Jimmie Troy and Tom Monsell were the first two to go on duty, on Sunday night I started with Tommie Mooney; he was a Corporal. We went on, at 12pm on Monday night. We had no real orders at the time, only to walk along the coast and watch it. We walked all the cliffs along by Ardo to Whitingbay Strand and back again by Terry's and the Round Tower and the New Line.[10]

Whelan's description shows that the Coast Watching Service initially differed little from the coastguard of the First World War. It hardly mattered; in September 1939 a watch had to be established on the coast as quickly as possible. It was little enough, and there were gaps as the remaining LOPs, mainly those in the far west, were not fully established until 9 September, but it all gave the impression that Ireland was serious about its neutrality.

3 SEPTEMBER 1939. THE BATTLE OF THE ATLANTIC BEGINS

In the North Atlantic Ocean the Second World War began just off the Rockall Bank, 250 miles north-west of Malin Head, on the evening of 3 September 1939. The Donaldson Line's 13,500-ton liner *Athenia*, chartered by the Cunard Line and bound for Montreal with 1,418 passengers and crew, was torpedoed without warning by U-30 commanded by Leutnant Fritz-Julius Lemp. *Athenia* was unarmed but she had been ordered to steer off her normal course and was zig-zagging to avoid U-boats. On sighting *Athenia* Lemp acted on recently received orders that war had been declared and attacks on enemy vessels were to commence in accordance with prize rules and without provocation. Though visibility was good and the sea calm, Lemp would later claim that he mistook the unarmed passenger liner for an armed cruiser and fired two torpedoes. One hundred and twelve of *Athenia*'s passengers and crew died in the attack, twenty-eight of them Americans sailing for home as war began in Europe. Three British destroyers and three freighters including a Norwegian vessel, *Knute Nelson*, rescued the survivors.

The Norwegian vessel signalled to the Irish authorities that it was en-route to Galway with survivors, the message being picked up by Malin Head radio, which had also picked up the distress signals from *Athenia*. On receipt of this advance warning the emergency plan for Galway city went into operation and hotels and schools were prepared to receive the survivors. *Knute Nelson* landed three

10 Siobhán Lincoln, *Ardmore: memory and story* (Ardmore, Co. Waterford, 2000), p. 219.

hundred and sixty seven survivors from *Athenia*, including its Captain, James
Cook, at Galway docks at dawn on 5 September. 'Expeditious and satisfactory'
arrangements were made for the disembarkation of passengers who were in 'a
very distressed state ... most of them only half clothed'.[11] The Army Medical
Corps and staff from local hospitals took charge of ten stretcher cases which
received priority treatment. Meanwhile Gardaí provided survivors with food,
clothing and, where necessary, additional medical attention. The government
sent a donation of £500 to the Mayor of Galway, Joseph Costello, 'towards
expenses connected with the care of the survivors of the SS ATHENIA'.[12] De
Valera wrote personally to the joint organizers of the relief committee, Mayor
Costello and the Archbishop of Galway, Michael Browne, that he was

> much impressed by the excellent arrangements made with so short a time
> for preparation. Thanks to well planned organisation and the public spirit
> of those who took part, nothing appears to have been left undone to
> alleviate the plight of the survivors.[13]

With the help of the Irish Army Air Corps, Captain Alan Kirk, United States
Naval Attaché in London, and Commander Norman Hitchcock, the United
States Assistant Naval Attaché for Air in London, flew to Galway to interview
American survivors. The American Minister to Ireland, John Cudahy also made
his way to Galway. Commandant Pádraig O'Duinnin, OC of the Defence Forces
1st Infantry Battalion, who was also present on the arrival of the survivors, wrote
to G2 that from the behaviour of the Americans it seemed that the Irish
authorities 'were not to be permitted to get the truth, and this was further borne
out by the eagerness with which they pursued anyone who said he saw a
submarine'.[14] Garda Superintendent Tomás O'Coileáin felt that Cudahy and
Kirk 'wished at all costs to establish that the SS Athenia had been sunk by a
submarine' and wished to report so to Washington.[15] Captain Cook later
confirmed to O'Duinnin that a torpedo had sunk his ship.

Secretary of State Cordell Hull instructed Cudahy to inform the Irish
government that the United States was 'deeply appreciative of the hospitable
assistance given to the American survivors of the S.S. Athenia by the authorities
and people of Eire'.[16] Cudahy had been present when *Knute Nelson* docked in
Galway and wrote to de Valera 'of the excellent arrangements made in Galway'
for dealing with the emergency.[17] They were 'a model of efficient organisation'
carried out in a 'competent and sympathetic manner'.[18] Anticipating further

---

11 NAI JUS 90/94/3, Cahill to Roche, 6 Sept. 1939.   12 NAI DT S11415, extract from
Cabinet minutes (G.C. 2/93), 4 Sept. 1939.   13 Ibid., de Valera to Browne, 11 Sept. 1939.
14 MA G2/X/431, O Duinnin to Archer, 6 Sept. 1939.   15 Ibid., Ó Coileáin to Murphy, 8
Sept. 1939.   16 NAI DFA 239/54, Cudahy to de Valera, 8 Sept. 1939.   17 NAI DT S11415,
de Valera to Browne, 11 Sept. 1939.   18 NAI DFA 239/54, Cudahy to de Valera, 8 Sept. 1939.

incidents the Department of Local Government and Public Health, on the instruction of the government, appointed Dr W. Sterling Berry, the department's Assistant Medical Adviser, as a 'special officer' for the conduct of all medical work and relief measures associated with 'emergencies such as arose recently in Galway as a result of the European War'.[19] The sinking of *Athenia* brought the battle of the Atlantic to the shores of neutral Ireland from the very outset of the Second World War. As the survivors arrived in Galway, their plight showed that, though neutral, Ireland could not isolate herself from the conflict.

Germany concealed Lemp's actions. Berlin feared the sinking of the *Athenia* would become another *Lusitania* and on 4 September ordered that there should be no further attacks on passenger ships. The German legation in Dublin sent External Affairs an aide memoire protesting that 'it was impossible that German naval forces took any part in the sinking of the ship. There were no German naval forces at all stationed in the area'.[20] There was no backlash in the United States and America maintained its neutrality. However, the sinking of *Athenia* began 'the longest campaign of the second world war and the longest and most complex submarine war in history'.[21] At the Admiralty in London Winston Churchill, returning triumphantly as First Lord after an absence of twenty-four years, decided that with war underway 'the prime attack appears to fall on the approaches to Great Britain from the Atlantic'. He anticipated unrestricted submarine warfare beginning in days. In the middle of 'the approaches to Great Britain from the Atlantic', at the point where convoys to and from Britain converged, lay neutral and defenceless Ireland.[22] Still seething at Chamberlain's return of the treaty ports to Ireland, the perceived impact of their loss to Britain in the battle of the Atlantic became an incubus to Churchill that would often destabilize British-Irish relations through the Second World War and which would place them in near crisis for the next twelve months.

In relaying Ireland's position on the outbreak of war in the Atlantic to London, Dulanty explained that de Valera had informed Eduard Hempel, the German Minister in Dublin, that 'he must not think that [the] Irish shore could be used for any German purposes – propaganda – espionage – etc.'.[23] Before the outbreak of hostilities the German Naval High Command had expected this, noting that 'with the exception of Spain and Japan, no benevolent attitude will be expected from *any neutral Power*'.[24] The use of the word 'any' indicated that

19 Garda Archives, 323/G/948/2/39, Ó Nualláin to Minister's Secretary, Department of Justice, 7 Sept. 1939. Through the Second World War Berry facilitated the care of persons shipwrecked on the Irish coast due to belligerent action. **20** NAI DFA 239/54. **21** Marc Milner, *Battle of the Atlantic* (St Catherines, ON, 2003), p. 8. **22** Martin Gilbert, *The Churchill war papers, volume I: at the Admiralty Sept. 1939–May 1940* (London, 1993), 'Winston S. Churchill: Notes of a Meeting', 4 Sept. 1939, p. 24. **23** TNA DO 35/1107/9 WX1/78, minute by Eden, 1 Sept. 1939. **24** Jak P. Mallmann Showell (ed.), *Fuehrer conferences on naval affairs, 1939–1945* (London, 2005), p. 35, Operational orders for Deutschland and Admiral Graf Spee, Berlin, 4 Aug. 1939. My italics.

even small neutral powers like Ireland were included in this strategic assumption. Hempel reported to Berlin that de Valera had told him that in the event of a war 'any violation either by Britain or by us of Irish territorial waters' would be taken very seriously in Dublin.[25] Emphasizing that Ireland would enforce neutrality and would defend itself to the best of its extremely limited ability against any attackers became Ireland's most important weapons to deter would-be invaders. Dublin informed Allies and Axis alike that the Irish coast would be under twenty-four-hour observation. This was hardly a real deterrent to invasion yet it might go some way towards minimizing clandestine contacts between Irish sympathizers and belligerents that could mushroom into incidents dragging Ireland into the wider conflict.

TRAINING THE COASTWATCHERS

Less than a week after the outbreak of the Second World War and with U-boats active off the Irish coast the Coast Watching Service existed only in rudimentary form. Its men were on active service but they lacked training and relied heavily on Garda support. Dunphy was guilty of underestimation when he told a Department of Finance official that there was 'much work to be done'.[26] Finance noted that 'some personnel' for the service had been recruited and the Department of Defence was taking over the aged fisheries protection vessel *Muirchú* and the deep-sea trawler *Fort Rannoch* for patrolling the coast, intercepting trawlers illegally fishing, and minesweeping.[27] The establishment of a General Headquarters staff to control the M&CWS was now 'an urgent necessity'.[28] Eight officers, headed by Colonel Seamus O'Higgins, were assembled to train and administer the landward section of what, following the establishment of the Marine Service on 6 September, would collectively be known to 1942 as the Marine and Coast Watching Service (M&CWS). The depot of the M&CWS would be at Fort Westmoreland on Haulbowline Island in Cork Harbour. The service would be administered at regional level from the depot in Cork and four sub-depots: one in Eastern Command at Portobello Barracks in Dublin, one in Curragh Command, in Waterford, and two in Western Command at Castlebar and at Killybegs. With support staff and two civilian technical advisors the headquarters staff of the M&CWS in September 1939 numbered fourteen. Colonel O'Higgins replaced Commandant Barrett as OC, though Barrett remained with the M&CWS. Dunphy continued as adviser and Commander O'Connell, a retired Royal Navy officer, was expected to be appointed as Chief Technical Adviser. In early October O'Connell's appointment was cancelled. Sir John Maffey, the newly appointed British Representative

25 *DGFPD: VII*, p. 471, Hempel to Foreign Ministry, 31 Aug. 1939.   26 NAI DF S4/84/38, minute on file, 5 Sept. 1939.   27 Ibid., minute of meeting with General MacMahon, 3.45 pm, 5 Sept. 1939.   28 Ibid., MacMahon to McElligott, 5 Sept. 1939.

in Ireland, 'gathered the impression, perhaps incorrectly that Commander O'Connell had become persona non grata'.[29] Finally in December Dunphy became Chief Technical Adviser on marine and naval matters. On 29 January 1940 Colonel Tony Lawlor succeeded O'Higgins as Chief Staff Officer in charge of the Marine and Coast Watching Service, remaining in command until April 1941 when he took command of No. 4 Mobile Brigade in Western Command, later becoming Chief of Staff in General Hugo MacNeill's 2nd Division. Commander Seamus O'Muiris replaced Lawlor as CSO of the Marine Service.

With the outbreak of war the reality finally dawned among the population of Ireland that the country might be under threat of invasion. Public interest in joining the Coast Watching Service increased as civilians sighted warships off the Irish coast and, after the sinking of *Athenia*, rumours circulated of U-boats operating in Irish waters. When travelling the east coast establishing LOPs Commandant Dominick Mackey of G2 reported that locals were 'helpful, friendly and anxious to help. There is no difficulty recruiting Watchers'.[30] Early logbooks and rosters show no problems filling shifts and shortage of numbers willing to serve was never a problem. When fully established the Coast Watching Service would comprise approximately 700 all ranks. Seven men led by an NCO manned each of the eighty-three LOPs. LOPs were grouped together in eighteen districts, with each district overseen by a district officer whose duty it was 'to visit the LOPs in his area at frequent and irregular intervals by day and night thus ensuring that the coast-watchers on duty are on the qui vive at all times'.[31]

Training for the first contingent of coastwatchers was almost non-existent. Raising the matter in the Seanad, Senator Frank MacDermott spoke of 'alarming stories' of the coastwatchers and claimed

> that the whole of this improvised coastguard system is a ridiculous farce ... [I]t is doing no good and could not do any good until some adequate arrangements are made for communications, for supplying the watchers with binoculars and for giving them some sort of training to enable them to recognise what they are supposed to have been placed there in order to see.[32]

In these circumstances Tom Kelly's experience of his first day's service at Power Head LOP on the east Cork coast cannot have been uncommon. He went on duty without any training or equipment and recalled that in three months spent with the Coast Watching Service, from September to November 1939, before joining the Defence Forces full time, he received no training in his duties.[33] Training was badly needed for the new force. Daily reports in the early months

29 TNA DO 35/548/25 E70/17, Maffey to Machtig, 4 Oct. 1939.   **30** MA G2/X/318, Mackey to Archer, 6 Sept. 1939.   **31** NAI DFA Secretary's Files P94, Memorandum on Coastal Observation, undated, but attached to Guilfoyle to Walshe, 20 Feb. 1943.   **32** *Seanad deb.*, vol. 24; col. 40, 6 Dec. 1939.   **33** Author's correspondence with Colonel Kelly, Oct.

of the Second World War were headed with the caveat that 'as no machinery is yet available to check the accuracy of these reports, they must be taken with reserve'.[34] An early report from Skerries LOP on the east coast north of Dublin shows the problems that arose due to lack of training when the LOP reported a 'vessel flying [an] unidentified ensign ... on the front of [the] ship was a big gun'.[35] Training schemes were needed to remedy such poor reporting and they were organized through the winter of 1939. Men went on a two-week course supplemented each year by one week's refresher training. By 1942 'it was found possible to withdraw most of the personnel in turn for refresher courses'.[36] Soon nearly all men had taken these courses and two special courses for NCOs were being run. The benefit was clear. The quality of the reporting from each post was not uniform, nor was it so throughout the service, but as training and experience improved there was a noticeable and sustained increase in the quality of reports from LOPs.

The handwritten notes kept by Volunteer John P. Burns of Ballina, Mayo, during his training in Dublin record the basic instruction given to coastwatchers. They show how coastwatchers were first taught to administer their post. The importance of the post logbook was paramount; it provided raw information in a standard format across the service, analysed by command intelligence officers and ultimately submitted for final analysis to G2 in Dublin.[37] LOP logbooks provide a record of what happened and when and where it happened around the Irish coast from September 1939 to June 1945. Yet they are only as reliable as the accuracy of those who kept them. While the information from some posts is extremely detailed, that from others is rudimentary at best.[38] These reservations aside, the logbooks are an extremely valuable historical source and are the most important legacy of the Coast Watching Service.

During basic training coastwatchers learned signalling, first aid, maritime practices and the identification of types of ships, submarines and aircraft, as well as basic meteorology and hydrography. Burns served at LOP 63 at Benwee Head above Portacloy on the north Mayo coast. He was attached to the post through the Emergency and was on duty when LOP 63 went 'off the air' at 1500 on 15 June 1945.[39] His training notes show that he consulted Admiralty charts to work out depths of the sea near his post and the distances to those points. The water in Portacloy Bay, immediately to the right of the LOP as Burns looked out to sea

2005.   **34** MA DRS No. 1, 2 to 5 Sept. 1939.   **35** MA DRS No. 21, 29 Sept. 1939.   **36** MA General Report for the Army for the year 1 April 1942 to 31 March 1943.   **37** The importance of the logbook is evident from May 1945 report that a coastwatcher at Ballycotton LOP was fined for tearing a page from the post log. The fine of 20*s*. also covered the offence of being absent from parade.   **38** In addition, logbooks by definition do not include examples of dereliction of duty such as falling asleep on duty, an offence with which many coast-watchers were charged. It is clear from charges on monthly reports that coastwatchers were liable to be slack on duty in the small hours of the morning.   **39** MA LOP 63, 15 June 1945.

towards the Stags of Broadhaven, was four fathoms; beneath the LOP, which was sited 200 feet above sea level, the sea was twelve fathoms; two miles away, inside the Stags of Broadhaven, the water was nineteen fathoms.[40] The trade route further out to sea was thirty fathoms.

Despite training, many LOPs lacked a full set of equipment in the first months of the war and coastwatchers could not practice their newly acquired skills. Captain Togher, Western Command IO, reported to the Department of Defence how equipment was 'urgently required especially Field Glasses as the C.W.S. judging by their reports cannot distinguish Markings on Ships, Aircraft, etc.'.[41] Captain Alexander B. Greig, the British Naval Attaché in Dublin, saw no evidence of signalling equipment in the posts he visited in Cork and Kerry in December 1939. He reported to the Admiralty that

> when the ratings go up to Dublin for their course they are taught the flags of the international code, and all had made little sketches of same in their notebooks. They also have instruction in Morse and Semaphore. At the moment I should say that their efficiency in signalling was practically nil.[42]

But Greig need not have worried. Commandant Robert L. Daly, Eastern Command IO, had already made this point in his weekly reports and deficiencies were being made good at local level. Training was refreshed through lectures given by the corporal in charge of each post and by district officers. The logbook for Toe Head LOP in Cork shows that coastwatchers received rigorous instructions from their NCO in the International Maritime Code and semaphore signalling, each training session being followed by an exercise. Training continued through the war and in Southern Command the NCOs took 'their men for Morse and semaphore signalling for two hours each day'.[43] Coastwatchers at Galley Head LOP practiced their semaphore rigorously, regular drill entries appearing in their logbook through the war. These were not simply training exercises for the sake of training. In March 1940 the Minister for Defence Oscar Traynor told the members of the Seanad of the actions of one coastwatcher

> on a very desolate portion of the south coast. He was on duty by himself and he saw what he believed to be a boat out at a great distance to sea. He got a glass and fixed it on the boat and decided on his own that it was a boat with shipwrecked sailors. He could only see one individual rowing. He immediately went to a nearby house, telephoned to the Gardaí and then telephoned to the command headquarters in Cork City. Again using

---

40 One fathom equals six feet. **41** MA G2/X/318, Togher to CSO G.3, Department of Defence, 7 Sept. 1939. **42** TNA DO 130/7, Greig to Slade, 27 Dec. 1939. **43** MA G2/X/315 Pt II, Monthly Report – Marine Service Depot, Haulbowline-Southern Command, Aug. 1941.

his own initiative, he asked the people in Cork City to send an ambulance as he believed this boat contained shipwrecked sailors. Command head-quarters accepted the message and sent an ambulance to the scene and this young Volunteer, by the aid of semaphore signalling, brought the boat into the only possible place it could have landed on that desolate coast. The sailors themselves who had come in the boat from the wrecked vessel tried to induce this young man to take whatever small amount of money they had on them as a mark of their esteem and appreciation for his initiative and extraordinary action.[44]

This was not an isolated case. On the morning of 24 August 1940, when the battle of the Atlantic was at its height off the coast of Ireland, the lighthouse keeper on Inishtrahull Island six miles north of Malin Head used semaphore to communicate with Malin Head LOP on the mainland that crew from the torpedoed cargo ship *Havildar* had landed on Inishtrahull. Near the end of the war, after the crew of U-260 came ashore near Galley Head LOP, the Marine Service sent torpedo boats to patrol the area. During the operation one of the boats 'pulled up stationary 1 mile south of post and semaphored to find out how many survivors landed here and at Courtmacsherry' and the coastwatcher on duty replied by semaphore that eleven survivors had landed.[45]

The most intricate drawings and notes in Burns' notebooks concern mines. These were 'the biggest and most deadly forms of explosive at the beginning of the war' and many hundreds were washed ashore along the Irish coast during the conflict.[46] As numerous accidents were to show, these mines would prove a dangerous hazard to military and civilians during the war. Burns recorded the exterior and variations in type due to nationality, making cross-section drawings in coloured pencil. He learned how mines detonated, how some floated free and others were anchored in position. Fixed mines could break free and drift from their intended position. A daily task of coastwatchers was to track the progress of mines and report their presence to Command ordnance officers. When a mine beached coastwatchers and LDF or LSF would be placed on guard to keep curious civilians away until ordnance officers rendered the mine harmless. In other cases mines observed out to sea were destroyed by rifle fire from patrol boats. Disposal of mines at sea was not always a simple task. The logbook of Brownstown Head LOP to the east of Tramore, Waterford, includes an entry from Private Brogan on to the attempted destruction of a floating mine that 'Private Condra and myself fired 25 rounds each [on] orders from O/C Dunmore East. Mine struck 7 (seven) times with no effect.'[47]

---

44 *Seanad deb.*, vol. 24; col. 751, 6 Mar. 1940.   45 MA LOP 29, 13 Mar. 1945.   46 Owen Quinn, 'Wartime Coast Watching', lecture to the Irish Maritime Institute, 27 Oct. 1988. I thank Joe Varley for giving me a copy of this lecture.   47 MA LOP 17, 26 June 1941.

There were a considerable number of serious injuries and deaths caused by exploding mines along the Irish coast during the Second World War. In January 1941, when the British minefield in St George's Channel disintegrated in winter storms, several mines beached on the Waterford and Wexford coasts. When one mine exploded at Cullenstown, Wexford, three members of the Defence Forces were killed instantly, one died later in hospital and a member of the LDF was injured. Patrick Scanlan, Assistant Keeper at Tuskar Rock lighthouse off the Wexford coast, was to die of injuries caused from the explosion of a drifting mine that hit Tuskar Rock; his colleague Assistant Keeper William J. Cahill was injured.[48] A mine washed ashore near Ballycotton LOP in April 1942 and exploded. Though there were no casualties, the explosion caused considerable local damage. The greatest loss of life through exploding mines during the Emergency was the death of nineteen men at Ballymanus near Annagry in Donegal on 10 May 1943. Warned of the hazard facing them by the local District Officer, they were among a group of about thirty onlookers who did not withdraw from the beached mine when ordered to move back at least 500 yards, the regulation safety distance. A number of the men, labourers who had returned from Scapa Flow, spoke with familiarity about mines and ignored the District Officer J.M. Dunleavy. Eighteen died instantly when the mine exploded, the final death occurred the following day in Letterkenny Hospital. The dead included three brothers and three pairs of brothers.

Initially coastwatchers were poorly drilled in recognition of aircraft. To the beginning of the Second World War aircraft were a relatively rare sight in Irish skies. The coastwatchers at first knew only silhouettes of the aircraft of the Irish Army Air Corps.[49] There was no training in recognition of British or German aircraft. In October Maffey wrote of the 'exclusion from instructions to coastal organisations of any mention of aircraft'.[50] This was to Britain's benefit as Maffey continued that 'today our aircraft are flying over the headlands of Eire, and even inland, and nothing is being said'. Recognition charts of British and German aircraft were acquired slowly and distributed to coastwatchers. District Officer MacLoughlin, inspecting Galley Head LOP in February 1940, noted the absence of the silhouette chart from an otherwise clean and tidy post. By March it was on display, MacLoughlin remarking that the post was now 'very good'.[51] This was not a situation peculiar to Galley Head. At the neighbouring Toe Head LOP MacLoughlin found that recognition charts had only been delivered in late February but visiting the post on 6 March he found 'charts displayed – orders and instructions in good order'.[52] When German aircraft bombed Campile and Ambrosetown in Wexford in August 1940, Volunteer Nicholas Redmond told

---

48 'Tuskar Rock Lighthouse', *BEAM magazine* (No. 30) at www.cil.ie (accessed 12 July 2005). 49 The Lysander, the Gloucester Gladiator, the Hawker Hind, the Avro Cadet, the Vickers Vespa, the Avro Anson and the Walrus Amphibian. 50 TNA DO 35/1008/11, Maffey to Eden, 26 Oct. 1939. 51 MA LOP 27, 22 Feb. 1940 and 6 Mar. 1940. 52 MA LOP 28, 6

questioners during his debriefing that though he had been a year on duty at his post at Carnsore Point, in other words, since the start of the war, he had 'no chart showing different types of aircraft and therefore had no means of comparing them to any known type by their appearance'.[53] By as late in the war as autumn 1943 the Defence Forces lacked recognition charts for United States aircraft, even though United States B-17 Flying Fortresses and B-24/PB4Y-1 Liberators were regularly seen in Irish skies. Training made up for such deficiencies as generic aircraft identification techniques were taught. Burns noted how an 'aircraft flies at 5 miles a minute' and a 'bomber at 4 miles a minute … bombers [had a] heavy volume tone [and] fighters [a] sharp tone'. He then noted the four physical characteristics to be recorded of any aircraft passing his post which he summarized as 'WEFT' or Wings, Engines, Fuselage and Tail. When Volunteer Redmond was asked to identify the aircraft he saw at Carnsore he used these techniques, describing

> two engines, single plane, glass in front on which the sun was shining … no visible undercarriage … the tail appeared to have a single upright fin. The engines were in the wing one on each side of the fuselage.[54]

On examining a set of silhouettes Redmond picked out the Luftwaffe He-111. On being questioned further he added that he saw 'a lot of aeroplanes from time to time but had not previously seen aeroplanes of the type which I saw on 26/8/40'.

If an aircraft crashed near a LOP, coastwatchers were to 'treat survivors kindly' and first 'call [a] priest or other such clergyman as is requested'.[55] They were then to 'render all possible assistance to personnel such as first aid … prevent civilians getting in touch with members of [the] crew' and, 'inform [the] survivors that they are in *Eire*'.[56] This important role of the coastwatchers was taught in detail and can be seen in practice when a German airman came ashore at Slea Head LOP on 28 November 1941 after he and his crew had come down in the sea close to Inishvichillaune. The coastwatchers took the German into custody until the military from Dingle arrived and took over. This hearts-and-minds approach had its tougher side. Training specified that the senior officer who searched a downed plane was to ensure that 'all maps and documents are to be collected [and] also pay books [,] identity disks etc.',[57] ensuring, if they had not been destroyed by the crew, a useful supply of raw intelligence material. This drill was followed on the morning of 5 February 1941 when a German FW-200 Condor crashed on a mountainside near Durrus, Cork, killing five of the six-man crew. Captain Florrie O'Donoghue, the IO at Collins Barracks Cork, and

Mar. 1940. 53 NAI DFA 221/147, statement by Nicholas Redmond (Vol. 206394), 3 Sept. 1940. 54 Ibid. 55 MA Owen Quinn Papers, training notes of Volunteer J.P. Burns. 56 Ibid. 57 Ibid.

Major Dan McDonald, OC West Cork Military Area, 'took possession of the maps and papers not destroyed by fire. They also searched the bodies for identity disks etc., and took possession of what they found.'[58] These items not only gave an indication of the identities of the crew but identified the squadron to which the aircraft was attached and its area of operation.

Coastwatchers were drilled that they were guarding the extremities of Ireland's territory. They were to control their beat and never leave their post. In carrying out these duties the coastwatchers were not usually armed but they received basic rifle training. Dunmore Head LOP logbook shows that on 1 May 1941 Volunteer Joseph Boyle reported to Fort Dunree 'for signal course and rifle marksmanship'.[59] Consideration was given in 1940 to issuing arms to all members of the Coast Watching Service. Under this plan, dating from the crisis months of May and June, coastwatchers were to receive rifles and Thompson sub-machine-guns 'to put up at least a minimum initial resistance' against invading forces but the plan was not pursued.[60] In the event of being issued with weapons coastwatchers had permission to open fire without warning in defence of their LOP and their comrades and to prevent themselves being disarmed.[61] On a day-to-day basis only the men at the LOP at Fenit in Kerry, which was located on a rocky outcrop that formed part of Fenit harbour, were armed.[62] This LOP, the only post to have a double complement of sixteen men, worked closely with troops at the Fenit military post in the defence of the harbour.

Some regular soldiers questioned the degree of soldiering undertaken by the unarmed coastwatchers, but it is significant that no arms were held in poorly defended LOPs. There is no record of IRA interest in the Coast Watching Service or attempts to disrupt duties at LOPs. This may also have been due to coastwatchers being former reservists from a force known to include many former IRA members. Individual coastwatchers may well have had specific political beliefs but they kept them to themselves. Guy Liddell noted in his diary that at either George's Head or Hag's Head LOP in Clare 'one of the men in charge of the local coast watching station is said to be an IRA deportee ... the local Civic Guard appear to be terrorised.'[63] It was a variation on a well-worn story. In the Dáil in November 1939 Fine Gael Deputy Michael Brennan damned the coastwatchers by reference to two of their number: 'Apparently the best qualification they had for the appointment was that they were strong supporters of the Government.'[64] Some days later independent Senator James MacLoughlin, in the course of a wide-ranging attack on Fianna Fáil defence spending, informed the Seanad that coastwatchers were 'simply numbers of

58 NAI JUS 90/119/296, O'Gara to Murphy, 5 Feb. 1941.   59 MA LOP 71, 1 May 1941.
60 MA EDP 20/5, Memorandum No. 4: Employment of CWS.   61 There are reports in G2 files of coastwatchers being fined for losing ammunition.   62 MA G2/X/315 Pt II, Monthly Report – Marine Service Depot, Haulbowline-Southern Command, Aug. 1941.   63 West, *Liddell diaries, vol. 1*, p. 58.   64 *Dáil deb.*, vol. 78; col. 416, 29 Nov. 1939.

untrained country lads – picked by minor Volunteer officers chiefly because of their political leanings'.[65] Local politics and family background may well have played a part in the selection of 'suitable' coastwatchers but if politics clouded the judgment or affected the operation of any LOP, then it is not evident from archival records. Nor is there any record of men being dismissed for political activities.

PRIMARY DUTIES OF COASTWATCHERS

Coastwatchers worked in groups of two on eight or twelve hour shifts. One man remained inside the LOP operating the phone, the other patrolled outside and the two would alternate this arrangement during shifts. The two men were not permitted to investigate incidents observed beyond their LOP; they were to contact the local military and the nearest Garda barracks to alert forces to deploy to the scene. Coastwatchers were aided from the summer of 1940 by the LSF who had among their specified duties supplementing the Gardaí and Defence Forces by assisting 'in the schemes of aerial observation [and] the maintenance of a coastal watch'.[66] As a non-combatant force the Coast Watching Service was to gather information about the enemy, record it and 'distribute it to the formation on the right, left and rear'. They were to 'know where the enemy is both strong and weak' and to 'assist in preventing [the] enemy from gaining information'. To this end, Volunteer Burns carefully noted the twelve duties of a coastwatcher in the notes taken during his basic training in Dublin:

1. To be always alert watchful and quick to report.
2. To ensure that messages and reports convey a true and accurate picture of [the] matter reported on.
3. Never relax vigilance during tour of watch.
4. To remain at their post until relieved.
5. To ensure that message and reports are definite, simple and brief.
6. To ensure they know the location of nearest telephone.
7. To understand his mission, what to report, how to report and to whom to report.
8. To avoid giving information on his duties or information on the CWS to unauthorised persons particularly as to the location of the report centre for his LOP.
9. To accurately report in post log book all events, messages and incidents that occur during tour of watch.
10. To establish the identity of all official visitors to the post before disclosing information or allowing inspection of post.

65 *Seanad deb.*, vol. 24; col. 12, 6 Dec. 1939. 66 NAI DT S11903, Organisation and Duties of Local Security Force, June 1940.

11. To prevent unauthorised persons from loitering in the vicinity of LOP.
12. To have no unnecessary exposure of light during night watches.[67]

When carrying out these duties coastwatchers at each LOP were to be equipped with a telescope, binoculars, silhouettes of aircraft and ships, a logbook, signal flags and lamps and a bicycle. A fixed-point compass card or bearing plate fixed on true north, and which included bearings and distances to local landmarks, was added to the list in the autumn of 1940 as the battle of the Atlantic intensified, allowing accurate bearings to be taken of 'attacks on vessels in the vicinity of our shores'.[68] Sometimes these items appeared at once from stores, such as at Galley Head where the men 'received from District Officer J MacLoughlin ... logbook and telescope, compass, bicycle, oil [skin] coats and hats also navigational intelligence book'.[69] In practice not all items appeared at the same time. Lamenting the lack of telescopes in LOPs in Eastern Command Commandant Daly realized that with the evenings closing in 'the instruments at the disposal of the CWS personnel are, on account of visibility conditions, totally inadequate for this type of work'.[70] Daly anticipated that the operational efficiency of the coastwatchers would be reduced if it was impossible for them to obtain basic details of incidents because they could not view them accurately. When reporting observations off the Mayo and Sligo coast in September 1939 Garda Superintendent Hunt of Easkey District made the damning though comical comment that the binoculars his men were using in their work assisting the coastwatchers were 'not powerful enough for this purpose, unless the Boat or Aircraft, as the case may be, happens to be very near to the person using the glasses'.[71] In September 1940 Volunteer James Brown at Carnsore Point LOP complained of having 'an old telescope ... not reliable especially for distinguishing colours or markings. It is only useful for giving an outline of the object'.[72] A year later the story was of haphazard progress as District Officers in Southern Command reported that men were 'making satisfactory progress in Morse, Semaphore, International Flags, but cannot practice with lamp[s] as batteries requisitioned for same have not yet been supplied'.[73]

The primary duties of the Coast Watching Service were thus passive defence and information gathering, keeping a constant watch along the coastline for air and naval activity, enemy forces poised to invade Ireland and potential fifth columnists who sought to assist invaders and who could be 'any unusual assembly of men, lorries or cars in the vicinity of the coast'.[74] Though 'initially

67 MA Owen Quinn Papers, training notes of Volunteer J.P. Burns.   68 MA G2/X/318, Archer to Lawlor, 20 Aug. 1940.   69 MA LOP 27, 1 Feb. 1940.   70 MA G2/X/315 Pt I, report by Daly for week ending 7 Oct. 1939.   71 NAI JUS 8/756, Hunt to Murphy, 27 Sept. 1939.   72 NAI DFA 221/147, statement by Volunteer James Brown (206392), 3 Sept. 1940. 73 MA G2/X/315 Pt II, Monthly report – Marine Service Depot, Haulbowline, Sept. 1941. 74 MA G2/X/318, Extract from report of visit of Major Flynn and Commandant Powell to Western Command Posts. Athlone, Galway and Castlebar, during period Jan. 17th–Jan. 19th,

intended for naval observation', the Coast Watching Service became 'the first service to report aircraft crossing the coast, which were then traced by reports from military posts, Garda stations etc.'.[75] The early-warning reports from the coastwatchers would give the ill-equipped Defence Forces valuable extra time to ensure that 'suitable defensive action may be taken' against invaders.[76] If warnings of an imminent attack were received, the Minister for the Co-ordination of Defensive Measures would summon 'a conference of the appropriate officers of the Defence Forces (including the Coast Watching Service and the Army Signals Corps) and the Garda Síochána'.[77] Reports received from observers including the Coast Watching Service would be important in beginning the early stages of transition to emergency decentralized government through Regional and County Commissioners acting subject to control by the military authorities in certain areas.[78] If an invasion occurred then the LOPs in the invasion zone, following their reporting of the invasion, were to regard their task as completed, destroy their equipment and withdraw, joining the nearest LDF contingent if possible. If a post was held up, then it was for off-duty personnel to 'slip past persons engaged in the operation and cycle to [the] nearest point to which phone or other contact could be made with the nearest military posts'.[79] This was probably easier said that done.

THE INSTALLATION OF TELEPHONES AT LOPS

Before the war began the Department of Defence maintained that 'the value of a Coast Watching Service will depend primarily on the rapidity with which it can transfer information to suitable centres'.[80] Bryan had written in 1936 that Ireland needed 'not only an effective Coast Watching Service, but also an effective Communications Service ... [I]t is obvious that military forces and a coast watching service dotted round the coast in a circle would need a network of communications through the country.'[81] Initially reports of belligerent action were conveyed by bicycle or by foot to the local post office where the coast-watcher concerned would report the incident to command headquarters. In the early months of its operations the lack of proper communications was the Coast Watching Service's weakest point. This greatly reduced efficiency in a manner highlighted by the British War Office *Manual of Coastal Defence*: 'Good information is the first requisite, but, unless there is an efficient system for

1940.   75 UCDA P71/171, Military Sections, rough notes by Bryan.   76 MA G2/X/318, Instructions for Personnel Manning Coast Watching Posts, Sept. 1939.   77 NAI DT S11903, minutes, Cabinet Committee on Emergency Problems, 15th Meeting, 11 July 1940.   78 This scheme of emergency administration and government in the event of the isolation or invasion of Ireland was approved by the government in July 1940 (see NAI DT S11980).   79 MA G2/X/318, Extract from report of visit of Major Flynn and Commandant Powell to Western Command Posts. Athlone, Galway and Castlebar, during period Jan. 17th–Jan. 19th, 1940.   80 MA 2/55390, Coast Watching Service, undated, probably Feb. 1939.   81 UCDA P71/8,

communicating information quickly to headquarters and those in a position to act upon it, much of its value is lost.'[82] The manual continued that 'too much stress cannot be laid on the necessity of establishing and perfecting this system in times of peace'.[83] Bicycles and the local post office or Garda station telephone were of no use for reporting a fast low-flying aircraft as the aircraft would be long gone by the time its presence was reported up the chain of command. Indeed in December 1939 it was estimated that using this system the 'time from sighting [to] despatching messages by telephone varied from 20 minutes to an hour'.[84] No matter how well its volunteers were trained, such a communications deficit meant that the Coast Watching Service was unable to distribute the information it was gathering efficiently and the information was losing much of its value. Other means of communication would have to be found and direct telephone communication from LOPs was the obvious answer.

In 1939 the Irish telephone network radiated out from Dublin to the main centres of population. There were few lines between regional centres and fewer lines, in places none at all, to the extremities of the state where the Coast Watching Service operated. Coastwatchers often had to travel great distances to the nearest phone to report incidents and this greatly hindered their efficiency. The installation of telephones at LOPs was expected to herald 'a vast improvement in the transmission of reports'.[85] However, few LOPs distant to centres of population were initially expected to get telephone lines as 'the expense of laying telephone communication to the remote parts of the state was prohibitive'.[86] Posts on the east coast were connected first with telephones being installed in Howth, Dalkey and Wicklow Head LOPs by mid-October 1939. This was early in the development of the Coast Watching Service but Howth and Dalkey LOPs were close to urban areas and Wicklow Head LOP was beside the lighthouse on the headland, all locations where phones were already installed. The three posts were thus relatively easy to connect to the phone network but they were also posts vital to the defence of Dublin against air attack and so the telephone was necessary at these locations to provide timely warning of air raids. North of Dublin, Ballagan Point and Dunany Point were connected to the telephone network by early November 1939 but beyond the east coast there were no telephones at LOPs and, despite the pleading of District Officers that the efficiency of the coastwatchers was being impaired, there was little likelihood of lines being installed. When he visited LOPs in Sligo and Donegal in March 1940 Captain Greig reported to Admiralty NID that none of the posts he had visited contained telephones and that 'the real weak spot in the organisation is communications'.[87]

Fundamental Factors Affecting Saorstát Defence Problem, May 1936.   82 TNA WO 287/84, *Manual of coastal defence* (London, 1939), chapter II, p.1.   83 Ibid., p. 10.   84 TNA ADM 223/486, Eire Coast Watching, 11 Dec. 1939.   85 MA G2/X/315 Pt I, report by Daly for week ending 7 Oct. 1939.   86 TNA DO 130/7, Greig to Maffey, 18 Nov. 1939.   87 TNA KV 4/280, Further visit to Eire Coastwatching Stations, 19 Mar. 1940.

Even where there were telephones available close to LOPs limited service at exchanges greatly reduced the efficiency of coastwatchers in outlying areas and excluded the possibility of rapid communications. On 9 May 1940 when a coastwatcher on duty at Roonagh, near Louisbourgh in Mayo, called at the local Garda barracks in the early hours to report the sighting of ships passing his post he 'waited over an hour ringing, unable to get through to CIO [and] was told by [the] Garda on duty that there was no connection possible till Post Office opened'.[88] This situation was untenable. Germany invaded the Low Countries the following day and with the war moving west and the possibility of an invasion of Ireland looming 'an entirely new situation' existed in which it was 'imperative that the LOPs along the south, south-west and part of the west coast should be connected to the telephone with the minimum delay'.[89]

A meeting to discuss the protection of vital points in the state was held on 17 May in the Department of Defence between representatives of that department and the departments of Justice and Industry and Commerce. The Chief of Staff of the Defence Forces and the Commissioner of C3, the Garda Special Branch, also attended the meeting. With the war in the Low Countries and France a week old coastwatchers were still expected to rely on Garda telephones. Towards the end of the meeting mention was made 'of the fact that many Garda Stations, including those on the Mayo coast' were without telephones. This was 'a distinct disadvantage' but the meeting concluded that 'the cost of installation in many such cases would be prohibitive'.[90] John Duff, Assistant Secretary at the Department of Justice, disagreed, writing to MacMahon at Defence that he was 'by no means sure' that it would be prohibitively expensive to extend phone lines to Garda stations in Mayo as the Department of Posts and Telegraphs were in the process of extending the telephone network to Belmullet. He asked MacMahon to amend the minutes of the meeting to read that

> from the point of view of defence it was essential that there should be facilities for rapid communication with all Garda Stations, and in particular, centres such as Blacksod and Belmullet ... [T]his is an urgent matter and should not be postponed by reason of considerations of expense.[91]

General Hugo MacNeill was thinking along more advanced lines and wrote to MacMahon that the use of Garda station telephones was not adequate. It was 'of vital importance in the present situation that information of hostile activities along our coastline should be reported ... with the utmost promptness' to command headquarters and GHQ.[92] The British evacuation from Dunkirk and

88 MA LOP 57, 9 May 1940. 89 MA EDP 20/5, MacNeill to MacMahon, undated, but May 1940. 90 NAI JUS 90/119/168, Protection of Vital Points, 17 May 1940. 91 Ibid., Duff to MacMahon, 22 May 1940. 92 MA EDP 20/5, MacNeill to MacMahon, undated,

withdrawal from Norway brought German encirclement of Britain closer and for Ireland the invasion threat grew. MacNeill continued that 'delay in reporting may make all the difference between our being in a position to meet such activities in their early stages and consequently frustrate them and being faced with a position which has developed to serious proportions'. The speed at which reports could be received depended largely on the distance between LOPs and the nearest telephone and, as matters stood, 'the telephone service at present available to our LOPs is entirely inadequate'. Many LOPs were between four and eight miles from a telephone and, perhaps with the Roonagh episode in mind, MacNeill added 'in many cases there is no night telephone service'. Another memorandum explained that LOPs are

> often five or six miles – in one case twelve – from the nearest telephone. Roughly speaking, the more important the LOP station the more difficult its communications inland. This fact ... greatly detracts from the value of the service from the standpoint of national defence.[93]

It was a 'very serious position' and the Chief of Staff was 'most anxious' that LOPs be linked to the national telephone system. The Army's Director of Signals, Major J.F. Gantly, had undertaken preliminary discussions with the Post Office who were prepared 'to put the work in hand immediately'. On 10 June it was agreed by representatives of Defence, Finance, Posts and Telegraphs and the Gardaí at an interdepartmental conference that 'telephone communication should be provided to all Look-out Posts ... irrespective of distances of a post from existing Garda or public service telephones'.[94] Presumably with rumours of U-boat activity in mind, Defence prioritised the provision of telephones at LOPs along the Cork and Kerry coast. Three days later MacNeill informed all commands that the Post Office was installing telephones at LOPs along the south and west coast. Accordingly, telephones were installed at most posts by the Department of Posts and Telegraphs during the summer of 1940. In the case of Roonagh the Post Office inspector called to the post in late June, six weeks after the incident at the Garda station, and the phone was installed.

If the LOPs were the nerve ending of the country's defences, the telephone system linking them to command headquarters, GHQ in Dublin and to each other became the nerves. The telephone ensured the rapid transmission of information leading to more accurate and timely intelligence assessments. In addition the telephone improved the security of posts and provided a psychological boost for men, particularly in the small hours, as they now knew they were not alone in carrying out their duties in isolated LOPs but were part of a wider network. The introduction of the telephone also ensured that the

but May 1940.   **93** Ibid., Memorandum No. 4: Employment of CWS.   **94** NAI DF S53/11/40, 'Emergency Communications', 10 June 1940.

Coast Watching Service played an important role in the development of the outlying regions of Ireland. The telephone numbers of individual posts illustrate how few telephones there were in these outlying areas. LOP 1 at Ballagan Point on the Cooley Peninsula in Louth was 'Greenore 7' while the neighbouring post at Dunany Point was 'Clogher Head 4'.[95] It was considered an event worthy of record by Volunteers Farrell and Doherty at LOP 64 on Downpatrick Head in Mayo that on 1 July 1940 'P. Murphy arrived at the post with telephone poles'.[96] Other LOPs noted the arrival of the telephone in their logbooks, with Malin Head phoning the military at Buncrana 40 at 2130 on 9 July 1940 'that the phone is now installed at the LOP'.[97] Test calls to exchanges and visits of linesmen became a regular feature of each post's daily routine. So too did the report of the District Officer as to whether there had been any non-official calls from posts under inspection. The importance of the telephone can be seen when a coastwatcher in Southern Command failed to answer a telephone test call and was fined thirty shillings.

Coastwatchers now had speedy communication with neighbouring LOPs, with local military posts and barracks, with command headquarters and with Defence Forces GHQ in Dublin. This greatly improved information gathering and incident investigation along the coastline. The phone enabled coastwatchers' reports of explosions, sightings of lights and the passage of unseen aircraft whose engine drone had only been heard to be investigated swiftly and comprehensively with greater ease and efficiency. It also allowed IOs to immediately interrogate coastwatchers, pass on orders, check up on LOPs during the small hours and distribute information on sightings, overflights and crashes with greater speed. For example, when an aircraft crashed on Inishtrahull at 2225 on 19 November 1944 the crash was not spotted by coastwatchers on Malin Head. Defence Forces GHQ in Dublin was alerted to the crash and was able to contact Malin Head LOP about the flight. The telephone brought the Coast Watching Service to life as a comprehensive observation system operating in real time on a countrywide basis.

Communication with neighbouring posts was just as important as communication with command headquarters or GHQ in Dublin. Just before midnight on 2 February 1943 Roonagh LOP 'sighted [a] glare about 8 miles south of post, rays directed skywards. Visibility poor. Called Rosroe Post re fire.'[98] Rosroe could offer no explanation. The trouble was closer to home; a barrel of petrol salvaged by a local had exploded as it was being divided out, burning down the man's house, injuring him and two of his family.[99] At Brownstown Head LOP in Waterford the practice of relaying messages from one LOP to another is vividly illustrated when on 20 September 1941 the LOP received a call from Hook

95 MA G2/X/315 Pt I, report by Daly for the week ending 11 Nov. 1939. 96 MA LOP 64, 1 July 1940. 97 MA LOP 80, 9 July 1940. 98 MA LOP 57, 2 Feb. 1943. 99 When a second barrel was washed up the following day, the Gardaí were notified immediately.

Head, the LOP to the east, that 'three internees has [*sic*] escaped from Isle of Man in a rowing boat' and all were thought to be Irish.[100] They noted the message and passed it in turn on to the next LOP to the west at Dunabrattin Head.

When a coastwatcher picked up his phone and used the magic prefix 'Defence Message – Priority', lines would be cleared by the operator and the coastwatcher would be patched through to command headquarters to deliver his message of sightings or landings.[101] Even in the worst cases, delays of over ten minutes were rarely experienced, very different from the bicycle dominated communication of the early months of the war. Commandant Quinn recalled that 'if we wanted to call right through to Castlebar, Athlone or Dublin … I'd only to say "Defence Call" and I got right through, I never had a break down, I never had a delay'.[102] A telephone operator at Western Command Headquarters at Athlone later told Quinn that she was 'very impressed by the accuracy, the clarity and the regularity of these reports coming in on the movement of craft, particularly aircraft, floating mines and so on and she realised that … these were our frontline troops'.[103] The quality of the lines was often poorer than Quinn remembered. The Curragh Command IO reported that along the entire coastal region of the command, between Kilmichael in Wicklow and Forlorn Point in Wexford, 'it is nearly impossible to hear conversation'.[104] Often dismissive of the Coast Watching Service, the verdict of RAF planners in January 1941 of the telecommunications network in wartime Ireland was as damning. When planning a theoretical air defence system for Ireland should Britain occupy the country, they noted 'the paucity and unreliability of telecommunications in Eire'.[105] Nonetheless, local and regional communications in Ireland improved because of the lines installed to facilitate the work of the Coast Watching Service. By 1943 only two posts, Parkmore and Foileye in Kerry, were without telephones, and they were to remain so for the remainder of the war. Here communication with the nearest telephone remained by bicycle. Parkmore used the telephone three miles away in Ventry post office and Foileye used the insecure method of despatching a runner to the telephone at Kells railway station, which communicated in turn with Cahirciveen station and thus on to the Garda station in the town.

Given the scarcity of telephones in rural Ireland a not so subtle piece of social history emerges from the Defence Forces memorandum 'Hints on the use of the Telephone', part of the handbook given to coastwatchers. Men were instructed to 'know the correct number of the person you are calling and your own number'

---

100 MA LOP 17, 20 Sept. 1941. The three internees were apprehended on the English coast.
101 MA G2/X/318, Instructions for Personnel Manning Coast Watching Posts, Sept. 1939.
102 Owen Quinn, 'Wartime coast watching', lecture to the Irish Maritime Institute, 27 Oct. 1988. 103 Ibid. 104 MA G2/X/315 Pt I, report by Daly to G2, 23 Oct. 1939. 105 TNA AIR 2/7233, minutes of a meeting held at the Air Ministry, 13 Jan. 1941.

and to 'speak clearly and distinctly into the mouthpiece … if you speak clearly it is rarely necessary to speak loudly'. In addition they received the rudimentary instruction that if they were using a dial telephone to 'lift the receiver and listen for a continuous low-pitched purring sound heard in the earpiece' and were warned 'do not replace the receiver or depress the receiver rest before the conversation is finished or you may be disconnected'.[106] Despite these hints, in Southern Command in late 1939 it was 'still not possible … to get the essentials of a message, except by question and answer and, with some personnel, it is impossible to carry on a telephone conversation and the help of a third party must be sought'.[107] With training, competency improved and the telephone brought the isolated LOPs along the Irish coastline into immediate contact with the central components of the country's defences, greatly improving the efficiency of the Coast Watching Service.

'THEY WENT UP LIKE MUSHROOMS' – BUILDING LOPS

With training underway and men in temporary accommodation at their positions in Army-issue bell tents, sites for permanent huts for LOPs, ideally within 200 yards of a road, were acquired under an Emergency Powers Order. Sites were 'carefully selected having regard to harbours, traffic routes, surroundings and the possibility of landings being attempted or anchorage being availed of in or near our territorial waters'.[108] In other words, LOPs were sited 'overlooking likely portions of our shores that are potential danger areas from the point of view of landings or anchorages for submarines, surface craft, or aircraft'.[109] Officers including Colonel O'Higgins and his colleagues and representatives from the OPW walked the coast and selected these locations. Their journey brought them to the most remote parts of the Irish coastline. At Bolus Head, Kerry, Captain Hough, Lieutenant Breen and Kenny and Blanchfield of the OPW pegged out a suitable site for the LOP. The landowner, Michael Murphy, lived 'some distance away under the mountain'.[110] He was an Irish speaker 'but the position was explained to him by an interpreter – Volunteer Patrick Fogarty' and it was agreed that the site could be used by coastwatchers. After this trip around Kerry, Hough wrote to Kenny, who evidently suffered during the site visits, that he sincerely hoped 'that you are recovered from your Coast Watching experience. We were very lucky with the weather.'[111]

Initial plans envisaged the construction of eighty-eight LOPs. Of these, a number were subject to local changes of location, being moved from one headland to a neighbouring one, others were dropped from the plans and a

106 MA G2/X/318.   107 MA G2/X/315 Pt I, report by O'Connell, 23 Oct. 1939. 108 NAI DFA Secretary's Files P94, Memorandum on coastal observation, undated, attached to Guilfoyle to Walshe, 20 Feb. 1943.   109 NAI DFA Secretary's Files A44, Beary to Walshe, 25 Feb. 1942.   110 NAI OPW D115/56/1/39, minute by Kenny, 30 Oct. 1939.   111 NAI OPW D115/54/39, Hough to Kenny, 20 Nov. 1939.

handful were added to the initial list.[112] The majority of the alterations and
amendments to locations were along the Kerry and Donegal coasts. Finally,
eighty-two posts were built or reconditioned in the winter of 1939 to 1940, the
eighty-third post being built later at Foileye on the south side of Dingle Bay and
opened in January 1942. Blueprints for LOP huts were completed by OPW
architect W.H. Howard Cooke and the Director of Military Engineering and
were approved by Colonel O'Higgins on 19 September 1939. Huts were built on
site to an identical design from 137 pre-cast blocks. Given their purpose and the
materials available for their construction, they were architecturally 'brutalist and
severe'.[113] 'Very solid', built of 'bricks being about 4" thick' they were nine foot
wide by thirteen foot long with a large bay-window made up of six angled
windows at the seaward end.[114] The two central windows faced directly out
ahead while on either side two sets of windows looked out to the left and right.
On the right wall at the rear was the door, which opened into a small interior
porch with another door at right-angles leading into the single room interior of
the LOP. In the centre of the rear wall was a small fireplace designed for coal
burning and often remarked upon by coastwatchers as being of little use for
burning local turf.[115]

It was a considerable logistical task to establish eighty-three posts around the
coast and the construction of LOPs was one of the most widely spread
engineering exercises overseen by the Defence Forces, in conjunction with the
OPW, during the Second World War. It involved planning and constructing
positions at strategic locations five to fifteen miles apart along a 1,970-mile
coastline from Ballagan Point in Louth to Inishowen Head in Donegal. Blocks
were transported to the vicinity of the post by Defence Forces' lorries and then
by local horse and cart. In some cases, such as at Erris Head in Mayo and
Carrigan Head Donegal, donkeys were required to move the blocks one by one
over difficult ground to the construction area as these posts were 'located in
places peculiarly difficult of access' on exposed headlands where the route was
over bog or along narrow and often precipitous paths.[116]

The OPW hoped that with tenders due by mid-October 1939 the huts could
be completed by mid-January 1940, with a substantial proportion to be
completed before Christmas 1939. After the pre-cast sections were delivered to
the site one hut could be constructed every three or four days. Due to wet
weather, logistical failings and excessively optimistic planning, construction was
slower than expected. Howard Cooke noted morosely on 14 November that he

---

112 The locations of the initial eighty-eight and the final eighty-three posts appear in
Appendix one.   113 Department of the Environment, Heritage and Local Government, *An
introduction to the architectural heritage of county Waterford* (Dublin, 2004), p. 119.   114 TNA
ADM 223/486, Eire Coast Watching, 11 Dec. 1939.   115 The coastwatchers had to arrange
locally for their own supply of turf.   116 MA 2/55390, Coast Watching Service, undated,
probably Feb. 1939.

was having the 'greatest difficulties at the moment … to get materials *only* to the sites'.[117] The Defence Forces were annoyed at the slow rate of progress; they were having problems with coastwatchers who were on duty for long shifts without proper equipment or accommodation. Nineteen thirty-nine into 1940 was 'a cold wild winter'[118] and one District Officer reported to Eastern Command that 'the men are complaining of the weather conditions … [U]nless the huts are erected soon, many of the men will be on the sick list.'[119] Other problems emerged. At Ram Head a local complained that the LOP being built on the headland would interfere with his and his family's privacy as they would be 'under the gaze and glasses of those look out men for ever'; he sought compensation of £25.[120] At Helvick Head in Waterford a local landowner would not let constructors make repairs to the existing First World War signal station on his property which was to be rebuilt as a LOP. It also proved impossible to recondition some of the other existing buildings. It was ultimately only in the most remote locations, such as Moyteoge Head, a 700-foot high promontory at the westerly extremity of Achill Island, that pre-1922 buildings were restored.

By 8 December only twenty huts had been completed and twelve were in the course of construction.[121] Where huts had been completed, such as Renvyle in Galway, or Bray Head in Wicklow, hasty construction in inclement weather resulted in poorly fitted windows and doors and smoking chimneys. The huts were prone to let in wind and rain. In Howth in Dublin it was reported that 'the window sashes do not fit well and there is air space around the sashes which is filled in with paper'.[122] The lengthy snag lists on OPW files show that many of the newly completed huts were uninhabitable. But as they were considerably better accommodation than bell tents, grateful coastwatchers had already occupied the huts by the time any defects became known. The OPW was more concerned with structural defects than the Department of Defence which noted that the

> huts while being provided mainly as shelters from wind and rain should be water-tight but they are not expected to be free from dampness or in very exposed positions percolation due to driving rain. The main object has been speed and to do this, erection has in most cases been carried out during wind and rain.[123]

The true state of affairs became evident when OPW officials visited newly constructed huts. At Bray Head in Wicklow 'at the time of inspection it was raining and the man on duty was brushing the water out continually'.[124] After

---

117 NAI OPW A115/1/1/1939, minute by Cooke, 14 Nov. 1939. 118 Author's telephone interview with Colonel Kelly, 21 July 2005. 119 MA G2/X/315 Pt I, report by Daly for week ending 4 Nov. 1939. 120 NAI OPW D115/6/39, McGrath to Secretary, OPW, 15 Dec. 1939. 121 NAI OPW A115/7/1/1939, minute on file, 8 Dec. 1939. 122 Ibid., A115/7/2/1939, undated minute on file re Howth and Rush huts. 123 Ibid., A115/7/4/1939, extract from undated Department of Defence letter (page 8). 124 Ibid., A115/7/2/1939,

visiting Mace Head in Galway an official remarked that 'during stormy weather, the walls and windows leak and [this] makes things very uncomfortable for the staff. This is a common fault with these huts'.[125]

The lives of coastwatchers were placed in danger as they took risks owing to their lack of permanent accommodation and the freezing winter conditions. In February 1940 a fire broke out at the improvised sod and earth structure used as a temporary post at Kerry Head on the south side of the mouth of the Shannon. A turf fire was kept burning on the earthen floor of the hut during duty hours with a milk churn extending through the roof providing a rudimentary chimney. Sacking attached to the churn formed a screen around the fire. During the early hours of 11 February the sacking caught fire and 'the Volunteer on duty in the hut had only time to remove a box containing the post records before the entire structure became alight'.[126] Permanent structures were essential to replace these jerry-built shelters before lives were lost.

Frost, exceptionally wet and windy conditions, poor construction, the lack of raw materials, especially tar for sealing roofs, and difficulties with the transport of the blocks for huts continued to hinder construction schedules. Contractor Patrick McGrath, who held the tender for works at Helvick Head, wrote to the OPW that he was 'sorry for the delay in not finishing as two of my chaps who worked there during such severe weather one got newmonia [*sic*] and the other reumaticfever [*sic*]'.[127] By 9 March all the planned new huts had been constructed and by mid-April work was completed on the existing buildings that were being reconditioned for coast watching purposes. Construction may have been slower than anticipated but in the memory of one coastwatcher it was the speed of the construction process that stood out: 'those huts, they built them all around the coast, they went up like mushrooms actually. The Army came, and lorry loads of cement blocks and got them up in a very short time.'[128] A March 1940 photograph of Aughris Head in Galway shows the newly completed LOP set against a barren landscape under a flat spring sky. The prefabricated nature of the LOP is visible as the exterior walls have not yet been covered with the light pebbledash common to all LOPs. A lone coastwatcher stands to the left of the post, cigarette in hand, grinning; his greatcoat fully buttoned with collar raised against the hilltop cold. He is a testimony to the wretched weather conditions in which LOPs were constructed.

It is initially hard for anyone now visiting a ruined LOP, vacant since the end of the Second World War, to imagine it in operation. Yet in the cracked plaster one can see the screw holes where the telephone was mounted and lines in the plaster where a nautical chart was once affixed. Shattered resistors where phone

minute on file, 3 Feb. 1940. **125** Ibid., minute on file, 2 Mar. 1940. **126** NAI DF S8/7/40, statement attached to MacMahon to McElligott, 11 June 1940. **127** NAI OPW A115/2/1/1939, McGrath to Connelly, undated. **128** MA Owen Quinn papers, interview with Ted Sweeney.

lines terminated remain in place on the outside of the post and inside corroded copper wire indicates the presence of the long silenced phone. The interior of the post can also be recreated from the post's inventory. The inventory was vital to the working of each LOP. It was so important that it was checked and certified to be in order at every change of watch. It contained the core equipment needed by the coastwatchers.[129] In the cramped, often damp and smoky interior of the LOP there was a table and chair, which had to be scrubbed three times a week according to post orders; the all-important logbook lay on the table and the telephone was affixed to the left hand wall of the hut near the window. Binoculars hung in a box on the whitewashed wall and a telescope stood on a stand for viewing ships, aircraft, flotsam, mines and bodies brought in by the tide. On the walls, further back near the fireplace, were local maps and charts of the silhouettes of ships and aircraft. A clock, often showing the wrong time, hung on the wall. It was notoriously difficult to synchronize the time between the eighty-three posts around the coast and a central location, but knowing the correct time was essential if overflights were to be reported accurately and plotted correctly by ADC in Dublin. This problem was solved after the introduction of telephones, with coastwatchers setting their LOP clock daily by reference to the clock at the local post office. Semaphore and Morse flags and lamps were crammed into the remaining space on small shelves beside the fireplace. Non-inventory items included turf baskets, scythes, brushes and shovels, the individual kit of the coastwatchers: heavy oilskins, rubber boots; pots and pans for cooking hung over the fire and among it all was a first aid kit, either for the men themselves or for administering to crash-landed airmen or shipwrecked sailors.

Pictures of LOPs often show a chair propping open the exterior door, a bicycle leaning against the side of the post, the heavy cowl on the chimney and the small square sections of window that opened to allow the use of the telescope in poor weather. Prominent too are the telegraph poles and the telephone wires, the communications system linking these lonely positions into the observation system for the country. As the war continued photographs show how LOPs became worn from continual use and from the effect of the environment on their exposed positions. In these photographs the ground around LOPs is bare from the tramping of patrolling coastwatchers. In some cases dry stone walls with barbed wire on top make the LOP into a small enclosure. Perhaps the walls were simply to prevent sheep and cattle from entering the vicinity of the LOP, on other occasions the walls were stronger, to shelter the LOP from gale-force winds and from the sea. The men at Ballagan Point LOP operated from within the walls of a disused coastguard station compound and the men on the day

---

129 See the logbook for Lambs Head for Dec. 1943 to June 1944.

watch had the additional chore of cutting the grass and clearing the weeds from the grounds within the walls around the hut.[130]

LOPs were spartan and functional and included no comforts for the men on duty. They were often built in harsh and unforgiving landscapes and those who manned them used ingenuity and brute force in an attempt to bring basic human comforts to their exposed positions. Further from the post, some photographs show an uncomfortable wooden latrine and in many western areas one can still see the ruins beside LOPs of small bunkers for storing turf. Other posts lacked a local water supply for drinking and cooking and water tanks were installed. They can be seen rusting at the post at Moyteogue Head, Achill Island. At Clogher Head LOP coastwatchers used local stone to lay a rough path around their post and a photograph from August 1940 shows that they had planted roses in small square white stone bordered flower beds around their hut. Possibly it was a testimony to the slow pace of the watch at that post. In contrast, at Dalkey LOP there was a light anti-aircraft gun and a searchlight at the post which was surrounded by an extensive system of barbed wire fencing and by Nissen huts built as accommodation for the searchlight operators and gun crews.

Throughout their operational life the LOP huts gave continual structural trouble. In March 1943 the officer commanding the M&CWS sub-depot in Cork, Lieutenant O'Riordan, wrote strongly about the impact shoddy construction and wartime exigencies had on the men who had been manning the posts for three years:

> The greatest difficulty is experienced in keeping the inside of the huts dry ... everything in the huts become[s] damp, rusty or soiled owing to dampness, and the men's health must be somewhat affected during their period of duty in this damp atmosphere where a fire has to be kept burning to boil water for men's meals [and] for drying clothes during inclement weather which lasts for practically nine months of the year.[131]

O'Riordan's description was very different from the photographs of the newly completed Aughris Head LOP described above. Photographs from February 1945 of Dunabrattin Head LOP in Waterford show the impact of wartime construction and five years of constant occupation. The single chimneystack has cracked its entire length, it has been repaired with tar and the cowl is missing. Heavy tarring is evident on the roof to keep out the rain, as are the repeated cracks along the join between the roof and the walls. The windowsills of the LOP are marked by the steady dripping of water from the roof overhang and the window hinges show heavy rust.

---

130 MA LOP 1, 23 Mar. 1945. **131** MA G2/X/315 Pt II, sub-depot, Marine Service, Southern Command, report for Feb. 1943.

MEN, MORALE AND CONDITIONS DURING THE FIRST MONTHS
OF THE COAST WATCHING SERVICE

Along the Irish coast coastwatchers and Gardaí kept watch as the Second World
War entered it first week. On Sunday 3 September at Glencolumcille in
Donegal, Corporal Colum Mockler went to Mass and then 'notified all the
Volunteers in his platoon that they were to do the Coast Watching'.[132] They had
to operate in trying and primitive conditions. Their Army bell-tent, issued as
temporary accommodation pending the construction of a concrete LOP hut,
proved ill-suited to the windy cliff top at Rossan Point where their post was
established. Tom Kelly, on Power Head in Cork, began duty the following day,
with Cork Harbour in darkness to the north-west as a blackout was put into
effect.[133] Kelly's post also operated from a bell-tent; it was 'blown down in the
first storm' of the winter of 1939.[134] Where they were without huts or tents
coastwatchers obtained such shelter as they could from their local surroundings.
Corporal Ted Sweeney, who commanded the LOP at Termon Hill overlooking
Blacksod Bay, 'started from scratch. We had no barracks, no hut or anything. We
worked an old British outpost that had been burned down, just a water tank left
there, a cement water tank, no shelter at all.'[135] As winter drew near the majority
of posts still were operating from poor condition tents which were, in the words
of Tom Kelly, 'very primitive and very rough' with the men cooking their food
outdoor on open fires and in Kelly's case, on a borrowed Primus stove.[136] In such
conditions 'the efficiency of these [LOPs] varied with the resourcefulness of the
crew in each individual post'.[137] The construction of new accommodation
became a matter of 'extreme urgency'[138] and 'the approach of colder weather'
put pressure on the OPW and the Department of Defence to speed up the
process of building LOP huts.[139]

At the 'bleak post' at Parkmore in Kerry, which was not fully established until
29 May 1940, those manning the LOP remained without shelter until the
autumn of 1941.[140] They adopted a novel approach that beat the reconditioning
plans of the authorities in Dublin. A testimony to the endurance and dedication
of the coastwatchers, they had 'to try and do duty under an upturned boat,
which they must crawl under to consult charts, etc.'. It was also an indictment of
the care shown to the men 'at this important post' by their senior officers. The
Officer in Charge of the Marine Service Depot at Haulbowline wrote to

132 Quoted in Breege McCusker, *Castle Archdale and Fermanagh in the Second World War*
(Irvinestown, Co. Fermanagh, 1993), p. 105.   **133** Author's correspondence with Colonel
Kelly, Oct. 2005.   **134** Ibid.   **135** MA Owen Quinn papers, interview with Ted Sweeney.
136 Author's telephone interview with Colonel Kelly, 21 July 2005 and correspondence, Oct.
2005.   **137** TNA ADM 223/486, Eire Coast Watching, 11 Dec. 1939.   **138** NAI OPW
A115/7/3/1939, Hyland (for MacMahon) to Secretary, OPW, undated.   **139** NAI DF
S7/2/40, MacMahon to McElligott, 8 Sept. 1939.   **140** MA G2/X/315 Pt II, Monthly
report – Marine Service Depot, Haulbowline, Sept. 1941.

Commodore Seamus O'Muiris, Director of the Marine Service, that 'the men at this LOP can hardly be expected to do duty efficiently' under such conditions as winter approached.[141] Later, with no concrete hut in sight, the men had built a shelter 'of sods and sandbags', but this stood little chance against the elements and 'every time it rains the walls cave in and the men on duty must stand watch for eight hours on the side of the hill in very inclement weather without shelter of any kind'.[142]

The practice of working eight-hour shifts did not go down well with coast-watchers who were farmers. Coastwatchers at Bloody Foreland in Donegal desired a return to twelve-hour shifts after their District Officer changed their roster. The men complained through their local Fianna Fáil Cuman to the Minister for Defence, Oscar Traynor. They argued that with travel distances of two to five miles to their LOP an eight hour shift gave 'them no time at home to do any work on there [*sic*] farms the result is that they have to pay for labour'.[143] For other posts twelve-hour shifts became a necessity if men reported sick or were unfit for duty. The coastwatchers were at full strength for the duration of the Emergency with no reserve force to call upon during crises, for this reason too, twelve-hours shifts were not unknown. On Sundays the shift system presented other problems. Arrangements were made to enable coastwatchers to attend to their religious duties. At some posts, such as Dunany Point in Louth, the corporal in charge ensured that a system of 'Mass relief' was in place. At other posts the district officer instituted a more rigid system. The men at Ballagan Point in Louth were ordered to have attended Mass before reporting for duty on Sunday mornings.[144] The spiritual welfare of Dalkey LOP was better catered for, the men being informed by ADC that the 'Rev Casey would be out to hear confessions' at the post.[145]

During the first months of the war district officers undertook that any problems were sorted out at a local level and that they stayed at local level. Overall levels of training remained a problem. In early October Commandant Daly, Eastern Command IO, reported to Archer that 'as regards the actual reports which I receive, it is obvious that they do not reach the required standard of efficiency, but that is only to be expected, as the personnel are not yet by any means trained'.[146] The matter of training and standards was raised in the Dáil. Fine Gael TD for Roscommon Michael Brennan painted a farcical picture of two coastwatchers:

> They were put into some old ruin on the western coast. They had not even glasses to enable them to carry out their duties and the nearest Guards' Barrack was five miles away. These two gentlemen go out to watch from

141 Ibid., Aug. 1941.   142 Ibid., Sept. 1941.   143 MA 2/55390, O'Gallcobhoir to Traynor, 6 Nov. 1940.   144 MA LOP 1, 17 June 1943.   145 MA LOP 7, 28 Sept. 1940.   146 MA G2/X/315 Pt I, Daly to Archer, 7 Oct. 1939.

9 o'clock in the morning until 5 o'clock in the evening. Between 5 o'clock in the evening and 9 o'clock in the morning, anybody and everybody who wants to do so, is welcome to come into our territorial waters and to land on our shores. Between the hours from 9 a.m. to 5 p.m., these two gentlemen, paid at the public expense, were to watch apparently without the aid of glasses. They were asked what they would do if they saw something that they did not understand or that they thought was a submarine and one of them said: 'We will tell the Guards.' The question was asked: 'How will you tell the Guards?' and the answer was: 'One of us would go back to the Civic Guards' Barrack.' He was then asked how he would get there, if he would walk, or cycle. The reply was: 'There is no road back; we would have to walk back five or six miles.' The next question asked was: 'What would the Guards do?' and the reply given was: 'We do not know. We go on at 9 in the morning and we finish at 5 in the evening.'[147]

This lack of training continued into early 1940 at many posts. Second Lieutenant Hugh Wren reported that when he inspected Brandon Point LOP at 0130 on 26 February 1940 the 'men on duty [were] keeping a good watch'; however, their 'knowledge of orders and instructions [was] poor'.[148] The coastwatchers at Brandon Point, in common with many others along the coast, simply lacked training. Such problems had been anticipated when the Coast Watching Service was being set up because it was impossible to train men in the operations of a branch of the Defence Forces which had no procedures because it did not as yet operate. The poor state of state training led to a virtual rebellion at Dunany Point in late September 1939. It was averted only by the men being given a severe lecturing by their District Officer, Sergeant Thornton, who reported with evident pride that 'I have definitely cleaned up Dunany now and I am sure that whoever comes after me will have no further trouble.'[149] Thornton moved on to sort out similar problems at Clogher Head and Howth. Lieutenant Wren sorted out the difficulties at Brandon Point, noting following a later inspection: 'Everything in order. Men alert and acquainted with their orders.'[150] Wren added that this had been achieved only after one unsuitable volunteer had been removed.

When the British Q-boat *Tamura* visited Blacksod in January 1940 her crew reported that 'the Coast Watchers now wear uniforms'.[151] It would seem that this had not been the case when *Tamura* had previously called at Blacksod in October 1939. It was evidence that the coastwatchers were beginning to become a coherent unit with a specific identity. In Southern Command the public image of the coastwatchers caused concern. Major J.P. O'Connell, Southern Command

---

147 *Dáil deb.*, vol. 78; col. 416, 29 Nov. 1939.   148 MA LOP 40, 7 Feb. 1940 to 29 June 1941.
149 MA G2/X/315 Pt I, Report by District Officer, 29 Sept. 1939.   150 MA LOP 40, 10 Apr. 1940.   151 TNA ADM 199/1829, Patrol by HMS/M H.43 in company with 'Tamura'

IO, wrote to his commanding officer that 'if the present emergency continues, our Coast Watchers will be continually in the public eye, particularly during the summer season, and it should be our aim to give them a high degree of training and discipline'.[152] At Dalkey LOP coastwatchers were continually in the public eye as their LOP was situated in a public park overlooking Killiney Bay. Close to Dublin, they were regularly inspected by senior officers. When the Assistant Chief of Staff inspected the men on the morning of 27 June 1940 he was accompanied by 'Press Camera Men' who 'made [a] film of [the] post'.[153] A posed still from the film shows a young coastwatcher purposely looking out over Dublin Bay towards Dalkey Island through a telescope while his colleague keeps a sharp lookout from inside the newly completed LOP hut, close to the telephone, the lines for which are clearly seen in the picture. Beside the hut, the post NCO is instructing two volunteers in the ways of coast watching. The picture is of a young alert force eager to learn. This was not the case at Galley Head LOP when District Officer MacLoughlin discovered during an inspection at the change of watch that one coastwatcher coming on duty was 'unshaven and minus waist belt and great coat buttons dirty' while his colleague was '15 minutes late[,] unshaven and buttons dirty[,] dressed in slacks'.[154] The condition of the LOP was 'OK', but for their poor appearance both men were to 'receive disciplinary action'. Word got around Galley Head of MacLoughlin's standards and inspecting the post the following day he noted 'everything correct [,] LOP clean [,] men alert'.[155]

Despite O'Connell's concerns and the media interest, it was Defence Forces practice to discourage public interest in the working of LOPs and entry by members of the public to LOP compounds was strictly forbidden. In cases where district officers inspecting posts found civilians in LOPs the men on duty were fined. Instructions were issued to coastwatchers to be on the look out for false identification cards used 'for the purpose of obtaining information from personnel'.[156] Bearers were to be 'detained if possible' and the Gardaí and the CIO were to be informed.[157] Coastwatchers also remained on guard for suspicious activity around their posts. Bryan himself interviewed a British naval intelligence officer, Michael H. Mason, who was detained near Wicklow Head LOP in October 1939. He volunteered that his task was to cover the east coast from Dublin to Courtown 'for the purpose of verifying certain rumours and letters ... regarding German submarine activities in the Irish Sea and St George's Channel'.[158] Personnel at Dalkey LOP on one occasion received information from the LSF that a man was photographing Coliemore Harbour, near to the Dalkey post. The Gardaí were contacted and decided that the man in question was 'doing no harm'; he turned out to be a Mr Clarke, from

– narrative. **152** MA G2/X/318, O'Connell to Costello, 23 Nov. 1939. **153** MA LOP 7. **154** MA LOP 27, 19 Mar. 1940. **155** Ibid., 20 Mar. 1940. **156** MA LOP 7, 1 July 1940. **157** Ibid. **158** MA G2/X/266, Notes on the activities of British agents in Ireland.

Palmerstown Gardens in Dublin, the Secretary of the Dublin Chamber of Commerce.[159] British officer, Captain Felix David, detained near Roskeeragh LOP was handed over to Gardaí at Lisadell. He was found to have in his possession a map and a pair of binoculars. It transpired he was merely carrying a tourist map and that he was 'an authority on wild geese and was in Sligo visiting the estate of Sir Gore Booth to see a famous flock of barnacle geese there'.[160] David was 'most apologetic' at the trouble he had caused. When Colonel Archer and Captain Greig inspected the LOPs on Inishowen the men on duty locked their LOPs and refused to answer questions from the Director of Military Intelligence. They had not been told in advance of the visit and were instructed by their district officer 'to have no conversation with strangers'. It transpired that the district officer had been recently reprimanded for not carrying out his duties 'with sufficient zeal' and had 'taken his reprimand to heart'.[161]

Through the Emergency there were questions asked as to the suitability of some of the members of the Coast Watching Service to undertake their duties. It is difficult to pin down the reasons why. Reported discipline problems were relatively minor. Certain coastwatchers might have had undesirable political views and it is clear that there was some laziness and lack of attention to detail. Recurring breaches of discipline included drunkenness, neglect of duty and not reporting for duty. Men were found asleep on duty; one report at least showing a sense of humour when dealing with the case of a coastwatcher found a 'short distance from L.O.P. in a reclining position'.[162] Coastwatchers were found absent without leave and some were constitutionally unfit to serve. In cases where NCOs were inefficient, they were demoted to volunteer rank and in severe cases dismissed, in similar cases volunteer coastwatchers were simply dismissed from the service. A very poor view was taken of coastwatchers who were found drunk at their posts and such men were fined. District officers normally dealt with these discipline problems. Therefore it was unusual when the suitability of Coast Watching Service personnel was raised at the inter-party Defence Conference. The Minister for Defence would only respond that an enquiry was proceeding into the matter and requested that discussion be postponed until he had received a report. In this case the possibility emerges that there was a serious breach of discipline at some point in the Coast Watching Service, but no other details are available as to the specific details of the case.[163]

159 MA LOP 7, 28 Sept. 1940.   160 MA G2/X/266, note by Guilfoyle, 13 Mar. 1941.
161 TNA KV 4/280, Further visit to Eire Coastwatching Stations, 19 Mar. 1940.   162 MA G2/X/315 Pt II, Monthly Report, Depot, Haulbowline, Southern Command, Apr. 1942.
163 UCDA P104/3534, Defence Conference, nineteenth meeting, 9 Oct. 1940.

CONCLUSION

Despite this rather varied start, surviving sources suggest that the morale, discipline and training in the Coast Watching Service were in general good in late 1939. Few major problems were reported up the chain of command and superior officers did not enquire too closely about local issues so long as observation reports were being made. Training improved during the spring of 1940 and by the summer the Chief of Staff reported that the Coast Watching Service was 'functioning satisfactorily. A considerable improvement in [the] type and accuracy of information reported has been noticed'.[164] There were problems to sort out. But with the belief current that a German invasion of Ireland was likely, if not imminent, there was a certain sense of a duty to be undertaken in the LOPs along the Irish coast.

In under a year the Coast Watching Service had been built up as a new wing of the Defence Forces and a comprehensive network of LOPs with a systematic reporting mechanism created. Coastwatchers were initially untried and untrained and their reporting structure was weak. Reports received were distributed 'with due reserve' as to their accuracy.[165] The coastwatchers were raw with many sharp edges to be knocked off them and it was left to district officers to ensure they were knocked off. Viewed from GHQ in Dublin the volunteer coastwatchers had become Ireland's frontline forces. The battlefield lay before and above them. Faced with vast expanses of grey sea and sky to monitor and with the Second World War only old days coastwatchers were warned to

> be alert and attentive and [to] guard against the feeling that nothing is likely to happen. Bear in mind always that you are the outpost of the Country's defences and on your alertness, powers of observation and quickness in sending information to the proper message centre depends the success of the defensive measures taken to defeat enemy activities.[166]

164 MA General report for the Army, 1 May 1940 to 30 Sept. 1940.   165 MA DRS No. 5, 11 Sept 1939.   166 MA G2/X/318, Instructions for Personnel Manning Coast Watching Posts, Sept. 1939.

CHAPTER THREE

The first ten months of the Coast Watching Service

'WE ARE IN THE CENTRE OF A THEATRE OF WAR'[1]

WHILE THE COASTWATCHERS TOOK up their positions and their LOPs were built, a crisis in British-Irish relations unfolded. Britain demanded reports on U-boat activity from neutral Ireland and Royal Navy access to Irish territorial waters to pursue German submarines. A final demand – never agreed Cabinet policy, often threatened but never formally made to Ireland – was the return to Britain of the treaty ports, particularly Berehaven. Dublin and London knew that if London made this demand it would be a doomsday scenario for British-Irish relations. It would lead to a British occupation of Ireland in the apparently inevitable event that Dublin turned down the request. In the highly charged atmosphere of the first months of the European conflict, British-Irish relations remained tense as both states began exploring the limits co-operation in the anti-U-boat war.

By the end of September 1939 the Admiralty had received no reports from Dublin of U-boat activity in Irish waters, a situation 'very unsatisfactory from the Admiralty point of view'.[2] At this time, co-operation between the British intelligence services over Irish affairs was poorly developed. Through its Dublin link, MI5 knew that G2 would investigate reports of submarine activity off Irish shores and that so far all reports investigated had been without foundation. Admiralty NID did not understand the formal nature of the MI5 Dublin link or the level of co-operation between G2 and MI5 and pressed for an SIS operation in Ireland. MI5 replied that this was not necessary. The appointment in October of Sir John Maffey as British Representative in Dublin improved British-Irish relations in this difficult period, though unsurprisingly it was reported in Germany as 'an attempt by the British to bring pressure on Ireland'.[3] As part of his brief Maffey ensured 'the maximum amount of practical contact and co-operation' on intelligence matters between Dublin and London.[4] Britain hoped that Maffey would be 'the link through which information of enemy activities

1 Eamon de Valera, Dáil Éireann, 27 Sept. 1939 (*Dáil deb.*, vol. 77; col. 269).   2 TNA KV 4/279, The situation in regard to coastwatching in Eire, 4 Dec. 1939.   3 NAI DFA 219/4, Warnock to Walshe, 30 Sept. 1939.   4 TNA DO 35/1107/9 WX1/5, Note for the guidance of Sir John Maffey, 19 Sept. 1939.

obtained from the coast-watching services in Eire could be made available to the Admiralty'.[5] Through Maffey, information from the coastwatchers was passed to the Admiralty through intelligence links augmenting the MI5-G2 link. To further strengthen co-operation on naval affairs, a retired Royal Navy officer, Captain Alexander B. Greig, was appointed British Naval Attaché in Dublin. Archer now had two links with the British intelligence community, through Liddell to MI5 and through Greig to NID at the Admiralty.

While these links developed, Britain continued, without Dublin's consent, to patrol Irish waters searching for the elusive U-boats believed to lurk beneath. The early months of the war saw U-boat scares off the Irish coast. Coast Watching Service daily summaries of activity show an abundance of partially surfaced submarines, fishermen fixated by rotating periscopes and suspicious activities in places where submarines were remembered in folk memory as having been sighted during the First World War. Coastwatchers suggested there were U-boats active off Dún Laoghaire, south of Dublin. These reports met with scepticism. When coastwatchers at Dalkey reported a periscope '800 yards off Dalkey Island. LMS Mail Boat arriving in Dún Laoghaire at the time', the captain of the mail boat 'stated there was nothing suspicious to report on voyage'.[6] Confirmed sightings of U-boats were few. Those few, including the landing by U-35 of the crew of a Greek ship at Ventry, Kerry, became celebrated examples that led to renewed demands from Churchill for Britain to retake the ports. In other cases the submarines sighted were probably British. While Churchill urged reoccupation of the ports, Maffey warned against such sabre-rattling. Britain would slowly learn that more information could be obtained from Ireland through co-operation. It was an argument proven through Maffey's contacts with de Valera and Walshe, and through Greig's relationship with Archer and O'Higgins. In Greig's case, soon after his appointment he toured LOPs in Cork and Kerry with Archer and O'Higgins and began to receive from the Irish authorities information on possible submarine sightings off the western and southern coasts – the very information that Britain had sought since the outbreak of the war. The question of Royal Navy rights of hot pursuit remained formally unresolved but de Valera made it known to Germany that, though neutral, it was 'inevitable for the Irish Government to show a certain consideration for Britain'.[7]

The previous chapter examined how the Coast Watching Service trained its men, built permanent LOPs and ironed out problems arising from its position as a newly established and widely distributed force. There was no formal British–Irish dimension to the operations of the Coast Watching Service but its establishment coincided with the period during which Dublin and London began to face up to, if not always understand, each other's position in the

5 Ibid. 6 MA DRS No. 5, 11 Sept. 1939. 7 *DGFP D: VII*, p. 471, Hempel to Foreign Ministry, 31 Aug. 1939.

unfolding conflict in the Atlantic. By early 1940 NID had, through Greig, a much stronger understanding than either MI5 or SIS of the role of the Coast Watching Service. However, MI5 through Archer and Bryan, had a wider degree of contact with Irish intelligence. The various agencies making up the intelligence services in London would continue to produce differing reports of events off the coast of Ireland through the war and hold differing views of the abilities of the Coast Watching Service but only Greig, and thus NID, had experience of the service in operation. Walshe and Dulanty stayed in close contact with the Admiralty in the first days of the war. De Valera sent Walshe on a special mission to London from 7 to 10 September to assure newly appointed Dominions Secretary Anthony Eden that the Taoiseach 'wished to be as friendly as he could, and to go as far as possible to assist Great Britain while maintaining the essentials of neutrality'.[8] Walshe explained that de Valera realised the 'particular difficulties arising from the nature of our Southern and Western Coast' in relation to submarines. He continued that Ireland would declare submarines forbidden from its waters but though the 'organisation' of the Coast Watching Service was complete, Ireland needed vessels, aircraft and weapons to enforce the declaration. Less than impressed, Eden wrote to Chamberlain that his contacts with Walshe and Dulanty had 'proceeded satisfactorily so far as they go'.[9]

While these high political moves took place, incident reports from Gardaí and coastwatchers began arriving with G2 and were collated and interpreted to provide an overview of the opening moves in the war around Ireland. Failings remained in Coast Watching Service operations, as its poor record observing the landing of German agents in Ireland in early 1940 will show. The coastwatchers also never got a satisfactory aerial counterpart as the Air Corps No. 1 Coastal Reconnaissance Squadron abandoned routine maritime reconnaissance in June 1940. Nevertheless, from September 1939 to May 1940 the final pieces fell into place in the plan for the Coast Watching Service devised by the Irish military in 1938–9 and the service began operations. Through the link between Archer, Walshe, Maffey and Greig, Dublin and London ultimately came to a loose understanding of how neutral and belligerent could co-operate as Britain and Germany fought the battle of the Atlantic.

BRITISH DEMANDS

On 12 September 1939 Dulanty presented an aide memoire to Eden containing notice that Dublin would close Irish territorial waters to all belligerent ships and aircraft. It was received with 'profound feelings of disappointment'[10] as London concluded that 'very detailed objectionable' orders were being drafted which

8 UCDA P150/2571, Visit of Secretary of the Dept. of External Affairs to London, 6th – 10th September, 1939.   9 TNA PREM 1/340, Eden to Chamberlain, 9 Sept. 1939.   10 TNA DO 35/1107/9 WX1/5, note by Maffey regarding meeting with de Valera, 14 Sept.

would have the effect of 'hampering' British activities in Irish coastal waters.[11] It was for Maffey to ensure that the Irish orders did not have this effect. Two days later Maffey unofficially met de Valera and discussed the problems created by the Irish memorandum.[12] As they spoke, de Valera's telephone rang and on concluding the call he turned to Maffey saying, 'There you are! One of your planes is down in Ventry Bay. What am I to do now?'[13] A patrolling British seaplane with engine trouble had made a forced landing off the Kerry coast. An hour later de Valera, with Maffey still present, received news 'that the plane had managed to get away – or rather had been allowed to get away'. Forlornly, Maffey concluded that 'problems of this kind lie ahead of us'. However, he did ensure that Dublin would 'leave matters alone' and make no difficulties for Britain on access to Irish territorial waters.[14]

At first, knowing only the numbers and the names of the locations of LOPs, Maffey's staff found it difficult to pinpoint LOPs exactly on the maps at their disposal. Neither, to the Admiralty's annoyance, did Britain have access to the information provided by the coastwatchers. Maffey was irritated that Britain had

> no contact with his [de Valera's] coastal watch. We may have difficulty in obtaining it as [de Valera] said a word to me about Eire not wishing to have the burden of our secrets. Co-operation in intelligence cannot work on that formula.[15]

While Maffey hoped that quiet persistent argument would move de Valera towards full co-operation in maritime matters, Churchill bluntly demanded that all information collected by the Coast Watching Service should be 'made available without delay' to Britain.[16] The Admiralty held that if the information were forthcoming there would be less need for British vessels to enter Irish waters. Anxious for a solution, Chamberlain wrote to de Valera that 'the submarine menace at the present time is one of the outstanding problems engaging our thoughts and energies'.[17] In his reply, de Valera made no mention of intelligence co-operation or the coastwatchers.

This lack of co-operation meant that the British authorities were quick to believe reports that German submarines were active along the Irish coast, their crews provisioned by locals or by tramp steamers 'despatched from Spain or elsewhere'.[18] The Admiralty requested the Ministry of Aviation assist in reconnaissance of the area. Under the guise of endurance tests and, with the

---

1939. **11** TNA ADM 1/11104, Maffey to Machtig, 25 Oct. 1939. **12** Maffey's appointment was announced in the House of Commons on 27 Sept. 1939. **13** TNA DO 35/1107/9 WX1/5, note by Maffey regarding meeting with de Valera, 14 Sept. 1939. **14** TNA ADM 1/11104, Maffey to Machtig, 25 Oct. 1939. **15** Ibid., note by Maffey regarding meeting with de Valera, 14 Sept. 1939. **16** Ibid., draft of war cabinet memorandum circulated as WP (39) 34, Appendix 1, 11 Sept. 1939. **17** Ibid., Chamberlain to de Valera, 19 Sept. 1939. **18** Ibid.

agreement of Dublin, using Foynes as a base, 'Mercury', the upper component of the 'Mercury-Maia' composite flying boat, patrolled off the west coast. The British civil aviation authorities were 'not prepared to be disingenuous' with Dublin 'in view of our frank relations with the Air Authorities in Eire' and asked only for permission to carry out a 'series of flights' from Foynes using 'Mercury'.[19] The Director of Civil Aviation, Francis Shelmerdine, minuted that he 'could not say what the real object of these flights was, but ... did not want to camouflage them under some pretext which would obviously have been seen through by the Government of Eire'.[20] When the Irish asked for further details, Shelmerdine and the Dominions Office agreed 'a specific pretext ... which we could subsequently substantiate'. Under the guise of test flights determining the 'effect of [the] carburettor heating system on fuel consumption at various altitudes', widespread anti-submarine reconnaissance took place during the winter of 1939 off the west coast of Ireland, with 'Mercury' joined by G-class Shorts flying boat 'Grenville' and S-Class flying boat 'Cameronian'.[21] The operations occurred in full view of the coastwatchers. On 11 October LOPs from Wexford to Waterford reported a 'large grey seaplane 3 miles off, moving in a westerly direction', which was confirmed the following day as 'the G-ADHJ (Mercury) proceeding to FOYNES.'[22]

External Affairs turned a blind eye to the real purpose of the 'test flights', Legal Adviser Michael Rynne writing to Walshe that 'if it is ascertained that the flights are being made with a view to collecting information for the British Government regarding German submarines, we might, of course, withdraw permission.'[23] Irish forces continued with their own air patrols to locate submarines. De Valera told Maffey that if information on a submarine's location was 'wirelessed at once, not to [Britain] specifically. Your Admiralty must pick it up. We shall wireless it to the world. I shall tell the German Minister of our intention to do this.'[24] Communications were a potent weapon against submarines as radio reports would give away the submarine's most valuable assets: concealment and surprise. In reality, there was 'no system – British or Irish – that could secure the hundreds of peninsulas and strands of the west coast [of Ireland] against a U-boat landing'.[25] While Maffey felt de Valera desired 'to make it thoroughly unhealthy for a German submarine to use Irish waters', he told de Valera 'that already tongues were beginning to wag' at what 'would happen in the secret places of the Irish coast'.[26] Churchill had already angrily

19 TNA AVIA 2/2623, Admiralty request for Air Reconnaissance off the West Coast of Ireland, 19 Sept. 1939.   20 Ibid., minute, Shelmerdine to Permanent Under-Secretary, 19 Sept. 1939.   21 Ibid., telegram, Shelmerdine to Leydon, 21 Sept. 1939.   22 MA DRS 32, 12 Oct 1939, and 33, 13 Oct. 1939.   23 NAI DFA Legal Advisers papers, Rynne to Walshe, 23 Sept. 1939.   24 TNA PREM 1/340, memorandum in the form of a diary by Maffey, 24 Sept. 1939.   25 Robert Fisk, *In time of war: Ireland, Ulster and the price of neutrality: 1939–45* (London, 1987 edition), p. 138.   26 TNA PREM 1/340, memorandum in the form of a diary

demanded a 'special report ... upon the question arising from the so-called neutrality of the so called Eire'.[27] Extrapolating from IRA bombings in London in 1939, rather than from concrete evidence, he asked 'what does Intelligence say about possible succouring of U-boats by Irish malcontents in west of Ireland inlets? If they throw bombs in London, why should they not supply petrol to U-boats.'[28] Letters sent to the Admiralty by retired Royal Navy personnel living along Ireland's coast reporting alleged submarine sightings backed up these views. One by a Lieutenant Commander Dring, who G2 suspected of co-ordinating British attempts at gathering naval intelligence along the south-west coast, concerning a submarine sighted between the Old Head of Kinsale and Cork made it to the British daily Naval Intelligence Summary for 15 September 1939.[29] G2 received a message from Old Head of Kinsale LOP at midday on 15 September that they had also sighted a 'submarine on [the] surface 3 miles out'. At the same time a 'steamer' appeared twenty miles offshore, whereupon the 'submarine submerged and went in direction of steamer'.[30] A Garda report on sightings off the Cork coast for the same day contains two similar reports from an unnamed 'Agent' of an unidentified submarine off the Old Head of Kinsale.[31] The submarine sighting produced results; the following day coastwatchers reported a seaplane, believed to be British, patrolling the area. Over the following week, Old Head LOP reported a twice-daily patrol by an unidentified seaplane, believed to be British, along their sector of the coast.

When prisoners from U-39 said they had been ashore in Ireland and were found to have in their possession Irish cigarettes, Churchill's beliefs were confirmed, at least to himself.[32] In a move that would be immediately noticed in the close-knit communities of the west coast of Ireland, Churchill continued in his *Boy's Own* manner to suggest that 'money should be spent to secure a trustworthy body of Irish agents to keep [a] most vigilant watch'.[33] Here lies an explanation of why G2 were reluctant to assign former Royal Navy personnel to positions in the M&CWS. They had suspicions and in cases proof that various individuals with naval backgrounds in coastal regions of Ireland were already working for the British.[34] Bryan knew the ways of the Irish countryside, writing that 'no one not even a native or local, could have secret activities or keep to himself in rural Ireland even if his next door neighbour was miles away'.[35]

by Maffey, 24 Sept. 1939.   27 Gilbert, *Churchill war papers*, p. 28, Winston S. Churchill to Admiral Pound and others, 5 Sept. 1939.   28 TNA PREM 1/340.   29 TNA ADM 223/79, Naval Intelligence Documents, Mar. to Sept. 1939, vol. 1, OIC daily report 15 Sept. 1939. Regarding G2 suspicions about Dring, see G2/X/266 Pt. II, note by Bryan entitled 'British Activities'.   30 MA DRS 10, 16 Sept. 1939.   31 NAI JUS 8/756, Emergency Order No. 1 – Matters for Report, Superintendent, Bandon to Murphy, 27 Sept. 1939.   32 Gilbert, *Churchill war papers*, War Cabinet minutes, 15 Sept. 1939.   33 TNA PREM 1/340, Churchill to Godfrey, 6 Sept. 1939.   34 See for example NAI DFA Secretary's Files A8, Archer to Walshe, 30 Apr. 1941, regarding Archer's suspicions surrounding the activities of the proprietor of Roches Hotel, Glengarriff.   35 UCDA P71/90, rough notes by Bryan.

Guy Liddell knew that it was 'difficult to get any very clear picture of what is going on in Eire' in September 1939.[36] There were 'a great many rumours' including stories of submarines with bases on the west coast. MI5 passed such rumours on to Archer for investigation and concluded that there did not seem 'to be much foundation for the allegations made'. Nevertheless, the MI5 section history on Ireland recorded the 'very strong pressure' brought on SIS by the Admiralty in autumn 1939 'to provide an organisation which could check the numerous reports of German submarines refuelling and landing personnel on the West coast of Ireland'.[37] SIS considered, but were unable to establish, 'a covert coast watching service in Ireland, and were reported to have increased their organisation so as to be able to provide some check on these reports'.[38] However, SIS agents had poor sources of information and little understanding of Irish affairs. Their organization, such as it was, was ineffectual and well known to G2. MI5 also had under consideration the establishment of 'a secret organisation' to report on submarine activities off the Irish coast but realized it would be difficult to establish and 'might vitally affect the existing relations between MI5 and the Eire Ministry of Defence ... the service they were now rendering to MI5 would cease in consequence'.[39] Instead, Archer again travelled to London to discuss 'the possibility of improving the coast watching service'.[40] Even so, the Admiralty persisted with another and less effective method of covertly watching the Irish coast.

TAMURA AND THE SEARCH FOR SUBMARINES OFF IRELAND

The Chief of the Naval Staff told the War Cabinet during September 1939 that there were British agents operating in Ireland and a trawler patrolling off the coast, both trying to substantiate rumours of U-boats operating from Irish waters. Guy Liddell wrote on 20 September of further 'frequent reports' of German submarine bases in the west of Ireland, adding 'there seems little doubt that something of the kind is going on'.[41] He later wrote of twenty 'large' German submarines 'based on a secret depot in the Atlantic, locality unknown'.[42] Though there was evidence of submarines of unknown nationality in Irish waters, Liddell's diary entries were pure fiction. Captain W.R. Fell commanded the trawler *Tamura*, one of a number of Q-boats active off Ireland. 'Showing resources and determination', Fell and his crew watched the west coast of Ireland from October 1939 to March 1940.[43] In their first mission submarine H-33 and *Tamura* were tasked 'with the object of destroying U-boats'.[44] From the account of the trip in Fell's autobiography *The sea our shield*, it is clear that

---

36 TNA KV 4/279, Liddell to Dykes, 17 Sept. 1939.   37 O'Halpin, *MI5 and Ireland*, p. 20.
38 Ibid.   39 Ibid. p. 47.   40 Ibid.   41 West, *Liddell diaries, vol. 1*, p. 25.   42 Ibid., p. 39.
43 TNA ADM 1/10138, HMS 'Tamura' and 'H.43'– Report of Proceedings, 3 Dec. 1939.
44 TNA ADM 199/1828, Operation orders for trawler 'Tamura' and S/M 'H.33', 1 Oct.

neither *Tamura* nor H–33 saw any U-boats and archive records amplify this to be the case with all *Tamura*'s voyages off Ireland.[45]

Armed with the latest naval intelligence on U-boats thought to be operating from Irish bases, Fell arrived off Ireland on 10 October, *Tamura* sheltering from a south-westerly gale off Crookhaven in west Cork. Close to Mizen Head with its lighthouse and LOP, *Tamura* only attracted the attention of local fishing boats. If Mizen Head LOP had spotted her, *Tamura* would have blended in as Fell's account includes reference to 'a small fleet of trawlers' fishing for hake south of the nearby Fastnet Rock.[46] Daily report summaries show that G2 and the coastwatchers were on the look out for suspicious actions by trawlers in September and October 1939 and were alert to possible contacts between trawlers and submarines off the Irish coast. On 3 October Sheep's Head LOP on the southern tip of Bantry Bay sighted a submarine ten miles to the west which 'appeared to be following a trawler about one mile away from it'.[47] It is unclear if this was Fell and H–33. While he did make a night rendezvous with H–33 off the Old Head of Kinsale and a nocturnal reconnoitre of the Kenmare River with *Tamura* 'carefully darkened', it brought no response from the Irish authorities. *Tamura* slid unnoticed by Lamb's Head LOP, raising the question that if she could do it as a surface vessel, could not a submarine also do it? Fell and his crew expected to meet a German submarine 'lying, charging its batteries' along the inlet.[48] Why they expected this may be explained by the sighting on 22 September by Lamb's Head LOP of a suspicious vessel believed to be a submarine which moved up the Kenmare River and was later spotted out to sea near the Skelligs. In anticipation of catching a U-boat, H–33 'lay almost submerged' at the mouth of the Kenmare River, unnoticed by the nearby Lamb's Head LOP. Fell saw nothing and left Irish waters after some poaching, with a catch of sole, turbot and brill. During this episode, one of his greatest fears was meeting an armed Irish fisheries protection vessel, which he nicknamed the 'Bogey Man'.[49] Fell added that 'running into him would have been more than awkward for us all'; a sign that London had not, at least to Fell's knowledge, provided Dublin with details of his trip.[50] With the return of poor weather, Fell led H–33 into Blasket Sound. Flares went up and torches shone from the cliffs on the Blasket side of the sound, in full view of Dunmore Head LOP. Islanders in a currach went out to *Tamura*, but as they spoke only Irish, Fell could do little other than gesture to them and he gathered they thought him shipwrecked. H–33 slipped away unnoticed.

When the poor weather passed *Tamura* continued north along the Kerry coast visiting Smerwick Harbour, Brandon Bay and Tralee Bay. Fell judged Smerwick to be suitable for submarines and missed Ventry harbour and Dingle Bay, locations where coastwatchers had already noted submarine activity.

1939. **45** W.R. Fell, *The sea our shield* (London, 1970 edition). **46** Ibid., p. 29. **47** MA DRS 25, 4 Oct. 1939. **48** Fell, *Shield*, p. 30. **49** Ibid., p. 31. **50** Ibid.

Continuing up the west coast *Tamura* passed Inishbofin and Clew Bay and sailed around Achill Island into Blacksod Bay. While planning to move north 'to patrol the entrance to the most likely bays where enemy submarines might replenish fuel or land survivors', Fell attracted the attention of coastwatchers from Termon Hill LOP on the north side of Blacksod Bay. He wrote simply that 'coast watchers came off to us in a rowing boat. They were extremely friendly and talkative.'[51] The text suggests that Fell was familiar with the Coast Watching Service. He never identified the coastwatchers as members of the Irish Defence Forces, nor did he explain their role to his reader. The coastwatchers gave Fell his first reliable intelligence information: 'a submarine had been sighted off the Iniskea Islands on 30 September but that nothing had been seen since and no ships that might have been carrying fuel or stores had been seen on the coast at all'.[52] This information directly countered Fell's Admiralty intelligence reports and shows a much more competent coast watching force on the west coast than on the south-west coast where references to the service were conspicuous by their absence in Fell's account and by their apparent inability to detect *Tamura* or H-33. An experienced seafarer, Corporal Ted Sweeney, Keeper of Blacksod Point lighthouse, led the coastwatchers on Termon Hill; they were in good hands in October 1939. So too were the neighbouring posts at Annagh Head, Erris Head and Lenadoon as contemporary events unknown to Fell established.

The sighting of the submarine off Iniskea marked the last in a five-day series of sightings of the vessel by coastwatchers. Lenadoon LOP first reported the vessel 300 yards offshore on the afternoon of 26 September. Three days later at 1300 on 29 September, coastwatchers on Erris Head sighted the surfaced submarine sailing towards the headland; 'when it came within five miles of the post it sailed in a southerly course towards Eagle Island and was lost to sight'.[53] Coastwatchers to the south at Annagh Head saw the submarine at 1600 and 1810, estimating it to be seven miles from land. An Air Corps reconnaissance aircraft patrolling the area at 1630 saw nothing. Whereas the men at Erris Head believed that the vessel was a submarine, but could not be categorical, those at Annagh Head had 'no doubt about it as they were using glasses and saw her very clearly, and could distinguish her Conning Tower'.[54] The episode shows that a submarine could loiter off the Irish coast for at least five days, much in the same manner as H-33 was doing in conjunction with *Tamura*, but that if it did, coastwatchers, despite their lack of training, would sight the vessel. It would be pure conjecture to suggest that this unidentified submarine was British, but Lenadoon LOP also reported the suspicious activities of a 'steam boat' off Downpatrick Head on 26 September. This in the context of British operations around Ireland suggests that Fell and his crew were not the only vessels seeking U-boats off Ireland in the autumn of 1939.

51 Ibid., p. 34.   52 Ibid. The Iniskea Islands lie to the west of Blacksod Bay less than ten miles offshore.   53 NAI JUS 8/756, Burns to Murphy, 6 Oct. 1939.   54 Ibid.

Tamura sailed north to Malin Head 'seeing nothing suspicious, but enjoying the most glorious scenery', turned, and was back off the Fastnet to rendezvous with H-33 on 18 October.[55] This time *Tamura* may not have been unobserved; on 17 October Mizen Head and Toe Head LOPs both reported the 'the activities of a submarine and a trawler' seen in close proximity and possibly in contact.[56] A trawler coming from the west, as Fell would have done, 'passed within fifty yards of [a] submarine which had [a] light on [its] conning tower'.[57] Again, it is not clear if this was *Tamura* and H-33, but it is verification that the coast-watchers were active and that at this early stage in the war Mizen Head was 'very well manned'.[58]

After his debriefing Fell wondered 'what all the anxiety and fuss of the past two weeks had been about'; he had seen nothing of the suspected German submarines.[59] A second patrol from 9 to 21 November proved equally fruitless. The shadowing submarine, H-43, showed greater caution on this trip and had 'not wanted to surface and show herself in sight of possible coast watches'.[60] This suggests that the British considered the Coast Watching Service capable of observing submarines in Irish waters. Irish documents show that they were definitely capable of doing so. A G2 code telegram to Southern Command warned coastwatchers to expect submarine activity off the Kerry coast while *Tamura* and H-43 were in the area.[61] H-43's report of the mission shows that her captain thought he had been observed at least once. When H-43 anchored off Schull, in Castle Island Sound, 'a perfect anchorage for a U-boat', light signals were seen from the mainland and H-43 slipped away quietly.[62] All this time Fell saw no U-boats. *Tamura* and other Q-boats undertook patrols off Ireland until May 1940. Their voyages were nothing more than 'a small boy's game played in the garden off the Irish coast'.[63]

Fell's account exposes as fiction British views on submarine activity around Ireland, such as Liddell's January 1940 diary entry of a 'disquieting report from SIS' of a submarine base at the mouth of the Doonbeg River in Clare where, it was alleged, 'a submarine comes in three times a week and is camouflaged with a canvas screen'.[64] *Tamura* and H-43 were sent to hunt and destroy U-boats off the west coast from 12 to 25 January 1940. Patrolling between Fastnet Rock and Donegal Bay, the highlights of the trip were a false alarm of U-boat activity in Blacksod Bay and H-43's chase of a phantom U-boat off the Blasket Islands following diesel engine noises heard by the submarine on her hydrophone. There

55 Fell, *Shield*, p. 34.   56 MA G2/X/315 pt I, report by Major O'Connell, 23 Oct. 1939. 57 MA DRS No. 37, 18 Oct. 1939.   58 MA G2/X/315 pt I, report by Major O'Connell, 23 Oct. 1939.   59 Fell, *Shield*, p. 35.   60 Ibid., p. 37.   61 MA G2/X/152, telegram, G2 to Southern Command, 18 Nov. 1939.   62 TNA ADM 1/10138, HMS 'Tamura' and 'H.43' – Report of Proceedings, 3 Dec. 1939. Greig contacted Archer to seek further information on these signals (see G2/X/152 Pt. I, Greig to Archer, 19 Dec. 1939). Archer thought the sightings had no significance.   63 Fell, *Shield*, p. 43.   64 West, *Liddell diaries, vol. 1*, p. 58.

was much of this rumour and speculation through the war but hard and fast evidence of U-boats rarely emerged. When the Revd James Little, a Unionist MP in the Westminster parliament, described by the Admiralty as 'a rabid Orangeman and a thorn in the side of the Security Service', alleged that crews from U-boats had landed on the Donegal coast, the Admiralty was categorical: 'Reports have been received at regular intervals since the outbreak of war about members of submarine crews landing on the south Donegal coast. These reports have all been thoroughly investigated and in no instance were they discovered to have any foundation'.[65] In retrospect, Godfrey wrote of such reports that 'at the time [they] seemed interesting and authentic, although, read in the light of after knowledge, they seem insipid, inconclusive and inconsistent'.[66]

On one occasion a British naval intelligence officer asked the Garda Chief Superintendent at Letterkenny, Donegal, whether there was any chance of submarines operating out of bays in north Donegal. He replied that this was 'an utter impossibility in view of our system of intelligence and vigilance and of the alertness of our coast watchers'.[67] The intelligence officer related the story of a corvette torpedoed about seventy-five miles off the Donegal coast and suggested that when ASDIC operators sought the attacking submarine, it had vanished, possibly into Irish waters. But when the Chief Superintendent replied that no submarine could be in Irish waters for any appreciable length of time the British officer replied 'We think that too, but this incident gave us a bit of worry. Let's forget about it.' The Irish police officer felt that the British were 'casting about in an attempt to save face for the failure to get the submarine'. It was a microcosm of British views towards Ireland when it came to their intelligence failings during the battle of the Atlantic.

CO-OPERATION ON COAST WATCHING OVERSHADOWED

On his return to the Admiralty Churchill demanded a study of 'the addition to the radius of our destroyers through not having the use of Berehaven or other south Irish anti-submarine bases; showing also the advantage to be gained by these facilities'.[68] He became fixated with the return of the ports, seeing their return as the panacea for all British weaknesses in the Atlantic theatre. Aware of the First Lord's single-minded view, Maffey hoped that Churchill would not act rashly as

> any mention at present of facilities at Berehaven would upset the applecart. As progress was being made by me on certain other lines, I thought it best not to jeopardise this progress and I hope the First Lord

65 TNA ADM 1/17089, minute by DNI, 31 Mar. 1944.   66 TNA ADM 223/486, Eire, memorandum by Godfrey, Aug. 1947.   67 NAI DFA Secretary's Files P94, Ó Coileáin to Murphy, 4 Dec. 1944.   68 Gilbert, *Churchill war papers*, p. 29, Churchill to Admiral Pound

will understand this. Action at Berehaven would undoubtedly shake the President's [sic] position. If such action is vital we shall have to take it. But we must think twice and count the gain and the loss.[69]

De Valera, conscious that the security of Ireland and Britain was interlinked, was slowly moving towards closer intelligence co-operation with Britain. Maffey knew that Britain 'must be careful not to deflect' this development.[70] In late September, with British losses rising in the Atlantic and with few German submarines sunk, Churchill demanded that the Royal Navy mount search and destroy patrols in Irish territorial waters. If Irish radio reports of submarine activity were received Britain would 'attack wherever the submarine happened to be' and Ireland would have 'to turn the blind eye'.[71] When informed of this Walshe made no response, a move Maffey took to signify grudging acceptance, London would get no formal agreement from Dublin for operations within Irish waters.

Maffey continued to appeal to de Valera for co-operation in naval matters, raising the danger of a headlong collision between Dublin and London over 'happenings off the Irish coast' if 'reasonable contacts and collaboration' in naval intelligence were not established.[72] He suggested to de Valera on 4 October 'the appointment in some unobtrusive way of a liaison officer' representing the Admiralty and 'promoting the efficiency' of the Coast Watching Service. De Valera 'after some consideration ... thought such an arrangement possible'.[73] It was an important breakthrough. The liaison officer would be appointed but his existence was not to be revealed to the Irish public. Britain was to officially state that it had 'every reason to be fully satisfied with the efficiency of the measures enforced by the Eire authorities' to monitor the Irish coastline.[74] Before the officer took up his posting British-Irish relations would go through another wartime crisis.

On the evening of 4 October Walshe informed Maffey that earlier in the day U-35 had landed the twenty-eight crew of the 4,990-ton Greek-registered *Diamantis* at Ventry in Dingle Bay.[75] In full sight of locals, the submarine remained about fifty yards offshore for one and a half hours while the crew of the Greek ship transferred in small groups to the beach by dinghy, the Germans calmly waving good-bye to Captain Panagos Pateras. The U-boat was leaving the harbour as Gardaí arrived, submerging in full view of the Irish authorities, which were powerless to stop the departing vessel. Walshe informed Maffey within thirty minutes of receiving news of the landing. Ever sceptical, the Admiralty 'declined to believe that the news had come through so quickly' and the Dominions Office 'had to reassure them three times it was true'.[76]

and others, 5 Sept. 1939.   69 TNA PREM 1/340, memorandum in the form of a diary by Maffey, 24 Sept. 1939.   70 Ibid.   71 Ibid.   72 Ibid.   73 TNA DO 35/548/23 E70/17, Maffey to Machtig, 4 Oct. 1939.   74 Ibid.   75 Gilbert, *Churchill war papers*, p. 205, War Cabinet Minutes, 5 Oct. 1939.   76 TNA DO 35/548/25, Machtig to Maffey, 9 Oct. 1939.

Maffey concluded that the episode 'aroused attention to the fact that the police, civil and military authorities have had no instructions whatsoever as to what their attitude should be in regard to a submarine which contravenes neutrality'.[77] An Emergency Powers Order drafted to deal with the matter was, Maffey considered, 'a woolly enactment'. But Walshe assured him that it did not contain objections to British surface vessels taking actions against 'hostile submarines in Eire territorial waters'.[78] What particularly struck the British Representative was that the Order was 'innocuous' and that its purpose was simply to 'satisfy [Irish] longings to have some legal enactment on the subject of neutrality'. If London were to 'wait longer or argue too much ... we may get something worse'.[79] In fact, London had received a remarkable degree of co-operation from Dublin on the draft Order. Walshe explicitly sought comments from London, hoping that Britain 'would look at it with a not too critical eye'.[80]

The newly appointed Irish High Commissioner in Ottawa, John Hearne, wrote to Dublin that 'the Kerry submarine incident has caused a good deal of adverse comment here'.[81] At a dinner given by Canadian Prime Minister Mackenzie King the French Ambassador to Canada, the Comte de Dampierre, had 'made no effort to control his impatience with our policy of neutrality'. MacKenzie King, who felt 'the interests of Eire itself would be better served by throwing in her lot' with Britain and the Commonwealth, did not mention the subject to Hearne.[82] Dublin telegraphed Hearne that the crew of *Diamantis* were 'presumably' landed in accordance with the terms of the London naval treaty of 1930, 'the humanitarian aspect of which [was] appreciated by [the] Irish Government'.[83] In threatening, though ultimately unenforceable, terms, the telegram concluded: 'Irish Government desire [the] exclusion [of] belligerent submarines from Irish waters and are prepared to use every means at their disposal to enforce'. Knowing that their diplomatic codes were not secure, Dublin may have intended this point for the attention of others. Hempel was conscious of the implications for Irish neutrality of the arrival of U-35 in Ventry. Perhaps also wary of provoking Britain he wired the German Foreign Ministry that 'Submarines should avoid Irish territorial waters, or at least where this is avoidable [unavoidable?] the greatest caution should be exercised.'[84] Contemporary Admiralty memoranda nevertheless reported German submarines in Donegal Bay and south-east of Mizen Head in Cork.

The U-35 incident showed that a submarine could not land unobserved along the Irish coast. The vessel had been sighted, reported and the authorities alerted with the information being passed swiftly to London. On 6 October a Coastal Command aircraft was despatched to locate and destroy U-35 off Ireland but it

77 TNA ADM 1/11104, Maffey to Machtig, 25 Oct. 1939.   78 Ibid.   79 Ibid.   80 Ibid., Antrobus to Machtig, 27 Nov. 1939.   81 NAI DFA Secretary's Files P4, Hearne to Estero, 31 Oct. 1939.   82 TNA DO 35/1008/11 WG 431/40, Campbell to Eden, 30 Oct. 1939. 83 NAI DFA Secretary's Files P4, Estero to Hearne, 31 Oct. 1939.   84 *DGFP D: VIII*,

was instructed not to infringe Irish territorial waters in so doing. The Irish had no weaponry to counter submarines, though motor torpedo boats ordered from Thornycrofts were on the point of delivery. The establishment of an Irish naval service was reported in the German press as a sign that the Irish 'doubt the ability of the British to keep even the seas around their own coast clear'.[85] Dulanty looked for more naval vessels from Britain, pointing out that the cost of 'submarine chasers and coast defence vessels' was putting a strain on Irish finances and that this worried the Taoiseach.[86] De Valera hoped that Britain would make these vessels available to Ireland at 'a decent cut rate'. Dominions Secretary Eden promised nothing. Britain was unlikely to have spare vessels given the need to protect 'our own and neutral commerce' against submarines and the wear and tear on destroyers and convoy escorts; a reference to the extra sailing required through lack of access to Irish ports. Dulanty countered that de Valera had asked him to find out 'whether the level of submarine activity was as great in this war as it had been in the last'. Eden took his cue and explained how activity was 'very serious' in the south-western approaches: 'on one day there were no less than three German submarines operating in this area'.

Eden considered that the strain on anti-submarine defences and on the Irish and British economies would increase as German submarine activity rose off Ireland and he agreed that Dulanty should pass these details on to de Valera confidentially. The Dominions Secretary could hardly have been hoping for a change of mind on de Valera's part. He told Lord Halifax that it was 'scarcely possible for "Dev" to square neutrality with the grant of the facilities for which the Admiralty ask'. With 'at least 80% of the Irish people' favouring neutrality this was, Eden concluded with considerable understatement, 'a pretty problem'.[87] Eden rejected Churchill's proposal that he should meet de Valera to discuss the use of the ports. Nonetheless, Eden continued to press upon Dulanty that submarines were operating in the south-western approaches, explaining bleakly that the British merchant ships being sunk by U-boats carried goods destined for Ireland. Maffey finally obtained 'an arrangement' with Dublin on 12 October that movements of submarines observed in Irish waters 'by the Eire coastal watch should be telegraphed to Dublin, Cork and then wirelessed by Dublin and Cork to the Eire airforce coastal patrol on a stated wavelength'.[88] It was another step forward for London, but access to the ports remained unresolved.

Churchill was not satisfied with these steps forward. On 17 October the Cabinet considered an Admiralty memorandum on using Berehaven as a base for vessels 'engaged in protecting our trade far out in the Western Approaches'. It proposed Berehaven as an anchorage for destroyers on convoy protection and

---

Hempel to Foreign Ministry, 8 Oct. 1939 p. 241. Query by *DGFP* editors.   **85** NAI DFA 219/4, Warnock to Walshe, 2 Dec. 1939.   **86** TNA DO 35/1107/9 X1–17, memo by Eden of talk with Dulanty, 18 Oct. 1939.   **87** Gilbert, *Churchill war papers*, War Cabinet Minutes, 18 Oct. 1939, pp. 260–1.   **88** TNA KV 4/279, Proposals for improving coastwatching reports

suggested that 'flying boats could also be based there'.[89] This would enable W
and V class destroyers to operate out to twenty degrees west and Coastal
Command to operate a further five degrees out over the Atlantic from present
limits. Draft minutes record that 'the time had come to make it clear to the Eire
Government that we must have use of' the ports 'and intended in any case to use
them'.[90] If Berehaven were taken by force Britain would gain a base 140 miles
closer to the scene of operations in the Atlantic than provided by the existing
facilities at Milford Haven. But in taking Berehaven, Britain would lose Irish
and, more importantly, United States and Dominions support in the war effort.
The Dominions Office warned that an invasion of Ireland to secure the ports
was 'entirely contrary' to the structure of the Commonwealth and was 'a
negation of the principles of freedom and opposition to aggression for which we
have entered the war'.[91] Though the War Cabinet took no final decision on
Berehaven, Churchill intended to keep the question alive during the coming
months. He encouraged the Admiralty 'to formulate through every channel
its complaints ... I will from time to time bring our grievances before the
Cabinet ... [O]n no account must we appear to acquiesce in, still less be
contented with, the odious treatment we are receiving.'[92] Churchill remained
unable to understand the depth of support in Ireland for neutrality. Indeed, he
doubted whether Ireland was even legally neutral, a view expressed in his famous
phrase that 'they "are at war but skulking"'.[93]

The Dominions Office urged caution as action against the ports would lead
to de Valera taking 'such hostile action against us as he dared, including no doubt
the cessation of such assistance as he is at present giving in relation to German
submarine activities'.[94] Maffey saw de Valera on 21 October and was told by the
Taoiseach that 'the creed of Ireland today was neutrality' and at its core was a
belief that the ports should not be given to Britain.[95] The same day the Irish
Chargé d'Affaires in Berlin, William Warnock, reported to Dublin that the
German press was 'full of accounts of the prowess of the German submarine
commanders, and their successful campaign against the British Navy and
Mercantile Marine'.[96] Dublin could be in no doubt that the situation in the
Atlantic was worsening for Britain but de Valera maintained that no government
in Dublin that attempted to give Britain the use of the ports would survive more
than twenty-four hours. In London, Dulanty softened this by suggesting that de
Valera 'would like to help us, but in this matter he was "in an awful jam"'.[97] The

from Eire, 26 Nov. 1939.   89 TNA DO 35/1008/10 WG431/19, draft war cabinet minutes,
17 Oct. 1939.   90 Ibid.   91 Ibid., memorandum for the War Cabinet, 17 Oct. 1939.
92 Gilbert, *Churchill war papers*, Churchill to Admiral Pound and others, 24 Sept. 1939, pp
143–4.   93 TNA FO 800/310, Churchill to Halifax, 20 Oct. 1939.   94 TNA DO
35/1008/10 WG431/19, note for Eden, 17 Oct. 1939.   95 TNA DO 35/1008/11, quoted in
Campbell to MacKenzie King, 26 Oct. 1939.   96 NAI DFA 219/4, Warnock to Walshe, 21
Oct. 1939.   97 TNA DO 35/1008/10, note by Eden, 23 Oct. 1939.

Irish did offer limited assistance to Britain over Berehaven but it was not in the end taken up. An armed British rescue tug was to be stationed at Berehaven from late 1939 but the Admiralty deployed the tug to the English coast.

When the War Cabinet met on 24 October Churchill maintained that Britain should challenge Irish neutrality using crude geopolitics. At the crux of his position was the belief that 'Eire was an integral part of the British Isles'.[98] He called for the mustering of dominion support and for Britain to 'insist on the use of the harbours'.[99] Chamberlain, unmoved, considered that 'it was difficult to maintain that the use of the ports in question was a matter of life and death'. The dominions would understand Britain's need for the ports but to seize the ports would, and Churchill should have realized this, 'have most unfortunate repercussions in the United States and India, where it would be hailed as a high handed and unwarranted action'. Eden supported Chamberlain: there would be no further threats to de Valera and 'he was well aware of our attitude'. In a huff, Churchill suggested that Britain now 'take stock of the weapons of coercion'. Dublin might think differently when it realized the consequences for trade and employment if Britain declared Ireland a foreign country. Lord Halifax concluded that if it came to Ireland being expelled from the Commonwealth 'it might not appear so long a step to demanding the return of the ports essential to our security'.

On the intervention of the DNI, who felt the situation was 'serious', Churchill brought a further memorandum to Cabinet naming Ireland as a 'potential source of enemy espionage, a centre of distribution of information helpful to the enemy and [a] Base for U Boats'.[100] Beginning that 'in no civilised part of the world is Great Britain less able to obtain vital information than in Eire',[101] the memorandum emphasized the 'unreliability' of the Coast Watching Service as, it contended, 'information about U. Boats was not being passed on' to Archer or to London.[102] Arguing that the coastwatchers either did not watch the coast properly, or did not report what they saw to G2, a third obvious point was not made: that Archer was canny enough not to pass certain information on to London as intelligence was a commodity which could be bartered. Churchill wondered instead if Archer did not report in order to save himself and de Valera's government the 'embarrassment' of having to account for U-boats found in Irish waters.[103] There is no evidence of this from Irish records. Slighted at Irish failure to comply with its wishes, the Admiralty dismissed MI5's Dublin link and again argued for the establishment of an SIS network in Ireland. To avert such a move Guy Liddell had a long talk with G.P. Slade, the officer co-ordinating Irish affairs at NID. He also wrote to Colonel Valentine Vivian at SIS

98 Gilbert, *Churchill war papers*, p. 285, War Cabinet Minutes, 24 Oct. 1939. 99 Ibid. 100 TNA ADM 223/486, Eire, memorandum by Godfrey, Aug. 1947. 101 Ibid., Intelligence Organisation in Eire, 2 Nov. 1939. 102 Ibid., Eire, memorandum by Godfrey, Aug. 1947. 103 Ibid., Intelligence Organisation in Eire, 2 Nov. 1939.

that he had 'convinced' Slade that 'our liaison with the [Irish] Ministry of Defence is worth preserving' and that it was 'desirable' to keep sending submarine reports to Archer for investigation.[104] Liddell felt the Admiralty were 'under a slight misapprehension' believing that the MI5-Dublin link was 'clandestine'; they were unaware that it had been established following an approach by Dublin and had de Valera's agreement. Rather than risk impairing the good relationship that existed between MI5 and G2, and aware that an SIS operation in Ireland would not receive information of the quality received through the Dublin link, the War Cabinet resolved to 'try again to get the Eire Government to co-operate ... "this might at least enable us to get a better picture"'.[105]

THE BRITISH NAVAL ATTACHÉ ARRIVES IN DUBLIN

When he met Maffey on 4 October de Valera had looked favourably on the appointment of a British naval attaché to Dublin. Contacts between the Dominions Office, the Admiralty and Dublin quickly reached agreement on the addition of the post to Maffey's staff. To Guy Liddell it was 'a step in the right direction'.[106] The post would not be referred to publicly as a naval attaché, though the officer would be attached to NID. Following briefings from NID and MI5, the new attaché, 51-year-old Captain Alexander B. Greig OBE, DSC, a retired submariner who had seen service in the Atlantic and the Baltic, arrived in Dublin on 3 November 1939. Now Britain had a man on the ground in Ireland with considerable experience in submarine warfare who could investigate rumours of U-boat activity off the Irish coast. His work would ultimately help discount the wild letters to the Admiralty from retired British naval personnel living along the Irish coast that they saw submarines offshore. Liddell knew of Greig that 'if he plays his cards well we should be able to get what we want, with the concurrence of the Eire authorities'.[107] Greig was soon in touch with Walshe to seek an interview with Archer. Walshe passed over reports of submarines spotted by Air Corps patrols and, unprompted, suggested to Greig that 'no doubt [he] would like to see the coast watching organisation at various parts of the coast'.[108] This was what MI5 hoped Greig would achieve swiftly, Liddell confiding to his diary that Greig 'may be able to make some progress on the submarine question'. MI5 also hoped that his appointment would calm extreme opinions in the Admiralty and remove any danger to MI5's Dublin link from Admiralty NID pressure on SIS to operate in Ireland.[109]

While Walshe organized the visit to a selection of LOPs, Admiralty Intelligence belatedly realized that they had not intercepted reports of U-boat

104 TNA KV 4/279, Liddell to Vivian, 26 Oct. 1939.   105 TNA ADM 223/486, Eire, memorandum by Godfrey, Aug. 1947.   106 TNA KV 4/279, Liddell to Vivian, 26 Oct. 1939. 107 Ibid.   108 TNA DO 130/7, Greig to Godfrey, 9 Nov. 1939.   109 West, *Liddell diaries,*

traffic radioed en-clair to Irish aircraft because of a mix-up over the transmission frequencies.[110] The Admiralty were keen to place the blame on the Irish, suggesting that they had not adhered to agreed frequencies or had transmitted at a low power that could not be received in Britain. They instructed Greig to find out whether 'they have in fact received at Dublin any reports either of sighting submarines from the shore, or of provisions being sent to submarines from the shore'.[111] Greig hesitated to ask for more submarine sighting reports. He did not want to push his luck further in such a short space of time. NID wanted G2 'confidentially' to pass all reported sightings of U-boats to Greig. This would not, they suggested, 'involve them in any risk of being charged with breach of neutrality' (though of course the action would have been a breach of neutrality).[112] When MI5 were alerted to Admiralty concerns about uncon-firmed reports of U-boats landing and provisioning on the Irish coast, they gruffly commented that 'if these cases had been passed to us we could have asked Archer and should probably have got a frank answer'.[113] The Admiralty continued to hold a low opinion of the coastwatchers in the first months of the war due to the communication breakdown with MI5 and the lack of confirmed sightings of U-boats. Had they used MI5's Dublin link the assessment might have been different. Slow to realize the value of MI5's links with Archer, the Admiralty preferred to believe that coastwatchers were not reporting U-boat sightings and that Archer was too embarrassed to admit this. They held that coastwatchers were 'badly paid ... badly equipped [and] recruited ... from unreliable personnel ... [T]hey keep little or no watch at night', the Admiralty expected Dublin to improve the efficiency of the Coast Watching Service and was, via Greig, willing to offer financial assistance for Dublin to do so.[114] Britain was unaware that the Irish military knew that their new force was untrained and inadequately equipped and that training was underway. The visit to the LOPs was a better option than talking down to Dublin on training. Greig planned in early December to visit posts between Tralee in Kerry and Skibbereen in Cork accompanied by Archer. Greig had been briefed on MI5's 'relations with Colonel Archer' and warned by Guy Liddell that 'it would be better he did not refer to our liaison in any conversation with Archer'.[115]

Greig's trip was of great importance for Archer as he had 'originally planned the whole coast-watching scheme [and] was very anxious to see for himself how things were functioning'.[116] None of the LOPs visited were briefed in advance

---

vol. 1, p. 37.   **110** The Admiralty were listening on 1110 kilocycles and the Irish were transmitting on 1110 metres or 270 kilocycles. With this problem solved, the British kept a 24-hour watch on the correct frequency.   **111** TNA DO 130/7, Slade to Godfrey, 15 Nov. 1939.   **112** TNA KV 4/279, Proposals for improving coastwatching reports from Eire, 26 Nov. 1939.   **113** Ibid., The situation in regard to coastwatching in Eire, 4 Dec. 1939.   **114** Ibid.   **115** West, *Liddell diaries, vol. 1*, p. 38.   **116** TNA ADM 223/486, Eire Coast Watching, 11 Dec. 1939.

that Archer, O'Higgins and Greig were making their tour. The three set off from Glengariff on 4 December 1939. They inspected ten LOPs between Toe Head and Kerry Head, all posts in the area except Bray Head on Valentia Island, Dunmore Head opposite the Blasket Islands, the relatively inaccessible post at Sybil Head and the armed post at Fenit which was part of the harbour control system. Archer questioned the coastwatchers in Greig's presence and, while Greig did not talk to them himself, he asked Archer in advance to put certain questions to the men and was present to hear the answers. Greig kept a detailed account of the men he saw on duty and how they were equipped and took particular notice of 'the excellence of their boots and leather leggings', noting their greatcoats, sea boots and oilskins.[117] There were only two oilskins per LOP and shifts swapped oilskins on changeover. The men he saw were aged between 18 and 45 and were 'drawn from the immediate neighbourhood and thus have local knowledge'. The NCOs were 'men of intelligence, and the same could be said of the majority of the crews seen'. Greig was taken by the 'very great keenness' the coastwatchers showed about their job, presumably not a trait he had expected to see. Only one man from each post had undertaken a training course in Dublin and these men were 'better equipped for their duties than those who had not done so'. As to equipment, Greig thought the Zeiss binoculars used by coastwatchers were 'quite good ones … I personally tested them in each post.'[118]

Greig's report was 'unexpectedly favourable' and marked a change in NID thinking on the Coast Watching Service. He found 'the personnel and equipment of the coastwatchers were better than had hitherto been supposed, but their accommodation and communications were primitive'.[119] The trip developed the professional relationship between Greig and Archer. Godfrey later wrote that it was 'very heartening' that these 'good relations' existed.[120] NID began to realize that the Irish coast watching system was developing, Guy Liddell minuting to the Director of MI5, General Vernon Kell, that Greig's report was 'quite satisfactory from our point of view'.[121] Greig reported that submarines had not been seen by any of the LOPs he visited, except one by Eask, overlooking Dingle Bay, on 2 November. This sighting had been radioed to Air Corps patrol aircraft but it was one of the transmissions the Admiralty had not intercepted. Greig was also able to use his new contacts to query reports of U-boats 'seen exhibiting bright red lights off the stretch of coast between Slyne Head and the Aran Islands' as well as reports of Belgian trawlers signalling to U-boats near Kinsale and Galway.[122] G2 investigated and found that the lights were due to local activity, they were of no importance, Greig agreed, writing to Archer that 'nothing of significance has come to light'.[123] The Naval Attaché

---

117 Ibid.   118 Ibid.   119 Ibid., Eire, memorandum by Godfrey, Aug. 1947.   120 Ibid.
121 TNA KV 4/279, minute from Liddell to Kell, 20 Dec. 1939.   122 TNA DO 130/7,
Greig to Archer, 22 Dec. 1939.   123 MA G2/X/152 Pt. 1, Greig to Archer, 22 Jan. 1940.

concluded that although the Coast Watching Service was 'an entirely new service brought into being in a great hurry, I think it can be said that the Eire authorities are making every effort to make it really efficient'.[124] After Greig's trip, Britain took the Coast Watching Service more seriously and the Admiralty was less inclined to favour SIS operations in Ireland. However, the British remained slow to accept the coastwatchers as an effective force.

THE FIRST TEN MONTHS OF THE COAST WATCHING SERVICE

Greig concluded that by December 1939 the Coast Watching Service had 'not reached the peak of its efficiency, but the raw material [was] gradually being developed'.[125] The authors of the MI5 section history on Ireland explained further that

> some of the controls which were to be operated by the Irish, such as the Eireann Coast Watching Service and Illicit Wireless Interception in Eire, had been under discussion before the war, but chiefly owing to the Irish attitude of self-sufficiency, desire to operate independently and lack of means, experienced personnel and equipment, these controls were not fully operating by the summer of 1940.[126]

In fact, a similar situation had existed in Britain where the Admiralty-operated coast watching service took some time to get up and running because it was 'inevitably, built on improvised foundations … [I]ts beginnings were – and had to be – in some ways haphazard.'[127] The slow start establishing the Irish Coast Watching Service affected its efficiency during its first months of operation. Daily Coast Watching Service summary reports of submarine activity included the caveat that 'other similar reports have been received but owing to the extreme improbability of their accuracy, they have not been included'.[128] Though gains in efficiency remained to be achieved, the coastwatchers were in the first months of the war forwarding to G2 a reasonably accurate picture of local shipping movements and of signalling between ships in Irish coastal waters. To Archer 'the collation and scrutiny of these reports [was] yielding valuable information'.[129]

Coastwatchers began keeping proper logbooks in January 1940 and only a few informal logbooks survive for the early months of the war. Detailed reporting from this period is rare, but reports by Gardaí, summaries of Coast Watching Service activity to G2 and initial entries in logbooks all indicate that the waters and skies around Ireland were relatively quiet from the outbreak of the war until

---

124 TNA ADM 223/486, Eire Coast Watching, 11 Dec. 1939. 125 Ibid. 126 O'Halpin, *MI5 and Ireland*, p. 51. 127 TNA KV4/376, Landing of enemy agents, 4 Jan. 1940. 128 MA DRS No. 1. Daily diary 2 September to 5 September 1939. 129 MA G2/X/318, Archer to Lawlor, 29 Sept. 1939.

the German invasion of France in May 1940. The east coast of Ireland in the Eastern Command region, from Louth to north Wexford, was particularly quiet. In Louth, Ballagan Point LOP and the neighbouring post at Dunany Point logged little unusual activity during their first months in operation. Coastwatchers saw signalling between ships but it related to 'ordinary and legitimate activities'.[130] Coastal trade declined but remained unmolested by U-boats. Occasionally a collier would pass towards Greenore or an Irish or British aircraft would fly overhead on routine patrol. These aircraft sometimes caused alarms, such as on 22 December 1939 when four aircraft 'believed to be British machines' crossed into Irish territory. They were, G2 later ascertained, only 'changing station from England to [the] Six Counties'.[131] There were no 'systematic naval operations, such as mine-sweeping [and] suspicious trawler activity' reported along the east coast. Nonetheless, G2 felt that submarine activity existed on the Dún Laoghaire to Holyhead mail boat route and south towards Bray and Wicklow.[132] The British also suspected this but considered 'vague reports of submarines in the Irish Sea ... to be unreliable'.[133] With movements 'confined to local shipping – colliers, cargo boats, trawlers, etc.',[134] this was all 'legitimate business'; there was greater activity in the three remaining command areas.[135]

Curragh Command, responsible for the strategic sector of coastline from Wexford to Waterford, reported occasional infringements of neutrality in the first months of the war. Gardaí were alerted to the activities of the crew of a trawler which landed at Dunmore East on 15 October and made inquiries about a submarine sighting, the number of troops in the area and the sympathies of the locals.[136] The trawler left Dunmore East on the morning of 16 October 'heading towards the English coast'.[137] Was this a vessel like *Tamura*? Coastwatchers also reported incursions into Irish airspace by seaplanes from RAF Coastal Command, solitary naval vessels on patrol and the dark silhouettes of escorted convoys hugging the distant horizon. Observed submarine activity was light and surface vessels numerous. The LOP at Greenore Point on the south-eastern tip of Wexford soon became an important post for the observation of convoys and naval vessels entering the Irish Sea from St. George's Channel bound for Liverpool and leaving coastal waters for the Atlantic.

By the beginning of 1940 a new trend was evident in the Wexford to Kilmore Quay region. Following attacks on the Rosslare to Fishguard mail boat by German aircraft, British aircraft were frequently observed patrolling St George's Channel to Irish territorial limits at Tuskar Rock to inhibit further attacks on shipping. The RAF were also using the easily identifiable Carnsore Point and

130 MA G2/X/315 pt I, Daly to Archer, 7 Oct. 1939.   131 MA DRS 93, 22 Dec. 1939.
132 Ibid.   133 TNA ADM 223/79, Naval Intelligence Documents, Mar. to Sept. 1939, vol. I, OIC daily report, 9 Sept. 1939.   134 MA G2/X/315 Pt I, report by Daly, 14 Oct. 1939.
135 Ibid., report by Daly, 4 Nov. 1939.   136 Ibid., report by Mackey, 23 Oct. 1939.   137 MA

Greenore Point on the south-east Wexford coast and Tuskar Rock lighthouse as rendezvous points for their patrols. Further aerial violations of sovereignty were expected in this region which was already high in the minds of Irish defence planners. It was a probable location for a seaborne invasion of Ireland and was a section of Coast Watching Service operations in which the Germans were interested. G2 had been watching the movements of a German with 'strong Nazi views', George Fassenfeld, who was resident in Ireland since 1935 and who was 'constantly in touch with the German legation' as Fassenfeld was 'interested in our Coast Watching Service in parts of the South East Coastline'.[138] It was suggested that an Air Corps base in the Wexford area be constructed, as had been done of the United States Naval Air Service during World War One. Although the suggestion was not followed up, the pier at Rosslare Harbour was laid with explosives, to be detonated should an invasion be imminent.[139] An inter-services reconnaissance mission of British officers that toured Ireland with Irish officers later reported that 'adequate arrangements exist for the demolition of the railway viaduct leading to the pier at Rosslare. Charges are placed and wired up to the firing key'.[140] To strengthen the harbour's defences pillboxes, machine-gun nests and light anti-aircraft positions were constructed in the cliffs overlooking the harbour. General Bill Callaghan, in 1940 a Second Lieutenant based in Wexford, recalled taking a group of soldiers to place barbed wire obstacles on the exits from beaches along the south east coast in an attempt to bolster the defences of the area.[141] During 1940 it looked as if these defences were about to tested when Greenore LOP reported a large fleet on a course set for the coast. Army engineers were saved the task of destroying Rosslare Harbour pier when the convoy changed course.

In command of Greenore LOP was Corporal Ibar Murphy. He emigrated to Britain after the war and following discussions with men who had served on coastal defences in England and Scotland realized that 'we saw more aerial and naval action at Greenore Point No. 13 off Rosslare Harbour and at Carnsore No. 14 ... than many of those chaps did'.[142] The Defence Forces were lucky that Murphy was in command of Greenore. The logbooks kept by his team are among the most competent in the Coast Watching Service and Murphy's men were clearly exceptionally well trained and led. When one man, Volunteer Green, was questioned by an intelligence officer as to the veracity of his observation of a German He-111 he maintained that 'although there are several

DRS 35, 16 Oct. 1939. **138** NAI DFA Secretary's Files P168, Whelan, for Bryan, to Boland, 19 Aug. 1949. **139** In Oct. 1940 Colonel P.A. Mulcahy OC, Air Corps, told Air Commodore C.N. Carr, AOC, RAF, Northern Ireland, that he hoped that a base for fighter aircraft would be built in the Wexford area (TNA AIR 2/5130, Carr to Air Ministry, 14 Oct. 1940). **140** TNA ADM 1/13032, Report to Commander in Chief, Western Approaches, 13 Dec. 1942. **141** Author's conversation with General Callaghan, Jan. 2007. **142** MA Owen Quinn Papers, Murphy to Quinn, 5 Apr. 1990.

types of low-winged monoplanes I am not mistaken because of the tail plane assembly and the tapering of the wings'.[143] His colleague Volunteer Goodall questioned as to why he identified the same aircraft as a He-111 replied 'my first reason for this conclusion was because of the way the wings were thrown back and the shape of the tailplane'.[144] He then pointed out the 'peculiar shape of wings and tailplane of the German Heinkel 111 and explained that they are identical with the appearance of the aircraft in question'. These men knew their duties and responsibilities. One series of entries from the Greenore logbook for the afternoon of 24 September 1942 further illustrates the command they had of their post. Log serial number 10,107 at 1426 recorded that they had seen '3 low-winged single-rudder single-engined monoplanes, British Spitfires ½ miles E of post travelling NW over land now reconnoitring 4 miles NW of post alt. 50ft viz moderate'. It was a textbook example of how to record an observation of an aircraft. The following entry developed the observation, adding that one of the aircraft bore the marking AH-OY.[145] It continued that the 'three aircraft reconnoitred overland, between Rosslare Harbour and Wexford town from 14.28 to 14.45 [when they] travelled south-west'. A final entry adds to the intelligence picture with the observation that the aircraft had 'inline engines and were of the cannon firing type, one cannon in each wing'.[146] The entries have a level of detail and authority not often seen in reports from coastwatchers.

Moving west from Greenore, during the first months of the war there was considerable activity along the south-west coast. Southern Command concluded that LOPs in the area were 'functioning fairly satisfactorily'.[147] Early on the morning of 5 September Garda McDonagh of Kinsale observed an 'unidentified warship of Cruiser type' five miles off Daunts Lightship south-west of Cork harbour.[148] Later in the month McDonagh and coastwatchers at the Old Head of Kinsale saw 'two Cruisers (flying the British flag) travelling in an easterly direction'.[149] Coastal Command seaplanes were a regular sight, as were patrolling aircraft of the Irish Air Corps' No. 1 Coastal Reconnaissance Squadron. There were regular sightings of alleged submarines from Cork to the Blasket Islands, in particular of partially surfaced submarines passing through the Blasket Sound. Reports came in of submarines in Dingle Bay and in Ballycotton Bay. In the latter case, a British destroyer searched the area with unknown results. One of the more credible reports of submarines in Irish waters in the first month of the war came on 22 September when a 'suspicious vessel believed to be a submarine' was seen moving up the Kenmare River off Lamb's Head. The

143 NAI DFA 221/147, statement by Volunteer P. Green (207682), 2 Sept. 1940.   144 Ibid., statement by Volunteer A. Goodall (205848), 3 Sept. 1940.   145 Though this would appear to be an incorrect identification.   146 MA LOP 13.   147 MA G2/X/315 Pt I, Report by O'Connell, 23 Oct. 1939.   148 NAI JUS 8/756, Emergency Order No. 1 – Matters for Report, Superintendent, Bandon to Murphy, 27 Sept. 1939.   149 Ibid.

Garda report described the vessel in almost childish terms as being 'long and low and high in the middle'. First sighted at 1000 on 22 September, later that day it was spotted heading out to sea 'off Cod's Head ... 18 miles approx from the shore near Western Skellig rock'.[150] This may have been the report that inspired *Tamura* to search the area in early October.[151] When Irish forces saw a submarine off the Blaskets on 2 November they broadcast its presence in a clear radio message giving details of the vessel and its position. Sporadic seaplane activity was sighted and as winter closed in British seaplanes hugged the coast on patrol for submarines in Irish waters.

In Western Command, steamers, warships of various types, trawlers and patrol vessels were sighted by coastwatchers ten to twenty miles out to sea. When crew from a Milford Haven trawler put ashore on Aranmore Island off Burtonport their suspicious actions led locals to contact the Gardaí as they believed that 'the captain expected to meet somebody on the shore' who had not turned up.[152] Was this another British Q-ship? A submarine, thought to be German, was sighted in Donegal Bay at the beginning of October 1939 close to Carrigan Head LOP and submarines were also seen in Galway Bay.[153] The most detailed account of a submarine spotted off the Irish coast at this stage of the war was covered above in connection with the voyage of *Tamura*.[154] Through the war, External Affairs regularly received reports from Maffey's staff of U-boats operating off the west coast. Submarines of unknown nationality definitely transited the west and south-west coasts of Ireland and U-boats operating outside territorial waters attacked and sank shipping in oceanic waters off the Irish coast. However, tales that they were operating from bases in the region were simply fiction and the vast majority of reports of submarines investigated by Western Command were false alarms. One report detailed the movements of a submarine operating north of Kildysart, Clare which 'took on 10 drums of oil and provisions' in the area through contact with a Kilrush local 'named (?) O'Flagherty ... who is in reality German born [and] came to Kilrush about 8 months ago with some local introductions'.[155] As with all good stories, it could not be verified and when checked it appeared that the fictional submarine had left the area and was now operating from nearby Doonbeg Bay. There were many other instances reported to G2 and investigated. All were either spurious or inconclusive. Such rumours also reached London. During 1940 and 1941 the Admiralty enlisted the services of Colonel the Honorable Angus MacDonnell, son of the sixth Earl of Antrim a businessman who frequently visited Ireland, to check such stories. Godfrey thought MacDonnell to be 'a very good mixer' and, as a fisherman, he 'knew the West Coast of Ireland well'.[156] When Godfrey

150 Ibid., Return showing messages transmitted on behalf of Military from Allihies Garda Station, undated, but Sept. 1939. 151 See above, p. 67. 152 MA DRS 14, 21 Sept. 1939. 153 Gilbert, *Churchill war papers*, War Cabinet Minutes, 1 Oct. 1939, p. 190. 154 See above, pp 68–9. 155 NAI DFA Secretary's Files A3, Antrobus to Boland, 1 June 1940. 156 TNA

received reports of U-boat activity in remote places along the west coast he would send MacDonnell to investigate under the guise of a fishing trip. He would 'very soon get to the bottom of the rumour which was invariably false'.[157] G2 speculated that a number of the 'U-boats' sighted off Ireland were British submarines. Coastwatchers in Western Command also logged regular reconnaissance flights by British Coastal Command seaplanes close to the shore and over Irish territory. Overlooking RAF bases near Derry, Inishowen Head, Glengad Head and Malin Head LOPs in Donegal soon became the busiest area of Coast Watching Service operations. Further south, G2 Western Command were concerned that it was not being properly informed of trial seaplane flights from Foynes and that by broadcasting details of such flights in the clear by radio they might be unintentionally imperilling them. As shown above, many of these flights were in fact British anti-submarine reconnaissance patrols.[158]

The Coast Watching Service provided local information from which G2 derived a national intelligence picture. To augment that picture G2 intercepted clear and coded British traffic from Malin Head and Valentia Island marine radiotelegraph stations. They learned from this source that in the early months of the war there was 'a fair amount of war traffic consequent on submarine actions around the coast' passing through both stations.[159] On 21 November Malin Head Radio received a clear transmission from an unidentified trawler that a 'submarine [was] attacking [a] trawler N.W. of INISHTRAHULL ISLAND; Submarine alongside trawler'.[160] Daily report summaries show that a submarine was active off Donegal at the time, with at least two trawlers sunk in the area. As 1939 ended coastwatchers' reports and intercepted radio traffic showed intensive belligerent activity off the western and north-western coast of Ireland. Monitoring marine radio transmissions provided the Defence Forces 'in almost every instance' with 'information as soon as an attack is made on a vessel in the Atlantic.'[161] These were matters, Archer informed E.J. Cussen, the Chief Telegraph Censor, 'in which the Taoiseach is specially interested.'[162] The effectiveness of the attack was not always apparent from the intercepted transmission but the Irish military anticipated that 'in about 50 per cent of the cases the attack does not mean the total loss of the vessel attacked'.[163] Other messages affirmed the loss of vessels known to have been attacked. On 13 February 1940 G2 intercepted a radio message relayed by Malin Head from the Belgian trawler *Jan de Waete* to the Swedish Consul in Belfast that it had taken

ADM 223/486, Eire, memorandum by Godfrey, Aug. 1947.   **157** Ibid.   **158** See above, pp 63–4.   **159** NAI DFA Secretary's Files A30, Telegraph Censorship, 8 Aug. 1940. British stations at Land's End and Portpatrick monitored Valentia and Malin Head broadcasts and communicated with each.   **160** MA DRS 66, 21 Nov. 1939.   **161** NAI DFA Washington Embassy, file 121, memorandum by Defence 'British Claims to Irish Ports', undated, but 1941.   **162** MA G2/X/318, Archer to Cussen, 23 Sept. 1939.   **163** NAI DFA Washington Embassy, file 121, memorandum by Defence 'British Claims to Irish Ports', undated, but

on board survivors from the Swedish vessel *Danaro*, torpedoed 135 miles off Tory Island on 12 February. The following day, as the radio traffic had indicated, twenty-nine survivors and the body of the captain, who had been killed in the attack, were landed at Buncrana. Twenty-eight of the crew left for Derry, the first mate remained in Buncrana awaiting instructions from the Swedish Consul in Dublin for the captain's burial. The codes to decrypt certain messages, normally Admiralty traffic, were not available to the Irish but logs of traffic, clear and encrypted, passing through Valentia and Malin Head were passed directly to G2 as 'the only means … of keeping informed of war actions, distress, etc., off the Irish coast'.[164] This is not to discount the role of the Coast Watching Service. It was limited by the horizon and by weather conditions. Signals intelligence from marine radio stations augmented the coastwatchers by giving warnings of events over the horizon. By March 1940 sinkings off the coast of Ireland had declined as U-boats were withdrawn from Atlantic waters in preparation for the invasion of Norway. The Irish could only infer from coastwatchers' reports and intercepted radio traffic that a change of some kind in the conflict in the North Atlantic was occurring, they did not know the precise nature of, or reason for, the change.

THE COASTWATCHERS FAIL TO DETECT GERMAN AGENTS LANDED IN IRELAND

Early in February 1940 coastwatchers in Western Command failed in one of their primary tasks as, on the night of 8–9 February, U-37 landed Ernst Weber-Drohl unobserved on the west coast of Ireland. The German agent, described by Bryan as 'a funny fish and a pest', was tasked to make contact with the IRA, deliver a sum of money and a radio transmitter and urge them to send a representative to Germany.[165] Weber-Drohl landed 'under the cover of a dark night [when] a strong westerly gale was whipping high breakers against the rocky coast'.[166] He and the U-boat crewman rowing him ashore were nearly drowned when their dinghy capsized attempting to make landfall. With his radio now lost, the German spy's second attempt to land was successful. It is uncertain where exactly Weber-Drohl landed. According to Mark Hull, in *Irish secrets*, U-37's log says Killala Bay.[167] Kenneth Wynn's *U-boat operations of the Second World War* says Donegal Bay, Eunan O'Halpin in *Defending Ireland* says Sligo and Robert Fisk in *In time of war* says Sligo Bay.[168] Taking the widest view of this area, there were LOPs at Kilcummin Head, Lenadoon Point, Aughris Head,

1941.   **164** NAI DFA Secretary's Files A30, Telegraph Censorship, 8 Aug. 1940. **165** UCDA P71/90, rough notes by Bryan.   **166** Enno Stephan, *Spies in Ireland* (London, 1965 edition), p. 66.   **167** Mark Hull, *Irish secrets: German espionage in Ireland, 1939–1945* (Dublin, 2003), p. 72.   **168** Wynn, *U-boat operations of the second world war*, I (London, 2003 edition) p. 26; O'Halpin, *Ireland*, p. 241; Fisk, *In time of war*, p. 138.

Roskeeragh, Mullaghmore and St John's Point. Weather conditions were such that no sightings were made of the submarine or the boat ferrying Weber-Drohl to the shore. For no LOPs to see and report anything was a poor result for the coastwatchers.

Coastwatchers failed a second time to intercept a German agent when, just over four months later, on the night of 12–13 June 1940, U-38 landed Walter Simon, on the Kerry coast between Annascaul and Dingle. According to Stephan, the landing was achieved 'by bright moonlight'.[169] Coastwatchers' reports from nearby Bray Head on Valentia Island show that visibility on the night was in fact moderate to poor with fog.[170] Garda reports to G2 suggest that U-38 was spotted before Simon landed, as on the afternoon of 12 June reports were received that 'civilians' had 'observed an unidentified submarine partly submerged at Doonsheen, Dingle Bay' which 'came within 100 yards of the coast then moved out to sea and disappeared.'[171] Simon intended to radio weather reports and observations of British convoy escort vessels in Lough Foyle to Germany. The landing of Wilhelm Preetz near Minard Head, Dingle at an unknown date in or about the night of 25–26 June 1940 also passed coast-watchers unnoticed, though the Bray Head logbook also mentions poor visibility for the night and the surrounding nights.[172] The details of Preetz's landfall were initially a mystery. Archer could only say that 'about the end of June an unknown man had landed on the coast of Kerry at a place called Minard, but the only clue we had was the finding of a rubber bag of peculiar type there'.[173] Intelligence from Garda sources showed that two LSF members had 'observed an unidentified submarine off ADRIGOLE, BANTRY BAY … proceeding on the surface towards BANTRY', at 0345 on the morning of 28 June, but there was no certainty that the submarine was connected with Preetz's landing, the distance being quite far removed from Dingle Bay.[174] Apprehended in Dublin, Preetz admitted that he had landed at Minard and that the bag contained a radio set. He had a similar mission to Simon, to report information to Germany of relevance to Operation Sea Lion, the planned German invasion of Britain.

These three failures in less than five months illustrate the limitations of the Coast Watching Service. However well they knew their stretch of coast and however well they trained, coastwatchers operating static posts on exposed headlands were not always operating in optimum conditions for sentry duty. The darkness of the night and low visibility simply raised the chances of evading capture for the landing party. Mobile patrols later instituted by the Gardaí and the LSF went some way to overcome this problem but the Irish coastline remained permeable for those who tried hard enough to come ashore unnoticed. The British authorities, often critical of the Irish Coast Watching Service, were

169 Stephan, *Spies*, p. 125.   170 MA LOP 35, entries for 12–13 June 1940 and days surrounding.   171 MA DRS 233, 13 June 1940.   172 See Mark Hull, *Irish secrets*, pp 113–9. 173 TNA KV 2/1303, Archer to Liddell, 5 Sept. 1940.   174 MA DRS 247, 29 June 1940.

in this case understanding. MI5 felt that the coastwatchers 'must not be unduly blamed, the difficulty of picking up a landing of that kind at night on the west coast of Ireland being insuperable; nor were the coast watchers in Great Britain any more successful, even on the south coast of England'.[175] A British military document added that 'the value of these coastal watchers in preventing or detecting landings made under cover of darkness' along the coast of England was 'very limited.'[176] The Department of Defence appreciated similar difficulties and admitted that while it could 'be stated with a reasonable degree of certainty that our look-out posts and maritime Garda Stations afford observation over all the islands and islets' on the Irish coastline, that was 'not to say, however, that every portion of our coastline is subject to constant observation'.[177] Again, their British counterparts agreed, maintaining that 'the ideal position would be to have an effective patrol maintained over the entire coastline for the full twenty-four hours', though it was also clear that 'this ideal could not be achieved in practice.'[178]

The coastwatchers did have one limited success assisting in the capture of three German agents who had landed in Ireland but they were, through a communications failure, responsible for hampering the counter-espionage operation to apprehend the spies. On the early morning of Sunday 7 July 1940 coastwatchers at Toe Head, Cork spotted a yacht, the *Soizic*, from which a dinghy sailed towards the coast and landed at Tralaspeen Strand. On board the dinghy were Herbert Tributh and Dieter Gärtner, both German South Africans, and an Indian, Henry Obed, all described as 'tough customers'.[179] The coastwatchers' record of the sighting of the dinghy indicated nothing as to its crew or intentions: '05.30. Sighted small boat 2 miles west of post going in direction of Tragumna, phoned Castletownshend. Visibility good, wind light NW, sky cloudy, sea calm'.[180] Despite a successful observation and contacting the Gardaí at Castletownshend, the reporting of the unfolding incident was imperilled by the coastwatchers' next action. The American Consul in Cork, William Smale, was told by Colonel M.J. Costello, OC Southern Command,[181] that the three men 'were observed after landing by a military outpost guard who happened to be alone at the time'.[182] This was standard procedure as one of the two-man

---

175 O'Halpin, *MI5 and Ireland*, p. 55.   176 TNA KV4/376, The landing of enemy agents from small craft, 1 Apr. 1941.   177 NAI DFA Secretary's Files A44, Beary to Walshe, 25 Feb. 1942.   178 TNA KV4/376, The landing of enemy agents from small craft', 1 Apr. 1941. 179 National Archives and Records Administration (hereafter NARA), RG 84, Dublin Legation, SSF, Box 3 (1940), Smale to Gray, 10 July 1940.   180 MA LOP 28, 7 July 1940. 181 Michael J. Costello (1904–86) joined the IRA in 1920, transferred to the National Army in 1922 at the rank of Second Lieutenant, promoted to rank of Colonel Commandant by Michael Collins; Director of Intelligence (1924–31); graduate of the United States Staff College at Fort Leavenworth, Texas; Director of Training (1931–2); Assistant Chief of Staff (1932–9); GOC Southern Command (1939–41); GOC 1st Division (1941–5).   182 NARA RG 84, Dublin Legation, SSF, Box 3 (1940), Smale to Gray, 10 July 1940.

team of coastwatchers on duty would patrol outside the LOP while his colleague manned the LOP and the phone. Following routine instructions the coast-watcher in the LOP phoned Castletownshend Gardaí, but inexplicably, as Costello told Smale and as the LOP logbook verifies, the coastwatcher failed to contact the Southern Command IO to inform him of the incoming craft. The coastwatchers had failed in a primary duty of being quick to report to the military authorities. The three agents made their way ashore unchallenged and onwards to Skibbereen from where they hitched a lift to Drimoleague. Gardaí in Drimoleague spotted them boarding a bus to Cork and they were arrested on their arrival in the city.[183] Though the coastwatchers were the first to sight and report the three agents, their failure to fulfil their duty was a grave one. Military posts were left unaware that the agents had landed in Ireland and so Southern Command was unable to alert other LOPs and warn them to keep a sharp look out for other similar landings. There was no indication at this stage that this was a one-off event. Had the three agents gone to ground, the failure on the part of the coastwatchers to inform the military would have been all the more significant as it lengthened the elapsed time before the military could react by deploying forces and cordoning off areas. The failure to call Southern Command also meant that the military were unprepared to respond immediately to any Garda call for assistance and that they and the Gardaí could not work in the close co-operation required under the circumstances.

As it happened the agents made no effort to hide themselves that Sunday morning and were seen making their way from Skibbereen to Cork. They even came to the notice of the Fine Gael TD for West Cork, Eamon O'Neill, who wrote in alarm to Walshe at External Affairs, with whom he was close friends, that while 'down west holding some recruiting meetings' he saw 'three very foreign looking fellows by the kerb awaiting the Cork bus'.[184] O'Neill knew that the Garda Sergeant in Drimoleague 'had them under his eye' and that the men were arrested before they reached Cork but he asked Walshe, 'What are our Coastwatchers doing?'. He urged Walshe to pass information on the episode on to the British. Since the Irish had only caught the men due to the ineptitude of the agents, and in spite of the ineptitude of the coastwatchers, the British 'may be able to do something about these "bucks" on the sea before they land at all'. Speculating that the men came off a French fishing boat which would be 'quite familiar to people on the coast here and would be regarded as very "innocent"', O'Neill tellingly concluded that in the dark days of the summer of 1940 'an incident like this yesterday should make us all feel how imminently near the war is to us'. Walshe, with the crisis of May and June 1940 just behind him, needed no reminding.

---

183 See Mark Hull, *Irish secrets*, pp 120–6.   184 NAI DFA Joseph Walshe semi-official correspondence 1928–1945, O'Neill to Walshe, 8 July 1940.

THE DEMISE OF NO. I COASTAL RECONNAISSANCE SQUADRON

In 1937 Defence Forces planners suggested that the Air Corps should consist of five fighter squadrons and five reconnaissance squadrons. By 1939 this scheme had not been put into effect. To assist coastal observation and defence the 1939 Army Re-organization Scheme envisaged an Air Corps maritime reconnaissance and patrol squadron of sixteen Avro Anson aircraft. The Anson entered RAF service in 1936 and though flown by ten out of nineteen Coastal Command squadrons in 1939 was obsolete by the outbreak of the Second World War. Judged a 'military aircraft by courtesy (or default)', it was slow, had a range of only 1,000 kilometres and was weakly armed.[185] Nine Ansons, three Walrus Amphibians (aging but 'admirably suited for Coastal Reconnaissance work') and, later, a single Lockheed Hudson, then one of the more up-to-date aircraft operating with the Air Corps, became No. 1 Coastal Reconnaissance Squadron operating from Rineanna and Foynes on 30 August 1939.[186] Dulanty had attempted to obtain 'more aircraft for coast watching' from Britain, however 'the Service Departments were, not exactly obstructive, but inclined to put Eire's requests rather low down in order of priority.'[187] By January 1940 three Ansons had been destroyed in forced landings and the attrition rate continued. By May 1940 only four were serviceable.[188]

In the first months of the war No. 1 Coastal Reconnaissance Squadron flew routine three-hour patrols along the west coast just outside Irish territorial waters. For example, on 12 September they flew patrols from Lough Foyle to Sligo Bay, along the North Mayo Coast and from Wexford to Kenmare, all areas where U-boats had been reported and RAF Coastal Command activity had been spotted. Reports of these patrols regularly appear in Coast Watching Service logbooks, with volunteers noting the passing of a single 'twin-engined monoplane, nationality Irish' as an Anson flew past; others simply reported the passage of a 'Home aircraft'. On 7 June 1940 Horn Head LOP recorded the squadron in operation as the *Eros* arrived in sight. They observed a 'battleship and a small boat in front [which] seems to be towing the third vessel[.] [S]he is apparently damaged.' They then logged an Irish military aircraft 'flying over the ships[,] circled over them four times and then flew off in a westerly direction'.[189] By the end of June 1940 routine maritime reconnaissance had 'been abandoned' as Ansons continued to be lost carrying out routine reconnaissance missions.[190] The RAF considered this 'a great error' and hoped that the Air Corps would at least re-establish maritime patrols on a reduced basis as a coastal anti-invasion patrol examining possible anchorages and points

185 Terraine, *Business*, p. 246. 186 TNA AIR 2/5129, The Defence of Ireland, undated. 187 TNA DO 35/998/10, memo by Price, 14 Oct. 1939. 188 TNA AIR 2/5130, report No. 1 by Lywood, 20 May 1940. 189 MA LOP 77, 7 June 1940. 190 TNA AIR 2/5130, Lywood to Air Ministry, 18 June 1940.

of disembarkation.[191] As aviation fuel became scarcer, routine coastal flights ceased entirely. Until its abolition in 1942 No. 1 Coastal Reconnaissance Squadron continued to work in conjunction with the Coast Watching Service. Routine patrols were replaced by flights to investigate incidents as called upon by coastwatchers. For example, Air Corps aircraft flew from Rineanna over the islands off Donegal on 10 and 11 December 1940 to search for survivors from the wrecked Dutch vessel *Stolwyk*. Colonel P.A. Mulcahy, OC Air Corps, who had 'within the limits of its resources built up an efficient and organised force', made no pretence at hiding his preference for the coastwatchers over the Air Corps in keeping watch along the Irish coastline.[192] Described by British intelligence as 'resolute and honest ... determined and realistically minded',[193] he reflected this character when he told Wing Commander Ralph W.C. Lywood, the British Air Attaché in Dublin, that the coastwatchers were 'carrying out quite effective work' and that 'in view of the small number of aircraft he has available for this duty he does not feel justified in using them for this particular duty'.[194]

CONCLUSION

The Coast Watching Service continued to gain experience during the first months of the battle of the Atlantic. These months saw 'the opening skirmishes before battle was joined' off the coast of Ireland.[195] The coastwatchers' efficiency increased as an untried group of amateurs became a trained force. Commandant Daly, Eastern Command IO, took a positive view of affairs in November 1939, writing to Archer that 'the LOP personnel are becoming accustomed to their duties, with a consequent increase in efficiency and, with a little training, they should be capable of dealing with any situation that might arise in that particular sphere'.[196] Such training took place through early 1940 during what turned out to be a lull in hostilities. Greig made a tour of LOPs in Sligo and Donegal in mid-March 1940, reporting that although he and Archer agreed that coastwatchers in both counties did not seem 'as intelligent as those of the posts previously visited in the South West ... the service is reasonably efficient and I think it is fair to say that it is improving', though communications remained problematic until the introduction of telephones in summer 1940.[197] Internationally, a system was in place to transmit information from the Coast Watching Service to Britain as Maffey 'was immediately informed and able to transmit reports direct to the Admiralty' and Greig, who remained in Dublin to

---

191 Ibid., Director of Plans to Lywood, 6 July 1940.   192 TNA AIR 10/3990, Air Intelligence Notes.   193 Ibid.   194 TNA AIR 2/5130, Lywood to Air Ministry, 18 June 1940.   195 Donald MacIntyre, *The battle of the Atlantic* (Barnsley, 2006 edition), p 28. 196 MA G2/X/315 Pt I, Daly to Archer, 4 Nov. 1939.   197 TNA KV 4/280, Further visit

February 1941, undertook day-to-day liaison with the Irish military.[198] The MI5-Dublin link continued to develop. Slade at NID asking Cecil Liddell, Guy's brother, who headed the Irish section of MI5, to find out from Archer in mid-March if U-boats had landed any ammunition for the IRA. He also inquired whether Archer had received 'through his coast-watching service, any reports of a U-boat seen off Spiddal at about the end of March or beginning of April'. He was also concerned to know 'whether anything more was seen of the U-boat' reported early on 5 April by coastwatchers off the Blaskets, and mentioned that the U-Boat had been described to an unidentified 'English visitor' by a 'uniformed coastwatcher'.[199] A 1943 G2 analysis of submarine activity off the Irish coast concluded that though 'during the earlier months of the war and the first year submarines were frequently reported by civilians ... subsequent enquiries in many instances proved that the depth of water was not sufficient to enable submarines to operate. Porpoises, whales, etc., were reported as submarines.'[200] U-35 was *'the only submarine definitely identified as German.'*[201] When he met Eden on 3 May 1940 Walshe told him that there now existed 'an elaborate coast watching system', adding that he believed the Admiralty were 'well satisfied' with its operation.[202] Well satisfied they may have been, but this did not stop NID operating a number of agents along the Irish coast. G2 knew about these agents and their identities and the quality of information they provided to the Admiralty was poor.[203]

Following the German invasion of the Low Countries on 10 May 1940 Warnock reported to Dublin that the mood in Berlin was that 'the war has at last begun. It has always been said here that Germany will win ... [E]verything will be over by next autumn.'[204] Speaking in Galway on 12 May de Valera condemned German action against Belgium and the Netherlands. Warnock worryingly informed Dublin that he had learned from Foreign Ministry sources that 'the Taoiseach's remarks on the invasion were not too well received' in Berlin.[205] The number of troops in coastal areas around Ireland was increased. The United States Consul General, John K. Davies, returning from a weekend trip to the west coast of Ireland saw 'numerous lorry loads of troops he estimated at one company' heading westwards.[206] When Davies inquired from a Garda as to why the troops were on the move the indiscreet policeman told him that 'they were bound for the west coast districts to strengthen present forces on coast

to Eire Coastwatching Stations, 19 Mar. 1940. **198** TNA DO 35/1107/12 WX1/76, memorandum of meeting by Eden, 3 May 1940. **199** TNA KV 4/280, Slade to Liddell, 13 Apr. 1940. **200** MA G2/X/152, Submarine Activity, undated, but March 1943. **201** Ibid., italics replace underlining in original. **202** TNA DO 35/1107/12 WX1/76, memorandum of meeting by Eden, 3 May 1940. **203** See three reports on TNA KV 4/280, Irish Affairs. **204** NAI DFA 219/4, Warnock to Walshe, 18 May 1940. **205** Ibid. **206** NARA RG 84 Dublin Legation General, Box 7 (1940), MacVeagh to Hull, 20 May 1940.

watching duty'. The situation became more critical on 24 May when the Defence Forces issued 'Operational Order No. 1' which anticipated an imminent German invasion along the south-west coast. The Coast Watching Service, for all its recent training and mixed operational experience, was about to face its first big test.

CHAPTER FOUR

The 'Happy Time' off the west coast of Ireland

'IF THE BOCHE DOES DESCEND ON IRELAND HE WILL DO SO WITH PRACTICALLY NO WARNING AT ALL'[1]

THE FALL OF FRANCE dramatically changed the nature of the sea and air war around Ireland as U-boats began to operate from French Atlantic ports and Luftwaffe reconnaissance squadrons flew missions over the Atlantic Ocean from captured airfields in western France. The Legal Adviser at the Department of External Affairs, Michael Rynne, wrote on 17 June, the day that France surrendered, that Germany was 'ready to enter *at once* on a new phase of the war. There are no longer any "Allies".'[2] Warnock had already reported to Dublin from Berlin that his colleagues from neutral countries in the diplomatic corps were 'astounded at the evident military unpreparedness of the Western Powers after nine months of war. The speed and thoroughness of the German advance must, undoubtedly, have knocked the Allies off their balance.'[3] Germany now commanded the continental Atlantic coastline from northern Norway to southern France. Walshe wrote despairingly to de Valera that

> Britain's defeat has been placed beyond all doubt ... [T]he entire coastline of Europe from the Arctic to the Pyrenees is in the hands of the strongest power in the world which can call upon the industry and resources of all Europe and Asia in an unbroken geographical continuity as far as the Pacific Ocean. Neither time nor gold can beat Germany.[4]

Britain was isolated on all sides except the west. Germany sought to close this remaining flank through a decisive U-boat campaign in the Western Approaches, cutting off Britain's maritime lifeline to her empire. Rynne expected air raids and a maritime blockade to commence as the precursor to a German invasion of Britain, with the country 'demoralised and disorganised beyond hope of successfully dealing with invading forces'.[5] Shipping would be 'ordered off the

1 TNA AIR 2/5129, Slessor to Richardson, 8 June 1940.   2 NAI DFA Legal Adviser's Papers, Appreciation of the Situation 17th June 1940.   3 NAI DFA 219/4, Warnock to Walshe, 28 May 1940.   4 NAI DFA Secretary's Office A2, Britain's inevitable defeat, no date, June 1940.   5 NAI DFA Legal Adviser's Papers Box 45, Appreciation of the Situation 17th

English Channel, the Irish Sea, the North Sea and the Western Atlantic as far as the west of Ireland'.[6] Ireland would be placed on the frontline of battle.

As the war moved west Ireland's neutrality appeared to count for little and invasion seemed more likely than ever. In the weeks following the invasion of France Irish defence preparations developed and British–Irish military staff talks took place. Though troops were deployed through the country and the defence of vulnerable points intensified, Ireland remained woefully under-defended. On raiding the house of Stephen Held in Dublin on 23 May Gardaí found evidence of German–IRA co-operation, such as maps of harbours along the south-west coast including Ventry and Dingle Bay. Walshe expected the Wehrmacht to invade Ireland soon, despite assurances from Hempel that 'the exclusive object of Germany's attack was Great Britain'.[7] The Defence Forces implemented plans to mobilise against a German landing on 24 May. On 25 May the Department of External Affairs began burning confidential files that might compromise British–Irish security relations, including files on pre-war contacts with the Admiralty. Concerned at Ireland's 'hopeless unpreparedness' to meet invasion, the leader of the Labour Party, William Norton, wrote to de Valera that it was 'dangerously absurd to imagine that we shall be given twelve months' notice of invasion; the other small countries didn't get twelve seconds notice'.[8] British sources predicted heavy air raids on Irish cities with German forces arriving on Irish soil by early July.[9] It was incorrectly believed that Germany had an armed fifth column in the south and west of Ireland. This assumption gained credibility with the discovery of the maps in Held's possession, though contemporaneous reports of submarines in Dingle Bay were discounted.[10] Irish forces noted how, in late May and early June, in an attempt to substantiate these rumours 'an intense reconnaissance of our eastern and south eastern coasts was carried out by aircraft, identified in several cases as British'.[11] On one occasion the military post at Spike Island reported a British aircraft that 'circled Templebreedy Fort and Cobh and was believed to be taking photographs'.[12]

Britain also responded to the heightened German threat to Ireland by increasing naval patrols off Ireland's west coast 'as a supplement to our inadequate intelligence sources in that Dominion'.[13] Cruisers HMS *Newcastle* and HMS *Sussex* took up position north-west of Loop Head to intercept vessels sighted off Iceland thought to be conveying German troops to Ireland.[14] The

June 1940. 6 Ibid. 7 NAI DFA Secretary's Files P3, memorandum by Walshe, Have we a guarantee against invasion from the German government?, 9 Aug. 1940. 8 NAI DT S11896A, Norton to de Valera, 11 June 1940. 9 This force was thought to be assembling in Vigo in Spain. 10 Though the majority of the material in Held's possession concerned so-called 'Plan Kathleen' for the German invasion of Northern Ireland. For details on the three U-boats see TNA ADM 223/82, Naval Intelligence Documents vol. iv, Apr.–June 1940, p. 262. 11 MA DRS 223, 1 June 1940. 12 MA DRS 222, 31 May 1940. 13 TNA ADM 223/486, most secret memorandum by Godfrey, 28 May 1940. 14 TNA WO 193/761, secret cipher from Commander in Chief of the Home Fleet, 9 June 1940.

Irish Marine Service continued its token attempt to defend Irish territorial waters. *Fort Rannoch* patrolled off Donegal, while *Muirchú* patrolled off the south coast with the Marine Service's single torpedo boat, *M1*, operational off the west coast. Bray Head LOP on Valentia Island recorded *Muirchú* regularly passing the post, patrolling from the Blasket Islands towards the Skelligs, a likely location for submarines close to where Held's maps suggested an invasion might begin.

Hempel informed Berlin that with the fall of France the fear in Ireland remained 'primarily' of a German invasion.[15] British Deputy Cabinet Secretary General Ismay considered 'everything' was 'ready for an immediate descent upon' Ireland by Germany through a simultaneous air and naval attack along wide sections of the coast.[16] German paratroops were devastatingly effective during the invasion of Norway. Dulanty obtained information through the Norwegian Shipping and Trade Mission in London on the deployment of these forces, emphasizing to Dublin 'the colossal concentration of fire power' in the weaponry the paratroops carried. They could 'get out and be ready for fighting in two minutes'; at one small aerodrome the Germans could land three thousand men in five hours.[17] A German paratroop attack on Collinstown or Rineanna was now a real fear, Archer producing an intelligence note analysing 'German Airborne Troops' and their tactics, using the occupation of the Netherlands and Norway as case studies. He concluded that though 'airborne troops are most vulnerable immediately before, during and after landing ... given a little time to consolidate their defences they are hard to dislodge'.[18] Both LDF and regular troops trained to counter parachute landings. The American Military Attaché in Dublin, Major Wofford, observed such an exercise later in the war and reported that 'the issue of orders and the deployment of the Infantry Battalion concerned ... were efficiently carried out and the men looked very fit and all ranks acted keenly.'[19] Though de Valera was 'organising the defence of the country with vigour and with all the means at his disposal',[20] Archer told British intelligence staff that a German airborne invasion of Ireland would be 'an extremely simple matter.'[21] Due to the poor equipment of the Irish Defence Forces, 'they would have no effective means of stopping the landing of troop carriers or parachutists'. He appealed to Britain to fulfil outstanding Irish contracts for military equipment, as did de Valera via Maffey. The Air Ministry had credible intelligence that German naval and air forces were considering 'attacking IRELAND and Faeroes to obtain air bases for an attack on Scotland, and air domination of North Atlantic'.[22] Britain did eventually release limited quantities of equipment to Ireland as the German threat to the country grew.

15 *DGFP D: IX*, p. 639, Hempel to Foreign Ministry, 19 June 1940.   16 TNA PREM 3/130, Ismay to Prime Minister, 29 May 1940.   17 NAI DFA Secretary's Files P12/14 (1), Dulanty to Walshe, 28 May 1940.   18 UCDA P71/37, Intelligence Note No. 19. German Airborne Troops, undated but summer 1940.   19 TNA WO 106/6045, Pryce to HQBTNI, 25 May 1941.   20 TNA DO 130/10, Maffey to Machtig, 15 June 1940.   21 TNA KV 4/280, Guy Liddell to Elliott, 20 May 1940.   22 TNA AIR 2/5129, telegram to Admiralty forwarded to

The British Combined Intelligence Committee, an inter-service committee established as a sub-committee of the Joint Intelligence Committee, considered all intelligence relating to an invasion of Britain and Ireland. At its first meeting on 31 May it was strongly influenced by the German invasion of Norway when considering how Britain and Ireland might next be treated: 'all landings appear to have taken place within a short time of one another … [Germany] will employ the same strategy of surprise, darkness, diversion and air protection'.[23] The CIC reported that 'extensive German plans for a descent on EIRE have been in preparation for a considerable time' but that an invasion of Ireland did not now appear imminent.[24] The following day the committee revised its view, an invasion was 'not only seriously planned and prepared with the help of the IRA but is imminent'.[25] With reports of aircraft flying the English Channel to unknown destinations to the west, the CIC agreed that 'Eire may be menaced'.[26] A seaborne invasion of southern Ireland from northern Spain had become a distinct possibility. In the following days Northern Ireland sources passed information to G2 that three submarines 'probably German' and which 'might be troop carriers' were off Donegal, though 'this was to be accepted with reserve'. Following up on the tip, G2 found that 'no reports from LOPs confirmed' such a presence, though 'subsequent British naval activity off Donegal suggest[ed] pursuit.'[27]

When Malcolm MacDonald, the British Minister of Health, met de Valera in Dublin on 17 June in an unsuccessful attempt to convince him that Ireland should join the war if Britain offered a united Ireland, he found the Taoiseach 'depressed and tired'.[28] As they spoke of 'the latest news from France' MacDonald held that after the experience of Denmark, Norway, Holland and Belgium, 'Eire would appear to be the next neutral country on the list'. CIC minutes suggest the contrary. Reports for the second half of June show greatly reduced concern over German intentions towards Ireland. A German invasion of Britain was expected in early July, but there was 'to be no bombing of Ireland at present'.[29] This was interpreted as a move not to antagonize 'certain Irish elements' and 'to avoid compromising surprise if invasion is intended'.

The situation remained fluid. A German landing along the west coast remained possible and, like the flying columns of the Anglo–Irish War, parties of fifteen to twenty soldiers were 'constantly patrolling the whole area from Donegal to Clare'; camping in the open each night they moved on a dawn.[30] At External Affairs Rynne considered that 'the emergency will, so far as this country is concerned, become greatly intensified during the next few weeks.'[31]

Air Ministry, 22 May 1940.   23 TNA ADM 223/846, CIC, Report No. 1, 1200 31 May 1940. 24 Ibid.   25 Ibid., CIC, Report No. 1, 1200 1 June 1940.   26 Ibid.   27 MA DRS 227, 6 June 1940.   28 TNA PREM 3/131/1, Note of conversation between Mr de Valera and Mr MacDonald, 17 June 1940.   29 TNA ADM 223/846, CIC, Report No. 36, 5 July 1940. 30 TNA WO 106/6043, Pryce to War Office, 21 June 1940.   31 NAI DFA Legal Adviser's papers, file 'Neutrality – General Papers', Suggested action in intensified emergency, 24 June

He did not think that Ireland would 'necessarily become involved as a belligerent in the war' but invasion scares continued. Information received by the Garda superintendent in Dundalk at 0205 on 3 July from the RUC district inspector in Newry suggested that the Germans were to invade by air at dawn. All military and Garda posts were informed by 0255. During the night unidentified aircraft were heard circling over Longford and Clonmel. At 0305 Dunmore Head LOP observed 'two vessels between the mainland and the Blaskets'.[32] A convoy 'in unusual formation' was sighted off Howth Head at 0320. At 0404 unusual lights were seen on the River Shannon near Rineanna and a suspicious aircraft was heard over Ballyduff, Tralee at 0525.[33] The Germans did not come that night, but it was one of suspense and uncertainty. Further flights along the Irish coast caused continuing concern. Between 1100 and 1200 on 13 July, during another invasion scare, Greenore LOP and later Dunany Head LOP sighted a seaplane of unknown nationality flying inside Irish territorial waters north along the length of the Irish east coast. The sightings were reported to Air Attaché Lywood and were in London that evening for the CIC to digest.[34] In Dublin McKenna remained convinced that 'the Germanic group is more likely to take the initiative against us'; de Valera ordered the Defence Forces to give priority to countering an invasion from Germany.[35] Fears reduced as July ended. On 20 July Walshe telegraphed the Irish Chargé d'Affaires in Berlin that the idea of a German invasion was 'no longer seriously entertained'.[36]

Dublin continued also to anticipate invasion from Britain.[37] At the end of July 'there was a general feeling that the British were about to invade'.[38] Walshe had been in urgent contact with Maffey about the intentions of British forces massing on the border outside Derry. Royal Air Force reconnaissance aircraft were spotted regularly over strategic Irish installations. On 30 July Bray Head LOP, Valentia recorded a 'monoplane 3½ miles west of post going east, 1000ft high, red, white, and blue on tail vertically divided and red circle on body, nationality British'.[39] Britain believed that any invasion would meet with little resistance from the Irish Defence Forces, who were considered in London to be in a state of 'considerable disaffection', despite strongly worded reports from Maffey and his Military Attaché, Major Meyric H. Pryce, to the contrary.[40] Pryce summed up by reporting to the War Office in London the 'determination' of the Defence Forces 'to fight bitterly against whomsoever first invades EIRE'.[41] Snippets of evidence from the coastwatchers show the Defence Forces making ready to counter what fate threw at them through the summer of 1940. Malin

---

1940.   **32** NAI JUS 8/840, Nangle to Murphy, 3 July 1940.   **33** MA DRS 250, 3 July 1940.
34 NAI DFA Secretary's Files A2, telegram, Air Ministry to Lywood, 13 July 1940.
35 Quoted in Brian Girvin, *The Emergency: neutral Ireland, 1939–45* (London, 2006), p. 154.
36 NAI DFA Secretary's Files P3.   **37** See Girvin, *Emergency*, p. 157.   **38** TNA WO 106/6044, Pryce to Clive, 3 Sept. 1940.   **39** MA LOP 35, 30 July 1940.   **40** TNA DO 35/1107/12 WX 1/78, Irish Affairs (Defence Forces in Eire), 9 Apr. 1940.   **41** TNA WO 106/6044, Pryce to Clive, 3 Sept. 1940.

Head LOP noted during a period of heavy British air activity around Inishowen that Fort Lenan on Lough Swilly was mounting extensive coastal artillery exercises.[42] Britain still had reason to invade Ireland. The German occupation of the French Atlantic seaboard led British planners to reassert their belief that a naval base in south-west Ireland remained 'a vital necessity'.[43] As shipping losses in the Atlantic rose dramatically, the Admiralty prepared to retake Berehaven by force. A small striking force of marines and reservists was 'available at short notice' to embark in 'a couple of destroyers to proceed and seize a vital point', thought to be Berehaven or Cork harbour.[44] As the summer passed, British planners turned their attention from Berehaven to the Shannon estuary as a naval base as Berehaven lacked a defensive air base. To protect the Shannon estuary the RAF drew up plans to operate from the partially constructed transatlantic airport at Shannon and the seaplane base at Foynes.[45] By the autumn of 1940 the Air Ministry and the Admiralty favoured the Shannon estuary at Foynes as 'a Main Fleet Base' with Lough Swilly as 'an advanced fuelling base for destroyers and light craft'.[46] These plans contained the significant caveat that they would be put into effect 'if Eire bases become available'; this remained wishful thinking.[47] Maffey again sought de Valera's agreement for British use of Irish ports and referred to improved defences at Berehaven and on the Shannon. But he reported to London that 'the mere mention of Berehaven in this connection gives a shock to the nervous system'; there had been no change in Irish attitudes.[48] Naively, the Admiralty hoped to use the Shannon estuary as it had not 'the odious treaty association which has the name of Berehaven'.[49] They would hope in vain.

Continued intelligence failings on German activities in Ireland did nothing to calm British nerves. Maffey warned the Permanent Secretary at the Dominions Office, Sir Eric Machtig, of his growing annoyance at these failings, telling London that

> with so many rumours and scares it is not surprising that the picture should get out of focus ... we get this sort of thing: 'Report just received Master of S.S. Kerry Head informed by reliable source German plane type unknown refuelled at Baldonnell Aerodrome on June 26. Can you confirm?' ... One asks who is authorised and by whom to send off such a ridiculous report. At this end, it looks like a case of disciplinary action.[50]

---

42 MA LOP 80, 1 Aug. 1940.   43 TNA ADM 116/5631, telegram to Maffey, 27 June 1940. 44 TNA ADM 223/486, minutes on file. The available troops were poorly trained and equipped and, on investigation, the destroyers were unavailable to convey the troops to Ireland.   45 See TNA CAB 84/11, AIR 2/7233 and ADM 116/5631.   46 TNA ADM 223/486, minute on file, 6 Sept. 1940.   47 Ibid., Phillips to Secretary, DCOS (AA) Sub-Committee, War Cabinet, 10 Sept. 1940.   48 TNA ADM 116/5631, Maffey to Machtig, 20 June 1940.   49 Ibid., Waldock to Garner, 23 June 1940.   50 TNA DO 130/12, Maffey to

Maffey knew that Wing Commander Ralph Lywood, the recently appointed Air Attaché on his staff, was responsible for the gaffe. Stupidly, Lywood had received this report from the Air Ministry and having been asked to investigate had 'mentioned it more as a joke than anything else' to Colonel Mulcahy, who had in turn passed the information to Walshe. It was not the last time that Lywood would act in such an unprofessional manner. With regard to the Baldonnell issue, Maffey reflected that 'if such a thing happened and I did not know about it I might as well pack up'.[51] The episode had 'made things difficult for British officials in Ireland, and increased the suspicions of Walshe and his colleagues' of British intentions towards Ireland.[52] Maffey's understanding of Irish affairs could defuse such incidents, though Pryce speculated that because of them 'the flow of information' from the Irish authorities 'may to a certain extent be dammed just when we began to hope for a flood'.[53] Fear of invasion from both belligerents continued in Ireland through the summer of 1940 as the war in the Atlantic took on a new intensity.

ON THE ATLANTIC FRONTLINE, THE 'HAPPY TIME',
JULY–DECEMBER 1940

LOP logbooks from the first half of 1940 show a quiet watch on all Irish coasts. Coastwatchers were not yet fully skilled in the art of recording what they saw from their positions but the general impression before June is of long periods where little happened along the coastline beyond routine coastal maritime traffic and passing Air Corps and RAF patrols. This changed dramatically on the fall of France. G2's daily reports summary for 22 June concluded that 'reports received indicate that the war on British shipping is again gaining momentum' in the western approaches and in the Bay of Biscay.[54] From July to December 1940 the battle of the Atlantic was waged directly off the west coast of Ireland. Increased naval activity was reflected in Coast Watching Service reports and in the 'marked revival' of war traffic from Valentia and Malin Head telegraph stations 'consequent on the revival of German submarine activities in the Atlantic, and, recently, of German aircraft activities'.[55] United States Minister to Ireland David Gray reported to Washington that he had heard from Colonel Lawlor, the officer 'in charge of coastwise intelligence' and in command of 'all the coast watchers and patrol boats', that 'the main effort' of U-boats was now 'directed to waters off Sligo and Galway'.[56]

All 'convoys and unescorted shipping with the exception of coasters and trawlers' were prohibited from entering or leaving the Irish Sea to the south via

Machtig, 15 July 1940. **51** Ibid. **52** TNA WO 106/6043, Pryce to Conyers-Baker, 13 July 1940. **53** Ibid., Report No. 13 (by Pryce), 16 July 1940. **54** MA DRS 241, 22 June 1940. **55** NAI DFA Secretary's Files A30, Telegraph Censorship, 8 Aug. 1940. **56** NARA RG 84 Dublin legation, SSF, Box 3 (1940), 1 Oct. 1940.

St George's Channel as the area was within striking distance from western France.[57] The prohibition on shipping was enforced by a minefield running from Milford Haven in Wales up to Irish territorial waters off Waterford and Wexford. On the Irish side the mines extended 'for about 60 miles from Mine Head (Co. Waterford) to Carnsore Point (Co. Wexford)'.[58] Dublin received 'no prior notification' that the minefield was in place.[59] When, on 24 July, Dublin first learned of the minefield, the Dominions Office alleged they knew nothing of the deployment, telling Dulanty that 'the first intimation … received from the Admiralty was … when the order to lay the mines had already been given'.[60] Nevertheless, they held that it might 'deter the enemy from attempting to pass surface forces through them'.[61] It certainly covered a good portion of the coast in areas where a German seaborne landing was anticipated.

From July 1940 the logbooks of Donegal LOPs showed a sharp increase in convoy traffic off the north Irish coast. There was not 'a single report of a convoy having been sighted from our South or West coasts. Prior to that date such reports were a daily feature, particularly from the Co. Wexford coastline'.[62] Convoys were now marshalled in a 'dangerous concentration' through the north-western approaches, well within the range of U-boats, which, as Lawlor told Gray, were routing up the west coast of Ireland to attack ships off Donegal.[63] Using the change in routes to criticise Irish neutrality, the British ambassador in Washington told the Irish Minister to the United States, Robert Brennan, that traffic was diverted north because Britain did not have access to Cobh and Berehaven; 'this makes [the] convoy [an] easier target because one line is more vulnerable than two'.[64] Dublin exposed the error of the ambassador's argument, replying that the 'route was selected because of proximity of German bases to southern route'.[65]

With shipping crowding into the seas off Malin Head the area became the prime hunting ground of U-boats during what their crews dubbed 'the Happy Time' from July to October 1940 when U-boats

> sank ships almost at will – at sea or within sight of land and safety, quietly or sending them up in huge fireballs. Sometimes nobody knew where a ship had sunk, sometimes everybody knew, for the wreckage would float for days and bodies would wash onto the beaches. Forty-two merchant ships, most of them carrying vital war cargo, were sunk in July [1940] alone, sixty-eight in August, sixty-six in September.[66]

57 NAI DFA Secretary's Files P35, British claims to Irish ports, undated, early 1941.   58 MA DRS 268, 24 July 1940.   59 NAI DFA Secretary's Files P3, telegram No. 54, Estero to Delegirland, Geneva, 25 July 1940.   60 NAI DFA Secretary's Files P12/14(1), Dulanty to Walshe, 24 July 1940.   61 NAI DFA Secretary's Files A10, extract from Machtig to Maffey, 16 Nov. 1940 provided by G2 to Walshe.   62 Ibid.   63 TNA ADM 116/5631, The use of air bases in Eire for North Atlantic operations, 4 Aug. 1941.   64 NAI DFA Secretary's Files A10, Eire to Estero (No. 296, Personal), 6 Dec. 1940.   65 Ibid., Estero to Eire (No. 197, Personal), 9 Dec. 1940.   66 Jordan Vause, *U-boat ace: the story of Wolfgang Lüth* (Annapolis, 2001

Losses of up to two ships daily from attacks by U-boats and their aerial partners the FW-200 Condors, which flew 'with impunity through Irish air space', made the roughly 250 square miles of sea off Bloody Foreland a cemetery for shipping.[67] On 1 August Hitler instructed that a complete blockade of all shipping with Britain be implemented and on 17 August shipping in the waters surrounding Britain and Ireland to 350 nautical miles west of Ireland was declared subject to German attack. G2 held that there was 'no indication' in the declaration 'that Irish territorial waters are immune from the blockaded area' and, accordingly, Ireland was, as Rynne predicted, now on the front line of the battle of the Atlantic.[68] Malin Head LOP's 1255 observation on 24 August of a damaged merchant ship being towed by a tug towards Lough Foyle included reference to 'an oil tanker semi-submerged half a mile west of them'. Fifty minutes later the LOP recorded that 'the tanker has disappeared probably sunk'.[69] This small incident reflected the wider situation off north-west Ireland as the 'Happy Time' continued and British shipping losses rose.

The Coast Watching Service was now better organized and trained, and the installation of telephones in most LOPs greatly improved efficiency. Their observations swiftly reflected the changing nature of the war off the Irish coast. An increase in incident reports from Western Command and a decline from Southern Command showed that the battle of the Atlantic was shifting to the north-west coast and that the tempo of battle was increasing. Western Command received 1,479 incident reports in July, a 'huge increase on the June total which was in itself much in excess of any previous month'.[70] There was now 'more or less continuous aerial reconnaissance' by British forces along the west coast of Ireland, 'but greatly more activity is noticeable where convoys are about to pass'.[71] August brought 1,838 reports and September a further increase to 2,367 reports. Between sixty and eighty percent of these reports were from the LOPs from Horn Head to Inishowen Head, the most northerly LOPs in Ireland. Reports increased at such a rate that

> the volume of messages ... is of such magnitude as to overtax the telephonic communications through our territory from Co. Donegal. At present there is only a single line connecting the Donegal telephonic networks to the rest of Eire.[72]

As the 'Happy Time' began to take its toll on shipping off Donegal, U-99 skippered by U-boat ace Otto Kretschmer passed along the west coast of Ireland on the early morning of 29 July. Kretschmer torpedoed the freighter *Clan*

edition), p. 56.   **67** UCDA P71/171, note by Bryan, Air and Marine [Intelligence].   **68** MA DRS 290, 20 Aug. 1940.   **69** MA LOP 80, 24 Aug. 1940.   **70** MA G2/X/315 Pt II, Report on M&CWS for July 1940.   **71** Ibid., Report on M&CWS for Aug. 1940.   **72** MA G2/X/318, Archer to Lawlor, 20 Aug. 1940.

Menzies, inbound from Sydney, Nova Scotia, with a cargo of wheat and zinc, 150 miles west of Loop Head. The vessel sank quickly, seven crewmen were killed and eighty-seven crewmen took to two lifeboats. They set off north-east and at 0635 on 30 July Erris Head LOP spotted one of the lifeboats four miles west of the post. The NCO in charge of Erris Head, Corporal Pat Reilly, along with a local Garda 'went out to direct them' into Broadhaven Bay where thirty-six men landed.[73] Western Command headquarters at Athlone sought detailed information from the survivors, who were described as 'Negroes' and who identified their ship and provided an account of its sinking.[74] As this debriefing was underway the LOP sighted an Irish trawler passing from the north-west heading north-east towing a second lifeboat.[75]

Another reminder of the grim reality of war in the North Atlantic appeared in the next entry in the Erris Head logbook: 'dead body floating ½ mile south of post 10 yards from shore'.[76] The coastwatchers reported the body to the Gardaí at Belmullet who investigated but could not recover the corpse because of the rough sea and overhanging cliffs. Sergeant Burns from Belmullet returned on 2 August with a number of Gardaí who brought with them grappling hooks and ropes. Sailing beneath the cliffs in a borrowed currach the Gardaí 'hooked the body and towed it in to Aughadoon' where they brought it ashore.[77] It was of a European male, badly decomposed and dressed in a blue pinstripe suit and a red striped cotton shirt. In his pockets were playing cards, cigarette cards, a second-class boat ticket, some English money and a small crucifix. An inquest was not required for casualties of war who died outside the limits of territorial waters. The man was buried that day in the nearby Termoncarragh graveyard in an unmarked grave. He was never identified.

There was no doubt on what ship the unidentified man had been sailing. He was one of the 743 Italian and German internees, guards and ships crew who lost their lives when the Blue Star line's 25,000-ton *Arandora Star*, sailing without an escort from Liverpool for St John's, Newfoundland, was torpedoed 75 miles west of Bloody Foreland at 0705 on 2 July 1940 by U-47 commanded by Gunther Prien. The ship sank in just over an hour. Sergeant Norman Price of the Worcestershire Regiment saw the end of the liner from the water:

> I could see hundreds of men clinging to the ship. They were like ants and then the ship went up at one end and slid rapidly down, taking the men with her … [M]any men had broken their necks jumping or diving into the water. Others injured themselves by landing on drifting wreckage and floating debris near the sinking ship.[78]

73 MA LOP 62, 30 July 1940.   74 MA DRS 273, 30 July 1940.   75 The vessel was most likely *Kyleclare*.   76 MA LOP 62, entry for 1535 30 July 1940.   77 NAI DFA 241/184, Burns to Murphy, 7 Aug. 1940.   78 'The loss of the *Arandora Star*', in Ian Hawkins (ed), *Destroyer: an anthology of first-hand accounts of the war at sea 1939–1945* (London, 2005,

Malin Head radio picked up distress signals from *Arandora Star* and retransmitted them to Land's End and Portpatrick but Britain did not immediately announce the loss of the ship. The majority of those who died in the sinking were Italian men above fighting age. The bodies of many of those drowned washed ashore on the Irish coast. On 30 July the body of 71-year-old Ernesto Moruzzi was found near Burtonport in Donegal. Four more bodies, including that spotted at Erris Head, were found that day. In addition to Moruzzi, two were identified, 60-year-old Luigi Paretti on Tory Island and 45-year-old Giovanni Marenghi near Belmullet. On 7 August Erris Head reported two more bodies sighted close to the shore. Volunteers Barrett and Lalley were ordered to find out for each 'whether [an] inquest will be held, how long he was in the water, what corps he belonged to if [a] soldier and all other particulars if possible (Colour of uniform whether a member of British air force or otherwise)'.[79] There was no inquest, the bodies were buried locally, and the lengthy and traumatic task of tracing the next of kin began in the Department of External Affairs as they worked closely with diplomatic missions in Dublin to make contact with the families of the deceased.

The two bodies spotted at Erris Head were not recovered at the headland, indeed they may never have been recovered, such is the way of currents and tides. Perhaps they were the bodies of 27-year-old career soldier Trooper Frank Carter from Kilburn, London, of the Royal Armoured Corps and 19-year-old Private Fred Chick from Martinstown, Dorsetshire, of the Dorsetshire Regiment. The two men lie buried in Belmullet, their bodies washed ashore at Annagh Head on 8 August. They were amongst the troops guarding the Italian and German internees on *Arandora Star* including Moruzzi and Marenghi. In total 33 of the 88 bodies washed ashore on the western Irish coast between July and the end of August were from *Arandora Star*. The true figure is probably much higher as a further forty-three bodies were never identified due to advanced decomposition or to lack of identifying papers or possessions. The old man washed ashore on 10 August at Buninver, Dungloe and buried in the cemetery at Mahergallon, Bunbeg and the unidentified Italian in his mid-40s found in the sea the same day at Easkey pier in Sligo were probably from *Arandora Star*. With these two cases, as with many more, Frederick Boland at External Affairs could only write that 'there would appear to be very little hope of ever establishing the identity of the deceased'.[80] Nationality did not matter in the icy waters of the Atlantic, a poignant illustration being the graves of Luigi Tapparo, a 42-year-old Italian internee from Edinburgh, and one of his guards on *Arandora Star*, 21-year-old John Connelly, from Oban in Argyleshire, a Trooper in the Lovat Scouts. They died on the same day and lie buried side by side in Termoncarragh graveyard outside Belmullet.

paperback edition), p. 137.   **79** MA LOP 62, 8 Aug. 1940.   **80** NAI DFA 241/184, Boland to Antrobus, 2 Dec. 1940.

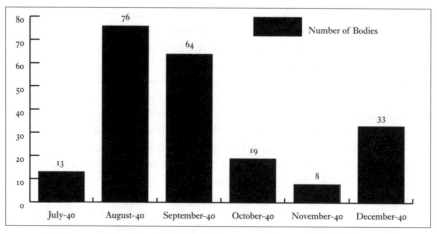

4.1: Bodies washed ashore: July–December 1940 (Source: NAI DFA 241/184)

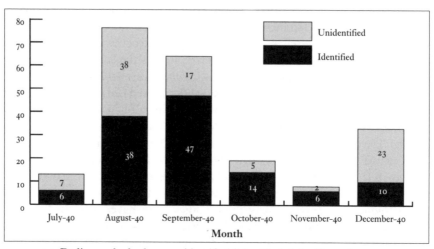

4.2: Bodies washed ashore, unidentified/identified: July–December 1940
(Source: NAI DFA 241/184)

    Through August 1940 bodies from *Arandora Star* washed onto Irish beaches. The Burtonport representative of the Shipwrecked Mariners' Society, James O'Donnell, anticipated that 'if the wind holds to the west and north west many of these poor men's remains will be cast in on this coast'.[81] These 'men that came in with the sea' show the rising death toll in the battle of the Atlantic over the summer and autumn of 1940 as the 'Happy Time' continued.[82] In August, 12 ships were torpedoed off the Irish coast and 41 lifeboats and 13 rafts put ashore on Irish territory with 132 survivors. On 12 August Malin Head LOP recorded

81 TNA DO 35/1107/16, O'Donnell to Sidebotham, 16 Aug. 1940.   82 NAI DH A116/33 vol. II, Kerrigan to Ruttledge, 23 Sept. 1940.

that 'there are at present four ships boats washed ashore and five floats ashore'; one of the boats being from *Arandora Star*.[83] Another contained the barest fragments of human existence: 'Naval cap band bearing the letters H.M.S. Transylvania, naval jackets bearing the names P. Hammil[,] McClean and R. Cecil. Photograph with the name Ward. Dial calendar with the date 10 August 1940'.[84] Amongst the flotsam, the Military Post at Rathmullen found a stark message in a bottle: 'Sole survivors of torpedoed ship 10 men in open boat, 5 wounded. Food for only six days more.'[85] Corporal Ted Sweeney at Blacksod LOP recalled how 'eventually we started to have rafts washed ashore and there were some dead bodies, there were rafts and old lifeboats coming, and, not many came ashore here, but there were quite a lot of bodies'.[86] From the end of July to the end of December 1940, 213 bodies washed ashore along the Irish coast to be found by the coastwatchers, the LSF and local inhabitants.

Of the 213 bodies, 196 were washed ashore between Slyne Head in Galway and Malin Head in Donegal: 114 in Donegal, with Mayo (in particular the Belmullet peninsula and the Iniskea Islands) following with 51, and then Sligo where 27 bodies were found. All were from ships. Of those that could be identified, 35 were from *Arandora Star*, 32 from *Mohamed Ali el Kebir* and 6 each from *Dunvegan Castle* and *Manchester Brigade*. A small number were from *Canton*, *Ville de Grand*, *Accra*, *Upwey Grange*, *Rendlesham*, *Patroclus*, *Glenmoor*, *Laurentic* and *Stolwyck*. One hundred and twenty-one of the dead were identified, while 92, most probably from *Arandora Star*, remain unidentified.

ARMING IRISH MERCHANT SHIPPING

It was only a matter of time before Irish vessels were caught in the rising battle off the Irish coast. Berlin warned Dublin that while Germany 'wishes that we maintain our strict neutrality and that we may count with absolute certainty on no violation by Germany … increased naval operations may unavoidably affect us adversely'.[87] Attacks on Irish shipping began on 15 July when *City of Limerick* sank after being bombed and hit by machine-gun fire off Cape Ushant, they continued with attacks on *City of Waterford* and *Kerry Head* inside Irish territorial waters off Cork. The sinking of the Limerick Steamship Company's *Luimneach*, though clearly neutral with 'EIRE' painted in large white letters on her sides, 260 miles south of Kinsale on 4 September by U-46 further emphasized that the German statement was not an empty threat. Coastwatchers and locals saw the German aircraft that mounted the final, fatal, attack on *Kerry Head* on 22 October off Sheep's Head. The aircraft was seen diving low over the

83 MA LOP 80, 12 Aug. 1940.   84 Ibid. The liner, converted as an armed merchant cruiser was torpedoed on 10 August 1940 by U-56 about 40 miles north-west of Malin Head. She was taken in tow but later sank.   85 MA DRS 337, 14 Oct. 1940.   86 MA Owen Quinn papers, interview with Ted Sweeney.   87 NAI DFA Secretary's Files P3, Warnock to Walshe, 20 July 1940.

vessel, there was 'an immediate explosion followed by a big cloud of black smoke. The plane was not seen again. The ship sank in a few minutes.'[88]

With attacks on Irish shipping growing, External Affairs investigated the practicalities of arming Irish merchant shipping against air and naval attack. They speculated that 'unless we are prepared to convert Irish-registered merchant ships into veritable men of war, there would seem to be strong reasons against interfering with their present condition'.[89] Submarines were sinking armed and unarmed merchant shipping and armament carried by a merchant ship did not 'necessarily ensure her safety'.[90] Armaments enabled British ships to take offensive action and cause German casualties where possible, but this was not a concern for a neutral state. When the B&I Line requested that defensive armament be fitted to their ships Walshe concluded that such a move would be 'a great mistake' and, consequently, the fitting of defensive armament to Irish merchant vessels 'cannot be authorised'.[91]

Strangely, External Affairs did not highlight air attacks on shipping, though evidence of attacks by FW-200s and Ju-88s formed a large component of coast-watchers reports. German aircraft were routinely observed off the Irish coast during the summer of 1940; on the morning of 27 July Toe Head LOP sighted an aircraft '1 mile north of post going north-west, black cross underneath wings, nationality believed to be German'.[92] German aircraft were also reported engaging shipping. On 20 August Ted Sweeney at Blacksod LOP received details of an attack on the British-registered *Macville* as she passed close to Black Rock lighthouse on the west Mayo coast en-route to Limerick with a cargo of coal. At 1300 a single German air FW-200 'machine-gunned and bombed' *Macville*. The vessel, armed with a Lewis gun, returned fire, whereupon the 'plane made off after a few bursts of gunfire'.[93] In the case of *Macville* lightly arming a ship against air attack had proved its value. German pilots knew that the Condor could not withstand much combat damage; so light was its armour that crews nicknamed it the 'Stannoil Bomber' or 'Tinfoil Bomber'.[94] Of civilian aircraft design, neither could it withstand the stress of low-level manoeuvres to avoid machine-gun fire. *Macville* saw off the attacker, but not without the loss of one crewman, Able Seaman Patrick Colbert from Tramore in Waterford. His body was taken ashore at Blacksod Harbour and he was buried at Termoncarragh.

A later minute, written in the context of the establishment of Irish Shipping in 1941, presented a new problem. External Affairs made the valid point that even if it was agreed that Irish merchant vessels were to be armed, 'we possess no suitable armaments [and] we have no men capable of operating armaments on board merchant ships'.[95] Nevertheless, in June 1941 Minister for Industry and

---

88 MA DRS 347, 25 Oct. 1940.   89 NAI DFA Secretary's Files P18, Arming of Irish Merchant Ships, 29 Aug. 1940.   90 Ibid.   91 Ibid., Walshe to Ferguson, 20 Oct. 1940. 92 MA LOP 28, 27 July 1940.   93 MA LOP 60, 20 Aug. 1940.   94 TNA AIR 40/154, K Report 318, 9 June 1941.   95 NAI DFA Secretary's Files P18, Rynne to Walshe, 11 Feb. 1941.

Commerce Seán MacEntee again attempted to bring the arming of Irish merchant vessels to Cabinet in response to a lightning strike by the crews of ships carrying the strategically important cargo of coal for the Dublin Gas Company. They had been attacked by German aircraft and refused to go to sea without defensive measures being taken to protect them. MacEntee recommended arming their ships. De Valera refused outright to entertain the proposal. Attacks on Irish ships had 'become a serious problem, from the practical no less than from the political point of view', but 'the political dangers of arming Irish ships would be out of all proportion to any practical advantages likely to be secured'.[96] Industry and Commerce regrouped and tried again to force the matter in September 1941. This time the Cabinet discussed the memorandum they produced, but agreed that 'weapons, rockets or kites for defensive purposes should not be provided for Irish ships'.[97] High visibility lighting and signage would be the only defences available to Irish merchant ships during the Second World War.

ATTACKS OFF THE SOUTH COAST

The main action in the battle of the Atlantic shifted to the north-west coast of Ireland during the summer of 1940, yet attacks continued on coastal shipping off the south and south-east coast. In late July *Rockabill*, en-route to Waterford, was attacked by an aircraft four miles north-west of the Saltee Islands. As it was outside Irish territorial waters the British-registered vessel opened fire with her anti-aircraft gun and the plane departed, it turned out, to mount an attack on the Belfast-registered *Carnalea*, outward bound from Waterford. The attacks were not limited to the south-east tip of Ireland. Distress signals picked up on 2 October from the British vessel *Latymer* indicated she had been bombed by an aircraft off the Blasket Islands. A lifeboat made for the vessel as she had caught fire and begun drifting out to sea. Six crew were lost in the attack and twenty-two survivors landed at Valentia. While these vessels may have been targets of opportunity, the attacks were premeditated. This was the case when 'a German bomber' attacked the unarmed Irish-registered *Edenvale* three miles off Helvick Head, Waterford on 17 October. The aircraft 'came in from the sea circled over the vessel and discharged a burst of machine-gun fire and then flew out to sea again'.[98]

The seas off the south-east and south coast of Ireland remained the location for German attacks through the winter of 1940. On 18 December a German aircraft bombed and sank the 1,010-ton British tanker *Orage*, east of the Arklow Lightship. The crew of twenty-one landed safely at Rosslare. The following day

---

96 Ibid., Walshe to Ferguson, 16 June 1941.   97 Ibid., Ó Cinnéide to Private Secretary, Minister for Industry and Commerce, 8 Oct. 1941.   98 NAI JUS 8/756, Nangle to Murphy, 18 Oct. 1940.

a German aircraft thought to be a Condor, and which had been sighted by LOPs from Howth Head to Hook Head, bombed and sank the Irish lightship tender *Isolda* south of the Saltee Islands, killing three of the crew and later allegedly machine-gunning survivors in a lifeboat.[99] In the days following the sinking, five British naval vessels were sighted cruising in the area where the ship went down. These two sinkings took place during a period when 'considerable air activity was observed' along the Wexford coast.[100] German aircraft also mounted attacks on two vessels off Forlorn Point on Christmas Day, though G2 did not know the result of these engagements.

Further west, German aircraft sought targets off the Fastnet Rock. When the Dubrovnik registered *Cetvrti* was bombed by two German aircraft south-west of Ireland[101] on 1 December the crew took to their lifeboats and abandoned ship. Ten men came ashore at Valentia and twelve at Ballinskelligs. *Fort Rannoch* was patrolling in the area and was despatched to *Cetvrti*, locating her in Dingle Bay two miles south of Ventry Harbour on the late afternoon of 4 December. A salvage party was able to raise steam in the boilers of the abandoned ship and brought her into Valentia Harbour. Following considerable repair work *Cetvrti* was renamed *Irish Beech*, and in May 1941 became the third vessel in the newly established fleet of Irish Shipping Ltd. However, she was in poor condition and was 'a source of continuous machinery and structural faults'.[102]

CONTINUING RUMOURS OF U-BOATS

From April to October 1940 'by far the greater number' of the submarines reported off the Irish coast 'were believed to be German although in no instance was definite identification possible'.[103] Not surprisingly, rumours of German submarines operating from Irish waters continued to spread, overshadowing actual attacks by German aircraft on shipping off the Irish coast. Attacks by combined British air and naval forces on suspected submarines gave credibility to the rumours. Through the afternoon of 9 September Malin Head LOP followed the progress of one anti-submarine operation, beginning at 1450 when the LOP sighted a British seaplane six miles to the north-east 'circling over same place for [the] past eight minutes'.[104] A second plane took the place of the seaplane 'and circled over the same place' at 1528 while – showing that the submarine threat was real – a 'large three funnelled liner' changed course away from the area. A destroyer arriving from the north and the continuous circling of two RAF aircraft brought the attack to its conclusion at 1620 when, with the destroyer 'circling', the 'seaplane dropped explosives'. Malin Head was unable

---

99 TNA ADM 223/486, Irish Affairs, 7 Jan. 1941. **100** MA G2/X/315 Pt II, Curragh Command, Monthly Report, C.W.S.–Month of Dec. 1940. **101** At 51°30′N, 11°52′W. **102** Frank Forde, *The long watch* (Dublin, 2000 edition), p. 39. **103** MA General report on the Army for the year April 1940–March 1941. **104** MA LOP 80, 9 Sept. 1940.

to report whether the attack was successful, or if a submarine had been located. British forces maintained a strong presence in the area for a further twenty-four hours, an action related to the arrival of a 'large convoy' heading out into the Atlantic sighted twenty miles to the north-east at 0730 on 11 September.

By the end of 1940 reliable reports of German submarines operating off Ireland were rare. However, the myth of German submarines refuelling in Irish waters continued to appear in anti-Irish British propaganda.[105] Not to be outdone, Dublin quoted a 23 October speech in the House of Lords by Lord Strabolgi back at British mythmakers. Strabolgi

> declared that such refuelling was physically impossible because submarines did not use gasoline but heavy fuel oil of which no submarine could carry an extra supply sufficient to refuel another vessel ... [S]uch supplies could only be carried in a surface ship which could not fail to be observed and reported.

Strabolgi demanded to know why the British government had allowed such false rumours to be circulated. Replying for the government Lord Snell could only say that he did not know why such stories had gone unchecked and that 'the Government had no evidence to the effect that enemy submarines were being supplied from Irish territory'. Following a singularly aggressive speech by Churchill on the need for the Irish ports, delivered as the Admiralty announced the sinking of the liner *Empress of Britain* sixty miles north-west of Erris Head in Mayo, an *Irish Times* editorial described Churchill's allegations of the refuelling of German submarines by Irish sympathizers as 'moonshine'.[106] De Valera declared that it was

> a lie to say that German submarines or any other submarines are being supplied with fuel or provisions on our coast. A most extensive system of coast observation has been established here since the war. I say it is a lie and I say further that it is known to be a falsehood by the British Government itself.[107]

Commenting on Churchill's speech, Walshe vented his anger at British suggestions of Irish complicity with Germany:

> the average Irishman felt that the British Premier was at a loss for something to say which might direct the attention from the real facts at the time, i.e. Britain was obtaining a first class trouncing on land and sea. Some excuse had to be put forward.[108]

---

105 Alleged submarines were often fantasy, porpoises or bull seals. **106** *Irish Times*, 6 Nov. 1940. **107** NAI DFA Secretary's Files P2, quote from a draft speech given to United States Senator Murray by Robert Brennan, attached to Brennan to Walshe, 22 Jan. 1941. **108** NAI

Irish neutrality sought to protect Ireland from the bullying of Churchillian policies and should not be confused with support for Germany. Churchill had overreacted in a speech designed for public consumption. Walshe's anger was justified, as 'for the lack of a better answer to the submarine menace the cry "return the ports" was then raised'.[109]

Despite such public British-Irish political clashes over submarines, privately close intelligence co-operation between the two states to identify U-boats operating in Irish waters continued. When Coastal Command aircraft spotted what they thought were submarines close to the Irish coast they passed the information to G2 to enable Irish forces investigate. A submarine sighted one mile west of Torglass Island, near Doagh Island, Donegal 'dived on the approach' of the investigating British aircraft.[110] A small rowing boat with two men on board was 'seen near a rock about 400 yards from [the] submarine' and it was thought that 'the men in boat may have come from [the] submarine and made contact with land'. The Gardaí at Letterkenny investigated but came to no conclusion. Captain Alan Kirk, who had visited Galway during the landing of survivors from the sinking of *Athenia* in September 1939, was later promoted to Rear-Admiral and appointed Chief of Staff to Admiral Stark, the Commander in Chief of the United States Navy in Europe. Based in London, Kirk remained in contact with Chief Superintendent Tomás O'Coileáin whom he had met in Galway and when O'Coileáin was transferred to Letterkenny he and Kirk met up when Kirk visited Derry. Kirk told O'Coileáin that 'he never believed the stories that were circulated at one period of the alleged assistance to German submarines from our shores in the West and South-West'.[111] A minute from British Naval Intelligence from early December 1940 concluded that 'no real evidence has been found that U-boats use bases in Eire'.[112]

BELLIGERENT OVERFLIGHTS

From summer 1940 LOPs from Achill Island to Malin Head reported rising numbers of overflights through Irish airspace of German and British aircraft en-route to the Atlantic battle zone. Flying one of these aircraft was 26-year-old Squadron Leader Arthur Maudsley, DFC, DFM, of 233 Squadron Coastal Command based at Aldergrove near Belfast. His logbook shows that he used Inishtrahull and Fanad Head as landmarks from which to take bearings as he began patrols over the Atlantic on convoy escort duty. In one entry Maudsley, and his co-pilot Sergeant Brown, took off from Aldergrove at 0810 in Hudson T9343. At 1,000 feet they flew a bearing of five degrees off Inishtrahull on a

DFA Secretary's Files P35, British claims to Irish ports, undated, early 1941. **109** Ibid. **110** NAI JUS 8/813, Nangle to Murphy, 28 Oct. 1940. **111** NAI DFA Secretary's Files P43/1, Ó Coileáin to Murphy, 27 July 1942. **112** TNA ADM 1/11104, minute by Montague for DNI, 2 Dec. 1940.

'strike' mission to 'disperse raiders on [a] convoy'.[113] Maudsley's log for 29 and 30 July 1940 also shows that he used Eagle Island off north Mayo, a useful land-mark with its lighthouse and radio navigation beacon, as a point from which to fly south-west on a dawn anti-aircraft patrol and a daytime anti-aircraft convoy escort. G2 and the coastwatchers knew the coast by Eagle Island, between Blacksod and Downpatrick Head, as the 'North Mayo Corner'. The five LOPs along the North Mayo Corner witnessed many attacks on shipping by aircraft during the summer and autumn of 1940, one being that by an FW-200 Condor on the British registered *Inistrahull* on 13 September. The aircraft strafed and bombed the ship and *Inistrahull* returned fire. Coastwatchers reported that none of the bombs scored a direct hit, though the ship suffered damage.

The Condor was never explicitly referred to as the FW-200 in G2 reports though the Irish should have known the aircraft as a variant of the pre-war civilian airliner the Kurier. One reason for the lack of precise identification of Condors is that they were former civilian aircraft and did not appear on standard Coast Watching Service aerial identification charts. Ibar Murphy, the corporal in charge of Greenore Point LOP in Wexford, wrote later that his post 'were the first to report a 4-engined Focke-Wulf Kurier long range Bomber, recognised from our chart, purchased out of our own pockets from Flight International, England'.[114]

In Southern Command Costello received regular reports from July 1940 of 'large and heavy' types or 'bomber or bomber type' of aircraft passing over Ireland at night.[115] He informed Archer that it indicated 'the passage of aircraft apparently going to and from definite objectives to the North East and North West of the command area'.[116] Costello was a 'forceful' and 'pushy' officer. Trained with the United States military, he showed a much greater strategic awareness of the implications of these incursions for Ireland's wartime neutrality than the officers commanding the three other Command areas. This characteristic vindicated the view of British Intelligence that Costello was 'a brilliant and energetic soldier ... reported to be the best officer in the Eire Army ... [H]e is said to compare favourably with the best senior officers of any army in Europe.'[117]

Condor flights initially operated almost to timetable as they passed over Ireland on routine patrols. However, from autumn 1940 they were 'losing the semblance of timetable regularity'.[118] To Costello this indicated that the German air patrols now 'operated ... on information concerning traffic on the North Atlantic shipping routes'.[119] Costello's assumption was correct. The crew of a downed Condor told their British interrogators that patrol routes were 'carefully worked out on a basis of their knowledge of convoy routes'.[120] By early 1941

113 TNA AIR 4/73.   114 MA Owen Quinn Papers, Murphy to Quinn, 5 Apr. 1990.
115 MA G2/X/315 Pt II, Southern Command, Coastal intelligence report of Sept. 1940.
116 Ibid.   117 TNA AIR 10/3390, Air Intelligence Notes, Nov. 1940/May 1941.   118 MA G2/X/315 Pt II, Coastal intelligence report of Oct. 1940, Costello to Archer, 1 Nov. 1940.
119 Ibid.   120 TNA AIR 40/154, Further report on F.W. Condor of KG40 brought down

tracks for five routes for FW-200 patrols were known to British forces. In
addition to flights from France that skirted the western Irish coastline and flew
on to bases in Norway, there were four routes 'carefully worked out according to
petrol consumption' and 'adhered to rigidly, at least on the outward course'.
British intelligence thought the return course 'dependent upon the activity in
the patrol area'.[121] Of these routes, two brought Luftwaffe reconnaissance
squadron KG40 close to Ireland. One routed from Brittany to Cornwall, across
the southern Irish Sea and 'then across Ireland, probably to Erris Head, from
which point they fly north-west for approximately 570km., and then back to
Bordeaux, sometimes by way of the Irish Sea and sometimes direct'.[122] The
second route was 'far out to sea, crossing only the south-west corner of Ireland,
or passing just off Mizen Head'.[123] Squadron Leader Maudsley also took part in
flights to intercept Condors on this route. Airborne out of Aldergrove at 0330
on 24 July 1941 he flew Hudson AM735 to the Bull Rock lighthouse off Dursey
Island, Cork. Maudsley's track took him over Irish territorial waters and then
out into the zone off the Irish coast where the Condors were expected by RAF
intelligence to cross on their outbound track. He headed south-west at altitudes
between 500 and 2,000 feet on a fruitless nine-hour flight tersely logged as 'anti-
aircraft patrol – condors'.[124] LOPs in Southern Command saw German
reconnaissance flights coming in from the Bay of Biscay and heading north. LSF
members at Ballyferriter, Kerry, watched 'through a powerful telescope' for the
passage of Condors off the south-west coast, identifying the aircraft simply as 'a
four-engined bomber with German markings.'[125]

Actual evidence of the activities of Luftwaffe squadron KG40 over Ireland
came on 20 August 1940 when a FW-200 commanded by Oberleutnant Kurt
Mollenhauer 'ground to a stop in level flight on the slopes of Mount Brandon in
County Kerry'.[126] Lost in low cloud and unaware of the hazard ahead of him,
Mollenhauer made a perfect wheels-up landing on the side of the Kerry
mountain. Though 'the fuselage of the plane was completely burned out, and
there was wreckage scattered for a distance of about one hundred yards all over
the mountain' he and five fellow crewmembers received only minor injuries.[127]
They were lucky, spending the war interned in the Curragh: Mount Brandon
and the Cork and Kerry mountains were the location of many fatal forced
landings during the war. The Kerry crash proved outright that the Condors of
KG40 were taking short cuts over Ireland on their way to the North Atlantic
convoy routes to begin their patrols 'at about 09.30 hours, while Venus is still
visible low down in the heavens'.[128] Mollenhauer appeared to have been on a

200 miles north-west of Ireland on 10 Jan. 1941. **121** Ibid. **122** Ibid. **123** Ibid.
124 TNA AIR 4/73, 24 July 1941. **125** MA DRS 304, 5 Sept. 1940. **126** Trevor Allen, *The
storm passed by* (Dublin, 1996), p. 19. **127** NAI JUS 90/119/295, Superintendent Ó
Laoghaire to Major O'Connell, 21 Aug. 1940. **128** TNA AIR 40/154, Further report on
F.W. Condor of KG40 brought down 200 miles north-west of Ireland on 10 Jan. 1941.

weather flight, the youngest member of his crew being a meteorologist. The remains of his aircraft were brought to Baldonnell where, Walshe told Maffey, 'Lywood would be given an opportunity of seeing it.'[129]

Maffey consulted de Valera on Condor flights in early October as 'no doubt [the Taoiseach] was aware of the frequency with which German aeroplanes flew over the territory of Eire'.[130] He felt that de Valera 'did not seem to be well informed' and 'told him of meteorological and shuttle flights between Brest and Norway'. Gray reported that the 'most reasonable interpretation' of the Condor flights was the collection of meteorological data, but he added that the American Consul in Cork, William Smale, had been told by Costello that it was 'possible … that these reconnaissance flights are preparatory to invasion'.[131] Costello was good friends with Smale and, according to Smale, the two had 'a tacit agreement that with respect to the conduct of the war the American Government should have all information needed by the American Government which is available to the British Government, and that the sources of my information should not be disclosed'.[132]

Ireland could not defend her airspace against Condor incursions and Bryan saw late 1940 as 'the period when the German Luftwaffe secured air superiority over Ireland'.[133] The Condor flights over Ireland to the Atlantic and the reconnaissance flights of RAF Coastal Command along the southern coast showed from autumn 1940 how 'the infringement of our neutrality' had become 'much more prevalent' and 'deliberate rather than accidental'.[134] Costello concluded there was 'a progressively increasing disregard for our neutrality by both belligerents'.[135] External Affairs sought information on how overflights were dealt with in other neutral states, asking the Irish Minister to Switzerland to report all infringements of Swiss neutrality 'by air or otherwise', the actions taken by the Swiss government and the reaction of the belligerents.[136] Following a protest to the German Foreign Office in November by Warnock at which he was 'instructed to talk … "earnestly and firmly" about the increasingly frequent infractions of our sovereignty by German aircraft', German violations of Irish airspace temporarily declined.[137] Berlin formally expressed regret for the incursions and issued instructions to the Luftwaffe to avoid intentionally flying over Ireland. Oberleutnant Konrad Neymeyer, the captain of a BV-138 flying boat which crashed off the Irish coast on 25 November 1940, 'stated explicitly

129 TNA DO 35/1008/9, Maffey to Machtig, 22 Aug. 1940.   130 TNA DO 130/12, Maffey to Machtig, 11 Oct. 1940.   131 NARA RG 84 Dublin Legation, General, Box 7 (1940), Gray to Hull, 9 Oct. 1940.   132 UCDA P71/120, Smale to Gray, 18 Mar. 1945, given by Dr Deirdre McMahon to Bryan in 1983.   133 UCDA P71/78, Archives: Brief Summary – Some Additional Notes. Bryan also noted the 'gradual decline of this superiority until the British (and the Americans) were again in control'.   134 MA G2/X/315 Pt II, Southern Command, Coastal intelligence report of Sept. 1940.   135 Ibid., Southern Command, Coastal intelligence report for Oct. 1940.   136 NAI DFA Secretary's Files P12/7, Estero to Cremins, 18 Nov. 1940.   137 NAI DFA 221/147A, Bombings in Ireland – Protests, 3 Jan. 1941.

that all German pilots had instructions to keep outside' Irish territory.[138] The impact of Warnock's protest wore off as a crewman from a Condor brought down by the British later told his interrogators that 'because of the possibility of English intervention if Irish neutrality were too blatantly violated' the Luftwaffe initially had orders 'not to cross Ireland except in case of emergency'. He added that that ban had been lifted and flights across Ireland became a 'frequent occurrence … unmolested by A.[nti] A.[ircraft] or fighters'.[139]

Normally German aircraft seeking targets off Ireland operated alone, but on the late afternoon of 29 December 1940 '5 or 6 planes which were probably German – in view of the course they followed' passed over Roscommon and Sligo and over Donegal Bay north west over the Atlantic.[140] Air raid sirens sounded in Derry and Strabane. The planes were on a reconnaissance flight and returned as anticipated, being sighted over Cavan, Longford and Westmeath between 1900 and 2035. These flights went unchallenged, but British aircraft were often seen to patrol the north-west Irish coast seeking targets at times when Irish ADC knew that German aircraft were passing over Irish territory. Reports of German reconnaissance flights over Irish territory appear regularly in British CIC reports on German preparations for the invasion of Britain and Ireland through the second half of 1940. They link British and Irish ADC operations and coastwatchers' reports. One case illustrative of many was of a flight covering 'the West end of the Channel, the sea area South of Ireland and the Southern Irish coast from Cork to Bantry Bay'.[141] Initially such flights were interpreted by Britain as reconnaissance for invasion landing sites, whereas the Irish interpreted them as meteorological flights due to their high altitudes. Ultimately the British also took this interpretation, CIC reports referring later to the flights as 'regular routine' meteorological flights.[142] Low-level German reconnaissance flights were irregular, one on 27 July being noted by the CIC passing 'from Head of Kinsale [*sic*] to Sheep's Head', that is, from LOPs 25 to 31.[143] CIC reports strongly suggest that much British information on German overflights along the south and south-west coast of Ireland during the summer of 1940 came directly from the Coast Watching Service via G2 and the Department of External Affairs.

Initially RAF analysts could only conjecture the outward track of Condors and concluded that this 'overrules the practicability of outward interception'.[144] Anti-shipping operations by the aircraft had become 'a serious menace' which British forces had been 'unable to deal with effectively'.[145] In November 1940 the only RAF aircraft available to counter the FW-200 was the Bristol Blenheim,

138 Ibid.   139 TNA AIR 40/154, Further report on F.W. Condor of KG40 brought down 200 miles north-west of Ireland on 10 Jan. 1941.   140 MA G2/X/315 Pt II, Western Command Monthly Report, Dec. 1940.   141 TNA ADM 223/846, CIC, Report No. 40, 9 July 1940.   142 Ibid., CIC, Report No. 54, 23 July 1940.   143 Ibid., CIC, Report No. 58, 27 July 1940.   144 TNA AIR 15/171, Suggestion for interception of Long Range Enemy Aircraft, 6 Nov. 1940.   145 Ibid., Interception of Focke-Wulf, 4 Nov. 1940.

then a relatively high-speed aircraft, but one ultimately too slow to catch a Condor. It was, Walshe explained to the Minister for the Co-ordination of Defensive Measures, Frank Aiken, 'no secret' that 'Britain possesses no long distance fighter aircraft to combat the Atlantic bomber'.[146] Air Chief Marshal Bowhill, OC Coastal Command, was willing to employ Blenheims against the FW-200, considering that 'if we can destroy one or two F.W.'s it will be an excellent thing'.[147] The availability of faster Mosquito fighter-bombers from early 1941 did not ease the problem, 'the area of the sea and sky being so vast it was not much good sending out' these aircraft 'because of the great difficulty of locating the target'.[148] Condor flight paths varied daily 'and so no advance information other than the start time' was ever received.[149] If the Condor flew out to sea without touching land, no direction of flight could be approximated. Through 1940 the RAF were unable to make a single interception of a Condor. The pilots of 245 Squadron at Aldergrove 'suffered from this frustration with the knowledge that Condors were frequently reported – too late – to be within range of their base'.[150] But in a further example of Irish wartime co-operation with Britain, the RAF wireless interception 'Y-service' knew that 'if the aircraft passes over Southern Ireland, some indication of the possible direction <u>may</u> be received from the reports of the Irish Observer Corps'.[151] The Irish assisted the RAF tracking Condor and other Luftwaffe flights, an RAF source explaining that for warnings of aircraft approaching from the south 'it is necessary to rely on broadcasts from the Eire Observer Corps'.[152] Table 4.3 shows how during the eleven days between 17 and 27 October 1940 the RAF factored information received from Irish sources into their calculations on aircraft thought to be FW-200s or the He-111s operating from Bordeaux on missions in the northwestern approaches.

Date	Origin of flight	Take-off time	Irish observation: location and time
17/10/1940	Bordeaux	0100	Arrived Waterford area. 0400 hours
21/10/1940	Bordeaux	Unknown	Arrived Waterford area. 0545 hours
22/10/1940	Bordeaux	0355	Arrived Fastnet area. 0700 hours
24/10/1940	Bordeaux	0325	Arrived Cork area. 0653 hours
27/10/1940	Bordeaux	0350	Arrived 30 miles south-east of Foynes. 0610 hours

4.3: FW-200 Condor flights over Irish territory, 17–27 October 1940 (Source: TNA AIR 15/171)

146 NAI DFA Secretary's Files P35, British claims to Irish ports, undated, early 1941. 147 TNA AIR 15/171, minute by Bowhill, 5 Nov. 1940.   148 NAI DFA 2006/39, Dulanty to Walshe, 31 Mar. 1941.   149 TNA AIR 15/171, minute, X Branch to D/S.A.S.O., 6 Nov. 1940. 150 Allen, *Storm*, p. 56.   151 TNA AIR 15/171, minute, X Branch to D/S.A.S.O., 6 Nov. 1940, underlining in original.   152 TNA AIR 16/984, Note on air raid reporting system – Northern Ireland, 16 May 1941.

In their continuing attempts to shoot down Condors the RAF predicted areas off the south-west Irish coast and over west Cork and west Kerry where Blenheims of 236 Squadron from RAF St Eval in Cornwall could expect to intercept and attack the German aircraft. The RAF was not going to respect Irish neutrality and seek out Condors only when they were well clear of Irish territory. When intelligence sources indicated that a Condor flight from Bordeaux was planned, St Eval would get twenty-four hours notice and three aircraft would be held ready for take off. Once airborne they would make 'landfall off the Coast of EIRE' and head for a position (51°N 13°W) 150 miles south-west of the Fastnet Rock.[153] Here they waited to attack Condors low on fuel returning from Atlantic patrols. The RAF then used Irish radio reports of traffic observed by coastwatchers to check the progress of their own flights seeking Condors. During one attempted interception the attacking Blenheims were recalled without making contact with the Condors, the RAF noting that 'Irish Observer Corps reported 3 unidentified aircraft flying SE over Dursey Island at 12.00 and again over Mizen Head at 12.05 hours. Aircraft were not in positions allocated at vital time'.[154] These aircraft were later confirmed as the Blenheims, whose crews had called off the search due to bad weather. Irish sources show that G2 did not know the true intention of the flights, believing them to be 'endeavouring to locate the survivors of the SS NESTLEA attacked by aircraft and abandoned by the crew ... approximately 70 miles south west of Mizen Head'.[155] However, a later report correctly understood that the flights were 'engaged on a patrol of the areas where most of the attacks by aircraft on shipping have taken place (200 to 300 miles N.W. and N.N.W. Mizen)'.[156] These search and destroy patrols for Condors were not successful; some at Coastal Command thought the FW-200 was fitted with an airborne radar enabling it to avoid the Blenheims, others suggested that an attack on the Focke-Wulf factories at Bremen would be more appropriate. The Condor still had to be hunted down. A further suggestion to counter the Condor was to station a trawler keeping radio contact with RAF St Eval 'near the Skelligs as a lookout for the Focke-Wulf'.[157]

British intelligence on the FW-200 remained very poor well into 1941. An oil cooler thought to have been from a Condor and picked up by a trawler in Bantry Bay at the beginning of February 1941 was eagerly analyzed by the Royal Aircraft Establishment at Farnborough. Lywood was then despatched to Bantry to retrieve more parts of the aircraft.[158] In a clumsy move described by Archer as 'very indiscreet – criminally so',[159] Lywood called on salvagers G.W. Biggs

153 TNA HW 2/71, Coastal Command Operational Instruction No. 90. Interception of Long-Range Focke-Wulf Aircraft, 16 Nov. 1940. 154 TNA AIR 15/171, teleprinter message, Johnson to Lloyd, 19 Nov. 1940. 155 MA DRS 369, 20 Nov. 1940. 156 MA DRS 371, 22 Nov. 1940. 157 TNA AIR 17/171, Interception of Focke-Wulf, 28 Dec. 1940. 158 TNA AIR 40/234, Examination of oil cooler, undated, but Apr. 1941. 159 NAI DFA

and Company of Bantry 'anxious to get information concerning certain types of equipment used on German long-range Focke-Wulf bombers which were operating in the Atlantic'.[160] He hoped that he could get 'early notification of any crashes' from the company so as to get to the site quickly.[161] When it transpired that the company representative Lywood was talking to, a Mr O'Keefe, was a member of the Maritime Inscription, the Irish naval reserve, and could not give out such information. Lywood bluffed that he had been given permission by Archer to visit crash sites, adding 'you know, though we are very short of stuff ourselves we are doing our best to arm you'.[162] Lywood would have done well to heed the advice of the United States Minister to Ireland, David Gray, who told Washington that 'any movement that any stranger makes in Ireland is closely followed'.[163] Once again Lywood had blundered, continuing his own small role in destabilizing British-Irish relations.

THE IMPACT OF THE 'HAPPY TIME' ON BRITISH-IRISH RELATIONS

Relations between Dublin and London improved somewhat during the early summer of 1940 as defence co-operation talks took place and London released 'further supplies of munitions to Eire to strengthen their resistance to a possible German invasion'.[164] Serious losses of merchant shipping during the late summer and autumn brought British minds back to the need for naval facilities in Ireland. October 1940 was for Britain 'one of the black months of the war at sea'.[165] Churchill was frightened by the successes of the U-boats and the Defence Committee of the War Cabinet again considered the reoccupation of the Irish ports. The use of the ports remained for Britain the 'one satisfactory solution' in the North Atlantic: 'the whole course of the war will depend on a safe and satisfactory base for our battlefleet'.[166] On 5 November Churchill told the House of Commons that the lack of the ports was 'a most heavy and grievous burden'.[167] It was 'a plain statement of an unpleasant fact designed to serve as a warning that it may not be possible to let matters rest as they are'.[168] De Valera replied that Ireland would continue to resist any effort to retake the ports and Maffey cautioned London against continuing the line contained in Churchill's statements, telling Dominions Secretary Viscount Cranborne that 'the question of the ports should be soft-pedalled to inaudibility. Our reproaches, far from doing any good, merely present Mr de Valera with opportunities and texts for his

Secretary's Files A8, Archer to Walshe, 30 Apr. 1941.   **160** Ibid., O'Donoghue to Archer, 28 Apr. 1941.   **161** Ibid.   **162** Ibid.   **163** NARA RG 84 Dublin legation, SSF, Box 5 (1942), Gray to Hartle, 20 Aug. 1942.   **164** TNA DO 35/1008/11, telegram No. 778, Cranborne to High Commissioner, Pretoria, 25 Nov. 1940.   **165** Terraine, *Business*, p. 269.   **166** TNA ADM 116/5631, untitled memorandum, 5 Oct. 1940.   **167** Carroll, *War years*, p. 71.   **168** TNA DO 35/1008/11, telegram No. 778, Cranborne to High Commissioner, Pretoria, 25

political platform'.[169] Neutrality had near universal support in Ireland. The leader of Fine Gael, W.T. Cosgrave, told Maffey that 'even among the ex-unionists there was no sense of disapproval ... [T]he country was so defenceless that nobody could find arguments for a policy involving the risk of bombing.'[170]

The improvement in British-Irish relations over the summer of 1940 dissipated following Churchill's speech. The Defence Forces refocused their planning to counter the renewed British threat, speculating that a German invasion was unlikely through the winter months. Walshe considered that 'if Britain seizes our ports merely because [it is] useful to win [the] war, she follows [the] example of her enemies and destroys [the] whole moral basis of her case'.[171] He discounted the value of the ports to Britain; they were useless in 'modern conditions'. With airbases in Northern Ireland, Britain would only gain ten or fifteen minutes flying time if she had bases in 'occupied' southern Ireland, making the invasion of Ireland of little strategic value. He considered British agitation to be 'based on [a] desire to find [a] scapegoat ... [The] composition of [the] Cabinet makes [the] situation uncertain and dangerous.'

Ireland's continuing refusal to open the ports to Britain led the War Cabinet to investigate new ways to pressurize Ireland. Political rhetoric had for the moment failed and, with shipping losses in the Atlantic mounting, Britain resorted to an economic squeeze on Ireland

> to find some means of drumming into the Irish consciousness that the question of the provision of facilities for naval and air bases in the South and West of Ireland is not, properly viewed, an issue between Eire and the United Kingdom. It is a problem in the solution of which the two countries are equally interested.[172]

The nature of British pressure on Ireland, as Churchill put it, to 'open the eyes of the Irish people to their true situation' was not likely to produce the results the British desired.[173] Churchill asked the Chiefs of Staff to consider the military consequences of the application of economic pressure on Ireland. He hypothesized as to what would happen in various scenarios, one of which was what if Ireland withdrew the 'watching facilities they have'.[174] The Chiefs of Staff felt the loss of reports from the Coast Watching Service 'would not be serious', however they argued against themselves, continuing that in the absence of reports from coastwatchers 'we might have to increase naval patrols to ensure that we received early reports of movement of enemy vessels off the coast of

Nov. 1940.   **169** TNA DO 35/1008/12, Maffey to Cranborne, 25 Nov. 1940.   **170** TNA DO 130/12, Maffey to Cranborne, 23 Dec. 1940.   **171** NAI DFA Secretary's Files P2, Estero to Eire, No. 196 (Personal), 5 Dec. 1940.   **172** TNA ADM 116/5631, memorandum by Cranborne to the War Cabinet, 3 Dec. 1940.   **173** TNA PREM 1/127/1 W.P. (41) 64, Necessity for base facilities in Eire, 19 Mar. 1941.   **174** TNA PREM 3/127/3A, Churchill to

Eire'.[175] On 2 January 1941 the War Cabinet agreed to put economic pressure on Ireland and withdraw shipping facilities made available to the country. In effect this would institute a slow blockade of Ireland by reducing the quota allocated to Ireland on ships delivering food to Britain and ending the chartering of ships for Ireland. Ireland would now have to provide for its own food imports. This would be communicated to Dublin as a move taken 'in no vindictive spirit' and only due to 'dire necessity' through pressure of space due to losses of British shipping.[176]

Between July 1940 and the beginning of January 1941 543 Allied ships were lost in the Atlantic. Of these, 'a large proportion of them went down within sight of the Irish coast or a few hours' sailing distance away'.[177] Such blunt figures explain Churchill's fixation on the Irish ports. He was convinced that vessels operating from them would aid the protection of convoys and help reduce these losses. Walshe expressed no sympathy. In January 1941 he wrote that it was an 'easy assumption that the possession of a few Irish ports would in itself win the war for Britain'.[178] Looking beyond the ports, it was more important to the outcome of the war that the United States hand effective control of its aeroplane and munitions factories to the British. Walshe looked to these new technologies from the United States as the way to win the war, not to Churchill's pre-1919 geopolitical world dominated by outdated naval technology.

CONCLUSION. THE COAST WATCHING SERVICE AND INTELLIGENCE GATHERING, JUNE–DECEMBER 1940

In October 1940 Colonel Lawlor told Commander Kilgour of the Northern Ireland Coastguard that 'our coast watching system is adequate to our needs, efficient, and that nothing could happen without our knowledge'.[179] The coastwatchers were now completing their training and were proud of their abilities. Michael Brick, a coastwatcher at Brandon Head LOP in Kerry, recalled that 'we would be right above any craft that entered our vicinity. A gannet could not land on the water unknown to us'.[180] But how well did the Coast Watching Service perform during the 'Happy Time', during the months when the Second World War first came to Irish shores? These months were the first real test of the coastwatchers' operational ability. Did the coastwatchers provide G2 with a reliable picture of events off Ireland's coast? Their competency had certainly risen; at the end of November 1940 Lawlor reported

Ismay, 3 Dec. 1940.   **175** Ibid., Chiefs of Staff to Churchill, 6 Dec. 1940.   **176** TNA ADM 116/5631, extract from cabinet conclusions, 2 Jan. 1941.   **177** Allen, *Storm*, p. 10.   **178** NAI DFA Secretary's Files P48A, Mr Gray's Memorandum: Notes Thereon, 17 Jan. 1941.   **179** MA G2/X/318, Lawlor to McKenna and Archer, 12 Oct. 1940.   **180** MA Owen Quinn Papers, Brick to Quinn, 10 July 1994.

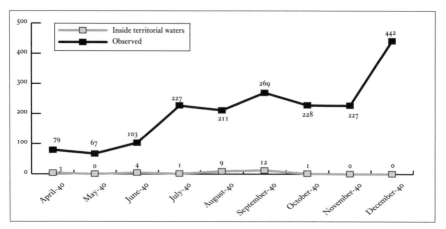

4.4: Belligerent surface craft observed (all Commands): April–December 1940
(Source: MA, Annual reports on the Army)

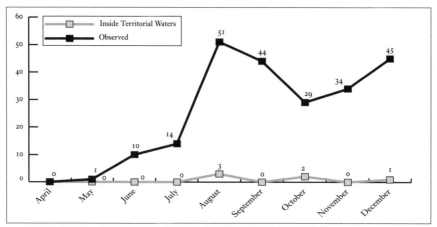

4.5: Observed attacks on shipping (all Commands): April–December 1940
(Source: MA, Annual reports on the Army)

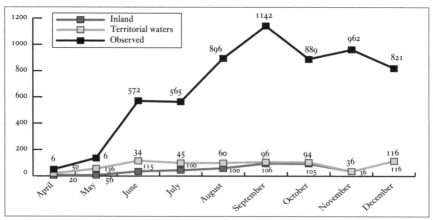

4.6: Overflights by British and German aircraft (all Commands): April–December 1940
(Source: MA, Annual reports on the Army)

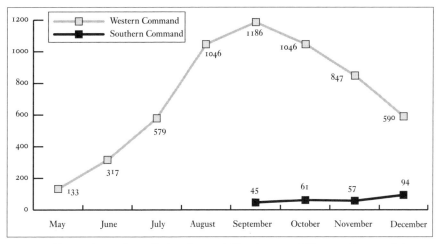

4.7: Comparison of overflights observed (Southern and Western Commands):
May–December 1940 (Source: MA, G2 X series files, partial data only available)

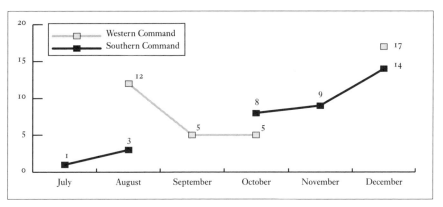

4.8: Comparison of sinkings observed (Southern and Western Commands):
April–December 1940 (Source: MA, G2 X series files, partial data only available)

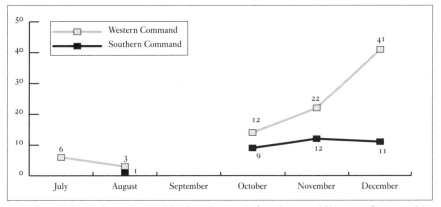

4.9: Comparison of attacks on shipping observed (Southern and Western Commands):
April–December 1940 (Source: MA, G2 X series files, partial data only available)

the vast improvement noticeable in the personnel stationed along the north west coast, particularly from Killybegs to Inishowen in Donegal. Since the transfer of the vast volume of British shipping activities from the southern to the northern route, the superior reports received from this area, in comparison with those of other centres, is particularly noticeable.[181]

Greig and Archer had not thought highly of these men when they inspected them in March and April 1940 – the busy summer of that year had made all the difference.

In compiling their intelligence assessments Archer and Bryan were interested in broad brushstrokes, 'pointing out tendencies' to provide 'a general picture of the situation rather than a record of all happenings'.[182] To this end Commandant Mackey, Curragh Command IO, exhorted the coastwatchers in his area to 'report everything, EVERYTHING'.[183] Mackey and his staff then filtered the material received, grouping events together to point out the general tendencies G2 were looking for.

In considering Coast Watching Service operations through summer 1940 some caveats are necessary. The primary duties of the Coast Watching Service related to events within the three-mile limit of Irish territorial waters and to overflights through Irish airspace. Coastwatchers were limited by day-to-day visibility and by the limit of the horizon. The course of events beyond the horizon had to be extrapolated by G2 from other sources, including reports transmitted by Lloyds of shipping sunk, marine radio messages intercepted by Fort Dunree, information from survivors, and reports from Gardaí and lighthouse keepers.

Considering these caveats, the increase in incidents reported by coastwatchers in Southern and Western Commands showed G2 that the battle of the Atlantic had intensified in the waters immediately off Ireland's southern, western and north-western shores following the fall of France. Activity reported from Western Command far outpaced that from Southern Command, placing the focus of belligerent activity off the north-west coast of Ireland. Eastern and Curragh Commands reported a drop in activity due to the St George's Channel minefield. The charts above group all Commands together and show rising observations of belligerent surface craft, attacks on shipping, and overflights as military activity around Ireland increased through the summer of 1940. There was no proportional increase in the number of vessels observed by coastwatchers inside territorial waters and G2 could conclude that belligerents on the sea were generally observing Irish neutrality. It was a different case in the air. Coastwatchers showed that aerial activity around and over Ireland had increased

181 MA EDP 20/5, (Ó Muiris for) Lawlor to CSO i/c Plans and Operations Branch, 21 Nov. 1940.   182 MA G2/X/315 Pt II., Archer to Command Intelligence Officers, 10 July 1940. 183 MA Owen Quinn Papers, Murphy to Quinn, 5 Apr. 1990.

through 1940 and overflights disregarding neutrality were by the year's end causing grave concern for the Irish military. While British flights were generally tolerated, the Department of External Affairs protested with limited success through the Irish Chargé d'Affaires in Berlin about the conduct of German aircraft crossing Ireland.

Combining Coast Watching Service reports with the wider sources of information mentioned above, G2 correctly concluded that the main conflict in the Atlantic was by autumn 1940 taking place off the north-west coast of Ireland, with a secondary theatre along the south coast. When sinkings and attacks on shipping are isolated, Coast Watching Service figures give a misleading figure for the true level of destruction of merchant shipping off the Irish coast during the 'Happy Time'. Alone, these figures show all waters off Ireland to be the location for a rising number of sinkings and attacks during the later months of 1940, but they do not give any conclusive evidence as to the location of the main concentration of the conflict. The number of sinkings and attacks observed off the south coast by Southern Command coastwatchers almost equals those seen by Western Command coastwatchers off the north and north-west coasts.

However, the details of coastwatchers' reports show that attacks off the south and south-west coast were predominantly sinkings of trawlers and coastal shipping, while those off the north-west coast were of larger ships sailing in convoy or larger faster liners such as *Arandora Star*. Intercepted radio messages and information from Lloyds backed up this conclusion. So too did information from survivors put ashore in lifeboats along the Irish coast. Sinkings off the north-west coast often occurred beyond the horizon and coastwatchers did not always see the actual attacks, merely the resulting flotsam and human remains, whereas the attacks themselves were often visible off the south and south-west coast. In his report for December 1940 the Western Command IO put the sighting of only six convoys in the Inishowen area through the month down to the fact that 'convoys are taking a course farther North in an effort to elude the numerous submarines of whose presence around our coast the list of shipping attacks ... affords ample confirmation'.[184] When Coast Watching Service incident reports, details of the type of shipping sunk, and information regarding the frequency and direction of overflights are factored into the air and marine intelligence picture the movement of the main theatre of the battle of the Atlantic to seas off the north-west coast is clear. Putting information from all sources together shows that from combined intelligence sources G2 correctly identified the killing ground of the German U-boats and FW-200 Condors, which extended five hundred miles off the Donegal coast, and the 'ceaseless patrol on the Northern shipping routes' by RAF Coastal Command.[185] They

184 MA G2/X/315 Pt II, Western Command Monthly Report, Dec. 1940.   185 Ibid., Western Command report for Nov. 1940.

also knew the routes and directions of German reconnaissance flights. The increased frequency, specific altitude and direction of overflights also showed that German aircraft were crossing Ireland to the north-west and this confirmed that the focus of military activity was taking place off the north-west coast.

These details were plotted on maps and were presented to meetings of the inter-party Defence Conference. In December 1940 Fine Gael's Richard Mulcahy told Maffey that the plots 'appeared to disprove the contention that the use of the ports was vital, since the sinkings were concentrated in the areas to the north-west' which were already commanded by Britain.[186] This was put in condensed form in a one sentence telegram to the Irish Minister in Washington: 'Almost all sinkings by planes and submarines take place between one hundred and six hundred miles from [the] north-west' coast of Ireland.[187] A briefing document given to Minister for the Co-ordination of Defensive Measures Frank Aiken for a meeting with American President Franklin D. Roosevelt showed the input of G2 and the Coast Watching Service. Countering British propaganda on the return of the Irish ports, the document explained how in late 1940 attacks on shipping off the coast of Ireland were

> all practically west-north-west. A few attacks were made by aircraft on trawlers off the South West coast, say in a line with Co. Kerry but these were made on the return flight by aircraft. In the Atlantic the field of operations of the submarine since July can be regarded as in a region from 300 to 600 miles west-north-west of our shores and the quadrilateral between the parallels 55° and 57° N and the meridians of 15° and 18° W was the area in which submarine attacks were most numerous. An occasional vessel was attacked near our shores, but such an attack was an exception.[188]

By December 1940 the British described the Coast Watching Service as being a 'fairly efficient' operation.[189] As the memorandum to Aiken and the information provided to Mulcahy and Brennan show, it was providing the Defence Forces and the Department of External Affairs with accurate and independent information on belligerent operations around Ireland. In doing so, the coastwatchers were playing an important part in implementing and bolstering Irish neutrality. The information they provided in the months following the fall of France gave an accurate if geographically limited view of the changing trends in the battle of the Atlantic in the summer and autumn of 1940 as the conflict around Ireland intensified.

---

186 TNA DO 130/12, Maffey to Secretary of State for Dominion Affairs, 23 Dec. 1940.
187 NAI DFA Secretary's Files P2, Estero to Eire (No. 196, Personal), 5 Dec. 1940.
188 NAI DFA Secretary's Files P35, British claims to Irish ports, undated, early 1941.
189 TNA AIR 10/3390, Air Intelligence – Ireland.

CHAPTER FIVE

1941: The battle of the Atlantic

G2 REPORTS FOR DECEMBER 1940 listed forty-five ships torpedoed, bombed and machine-gunned in the North Atlantic from off the Irish coast to 1,100 miles west of Ireland. In January 1941 Costello in Southern Command extrapolated 'from intercepted reports' that 'the principal attack area in the Atlantic' was 'between 56 and 60 degrees North latitude', placing the majority of attacks off the north-west coast of Ireland.[1] U-boats and German aircraft were moving west from their 'Happy Time' limits off the Irish coast into the weakly defended mid-Atlantic. Continuing the trend begun in mid-1940, air and marine intelligence reports through 1941 show a marked contrast between Southern Command and Western Command. While both Commands faced into the theatre of Atlantic operations, Western Command continued to see far more action than Southern Command. Incident reports from LOPs in Western Command almost tripled from 1,760 in December 1940 to 4,649 by April 1941, illustrating the still rising levels of belligerent activity off the north-west coast. G2 knew as 1941 began that convoy traffic remained concentrated off Donegal. In contrast, Southern Command saw a decrease in activity over the same period. There was 'not a ship's stack to be seen in Cork'.[2] Statistics on incident reports were not kept in Southern Command and the lower levels of activity can instead be seen from comparing figures for overflights between the two areas. Overflights across Southern Command rose from fifty-six in February to 123 in April. This was far behind Western Command's equivalent of 981 overflights for February and 1,954 for April. Increased patrolling by Coastal Command aircraft operating from Northern Ireland caused this rise in aerial activity. As in 1940, Western Command bore the brunt of Coast Watching Service operations through 1941. So many British aircraft were sighted off the north coast that LOPs on Inishowen were instructed that there was 'no necessity to give [the] nationality if plane British'.[3]

THE 'BATTLE OF THE ATLANTIC'

In January 1941 Britain held 'that whoever was running the German submarine campaign was very good at his job'; unknown to London, Admiral Dönitz was

---

1 MA G2/X/315 Pt I, Western Command Monthly Report, Jan. 1941. 2 NAI DFA Secretary's Files A8, untitled memorandum attached to Archer to Walshe, 13 Mar. 1941. 3 MA LOP 80, 12 Mar. 1941.

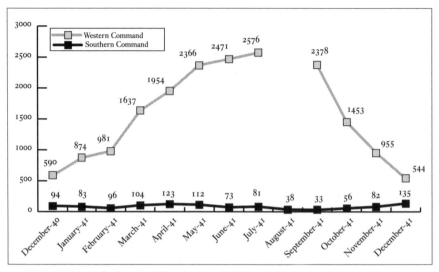

5.1: Aircraft observed (Southern and Western Commands): December
1940–December 1941 (Source: MA G2/X series)

actually critically short of serviceable U-boats and submarine activity temporarily fell in early 1941.[4] The return of German surface raiders to the North Atlantic partially concealed the absence of submarines. Western Command G2 speculated that an unidentified 'vessel of the cruiser type' sighted off north-west Mayo on 16 January was a German surface raider. This seems unlikely, as the main German capital ships were not in the North Atlantic around this date. Torpedoing by U-boats and bombing by the Luftwaffe, rather than attacks by German surface raiders, remained the most common form of German attack off Ireland through 1941. Yet, reliable U-boat sightings off the Irish coast were few. The majority of sightings of German forces were of aircraft (FW-200s, He-111s and Ju-88s) seeking shipping to attack. The lighthouse keeper on Inishtrahull graphically recounted to coastwatchers on Malin Head an attempted attack that began as he

> observed a convoy consisting of 19 freighters 7 tankers 2 destroyers and four corvettes 4 miles north east of [the] island going east. The visibility was moderate with low hanging clouds. A German plane (Ju-88) appeared out of the clouds and came down to 500ft. The escorting warships immediately opened a terrific barrage of Ack-Ack fire some of the shrapnel falling on the island. The plane then went off in a north-easterly direction without dropping any bombs.[5]

4 NAI DFA Secretary's Files P12/14(1), Dulanty to Walshe, 30 Jan. 1941.   5 MA LOP 80, 14 May 1941.

In late January Dulanty reported that 'there were not today so many ships afloat [and] the Admiralty were seizing every vessel on which they could lay hands'.[6] The shipping situation became critical by March as U-boats sent vital merchant vessels to the seabed. In response, Churchill issued his 'Battle of the Atlantic' memorandum, grandly stating what was already clear, that

> the Battle of the Atlantic has begun. The next four months should enable us to defeat the attempt to strangle our food supplies and our connection with the United States ... we must take the offensive against the U-boat and the Fockke Wulf wherever we can and whenever we can.[7]

More destroyers and more anti-aircraft guns for merchant ships were necessary, catapults for launching fighters from ships against attacking aircraft were required and damaged ships lying in British ports had to be repaired. With these measures in place Churchill predicted that 'the U-boat menace will soon be reduced [and] the Fockke Wulf and, if it comes, the Ju-88, should be effectively grappled with'. This final exhortation had considerable bearing on Ireland as overflights and air warfare increased over Irish territory through 1941.

Forty-eight hours after Churchill's memorandum the War Cabinet received a memorandum from the Chiefs of Staff on the necessity for naval bases in Ireland. The bases were deemed vital due to the precarious merchant shipping situation and the need to protect Britain's 'vital security in home waters'.[8] Proposed locations included the Shannon estuary as a main naval base, with Berehaven demoted to an alternative anchorage. British heavy surface forces based on the Shannon would be relatively safe from air attack and 'in a far better position to intercept enemy surface forces in the Atlantic than from Plymouth or Milford Haven'.[9] Reconnaissance aircraft ranging out into the Atlantic and fighter squadrons providing air cover to re-open the south-western approaches to shipping would operate from Irish airbases. The memorandum led Lord Cranborne to re-examine British policy towards Ireland. He considered that the economic squeeze adopted in January 1941 had done its job. The Cabinet did not agree; the policy of restricting supplies to Ireland would remain and was 'consistent with our own needs'.[10] But in considering the requirements for facilities in Ireland Cranborne correctly synopsized that the Chiefs of Staff were calling for 'something approaching a military occupation, something which, even in these days, could hardly be described as compatible with neutrality'.[11]

The rising intensity of the war in the Atlantic and Churchill's response, of which the renewed call to occupy the Irish ports was a part, masked crucial

6 NAI DFA Secretary's Files P12/14(1), Dulanty to Walshe, 30 Jan. 1941. 7 TNA PREM 3/60/2, The Battle of the Atlantic. Directive by the Minister for Defence, 6 Mar. 1941. 8 TNA PREM 1/127/2, W.P. (41) 59, Necessity for bases in Eire, 8 Mar. 1941. 9 Ibid. 10 TNA ADM 116/5631, conclusions of War Cabinet 31 (41), 24 Mar. 1941. 11 TNA PREM 1/127/2, W.P. (41) 64, Necessity for base facilities in Eire, 19 Mar. 1941.

developments in the first half of 1941 leading to the eventual defeat of Germany in the Atlantic theatre in mid-1943. In March, Dönitz lost three of his top U-boat commanders: Gunther Prien (U-47) and Joachim Schepke (U-100) killed and Otto Kretschmer (U-99) captured. The RAF shot down four Condors in April, one by a Blenheim of 252 Squadron fifty miles west of Erris Head on 16 April. These attacks broke the Condor's psychological hold over Coastal Command. Then, in May, British warships forced the surrender of U-110, captained by Fritz-Julius Lemp, and captured a working enigma machine along with code keys valid for three months. It was a major breakthrough for naval intelligence. The British were soon reading German code naval traffic and were able to route convoys away from known U-boat locations. As a result, through May and June Allied shipping losses fell. It was relatively quiet in the mid-Atlantic until 23 June when ten U-boats attacked convoy HX133 south of Greenland. In June sixty-one ships were lost, in July only twenty-one ships and in August twenty-three. Though Dönitz had now more submarines at sea, the loss of experienced commanders, increased Allied anti-submarine and anti-aircraft operations and the impact of the capture of Lemp's enigma machine on the quality of British signals intelligence meant that the 'Happy Time' of autumn 1940 was truly over.

NAVAL AND AIR ACTIVITY OFF THE NORTH AND
WEST COAST, JANUARY—MAY 1941

To cope with the increase in belligerent air and naval activity off Inishowen in early 1941 the three LOPs on the peninsula began phoning reports to a new filtering centre at Fort Dunree. The filtering centre transmitted digests of incidents to Western Command headquarters in Athlone. For most months, the combined number of reports from Inishowen equalled the combined number of reports from the thirty-two other LOPs in Western Command. The phone exchange at Buncrana was hard pressed relaying the condensed reports to Athlone but the filtering centre greatly reduced onward pressure on the telephone system. Although the centre 'carefully sifted' reports, further increases in belligerent activity over the summer were such that by October it took the filtering centre an average of seventy-five minutes to pass reports, whereas the direct line took on average six minutes, if a line was clear.[12] The centre simply changed the nature of the bottleneck in the system, actually resulting in a reduction in the efficiency of the Coast Watching Service in one of its most important areas of operation.

Reports from Inishowen and elsewhere in Donegal for early 1941 indicated that German submarines and British surface vessels remained operational in the north-western approaches. Coastwatchers from Aranmore north to Malin Head

12 MA G2/X/315 Pt II, Western Command Monthly Report, May 1941.

frequently heard gunfire out to sea. It was most noticeable when they observed any 'large convoy' passing or 'the presence of German aircraft off the North coast'.[13] Explosions were 'heard almost daily' off Inishowen, some from mines being destroyed by Irish naval patrols, others evidence of training by British forces.[14] In April, Inishowen coastwatchers spotted 'a new type of escort consisting of a Spitfire aircraft carried aft on escort vessels' and G2 correctly deduced that 'these vessels are apparently equipped with catapult apparatus for launching the aircraft'.[15] A further report described 'single aircraft being carried by escort vessels. The deck of the vessel seems to be equipped with a type of runway. Possibly this is a new type of defence to be used in protecting shipping from long range German bombers.'[16] The coastwatchers had sighted Hurricane fighters mounted on 'Catapult Aircraft Merchantmen', naval auxiliaries sailing within convoys and used to counter Condor attacks. Introduced in April 1941, the coastwatchers immediately picked up the 'CAM' system. Later reports show that coastwatchers' knowledge of 'CAM-ships' improved and they became aware that the aircraft was a Hurricane and not a Spitfire. G2 also received reports of new aircraft from coastwatchers and drew incorrect conclusions. When Inishowen Head LOP noticed a 'plane carrying [a] searchlight',[17] the so-called 'Leigh light', '4 miles south of post flying north east, circling and dropping flares close to the post', G2 thought that this was 'an attempt to solve the problem of the night bomber'.[18] In fact, the Wellington bombers adapted to carry the Leigh light were testing a system for obtaining final visual fixes on U-boats during night attacks initiated by radar. G2 lacked suitable technical intelligence to understand the role of these new weapons, so they misinterpreted the Leigh light test flights. The Inishowen report was from May 1941 and trials of the Leigh light had begun out of Limavady in Derry, in full view of Inishowen Head LOP, in late April 1941. Like the CAM-ships, the coastwatchers spotted and relayed to G2 the existence of the Leigh light immediately trials began. The sightings of CAM-ships and the Leigh light tests illustrate the timely transmission of information on weapons development from coastwatchers to G2 but mistakes in analysis of the reports show the limitation of G2's capabilities.

Through 1941 G2 Western Command continued to receive daily reports of sinkings and attacks on shipping off the north and west coasts. An aircraft attacked the 5,266-ton Belgian vessel *Olympier* 240 miles west of Achill Head on 30 January. Fifteen of the crew of forty-two landed in a lifeboat at Melmore Head, Donegal on 2 February; five were in a poorly condition. A second lifeboat was missing and all posts on the west coast were instructed to keep a sharp look out. The same fate befell the 7,200-ton Norwegian *Ostvard*, attacked on 30 January 150 miles south-west of Ireland 'by a four-engined German bomber'

13 Ibid., Jan. 1941.   14 Ibid., May 1941.   15 Ibid., Apr. 1941.   16 MA DRS 507, 30 Apr. 1941   17 MA LOP 82, 2 May 1941.   18 MA G2/X/315 Pt II, Western Command Monthly Report, May 1941.

and suffering five direct hits.[19] With five of the crew killed, eight put to sea in two lifeboats. Six survived to put ashore between Sybil Head and Dunmore Head in Kerry, two had died of exposure and were buried at sea. Fort Dunree maintained a watch on marine radio frequencies, intercepting distress signals from torpedoed and sinking vessels and widening G2's intelligence perspective from the local reports received from coastwatchers. One message, intercepted on 28 February 1941, 'cannot last much longer', was thought to be from the 2,085-ton *Memphis*.[20] The engines of the Egyptian-registered vessel had become disabled in heavy weather and she foundered, sinking that day, 136 miles off Bloody Foreland with the loss of all hands.

Following the rise in sinkings, there was an increase in the number of bodies and of empty lifeboats and flotsam of war washed up on the western Irish shoreline. The Chief of Staff's report on the Army covering 1940 and early 1941 referred in a matter-of-fact manner to the 'hundreds of dead bodies … washed ashore as well as life-boats, rafts, etc.'.[21] Department of External Affairs figures record eighty corpses found along the Irish coast through 1941. During July alone 28 bodies, 16 of which remain unidentified, washed ashore. Many were from the troopship *Nerissa*, torpedoed ninety-two miles north-west of Bloody Foreland by U-552 on 30 March. *Nerissa*'s dead included 83 Canadian soldiers, almost an entire class of graduating RAF Commonwealth Air Training Scheme pilots and 11 American pilots who were ferrying aircraft between Britain and North America. The body of one American pilot, Robert G. Smith from Warsaw, Indiana was found on the Aran Islands and the bodies of seven Canadian soldiers washed ashore at points between Donegal and Clare. The body of one unidentified airman, found near Malin Head LOP on 17 July and dressed in a British RAF sergeant's uniform, was buried the following day in Malin Church of Ireland graveyard with Irish officers Commandant Farrell and Lieutenant Farrell and two British officers from Northern Ireland present.

The suffering beyond the horizon must have been obvious to those who found an empty lifeboat washed ashore at Omey Point in Mayo. G2 starkly recorded that the lifeboat 'would hold 37 passengers. Boat found to contain numerous bullet holes.'[22] When the military at Kilrush in Clare secured a lifeboat which had been reported drifting up the Shannon by Kilcreadun LOP, they discovered that the oarless boat 'contained the bodies of two men who had been dead for some time'.[23] Believed to be Belgian seamen aged approximately 30 and 50 from the Belgian ship *Adolphe Urban*, their identities remain unknown and they are buried in Shanakyle cemetery at Kilrush. *Adolphe Urban* was sunk after being attacked by a German aircraft thirty miles off Greenore Point, Wexford, on

19 NAI DFA 206/79, note by Butler, undated.   20 MA G2/X/315 Pt II, Western Command Monthly Report, Feb. 1941.   21 MA General report on the Army for the year April 1940–March 1941.   22 MA G2/X/315 Pt II, Western Command Monthly Report, Aug. 1941.   23 Ibid., Southern Command, Monthly Report on Coastal Intelligence – Mar. 1941.

8 March 1941. The lifeboat with the doomed men onboard had covered the southern and south-western coast of Ireland before finally being brought ashore at Kilrush. The lack of emotion in these reports makes them chilling reading. Chilling reading too is a later report that after nineteen survivors from three ships torpedoed 800 miles west of Brest on 26 September 1941 came ashore on 10 October after two weeks in a lifeboat 'in an exhausted condition' at Slyne Head in Galway, the 'sole surviving member of the *Cortez* crew died in Clifden hospital the following day'.[24] The eighteen others on the lifeboat 'entrained for Dublin when fully recovered'.[25]

SUBMARINES IN IRISH WATERS

The myth of U-boats operating from Irish bases simply refused to die. Raymonde Kerney, wife of Irish Minister to Spain, Leopold Kerney, heard in March 1941 from the British Ambassador in Madrid that there were German submarine bases on the Irish coast 'perhaps without knowledge of interested people' but he quickly added that he had 'better not discuss that question' when he saw Mrs Kerney's 'incredulity'.[26] Using reports from the coastwatchers, Dublin replied to Kerney that there was no evidence for such allegations, adding that the British naval staff in Dublin 'freely admit that such stories are complete fabrications'.[27]

Instead, it was the activities of British submarines in Irish territorial waters that concerned command areas through 1941. In Western Command the opening of a British submarine base on Lough Foyle in November 1940 accounted for a large rise in submarine sightings by coastwatchers as 1941 began. British submarines trained from Lough Foyle and coastwatchers saw that they operated off Derry with Dutch and Norwegian vessels. Submarine activity from Lough Foyle ebbed and flowed through the year. From November 1940 to March 1941, 155 out of the 163 submarines reported by coastwatchers were British; of the remaining 8, no outright identification was possible. By August 1941 submarines were sighted every day, 'all were British and appeared to be carrying out training missions'.[28] No warlike activity by these craft was noted.

Lough Foyle was a safe haven for Allied naval vessels. German submarines were never identified in the Foyle during hostilities but there were scares in the approaches to the Lough. An 18 July 1941 report from Western Command identified a German submarine sighted off Malin Head explicitly as an 'enemy submarine'. The British Hudson and Whitley aircraft of Coastal Command which 'circled 8 miles west of [the] Post and dropped bombs' were left without nationality or a judgment of whether they were friend or foe, the familiarity with

---

24 MA G2/X/315 Pt II, Western Command Monthly Report, Oct. 1941. 25 Ibid. 26 NAI DFA Secretary's Files P12/4, Kerney to Walshe, 21 Mar. 1941. 27 Ibid. 28 MA G2/X/315 Pt II, Western Command Monthly Report, Aug. 1941.

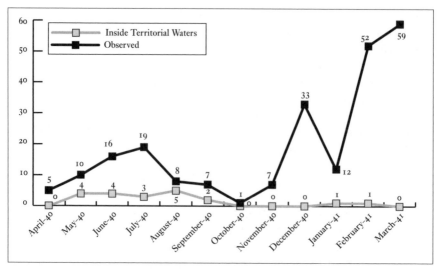

5.2: Submarines (All Commands): April 1940–March 1941
(Source: MA G2/X series files)

them suggesting the former.[29] A protective boom was built across Lough Foyle in 1941 as U-boats were suspected to be operating nearby. The boom worried External Affairs as a German attack on it would put Irish territory in danger. Walshe took up the matter with de Valera and the Department of Defence but also clandestinely contacted Bishop Farren of Derry who told him that the district was lit 'sufficiently so to enable the Germans to distinguish the neutral from the belligerent area'.[30] Despite the construction of the boom, reports of German submarines near Lough Foyle continued. The boom was removed in May 1942 and transferred to Larne, G2 commenting that 'the boom was never a success in the Foyle'.[31]

Small numbers of suspected German submarines were active off the south-west coast through 1941. Maffey continued to send information on these vessels to External Affairs for the military to investigate. Information was often sparse, such as the report from Eask LOP on 29 August that 'a submarine was sighted 4 miles SW of Post going west at 22.10'.[32] The significance of this report is that it placed the submarine in the middle of Dingle Bay heading into the Atlantic Ocean at dusk and suggested that the craft had been in Dingle Bay for a number of hours. Submarines in this area had been responsible for landing German agents, as in the cases of Weber-Drohl and Simon in 1940. Bray Head LOP on Valentia Island and Bolus Head LOP observed surfaced submarines or the periscopes of submarines between Puffin Island and the Skelligs on the southern approaches to Dingle Bay but were unable to provide positive identification.

29 Ibid., July 1941. 30 NAI DFA Secretary's Files A22, note by Walshe, 26 June 1941. 31 MA G2/X/315 Pt II, AMI, Western Sector, Monthly Report – May 1942. 32 Ibid.,

Eventually five LOPs and four LSF 'shelters' guarded Dingle Bay, Ventry Harbour and Dingle Harbour in the hope of preventing further landings from these unidentified submarines.

THE GROWING IMPORTANCE OF DERRY AS A NAVAL BASE

Through the winter of 1940 into 1941 coastwatchers on Inishowen Head had a clear view of all vessels entering and leaving Lough Foyle, giving G2 an insight into the growing role of the naval base at Derry in Atlantic operations. On 10 January 1941 G2 Western Command was notified of the passage of a convoy of seventy-four ships, 'the largest yet seen off this coast'.[33] To protect these convoys, packs of destroyers, with armed trawlers acting as auxiliaries, worked in conjunction with destroyers on patrol and escort duties out of the Foyle. Destroyers given to the British by the United States in the late autumn of 1940 began arriving in Derry in February 1941. Walshe told Aiken how the arrival of these 'obsolescent American destroyers discloses the scarcity of this type of craft' available to Britain.[34] The significance of the heavy escort work took another month to ascertain and by the end of February G2 knew that 'the strength of the protection given' to convoys 'would appear to depend more on the nature of the cargo carried than on the number of vessels as large merchantmen and liners were on several occasions better escorted than convoys'.[35] The examination by G2 of convoy patterns showed that when a convoy arrived off the north-west Irish coast a fresh destroyer escort moved out from Derry to meet it, relieving the old escort. This was particularly noticeable on 11, 12 and 13 June 1941 when large convoys arrived from North America. As the year progressed escort work from the Foyle remained on a heavy scale and the observation by coastwatchers of the commencement of intensive air and naval patrolling indicated to G2 that large convoys were due to pass the northern Irish coast.

By the summer of 1941 the Foyle was 'full of Warships'; a Garda who visited Derry watched destroyers and corvettes 'getting ready for sea placing their depth charges and guns into position'.[36] In the context of British-Irish relations, the decision to use Lough Foyle indicated that despite the fulminations of Churchill, the Admiralty had decided to build anew rather than occupy the southern Irish ports. Designated HMS *Ferret*, and built at Lisahally on the eastern bank of Lough Foyle, the Derry base eventually included a 2,300-foot jetty to accommodate the large number of escort vessels protecting Atlantic convoys.

Crosbie to Lawlor, 8 Sept. 1941.   **33** MA G2/X/315 Pt II, Western Command Monthly Report, Jan. 1941.   **34** NAI DFA Secretary's Files P35, British claims to Irish ports, undated, early 1941.   **35** MA G2/X/315 Pt II, Western Command Monthly Report, Feb. 1941. **36** NAI DFA Secretary's Files P43/1, British and American Forces in Northern Ireland, undated, attached to Carroll to Walshe, 16 July 1941.

Garda Crime and Security Branch estimated that by July 1941 up to 1,500 United States technicians had arrived in Derry to supervise the construction of a further base being built under the lend-lease agreement. G2 felt the figure to be somewhat exaggerated and Garda sources later reduced it to less than 400. Sources from Northern Ireland made it 'quite definite that the United States are doing something in Derry'.[37] Americans continued to arrive, some seen 'rushing through the City causing great confusion occasionally driving on the right-hand side of the road'.[38] Information collected by Gardaí sent specially to Derry to report back on developments led Garda Chief Superintendent MacMághnuis to report that there was 'no reason to doubt that Derry will be an American Naval Base; the arrival of American Marines is expected daily and the first contingent is expected to number about 2000'.[39] This information was passed on to External Affairs and Walshe reported it to de Valera. The Taoiseach was worried by the implication that troop deployments signified American acceptance of partition. De Valera's initial protest to the State Department to 'strongly emphasise the concern' of the Irish government at the imminent arrival of United States forces in Northern Ireland was made before the attack on Pearl Harbor.[40] It is uncertain what the response would have been had it been immediate, but coming after the United States had entered the war Washington valued strategic goals over Irish sensibilities. When Irish Minister in Washington, Robert Brennan, further protested that the deployment had political ramifications, he was informed that it was 'merely movement of troops in accordance with needs of war'.[41] Troops began to arrive from January 1942 and destroyer repair facilities, a hospital, radio station, oil tanks and ammunition dumps were constructed with 'much activity … being shown in efforts to complete the work'.[42] Walshe viewed the arrival of these forces 'without consultation or warning' in negative terms, they had 'caused deep disappointment and a certain degree of resentment throughout the country.'[43] This mattered little to the Allies: on 5 February 1942 United States Naval Operations Base Londonderry was commissioned. By 1943 Derry had become the largest escort base in Britain.

INVASION SCARES AND OVERFLIGHTS

Establishing patterns of overflights through Irish airspace was a common task for all command intelligence officers. Logging the arrival and departure of these aircraft was one of the most important tasks undertaken by coastwatchers.

37 Ibid., Bryan to McKenna, 11 July 1941.   38 Ibid., British and American Forces in Northern Ireland, undated, attached to Carroll to Walshe, 16 July 1941.   39 NAI JUS 8/832, MacMághnuis to Commissioner C3, 23 Sept. 1941.   40 NAI DFA Secretary's Files P43, telegram 307, Estero to Irish Legation, Washington, 6 Nov. 1941.   41 Ibid., telegram 71, Brennan to Estero, 6 Feb. 1942.   42 NAI JUS 8/832, MacMághnuis to Commissioner C3, 23 Sept. 1941.   43 NAI DFA Paris Embassy P48/2, Walshe to Murphy, 12 Feb. 1942.

Making sense of overflights started with G2 grouping together coastwatchers' individual observations to indicate flight paths. Loose patterns of activity were established and tentative conclusions drawn on the purpose of flights. Intelligence attempted to link the timings and routes of aircraft to events known to have occurred in the Atlantic theatre. In January 1941 Western Command contended that the association between unidentified aircraft spotted over Irish territory and attacks on shipping in the Atlantic 'holds good ... in practically every attack on shipping' summarized in a list sent to GHQ for that month. An unidentified flight on 17 January thought to be a German plane 'which reconnoitred the north-west coast of Mayo and Donegal Bay' from Achill Island to Crohy Head appeared to be 'the origin of two bombing attacks on the Northbrook in a position about 120 miles north-west of Erris'.[44] By the end of February the association noted in January had become an established pattern for flights sighted between Galway Bay and Malin Head. G2 further developed their argument as 'activity in these places by British and unidentified aircraft coincided on twelve different dates and was particularly noticeable on 21st on which day a large number of planes were over our territory'.[45] Such information gave G2 the approximate tracks of German aircraft attacking shipping off the Irish coast and put them in a position to estimate the British response.

From this analysis of overflights, the Chief of Staff's annual report for 1940–1 explained that both British and German aircraft were active over Ireland, adding that ground defences opened fire on unidentified aircraft nine times since April 1940. Western Command generally tolerated overflights but not all flights went unchallenged. In December 1940 the anti-aircraft defences at Fort Lenan and Buncrana twice opened fire on a patrolling British Hudson as it passed for the second time over Irish territory; 'the fire was effective as the plane appeared to be in difficulties', though it continued out to sea.[46] On 24 January 1941 Fort Dunree fired on an aircraft which 'came down the Swilly and wheeled back over Fort Dunree and Leenan'. The target was not hit, though this was not always the case. On 12 July the ground defences at Finner opened fire on 'a British Bomber which was flying east over the Camp'. The defences were on target as it was reported that 'the plane appeared to be hit as it shook in mid-air, and altered its course'.[47] Unconfirmed reports from a separate source suggested that this aircraft crash-landed in Northern Ireland and the pilot was killed. This was not an isolated case. A month earlier, in June 1941, ground defences at Finner had fired on a bomber and two seaplanes and were judged to have hit the bomber.

Through 1941 Western Command tracked Coastal Command aircraft on 'reconnaissance and patrol work' from the newly constructed air bases in Northern Ireland at Limavady, Eglington and Ballykelly.[48] Located high above Lough Foyle with a commanding view over the airbases in Northern Ireland on

44 MA G2/X/315 Pt II, Western Command Monthly Report, Jan. 1941.   45 Ibid., Feb. 1941.   46 Ibid., Dec. 1940.   47 Ibid., July 1941.   48 Ibid.

the opposite side of the Lough, the LOP on Inishowen Head had a vital role gathering information on these bases. Off-duty Gardaí undertook on the spot reconnaissance of the bases. During a visit to the construction sites at Eglington and Limavady in the summer of 1941 a Garda found runways

> miles long and as broad as O'Connell Street ... [A]ll around the place are machine-gun nests ... [M]en in Air Force Blue uniforms standing guard with rifle and bayonet everywhere in the base ... [L]ooking from this base away down the Foyle you can see out into the open Atlantic.[49]

Further reports expanded on the numbers and types of aircraft stationed at each base, estimated at a total of 200 Whitleys, Hudsons, Blenheims and Wellingtons. Inishowen LOP first tracked the flights of these aircraft as they took off heading for 'the open Atlantic', Malin Head LOP then picked up the aircraft as they flew towards the north-western approaches. Flight patterns showed that 'aircraft which passed Malin Head LOP apparently either veered North or circled back East as, otherwise they would have been observed by the LOPs along the North coast of Donegal'.[50] G2 concluded that aircraft reported at the same time along the Mayo coastline must therefore come from the seaplane base at Castle Archdale on Lough Erne. The number of flights from bases around Derry rose through 1941. By April 'activity was maintained almost without cessation from the early hours of the morning till late at night'.[51] With the onset of summer increased night flying began and G2 found it hard to fix any schedule to flights. Co-ordinated attacks on suspected U-boats by these aircraft working with destroyers and armed trawlers were seen daily through 1941 and coastwatchers heard gunfire and explosions of depth charges during attacks. Often only the start and end points of engagements were visible. On 5 March at 1715 Crohy Head LOP in west Donegal heard 'about twelve aircraft, apparently flying in different directions'.[52] Neighbouring LOPs observed a large amount of merchant shipping in the area at the time. Almost a week later, on 11 March, Glengad Head and Malin Head LOPs heard bursts of gunfire and the sound of planes between 1634 and 1717; there was an engagement underway nearby between British and German aircraft.

The German navy now controlled the activities of Condors which ranged 'far out into the Atlantic to the limit of their endurance in search of convoys'.[53] First observed in summer 1940, these long-range flights continued over Ireland through 1941. Western Command reported 'that on many occasions they followed similar courses and in every instance covered areas which have been

---

49 NAI DFA Secretary's Files P43/1, British and American Forces in Northern Ireland, undated, attached to Carroll to Walshe, 16 July 1941. 50 MA G2/X/315 Pt II, Western Command Monthly Report, Dec. 1940. 51 Ibid., Apr. 1941. 52 Ibid., Mar. 1941. 53 Allen, *Storm*, p. 82.

frequented by German aircraft in the past'.[54] Southern Command first picked up these German overflights as they flew north from Biscay and crossed the Irish coast near the Old Head of Kinsale, 'on all occasions' between 0845 and 0915, and left Irish airspace between the mouth of the Shannon and Galway Bay. Flights were 'usually associated with attacks on shipping in the north Atlantic'.[55] The aircraft were identified as Condors as they 'appeared to be bombers – judging by the heavy sound invariably reported'.[56] Returning German anti-shipping flights came 'inland about the mouth of the Shannon ... striking south for Bantry Bay or Valentia' between 1230 and 1330, though return flights were much less frequent, indicating that 'some of these planes keep off shore on the return flights'.[57]

Further proof of Condor flights through Irish airspace came at 0830 on 5 February 1941 when a FW-200 was heard coming in from the sea at low-level over Hare Island and Roaring Water Bay at Baltimore heading, as predicted by Costello's intelligence staff, towards the mouth of the Shannon. Attempting to get its bearings in 'very bad visibility' in heavy rain and dense fog the aircraft, flying at about 850 feet, struck the top of a mountain at Cashelane near Durrus in west Cork.[58] It 'travelled some distance on the side of the mountain before breaking up'.[59] An enthusiastic reporter from the *Southern Star* wrote of 'its barred framework blackened and fantastically twisted ... silhouetted against the sky, like the remains of some prehistoric monster'.[60] Wreckage and live bombs were scattered for over 500 yards across the mountain. A combined Garda/LSF/LDF party 'proceeded to the scene, carrying a number of rifles and a quantity of ammunition'.[61] They found that five of the six-man crew had been killed in the crash, their bodies 'strewn over a wide area'. The sole survivor, 25-year-old Feldwebel Max Hohaus, badly burned and with a broken leg, was seriously injured. A local girl, Mary Nugent, attended to him and 'showed very considerable bravery as the ground for some hundreds of yards round on all sides was littered with all kinds of munitions and other debris'.[62] When approached by LSF members, Hohaus asked in broken English 'England, Ireland'. William Johnson of the LSF replied 'Ireland and he said good'.[63] Hohaus was later interned. Earlier in the war all belligerent personnel found crash-landed on Irish territory had been interned. By 1941 the pro-Allied nature of neutrality was apparent when it came to internment. While Germans like Hohaus were interned Allied airmen were increasingly and secretly released across the border. On 23 December 1940 when two British naval ratings were

54 MA G2/X/315 Pt II, Western Command Monthly Report, Dec. 1940. 55 Ibid., Southern Command, Monthly Report on Coastal Intelligence – Jan. 1941. 56 Ibid., May 1941. 57 Ibid., Jan. 1941. 58 Ibid., Feb. 1941. 59 NAI JUS 90/119/296, Superintendent O'Gara to Commissioner C Division, 5 Feb. 1941. 60 *Southern Star*, 15 Feb. 1941, report contained in NAI DFA Secretary's Files A8. 61 NAI JUS 90/119/296, Walsh to Superintendent, Bantry, 6 Feb. 1941. 62 Ibid. 63 Ibid., Statement by Johnson, 5 Feb. 1941.

apprehended near Fort Dunree, 'the authorities at Dunree were instructed by G.H.Q. to use their own discretion as to holding the prisoners or sending them quietly over the border'. In an unusually open comment, G2 Western Command recorded that in this case 'the latter course was adopted'.[64] The procedure, Wing Commander Begg, the British Air Attaché in Dublin remarked, 'does rather stretch the interpretation of neutrality almost to breaking point.'[65]

There was a sharp reduction in cross-country Luftwaffe flights from January to March 1941 but flights rose through March as weather improved and Southern Command observed aerial activity almost every day. On 5 March two British aircraft attacked a German aircraft ten miles south of Mizen Head. Mizen Head LOP reported 'six bursts of machine-gun fire'.[66] At an altitude of about six hundred feet 'the attacked plane flew towards the land, and was pursued to territorial limits by the attackers, who then withdrew Eastwards'. Perhaps the British aircraft had simply run out of ammunition but it was a clever move by the Germans. They were close to Irish territory and used it as a safe haven. When the coast was clear 'the attacked plane circled over Mizen Head and flew South' back out to sea.[67] During April German flights increased along the south coast, one crashing into the sea between Clear Island and Schull on 18 April though its six-man crew were rescued.

Aerial activity continued over Southern Command as summer began, following the established pattern of 'frequent' flights 'in the early morning hours, striking inland between the Fastnet and the Old Head of Kinsale' and flying towards the mouth of the Shannon.[68] Less frequent southbound flights traversed the same areas in the early afternoon. These took place in daylight but were at high altitude, so no positive identification was possible. For May, Costello's successor, Colonel James O'Hanrahan, reported that 'there were few days when belligerent activity was not reported'.[69] Southern Command remained concerned by what Costello had described as 'deliberate infringements of our neutrality' by German aircraft 'associated with attacks on shipping in the Atlantic'.[70] Ireland left itself open to accusations from Britain that it was assisting German attacks on British shipping in the Atlantic by allowing the Luftwaffe take high altitude shortcuts over Ireland. Southern Command did little to interfere with these flights, it lacked the weaponry to do so and the Irish Air Corps had no suitable fighter-interceptor aircraft. However, on 4 January 1941 fire was opened by ground defences on an unidentified aircraft flying over Spike Island in Cork harbour but 'it did not appear to have been hit, and rose immediately to a greater height and flew out to sea'.[71] What was perhaps the

64 MA G2/X/315 Pt II, Western Command Monthly Report, Dec. 1940. **65** TNA DO 35/1109/14, Begg to Assistant Chief of the Air Staff, 26 Nov. 1942. **66** MA LOP 30, 5 Mar. 1941. **67** MA G2/X/315 Pt II, Southern Command, Monthly Report on Coastal Intelligence – Mar. 1941. **68** Ibid., Dec. 1940. **69** Ibid., May 1941. **70** Ibid., Jan. 1941. **71** MA G2/X/315 Pt I, Southern Command, Monthly Report on Coastal Intelligence-Jan. 1941.

most serious incident of this kind took place in Curragh Command on 27 May 1941. That day, during a period of considerable German air activity over Ireland, including the bombing of Belfast and Dublin, a German He-111 which had been involved in a low-level flight the length of the east coast from Carnsore Point to Dalkey, flew over the Rosslare Military Post in the Curragh Command area and the post opened fire at 1257. Commandant Mackey, OC Curragh Command G2, commented simply that the aircraft was 'fired upon by the ground defences. Hits were observed.'[72]

As the number of German flights increased off the south coast Southern Command observed a related rise in RAF Coastal Command flights. These flights 'flew inland, circled over particular areas, and returned to [the] coastline almost at the exact point at which [they] came inland'.[73] They followed a distinct and different pattern to the straight track flights of the Germans. One British flight which caused Costello concern reconnoitred the Shannon Estuary where the Foynes seaplane base, the partially constructed airport at Rineanna and the site at Ardmore Point near Tarbert for the soon to be constructed Fort Shannon, were all located. Through 1941 the RAF was particularly interested in the Shannon area as the Admiralty and the Air Ministry planned to use the Shannon estuary as an anchorage for naval vessels and Rineanna airport as an RAF Fighter Command base.[74] The Department of Defence, in a memorandum to the government, described Shannon airport as 'one of the principal military objectives in the event of a main attack against the South, due to its extensive landing grounds and its location in relation to the Shannon'.[75] The airport's partially-constructed concrete runways were 'a menace to the defence of the Aerodrome and an inducement to an enemy to make use of it as a base for operations'. When a Condor made a low level 'close survey' of the airport there was nothing Irish forces could do to hinder its progress. Fearful of possible German attacks when flying boat flights resumed from nearby Foynes to Lisbon, Maffey suggested Britain provide Ireland with a squadron of Hurricane fighters to base at Shannon so that 'a few of these with enthusiastic Irish pilots at Rineanna would provoke a desirable incident' should the Luftwaffe return.[76] Though the runways were obstructed the fear remained that night flights of heavy aircraft heading towards Limerick might be the start of a paratroop drop to secure Rineanna, marking the beginning of an invasion.

A German paratroop attack on Ireland still remained a real possibility in 1941. The Minister for the Co-ordination of Defensive Measures, Frank Aiken,

72 Ibid., Curragh Command, Monthly Report on M&CWS–Month of May 1941.   73 Ibid., Southern Command, Monthly Report on Coastal Intelligence – Feb. 1941.   74 TNA ADM 116/5631 covers the discussions of Cabinet Committee 455 through 1940 and 1941 on the acquisition of a defended base on the Shannon.   75 NAI DT S11403, Protection of Rineanna Aerodrome in the event of hostilities, 8 July 1941.   76 TNA DO 35/1109/5, Maffey to

was briefed on the need to respond to forces using tactics similar to those used during the invasion of Crete: 'highly trained troops armed with machine-guns landing in groups from the air'.[77] Fine Gael's James Dillon and Richard Mulcahy both raised the issue at the inter-party Defence Conference. Dillon scathingly commented that the LDF, who were being trained to meet such an attack, were 'receiving rifle training only'. Basic it might have been, but Dillon underestimated the level of commitment in this poorly equipped force as a series of orders given to the Group Leader of the LDF in Annagry in Donegal on 15 March 1941 by his District Leader reveal. An important background detail to understanding these events is that on 10 March General McKenna met senior officers from the British army in Northern Ireland to discuss the possibility of a German invasion of north-west Ireland. Churchill had four days earlier issued his 'Battle of the Atlantic' directive to counter the increasing German stranglehold on Britain. With German aircraft daily engaged in action with British forces off the Donegal coast, and with the number of German flights over Ireland increasing, it seemed that the Luftwaffe were taking a new interest in the north-west coast of Ireland and invasion could not be ruled out.

Accordingly, on Saturday 15 March the LDF District Command in Dungloe received information that suggested a paratroop drop along the coast was likely that night. James Sharkey, LDF Group Leader in Annagry, was ordered to place a patrol of five men on Mullaghderg Strand, a local beach, from 2000 on 15 March to 0800 on 16 March. It was a bank holiday weekend, Monday 17 March being St Patrick's Day. The members of the patrol would each carry a loaded rifle and have with them forty-five rounds of ammunition. The 'urgent and confidential' orders given to the patrol were stark:

> 1: Shoot to kill all persons attempting to land by parachute or from aeroplanes. Such persons should not be challenged.
> 2: Fire to hit all aeroplanes passing over the land.[78]

If this was an exercise, it was a high stakes one. The order to shoot first and ask questions later could give rise to fatal accidents in the case of any misunderstanding by a nervous volunteer. Dangerous times called for this small deployment to receive such orders. How could a force of five men overcome well-armed professional paratroops? It was unlikely, if the expected force had arrived, that any of the patrol would have survived to carry out their final order: to report by phone to Dungloe on the details of the engagement, and the movements of any associated ships and supporting craft. The LDF would have had limited success in delaying any invader, in reality it would be a British force,

Machtig, 22 Apr. 1941.   77 UCDA P104/3534, Defence matters raised at meeting of Defence Conference held on 11th June, 1941.   78 James Sharkey personal papers (in the possession of Hugo Sharkey), Boyle to Sharkey, 15 Mar 1941.

called in by Dublin from the strengthened Northern Ireland garrison, which would counter a German invasion of Ireland. More confident than in 1940, the Admiralty concluded that after an initial landing by sea and air in south-west Ireland Germany would face serious difficulties reinforcing and supplying its troops. These could be contained and overcome by forces from Northern Ireland in 'a matter of weeks'.[79] The problem was that within those weeks the Germans would gain access to Irish aerodromes and operate from them 'with considerable effect against our West coast ports'.[80]

Western Command reported that 'activity off our [north-western] coasts was particularly intense' during the first week of May and 'on many occasions German aircraft were observed, often in the vicinity of British air bases'.[81] Two waves of planes were observed heading overland towards Derry on 5 May. German aircraft were also spotted passing along the north Mayo coast on the same day. Air raid warnings sounded in Derry, Strabane, Portrush and Portstewart and as they sounded explosions were heard at the mouth of Lough Foyle. Bombs were dropped into the sea west of Malin Head and on Irish territory near Malin Head but without causing serious damage. G2 concluded that these incidents were 'probably connected with the air raids on Belfast and other Northern Ireland towns' on the morning of 5–6 May.[82] After the raids on Belfast air 'activity resumed normal proportions'.[83] The charts of flights forwarded to G2 in Dublin were 'not unfamiliar' as they bore a 'similarity to those which were a feature of this report some months ago'.[84] Summer weather caused problems for coastwatchers as 'recognition was rendered difficult because the sun's rays were between the LOP and the plane'.[85] But as the summer of 1941 began Southern and Western Commands had an accurate picture of aerial incursions over Irish territory and knew reasonably well what could be expected in the coming months.

THE DONEGAL CORRIDOR, CASTLE ARCHDALE AND THE SINKING OF BISMARCK

In late 1940 the RAF had begun the construction of a seaplane base at Castle Archdale on the shores of Lough Erne in Fermanagh in Northern Ireland. With the agreement of the Irish government, flights from Castle Archdale were given access to the Atlantic Ocean through an air corridor beginning at the border at Belleek, passing over eight miles of Irish territory to the sea at Ballyshannon and out over Donegal Bay to the edge of the Irish territorial waters. The diplomatic groundwork to allow the RAF to fly along the 'Donegal corridor' took place in discussions between External Affairs and the Air Ministry in December 1940

79 TNA ADM 1/11330, minute, 5 Apr. 1941. 80 Ibid. 81 MA G2/X/315 Pt II, Western Command Monthly Report, May 1941. 82 Ibid. 83 Ibid. 84 Ibid., Apr. 1941. 85 Ibid., Southern Command Monthly Report, Aug. 1941.

and January 1941, the details of the arrangement being finalized in a meeting between de Valera and Maffey. Aircraft using the corridor would fly at as great a height as possible over Irish territory and avoid the military installations at Finner Camp to the south-west of Ballyshannon as aircraft flying too close to Finner were liable to be fired upon by the light anti-aircraft positions at the camp. To Maffey, the creation of the corridor showed 'a desire to help in directions which do not involve obvious dangers here of German reprisals'.[86] The first flight from Castle Archdale along the corridor took place on 21 February 1941 when a flying boat was dispatched to escort a crippled merchant vessel to port.

Coastwatchers had reported little belligerent activity along the north Mayo coastline during December 1940 and January 1941. From late February coast-watchers in south Donegal, Sligo and Mayo began to report daily flights from Castle Archdale. The opening of the air corridor was immediately reflected in an increase in aerial activity over Donegal Bay, with the logbook for St John's Point LOP from 21–2 February 1941 containing several entries each day detailing sightings such as 'monoplane 5 miles S. East of L.O.P. flying low in a Westerly direction'.[87] St John's Point became the most important LOP for the observation of flights through the air corridor. By April the patrol areas of these aircraft were known to be between Annagh Head in Mayo and Rossan Point in Donegal and then westward over the Atlantic. The intelligence picture was still partial. G2 could not explain why 'more planes are reported going west from the Erne than actually return by this route'.[88]

In the historiography of Irish wartime co-operation with the Allies a fairly simple interpretation exists of the 'Donegal Corridor'. It allowed Allied aircraft to gain easier access to the North Atlantic by crossing neutral Irish territory instead of flying north to Lough Foyle. Access to the ocean along the corridor saved a trip of almost 200 miles and approximately two hours flying time to get to the same position west of Donegal Bay. But what did this shortcut achieve? Did the operation of the 'Donegal Corridor' significantly benefit the British war effort? De Valera clearly felt that it did as evidenced in his suggestion in May 1941 that access to the air corridor would be ended if Britain proceeded to introduce conscription in Northern Ireland.[89] One episode provides an answer. The 'Donegal corridor' and the flying boat base at Castle Archdale played a central role in the sinking of the German battleship *Bismarck* on 27 May 1941 in one of the most memorable naval engagements of the Second World War.

Since receiving a 20 May intelligence report from the British naval attaché in Stockholm that two German battleships had entered the North Atlantic from the Baltic, British aircraft, battleships and cruisers had been seeking *Bismarck* and

86 TNA PREM 3/131/3, memorandum by Maffey of meeting with de Valera, 20 Jan. 1941. 87 MA LOP 70, 22 Feb. 1941.   88 MA G2/X/315 Pt I, Western Command Monthly Report, Apr. 1941.   89 TNA DO 35/1109/20, Maffey to Machtig, 27 May 1941.

the cruiser *Prinz Eugen*. The two ships had attempted to pass unnoticed through the Denmark Strait between Greenland and Iceland into the North Atlantic to attack Allied merchant shipping. *Bismarck* sank the battleship *Hood*, the most famous ship in the Royal Navy, and badly damaged the battleship *Prince of Wales* on 24 May. She escaped an air strike from Swordfish aircraft from the aircraft carrier *Victorious* on 25 May and, after evading pursuing British vessels for almost a day, seemed to be heading for the certain safety of France. For the British ships hunting *Bismarck*, 'the question of fuel was becoming acute' and they needed to find *Bismarck* before they were forced to reduce speed, an action that would make them prey to U-boats and most worryingly, allow *Bismarck* to escape.[90] It was of the utmost importance that the British find and sink *Bismarck* before she reached the range of Luftwaffe air cover over the Bay of Biscay.

As part of 'a comprehensive scheme of air search'[91] to regain the trail of *Bismarck*, two 'crossover patrols' by Catalina flying boats of Coastal Command based at Castle Archdale were to patrol a 328-mile stretch of ocean between 52°N 19°.30´W and 48°N 23°.30´W which was thought to include the track of *Bismarck*'s probable course, 'it being appreciated that [the] enemy force [was] probably making for BREST or ST NAZAIRE'.[92] A sweep by Coastal Command out to 30° west on the evening of 25 May had failed to locate *Bismarck*. The precedents were not promising for this new patrol. The first Catalina, Z of 209 Squadron, a squadron operating from Castle Archdale since late March 1941, took off at 0330 on 26 May in search of *Bismarck* and was airborne at 0345.[93] Flying Officer Denis Briggs flew Z/209 with co-pilot Ensign Leonard 'Tuck' Smith. Smith was an American Navy pilot attached to 209 Squadron as a 'Special Observer' since only 13 May, familiarizing the squadron with the Catalina, itself just one month in British service and one of the newest aircraft operating with Coastal Command. Smith, an airman from a still neutral state, was now flying a combat mission with Coastal Command. A second Catalina, M of 240 Squadron, flown by another American Navy pilot, Lieutenant James E. Johnson, took off from Lough Erne an hour later. Tasked by the head of Coastal Command, Air Marshal Sir Frederick Bowhill, to scout for *Bismarck* in an area to the west of Brest and south-west of Ireland, both aircraft flew along the Donegal Corridor and out over Donegal Bay. They climbed and turned west. Z/209 climbed to 3,000 feet through an overcast sky before proceeding to the west coast of Ireland and descending to 500 feet due to poor visibility. The Catalina then took a westerly course off Eagle Island at 0430 to the start of its patrol point 400 miles to the south-west.[94] M/240 followed almost an hour later.

90 TNA ADM 234/322, Battle Summary No. 5 (1950 edition), p. 20.   91 TNA ADM 234/321, Battle Summary No. 5 (1942 edition), p. 18.   92 TNA AIR 20/1329, Extracts from Coastal Command Summaries, 26 May 1941.   93 TNA AIR 27/1294, 209 Squadron Operations Logbook, entries for 26 May 1941   94 Report of Scouting and Search of PBY-5 No. AH545 'Catalina' for *Bismarck* 26 May, 1941, at www.history.navy.mil/faqs/faq118-3.htm (accessed 30

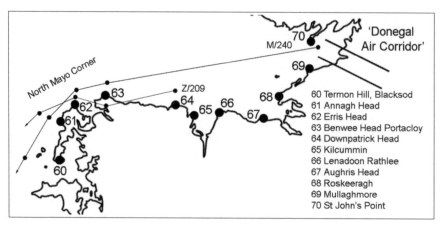

5.3: Tracks of Z/209 and M/240 along the north Mayo coast

The LOPs along the north Mayo coast each saw two Catalinas passing their positions on the night of 25–6 May 1941 and that night 'only two Catalina aircraft at Lough Erne were immediately available to cover the courses to the French Ports'.[95] The weather was moderate in north Mayo and all accounts agree on a cloudy sky and wind from the north-west. Despite poor to moderate visibility, the LOPs along the south Donegal and north Mayo coast observed and tracked the Catalina flying boats ordered from Castle Archdale to search for *Bismarck*.

Before examining the facts, one point is necessary to reconcile sources. During the Second World War Britain and Northern Ireland adopted British Double Summer Time (BDST), keeping clocks two hours ahead of Greenwich Mean Time during the summer months. In 1941 BDST began on 4 May. Ireland did not adopt this version of summer time during the war, with clocks set one hour ahead of Greenwich to Irish Summer Time (IST) during the summer months. Coastwatchers' reports were phoned to Command head-quarters in local time, while Coastal Command reports of the engagement with *Bismarck* generally show reporting of times in BDST, though this is not always clear. In the remainder of this section, times are clearly identified as belonging to specific time zones when correlation is required.

Z/209 was airborne at 0345 BDST (0245 IST). Downpatrick Head LOP spotted an aircraft at 0327 IST[96] passing three miles north of the post heading west at an estimated altitude of 4,000 feet. Seven minutes later and seventeen miles to the west, Benwee Head LOP saw the same aircraft. Erris Head LOP

March 2006).   **95** TNA AIR 20/1329, Coastal Command aspect of the Bismarck Episode, undated.   **96** All times and descriptions are from the post logbooks.

then picked up this aircraft, identifying her in the pre-dawn twilight of a short summer night as a twin-engined high-winged monoplane, a good description of a Catalina, flying at approximately 1,000 feet. The final sighting was from Annagh Head LOP at 0348 IST, as Z/209 passed south-west in moderate visibility at approximately 2,000 feet an estimated six miles to the north-west. The coastwatchers were unaware of the role played by Z/209 in the hunt for *Bismarck* and afterwards G2 remained unaware that such an important part in the hunt for *Bismarck* had taken place off Ireland's shores. As far as the Irish were concerned, Z/209 was just another Coastal Command patrol; they never realized the importance of the aircraft or of the second Catalina, M/240, which followed almost an hour behind. St John's Point LOP picked up M/240 at 0355 IST, passing one mile to the south-east of the post 'flying low over [the] sea [and] going west'. Flying further out to sea than Z/209, M/240 was not observed by Downpatrick Head LOP but was sighted by Benwee Head LOP at 0430 IST. It was by now almost bright and the post logged a high-winged monoplane six miles to the north, flying to the west at 2,000 feet, well out to sea beyond the Stags of Broadhaven. When two minutes later she was picked up by Erris Head, flying four miles to the north of the post, she was turning south-west and had descended to an estimated 200 feet. The manoeuvre was complete when Annagh Head picked up the trail at 0439 IST, the Catalina now having descended to an estimated 280 feet, probably to fix her position in the poor visibility before heading out into oceanic airspace. Blacksod Bay LOP, in the hands of experienced coastwatcher Corporal Ted Sweeney, did not see or hear the first Catalina; her track from Annagh Head shows that she was heading well out to sea out of range of Blacksod Bay LOP. But at 0440 IST that post did hear an unidentified aircraft to the 'far west of [the] post going south west', a time and location fitting the path of M/240. The flightpath of Z/209 and M/240 using the Donegal Corridor and along the north Mayo coast through Irish airspace allowed Bowhill to fulfil his plan of pushing his reconnaissance effort further south than the Admiralty had desired. Had the aircraft not been able to use the 'Donegal Corridor' they would have had to fly north through Northern Ireland and around the Donegal coast wasting valuable time in their search for *Bismarck*. This would have allowed the German battleship time to sail further east and closer to the long-range Luftwaffe air cover and U-boat cover that would protect her across the Bay of Biscay and into Brest.

Z/209 reached the search area at 0945. At 1030 in poor visibility and flying below cloud at 500 feet the Catalina's crew spotted 'a dull black shape, which gradually took on the contours of a large warship' steaming to the south-east.[97] Exploding anti-aircraft shells left no one mistaken; Z/209 had found *Bismarck*

97 Ludovic Kennedy, *Pursuit: the sinking of the Bismarck* (London, 2001 edition), p. 152.

and radioed her position at 49°36′ North, 21°47′ West, almost 600 miles to the south-west of Annagh Head where her crew had last seen land at 0430 over neutral Ireland. This report, picked up by the battleships *King George V* and *Renown*, placed *Bismarck* 690 miles from Brest. It was the first sighting of *Bismarck* since 0213 on the morning of 25 May and 'a wave of hope surged up in every ship'.[98] The British force could alter its course for direct contact with *Bismarck*. Once the Catalinas had located *Bismarck*, it became 'a race against time' to slow her down so naval forces could converge on the battleship and sink her.[99]

At 1510 Z/209 had to return to Lough Erne. M/240 shadowed *Bismarck* through the afternoon of 26 May as British naval forces converged on the battleship. With M/240 and (following receipt of Z/209's position report) aircraft from the aircraft carrier *Ark Royal* shadowing *Bismarck*, a Catalina from 210 Squadron at Oban was tasked with 'a special long distance job'.[100] Taking off at 1220 the Catalina 'set out at high airspeed to combat a headwind' to take over the aerial shadowing of *Bismarck* from M/240.[101] O/210 sighted *Bismarck* at 2344, picking up 'in the dusk a large warship almost immediately below us' and kept shadowing the battleship until 0404 on 27 May.[102] Running short of fuel, O/210 signalled she was retuning to base. She 'made landfall at the Fastnet' and 'crept up the West coast of Ireland', landing at Oban at 1428 on 27 May after a flight of 25 hours and 13 minutes.

After the aircraft from Lough Erne had spotted *Bismarck* it was feared that at a speed of 21 knots she would reach Brest by 2130 on 27 May. She had to be slowed down. A torpedo attack from Swordfish from the aircraft carrier *Ark Royal* jammed one of *Bismarck*'s twin rudders allowing British ships to catch up with her. *Bismarck* was finally sunk at 1101 on the morning of 27 May by a British naval force made up of the ageing battleship *Rodney*, the battleship *King George V* and the cruisers *Norfolk* and *Dorsetshire*. The following day, during a period of otherwise routine observations, two British battleships, one of which was thought to be *Rodney*, the other *King George V* accompanied by nine destroyers, were observed by LOPs heading north along the Donegal coast. The distinctive profile of the *Rodney* was easily recognizable to coastwatchers. British charts show *King George V* passing along the Irish coast from Belmullet to Malin Head from 1200 to 1800 on 28 May.[103] While the sighting of *Rodney* and *King George V* was an important observation for Irish forces, the action that the British ships were en-route from was a defining point in the war in the Atlantic. The brunt of the battle of the Atlantic would now fall on the U-boats and the role of the surface raider would decline.[104]

98 TNA ADM 234/321, Battle Summary No. 5, p. 19.   99 Ibid.   100 TNA AIR 20/1329, The Bismarck. Flight Lieutenant Hatfield, Captain of O/210–26/27 May 1941.   101 Ibid. 102 Ibid.   103 TNA ADM 234/321, chart Bismarck Operations, May 23–26, 1941. 104 *Prinz Eugen*, *Scharnhorst* and *Gneisenau* remained to be attacked. The ships attempted to

One of the three Tribal class destroyers operating as an anti-submarine escort to *Rodney*, HMS *Mashona*, was 'heavily attacked' by German Ju-88 aircraft on 28 May and later sank ninety miles north-west of Loop Head, Clare.[105] Forty-seven men and one officer were killed in the attack. The Admiralty were quick to put the loss of the ship down to Ireland's failure to allow the Royal Navy use of Irish ports and air bases, tersely concluding that

> once again we see this most distressful country operating to advantage against us. Control of West Coast ports would have:– (a) Given the fleet a base close at hand; (b) Given us air bases from which to protect our fleet as it returned home. MASHONA would never have been sunk, and fuel would have given us no undue anxiety.[106]

It took almost a month for the bodies of six of the men lost in the sinking of *Mashona* to be washed up on the shores of Mayo and Galway. The bodies of 17-year-old Boy Seaman (First Class) Peter McGlade and 34-year-old Electrical Artificer (First Class) Frederick Wheeler were found on 27 June, McGlade at Surgeview, Blacksod and Wheeler at Achill Sound. A third body, unidentified, was washed up at Achill Sound the following day. Leading Seaman Jack Johnson's body was found on Iniskea North Island on 29 June, that of Ordinary Seaman Ronald Woodward, at An Clochán, Galway on 1 July. Finally, on 3 July, the body of Petty Officer Jack Tweed was taken from the sea two miles off Clare Island. On Johnson's body was found a copy of a cypher radio message, a poignant reminder of the epic battle he had witnessed but not survived. It was from HMS *Dorsetshire* to Admiral Sir John Tovey, the Commander-in-Chief of the Home Fleet, and read: 'I torpedoed Bismarck both sides before she sank. She had ceased firing but her colours were still flying. 1107. 27/5/41'.[107] The telegram was sent half an hour after *Bismarck* sank. Perhaps Johnson had hoped to show this memento to his wife Minnie at home in Dagenham in Essex when he was next on leave and tell her of his part in the epic battle.[108] Instead, Johnson became another casualty of battle of the Atlantic.

In an exchange of telegrams immediately after the sinking, the Admiralty congratulated Bowhill and acknowledged 'the part played by reconnaissance of

make a dash along the English Channel on 11 Feb. 1942. Spotted, *Scharnhorst* was seriously damaged as it reached German waters on 13 Feb., *Gneisenau* was attacked in Kiel on the night of 26–7 of Feb. 1942 and *Prinz Eugen* was torpedoed on its way to Trondheim in Norway on 23 Feb. 1942, but survived the war. The British press had, at the time, speculated on the possible use of the radio set in the German legation in Dublin in aiding the flight of the two ships (see Walshe to de Valera, 15 Dec. 1943 (NAI DFA Secretary's Files A2) and Walshe to de Valera, 17 Feb. 1942 (NAI DFA Secretary's Files, A25)). **105** TNA AIR 20/1329, Bismarck Timetable. **106** TNA ADM 199/1187, minute, 3 June 1941. **107** NAI DFA 241/184A, text of telegram in to Burns to Commissioner, C Division, 4 July 1941. **108** Information on Johnson from www.cwgc.org (accessed 7 Feb. 2006).

the force under your command which contributed in a large measure to the successful outcome of the recent operations'. Bowhill replied that 'it was a great hunt and we are eager and ready for more'.[109] The Admiralty's own account of the hunt and sinking of *Bismarck* maintained that 'on no occasion had the value of aircraft been so clearly demonstrated for it was aircraft that found her when she was lost and made the decisive attack'.[110] The two aircraft from Lough Erne had started the clock ticking in the final hunt for the German battleship. With *Bismarck* located far from safety in port in France and far from the safety of Luftwaffe air cover her vulnerability to attack increased. Had they not been able to fly the 'Donegal corridor', the Catalinas would have arrived much later at their area of operations and, arguably, not discovered the *Bismarck* at all. The spotting of *Bismarck* by the two Coastal Command Catalinas gave the British more time to get their naval forces into position. This was crucial since the British vessels were running low on fuel and almost at their limits of operation.[111] Subsequent British accounts of the sinking of *Bismarck*, dominated by Admiralty thinking, have downplayed the role of airpower. They have also been dominated by a desire to camouflage 'the fact that the Bismarck was lost by the Royal Navy and subsequently found for them again by the RAF'.[112] This was not the contemporary view. In a letter of 31 May 1941 Captain R.A.B. Edwards at the Admiralty wrote to Bowhill to congratulate him 'on the part your Command took in the destruction of the Bismarck. It is no exaggeration to say that without them it would never have been accomplished'.[113] Coastal Command was the 'Service which probably saved the day' for the Royal Navy.[114] *Bismarck* was found when she was in a vulnerable position because the Coastal Command aircraft were able to take a shortcut over neutral Irish territory with the agreement of the Irish government.

Use of the 'Donegal Corridor' became routine by the autumn of 1941. By the end of the year, British aircraft were 'observed almost daily off the coast of Mayo, Sligo and Donegal and crossing our territory between Ballyshannon and Finner when moving to and from their base in Lough Erne'.[115] These flights underlined Ireland's significant geopolitical position for Coastal Command operations and showed the operational importance to Britain of the Lough Erne base. They also show the strategic value of the secret wartime co-operation between Dublin and London. When he met three members of de Valera's cabinet for lunch on 27 May Sir John Maffey reported to London that Seán T

---

109 *The Times*, 29 May 1941.   110 TNA ADM 234/321, Battle Summary No. 5 (1942 edition), p. 19. This passage does not appear in the conclusion to the 1950 edition which instead concentrates on the co-operation between the various forces 'including aircraft of Coastal Command' (p, 37).   111 *King George V* was down to 1,200 tons of fuel (32%) and *Rodney* reported she would have to leave the chase by 0800 on the morning of 27 May.   112 TNA AIR 15/204, Slatter to Brown, 3 Sept. 1946.   113 Ibid., minute, McGrath to Air Intelligence, 29 Aug. 1946.   114 Ibid., minute no. 9, Air Tactics to CIO, 23 Aug. 1946.   115 MA G2/X/315 Pt II, Western Command Monthly Report, Nov. 1941.

O'Ceallaigh, Seán MacEntee and P.J. Ruttledge were 'equally divided' over the sinking of *Bismarck*.[116] If the three men held divided opinions over the sinking of the German battleship, how more would they have been at odds had they known the role Irish airspace played in the sinking?

THE 'ROBERT HASTIE'

Increasing Coastal Command operations from Castle Archdale raised the possibility of aircraft getting into difficulties on approach to or departure from the base. The possibility of combat-damaged aircraft ditching off the west coast was also likely and search and rescue craft were needed near Lough Erne to pick up survivors. In February 1941, on Maffey's suggestion, the Air Ministry and Coastal Command entered into discussions to station a rescue boat, a tug manned by civilian personnel and flying the red ensign of the merchant navy, in a location suitable for picking up downed aircrews. Coastal Command considered that 'the best base for this tug will have to be decided in the light of local knowledge gained'.[117] This meant that the tug would have to be based on the western Irish coast as Lough Foyle was too far north of the tracks of aircraft using Lough Erne. It was now a question of getting Irish agreement. Though the Irish were 'sympathetic' to the British proposal, the necessary negotiations were delicate.[118] In July 1941 Boland told the Department of Defence that 'after various consultations, permission was, I understand, granted and conveyed verbally by Walshe to Maffey'.[119] There is no written record on the Irish side of this agreement.

The British were supposed to tell the Irish when the tug was due to arrive in Irish waters. No communications were received, a situation politely put down by Boland to a 'misunderstanding'.[120] It was only when the Garda Chief Superintendent in Letterkenny was informed by the County Inspector of the RUC in Derry that the vessel, the trawler *Robert Hastie*, had left Derry for Killybegs on 11 July that the date of ship's arrival was known. On arrival customs officers boarded the ship and sealed two machine-guns, seven rifles and four revolvers. External Affairs were not unduly worried by the presence of these weapons, telling Defence that 'provided they are not visible' while the ship was in port in Ireland 'we do not think that any action need be taken'.[121] *Robert Hastie*'s captain was warned that weapons were not to be used under any circumstances in Irish territorial waters. Bryan considered such a warning 'very apt'; Carrigan Head LOP later saw *Robert Hastie* fire three bursts from a Lewis gun on the border of Irish waters on the afternoon of 17 September. Later an

116 TNA DO 35/1109/20, Maffey to Machtig, 27 May 1941. 117 TNA AIR 20/1329, Bromet to Under-Secretary of State for Air, 20 Feb. 1941. 118 Ibid., minute by Howe, 6 Mar. 1941. 119 NAI DFA Secretary's Files A32, Boland to Beary, 24 July 1941. 120 Ibid. 121 Ibid., Walshe to Beary, 13 Sept. 1941.

aircraft dropped depth charges into the sea outside Irish waters seven miles west of Carrigan Head and forty-five minutes afterwards a trawler, believed to be the British rescue ship, was observed by coastwatchers at Carrigan Head 'three miles south-west … going southwards'. This contravened the orders the ship's captain had received that weapons were for defensive use only. When questioned he had no recollection of the incident involving the aircraft and the depth charges and replied that the firing was for training, as he thought he was outside territorial waters. Walshe was worried what would happen if the British vessel 'happened to sight a German aeroplane while she was inside our territorial waters entering or leaving Killybegs'. He hoped to avoid a statement to Britain on this question, but added 'if such an attack did occur it would be for us to deal with it'. Ultimately Walshe felt that 'if the "Robert Hastie" were attacked within our waters, it would defend itself and it would be hard to blame it for doing so'.[122]

The presence of weapons on a ship docked in a neutral Irish port and which was undertaking tasks 'not genuinely humanitarian in character' was, Rynne observed, 'rather delicate'.[123] He suggested that Dublin must 'face the fact that the "Robert Hastie" is a belligerent public ship' armed for war and 'treat her as a warship', allowing her access to Killybegs only for twenty-four hour periods at 'decent intervals'.[124] Rynne was taking a strictly legal position and cautiously relented that 'on the other hand', Dublin could 'ignore the vessel's ownership and usual activities altogether (we could not make much of a case for our attitude if challenged by the German Government!)'. This became the adopted practice, but using the LOPs at Carrigan Head, St John's Point and Mullaghmore, Dublin kept watch from a distance on the British rescue vessel.

Initially, *Robert Hastie*'s radio set and armaments were sealed, but the Irish authorities later arranged with Britain that the radio would remain operational. The set was essential to allow the vessel carry out searches. She was told to remain in Killybegs at one hour's notice to put to sea, maintaining a constant listening watch on marine radio frequencies, until called for by radio 'to investigate any rafts or floating objects off the coast and to go to the assistance of any person in difficulties whether German, Italian, British, etc.'.[125] The ship was to undertake occasional safety patrols between Killybegs and Eagle Island. Otherwise, she was to return to Derry every ten weeks for supplies and repairs and while at anchor in Killybegs Bay was to keep good relations with locals and facilitate the Irish authorities. An interview with the captain revealed that 'he appeared to be more interested in floating objects' than rescuing survivors as flotsam could provide useful technical intelligence. Rescued survivors from aircraft or merchant and naval vessels were to be landed in Northern Ireland but,

122 Ibid., Walshe to Bryan, 10 Nov. 1941.   123 Ibid., minute from Rynne to Walshe, 19 July 1941.   124 Ibid.   125 Ibid., Report of visit to British Rescue Vessel 'Robert Hastie' at Killybegs, on 11 Oct. 1941.

1 Newly constructed Aughris Head LOP, March 1940 (National Archives of Ireland)

2 Dunany Head LOP, Louth, February 1940 (National Archives of Ireland)

3 Clogher Head LOP, Louth, February 1940 (National Archives of Ireland)

4 Kilcreadun LOP, Clare, July 1941 (National Archives of Ireland)

5 Hag's Head LOP, Clare, January 1942 (National Archives of Ireland)

6 Dunabrattin Head LOP, Waterford, February 1945 (National Archives of Ireland)

7 LOP 63 and 'Eire Sign', Benwee Head, Portacloy, Mayo, April 2003 (M. Kennedy)

8 Shrapnel from a German bomb dropped at Dundalk, 24 July 1941
(National Archives of Ireland)

1st ATTACK
1 UNEXPLODED BOMB
2 DEMOLISHED BUILDING, KILLING THREE GIRLS
3 CRATERED RAILWAY SIDING
2ND ATTACK
4 DAMAGED WATER MAINS

9 Aerial photograph showing damage to Campile Creamery, Wexford by German
bombs, 26 August 1940 (National Archives of Ireland)

10 3.7" Vickers heavy anti-aircraft gun (Military Archives, Cathal Brugha Barracks)

11 Bofors-40 light anti-aircraft guns (Air Corps/Army Press Office)

L.O.P. LOG BOOK
L.A. 109

Wicklow Head Post 9
No. 1 District

Serial No.	Date	Time	EVENTS, MESSAGES, INCIDENTS — Details	ACTION TAKEN	REMARKS

12 Pages of the logbook of LOP 9 (Wicklow Head) for 30–31 May 1941
(Military Archives, Cathal Brugha Barracks)

L.O.P. LOG BOOK
L.A. 109

Wicklow Head Post 9
No. 1 District

Serial No.	Date	Time	EVENTS, MESSAGES, INCIDENTS — Details	ACTION TAKEN	REMARKS

13 Pages for the logbook of LOP 9 (Wicklow Head) for 31 May–1 June 1941
(Military Archives, Cathal Brugha Barracks)

14 LOP 63, Benwee Head, Portacloy, towards the Stags of Broadhaven, April 2003
(M. Kennedy)

15 LOP 59, Moyteogue Head, Achill Island, April 2003 (M. Kennedy)

16 Blacksod Bay Lighthouse, Mayo, 21 August 2007
(M. Kennedy)

17 LOP 38, Slea Head, Kerry, towards the Blasket Islands, January 2004
(M. Kennedy)

18 LOP 40, Brandon Point, Kerry, January 2004 (M. Kennedy)

19 LOP 14, Carnsore Point, Wexford, November 2003 (M. Kennedy)

20 LOP 71, Carrigan Head, Donegal, towards Benbulbin over Donegal Bay, June 2004
(M. Kennedy)

21 Colonel Dan Bryan, Director of G2. Described by the British Military Attaché in Dublin as 'very good indeed at his particular line of work and very little misses him'. (TNA WO 106/6045, Pryce to Bolster, 14 Oct. 1941) (Military Archives, Cathal Brugha Barracks)

22 Oscar Traynor, Minister for Defence, Captain Albertas, French Naval Attachés
Lieutenant General Dan McKenna, M. Xavier de Laforcade, French Minister to
Ireland, Colonel Liam Archer. Image (courtesy of the National Library of Ireland).

23 LOP 32, Dursey Head, Cork, October 2003 (M. Kennedy)

24 'Eire Sign', LOP 62, Erris Head, Mayo, April 2003 (M. Kennedy)

25 'Eire Sign', LOP 80, Malin Head, Donegal, August 2004 (M. Kennedy)

26 LOP 62, Erris Head, Mayo, April 2003 (M. Kennedy)

27 LOP 21, Knockadoon Head, Cork, August 2006 (M. Kennedy)

28 LOP 45, Loop Head, Clare, December 2003 (M. Kennedy)

29 LOP 80, Malin Head, Donegal, August 2004 (M. Kennedy)

30 LOP 30, Mizen Head, Cork, October 2003 (M. Kennedy)

31 LOP 70, St John's Point, Donegal, June 2004 (M. Kennedy)

32 War graves, Cruit cemetery, Donegal, June 2004 (M. Kennedy)

33 War graves, Termoncarragh cemetery, Belmullet, Mayo, May 2004 (M. Kennedy)

if this was not possible, RAF personnel or members of the armed forces landed in neutral Ireland were to wear seamen's kit in order to avoid internment.

The Coast Watching Service played a significant role in the first serious operation undertaken by *Robert Hastie*. On 6 February 1942 an RAF Coastal Command Sunderland flying boat (W3977) 'ZM-Q' of 201 Squadron crashed into the sea an estimated nine miles north of LOP 72 at Rossan Point in Donegal.[126] Coastwatchers reported the crash and location and GHQ relayed it to the RAF. In analysing the crash, the RAF obtained detailed reports from the logbooks of the Coast Watching Service. Rossan Point LOP heard the sound of an aircraft at 0020 and then heard explosions and 'two minutes later saw fire on the water' at an estimated nine miles north of the post.[127] The LOP north of Rossan Point at Dunmore Head did not hear the aircraft, but 'heard explosions' at 0015 and 'saw what appeared to be a ship on fire 12 miles west of the post at 0017', the fire being visible for five minutes.[128] North of Dunmore Head, Crohy Head LOP heard an aircraft to the south-west of the post at a distance of ten miles and heard two loud explosions, followed by 'fire on the surface in [the] same position'. The reports tallied, though not all posts agreed upon what had actually exploded, as the lack of an aircraft observation incorrectly led Dunmore Head to deduce that a ship had exploded.

Local police notified the captain of *Robert Hastie* about the explosions at 0120 on 6 February and they also made contact with the RAF at Castle Archdale. The initial response was telling of life in partitioned Ireland as Castle Archdale asked 'which police', to which the reply was 'Killybegs, notified by Rossan Point'. Critical here is that *Robert Hastie* was informed of the crash directly by the Killybegs gardaí and, contrary to orders, 'went to sea at once on hearing a vague report from the local police, without waiting for orders from Lough Erne'.[129] The channel of communication was supposed to be from Castle Archdale through the British Representative's Office and the Department of Defence. This would have wasted time and so the crew took matters into their own hands.

Reaching the scene of the crash at 0600 on 6 February *Robert Hastie* found nothing during a search in conjunction with an RAF Sunderland which lasted until 1510 on 7 February. Coastwatchers were told in advance of this operation, St John's Point LOP being informed that 'two British Sunderland flying boats will operate in vicinity of LOP (starting 0900 hrs) 7.2.42. LOP will report as usual'.[130] LOPs between Downpatrick Head and Dunmore Head sent in seventy-seven sightings of Sunderlands and Hudsons searching for survivors. Pieces of wreckage including an airman's lifejacket were washed up some days later on the Donegal coast. *Robert Hastie* would never have found any survivors

126 TNA AIR 2/4735, Tupholme to Rossmore, 13 Feb. 1942.   127 Ibid., memorandum Loss of Sunderland a/c 6.2.42.   128 Ibid., the lack of precision in timing between LOPs was due to the lack of complete synchronisation of clocks between LOPs.   129 Ibid., minute to Director General Air Safety, 19 Feb. 1942.   130 MA LOP 70, 6 Feb. 1942.

as an investigation concluded that 'the machine caught fire [and] had two major explosions visible 10 to 12 miles, and then burnt out on the water'.[131] None of the local LOPs heard a circling aircraft or saw distress flares; it is most likely that the aircraft flew straight into the sea.

Later searches by *Robert Hastie* also show the role of the Coast Watching Service in assisting the rescue vessel. The crash of a Lockheed Hudson (FH233) into the sea in the south of Donegal Bay during rough weather was reported by RAF Northern Ireland to the Air Ministry as having taken place five miles north-east of Lenadoon Point, Sligo, the location of LOP 66. The LOP reported that the aircraft sank in ten minutes and an initial report that one man got out was later discounted as all three crew were killed in the crash. Dublin gave permission for a surface and air search within Irish territorial waters but no wreckage was found. Coastwatchers continued to keep a careful eye on *Robert Hastie*, her movements made up a significant portion of Western Command/ Western Sector intelligence reports. The Irish authorities also co-operated with the British to assist the rescue boat, passing weather reports from around the Irish coast to the ship's captain as he was about to sail.

OVERFLIGHTS IN THE SECOND HALF OF 1941

By June 1941 overflights through Southern Command had settled into identifiable patterns. Aircraft spotted flying high and fast were en-route to objectives far out over the Atlantic. Local flights were of more interest to intelligence officers, particularly single aircraft sighted off the south coast at low altitude – on average between 200 and 800 feet, and on occasion as low as 50 feet, when 'the planes appeared to almost lick the surface'.[132] They indicated anti-shipping operations underway in the area. Though O'Hanrahan flagged the 'greater effort to evade our territory' made by these flights, and many were far off the coast and barely visible to LOPs, during June and July 1941 Ju-88s were regularly seen within half a mile of the Irish coast.[133] These German aircraft, whose release to operate as heavy fighters over the Atlantic Dönitz had recently obtained from a reluctant Hermann Göring, were assumed to be looking for British ships to attack as 'large numbers of Howth trawlers with Kinsale as headquarters have been fishing off the South coast [and] in no case was their activity interfered with'.[134] Nevertheless, their flights had repercussions for Irish-German relations. Henning Thomsen, the Chargé d'Affaires at the German legation, called to see the Boland on 15 July, telling him that between 1622 and 1627 on 22 June a German aircraft had noticed trawlers off Skibbereen which 'had new wireless aerials which they seemed to be using [and] judging

131 TNA AIR 2/4735, minute to Director General Air Safety, 19 Feb. 1942.   132 MA G2/X/315 Pt II, Southern Command Monthly Report, Dec. 1941.   133 Ibid., Southern Command, Monthly Report on Coastal Intelligence – July 1941.   134 Ibid., June 1941.

from the speed they were going they were not fishing'.[135] Boland was sceptical. Thomsen emphasized that he was not making 'any complaint or protest about this matter', he was merely bringing it to Boland's attention. The implication was that British Q-ships patrolling off the Irish coast were sending reports from within Irish waters. Boland judged Thomsen's intervention 'a rather curious one' and asked the Department of Defence to investigate.

Assistant Secretary at Defence Matt Beary based his response directly on information from the Coast Watching Service. Baltimore LOP reported a trawler of unknown nationality passing westwards just outside territorial waters at 1630 and at 1500 had observed a British trawler (LT647) two miles south of the post also heading west. This vessel subsequently entered Baltimore harbour. Baltimore saw a further unidentified trawler at 1945, heading west three miles south-east of the post. In the same area Mizen Head, Toe Head and Galley Head all logged single trawlers between 1740 and 1900 the same day. It would appear from the reports from LOPs that British trawlers were operating off the Cork coast near Skibbereen on the afternoon of 22 June. They passed close to or just inside territorial waters but Beary informed Boland that 'nothing suspicious was observed about either of these crafts'.[136] Defence did not think the information supplied by Thomsen was in any way suspicious. Vessels moving at speed were normal in the area as 'most trawlers sighted in that vicinity would be normally moving towards or returning from the usual fishing grounds off the S.W. coast'.[137] Beary added a further detail illustrating the value of the Coast Watching Service. LOPs between Galley Head in Cork and Forlorn Point in Wexford reported a German aircraft flying eastwards outside Irish territorial waters between 1625 and 1654 on 22 June. The details tallied exactly with Thomsen's reported times for the Luftwaffe aircraft which had seen the trawlers. The coastwatchers had acquitted themselves well and played an important role in this small chapter of wartime Irish–German relations.

From the late summer of 1941 into early autumn Southern Command noticed a 'progressive decline' in aerial activity along the south-west coast.[138] A handful of Ju-88s were among the few positively identified aircraft. One Ju-88 crash-landed at Belgooly, Kinsale on 26 August; the crew, none of whom were injured, destroyed the aircraft. Leutnant Rudolf Lauer told Gardaí who arrived at the scene that 'his plane was engaged by two Spitfires over our coast some distance out to sea.[139] With one engine shot out of action, the crew 'realised they could not return to Germany and decided to proceed to Eire'.[140] British Blenheims, Hudsons and Sunderlands were sighted off the south coast, but in reduced numbers. They often entered Irish territory, particularly around Cork Harbour.

135 NAI DFA Secretary's Files P47, Boland to Beary, 19 July 1941.   **136** Ibid., Beary to Boland, 31 July 1941.   **137** Ibid.   **138** MA G2/X/315 Pt II, Southern Command Monthly Report, Aug. 1941.   **139** NAI JUS 90/119/297, Nangle to Murphy, 27 Aug. 1941. **140** Ibid., Doyle to Murphy, 27 Aug. 1941.

Harbour. A British aircraft escorting an eastbound collier did so on 24 September, though staying far enough out to sea that 'it did not come within range of the anti-aircraft guns which were in readiness for action'.[141] A more sinister aircraft overflew Cork city just after midnight six weeks later. It was observed signalling K.A.I. by Morse lamp, an abbreviation of 'Kill All Irish', a term used as graffiti in Loyalist areas in Northern Ireland.

Flying conditions improved during September and, though 'there was nothing to hinder increased activity', the level of overflights and coastal flights remained unusually low.[142] With foreign trawlers present off the Irish coast and almost all aircraft observed being British or Allied, O'Hanrahan felt that 'this should normally call for increased German activity'.[143] But the Germans did not appear. In his report for October O'Hanrahan referred to 'the almost complete absence of rain, drizzle, fog, and all natural or phenomenal features that ordinarily act as deterrents to aircraft'.[144] Yet there were few flights reported. The question must have been raised as to whether the coastwatchers were at fault because O'Hanrahan continued that 'these conditions were also helpful to coast watchers and there is no reason to believe that the personnel of the LOPs were not continually vigilant'. Then, in November, aerial activity slowly began to increase despite the weather being 'almost uniformly bad' and heavy rain and strong south-west winds constituting 'a serious handicap to flying conditions'.[145] The rise in operations continued as Christmas 1941 approached and weather improved to 'facilitate both reconnaissance and patrol' flights, and, night flying, absent for some time, now returned.[146] Low-level patrolling off the south-west coast rose but figures never returned to the May peak. G2 never worked out a reason for the fluctuation in flight levels.

Unlike Southern Command, air patrolling increased in intensity in Western Command through September 1941 as 'routine patrols of British aircraft were observed off our North-West and Northern coasts daily'. In addition to the expected infringements around north-Donegal, incursions occurred across Galway, Mayo, Sligo and Leitrim 'in a north-easterly direction towards Northern Ireland, and were "short cuts" taken by British aircraft to their bases'.[147] Colonel Delamere's contacts in Northern Ireland had warned him to expect these developments and he told Archer that 'air activity will increase during the summer months [and] much of it will pass over our territory'.[148] The information given to the Irish to expect these flights suggests they were planned well in advance and were probably flights of aircraft being ferried across the Atlantic to Britain, a new development which will be covered in the following section.

141 MA G2/X/315 Pt II, Southern Command Monthly Report, Sept. 1941.   142 Ibid.
143 Ibid.   144 Ibid., Oct. 1941.   145 Ibid., Nov. 1941.   146 Ibid.   147 Ibid., Western
Command Monthly Report, Sept. 1941.   148 NAI DFA Secretary's Files A3, Archer to
Traynor, 27 Mar. 1941.

Month	August	September	October	November	December
Overflights	2,657	2,378	1,453	955	544

5.4: Overflights reported (Western Command): August–December 1941 (Source: MA G2/X series files)

With the exception of ferry flights, the decline in overflights first noted in Southern Command in late summer spread to Western Command by October with flights falling well 'below the normal average for the last few months'.[149] Routine patrolling continued at a reduced level. Termon Hill LOP reported a Coastal Command aircraft on 1 October as a 'British Whitley bomber' which passed nine miles west of the LOP at an estimated 2,000 feet and 'circled over B[lack] Rock lighthouse' before flying north.[150] Curiously, aircraft were not showing when convoys were sighted. Castle Archdale was unexpectedly quiet and 'the majority' of Atlantic patrols were 'carried out by aircraft stationed around Derry', a further sign of the growing role of Limavady and Ballykelly airbases.[151] The whole focus of battle seemed to have shifted much further north of Ireland. In December 1941 Western Command LOPs reported only 544 aircraft and 'no German activity by aircraft or submarines in the immediate vicinity of our North and North West Coasts'.[152] The end of 1941 saw quiet skies over Irish coastal waters, activity remained well down on late summer, sinkings were few and almost all of the activity observed was British. There was one new area monitored by coastwatchers. One that would, by 1942, vie with Coastal Command flights as the main of aerial activity along the Irish coast. That was overflights by aircraft of the newly formed Ferry Command striking inland on their landfall along the Mayo-Galway coast.

FERRY FLIGHTS

In July 1940 the Air Attaché at the British Embassy in Washington, Group Captain Pirie, asked George Woods-Humphrey, a former Director of Imperial Airways then resident in the United States, to form a team to ferry fifty Lockheed Hudson aircraft from the United States across the Atlantic Ocean to Britain. The RAF opposed the plan but the Ministry of Aircraft Production and its energetic head, Lord Beaverbrook, drove the proposal forward. Using civilian pilots, the embryonic ferrying organization, administered by Canadian Pacific Railway and known as its Air Service Department, formed at Montreal. The first

149 MA G2/X/315 Pt II, Western Command Monthly Report, Oct. 1941. **150** MA LOP 60, 1 Oct. 1941. **151** MA G2/X/315 Pt II, Western Command Monthly Report, Nov. 1941. **152** Ibid., Dec. 1941.

delivery flight left Gander on the evening of 10 November 1940 with Captain Don Bennett flying the lead aircraft. All seven aircraft arrived safely into Aldergrove in Northern Ireland. Bennett arrived first having descended 'through a fairly low cloud base with beautiful scenery below, and steamed round the north coast of Ireland at low level into Aldergrove'.[153] What was to become the Atlantic Ferry Organization (ATFERO) had achieved the first crossing of the North Atlantic by United States designed land planes: 'experts had reported that the Atlantic could not safely be flown in winter. "ATFERO" proved that it could.'[154] The regularity of ATFERO's activities, a product of wartime pressures, 'ushered in a dramatic new era in aviation'.[155]

On 20 July 1941 ATFERO was renamed Ferry Command, and placed under the former head of RAF Coastal Command, Air Chief Marshal Bowhill.[156] Ferried aircraft landed in Prestwick in Scotland or Aldergrove, and were regularly observed by coastwatchers in the last stages of their crossing. Aircraft making direct crossings used the UU7 radio beacon at Derrynacross on the northern shore of Lough Erne in Northern Ireland and could confirm their position visually over 'the rugged coast and dark, steep cliffs of north-east Ireland', a procedure which brought the aircraft across neutral Irish territory.[157] Ferry Command flights passed Achill Island, the Belmullet Peninsula and Malin Head, tracked by coastwatchers along that section of coast. Australian-born navigator John Butler Wood recalled using Tory Island and the Inishowen Peninsula as navigation waypoints.[158] Irish Lights controlled the radio navigation beacon on Tory Island. Colonel Delamere gathered from discussions with RAF Group Captain McDonald, whom he had met in Belfast and who visited Delamere when he was on leave in Dublin, that 'this station was of considerable importance to them, as British aircraft operating in the Atlantic used it for "homing" on'.[159] Because of German raids over Britain, most British beacons were turned off and there were almost no navigation aids available except those in neutral Ireland. Pilots came to rely on 'the one little marine beacon on Tory Island, a little rock off the north coast of Ireland. It came on ... for two minutes every twenty minutes and that was the one navigation [flights] could home on'.[160]

G2 understood the purpose of transatlantic Ferry Command flights almost as soon as they began. Through summer 1941 they pieced together information about these new flights collected from LOPs. First it was noticed that 'a much greater number fly East than West. This would lead one to believe that a large

153 D.C.T. Bennett, *Pathfinder: a war autobiography* (London, 1958), p. 106, quoted in Carl A. Christie, *Ocean bridge: the history of RAF ferry command* (Toronto, 1995) p. 55.   154 TNA AIR 24/205, Ferry Command Operations Record Book, p. 1.   155 John Butler Wood, *Uncharted skies* (Sydney, 1999), p. 216.   156 In March 1943 Ferry Command was incorporated into the newly formed RAF Transport Command and reduced in status to 45 (Transport) Group.   157 Wood, *Uncharted skies*, p. 89.   158 Ibid., p.107.   159 NAI DFA Secretary's Files A3, Delamere to Archer, 2 Apr. 1941.   160 Dr Patrick D. McTaggart-Cowan quoted in Christie, *Ocean bridge*, p. 54.

number of planes are being flown across the Atlantic and landing in Northern Ireland.'[161] The G2 officer at Foynes established that 'the number of planes now arriving in England from the USA was "incredible" – they were pouring in daily'.[162] G2 at Foynes also sighted American pilots who appeared to be returning to the United States after ferrying aircraft to Europe. Nine USAAF pilots with special passports and returning from Britain were 'very reticent' while in Ireland, though G2 learned from 'conversation with other passengers ... that they had been flying bombers from Canada and the US'.[163] Intelligence reports from Foynes through 1941 emphasized 'the very great number of American aircraft arriving by the Atlantic Ferry Service'.[164]

Proof of ferry flights was always welcome. On the morning of 21 July 1941, less than twenty-four hours after the commencement of Ferry Command operations, a Hudson with a crew of three landed at Roskeeragh Strand in Sligo. One of twelve that had left Newfoundland, it was running short of fuel and made a forced landing. The plane was unarmed but was carrying an unknown cargo in large wooden crates. However, it was soon refuelled and left quickly for Limavady without the interference of the Irish authorities. Less fortunate was a 'trans-Atlantic aircraft' that went missing off the Irish coast on 1 September 1941. At 2020 Mayo and Galway LOPs received a message from the military at Castlebar that 'a British bomber on flight from Canada to Scotland is overdue and [has] possibly landed in Ireland, keep a sharp look out and report immediately to Castlebar'.[165] The aircraft was Liberator AM915 which crashed on Arinarach Hill, Campbeltown, Scotland, killing the crew of four and six passengers. These included military officers, technical personnel, Count Baillet la Tour, Economic Counsellor to the Belgian Ministry for Colonies, and R.B. Mowat, Professor of History at Bristol University, who was returning from lecturing in the United States.[166] A phial of radium on board was never recovered. Maffey wrote to de Valera on 8 September on behalf of the Air Ministry to convey their 'grateful thanks ... for the prompt co-operation of the Eire authorities' in searching for the plane. But the secrecy of the Irish involvement is evident from a marginal note by Walshe's private secretary Sheila Murphy that Maffey's letter was 'the only written communication on this subject. Everything else was arranged by telephone.'[167]

Dublin was anxious to suppress knowledge of Irish involvement in aiding ferry flights. On 28 August 1941 the *New York Times* published a detailed account by the British Ministry of Aircraft Production of the delivery flight of a Liberator from Newfoundland to Ireland. The Irish Minister in Washington,

161 MA G2/X/315 Pt II, Western Command Monthly Report, July 1941.   162 NAI DFA Secretary's Files A8, Reports from IO at Shannon Airport, Foynes. Period 3rd–8th July, 1941, 12 July 1941.   163 Ibid., Period: 9th–29th July, 1941, 30 July 1941.   164 Ibid., Period: August 1941.   165 MA LOP 60, 1 Sept. 1941.   166 TNA AIR 15/505, p. 8.   167 NAI DFA Secretary's Files A10, marginal note by Murphy on Maffey to de Valera, 8 Sept. 1941.

Robert Brennan, sent a telegram to Dublin giving the details and adding that the 'places of landing in Ireland [were] not stated'.[168] This gave the impression that flights were landing in neutral Ireland. This was uncomfortably close to the truth. Hudson AE577, en-route to Prestwick in Scotland from Gander, landed at Baldonnell on 27 September and was secretly refuelled before proceeding. The aircraft crashed at Jenkinstown near Dundalk, killing the crew of three. By the autumn of 1941 the majority of inland flights over the west and north of Ireland were ferry flights, like the ill-fated AE577, coming in from the west and flying to the north-east 'across Galway, Mayo, Donegal to Northern Ireland'.[169]

EASTERN AND CURRAGH COMMANDS

LOPs in Eastern and Curragh Commands reported widespread belligerent air activity through 1941. As marine activity off the east coast declined, they reported these air incursions directly to ADC in Dublin Castle, rather than to G2. The Holyhead to Dún Laoghaire mail boat was often attacked by German aircraft. One vessel on the route, *Cambria*, had been strafed and bombed by a German aircraft on 18 December 1940; the third officer was killed and two female passengers injured. The region from Tuskar Rock west to the Saltee Islands and Waterford became a regular hunting ground for German aircraft strafing and bombing local shipping. Coastwatchers saw two large oil tankers on fire fifteen to twenty miles south of Tuskar Rock on 2 April 1941. The skies from Wexford town and around the coast past Rosslare to Kilmore Quay saw continual overflights by both British and German aircraft through the year, with a number of crashes of He-111 bombers in the Carnsore area. A more unusual encounter in Curragh Command was a dogfight between two seaplanes and two fighters, all of unknown nationality, observed ten miles or so south-east of Forlorn Point LOP. One of the fighters was shot down by the seaplane but the Kilmore Quay lifeboat found neither survivors nor wreckage.

German aircraft attacked the Rosslare to Fishguard mail boat *St Patrick* five miles south east of Tuskar Rock on 13 May. Though the ship was damaged there were no injuries to passengers or crew. Commandant Mackey, OC G2 Curragh Command, reported to Archer that the crew members who arrived in Rosslare were interviewed by his staff but were 'not inclined to give any information. Army and Garda have endeavoured to get statements from them but they are very reticent'.[170] A Ju-88 attacked the Limerick Steamship Company's *Kyleclare* off Brownstown Head, Waterford on 30 May. A bomb exploding in the water near the ship caused extensive damage to plating and the ship made for Waterford where repairs were carried out. When on 18 June a German aircraft

168 NAI DFA Secretary's Files P12/6, Brennan to Estero, 28 Aug. 1941.   169 MA G2/X/315 Pt II, Western Command Monthly Report, Aug. 1941.   170 MA G2/X/423 Pt II, Mackey to Archer, 16 June 1941.

spotted *Hull*, trading between Cork and Glasgow, it dropped four bombs on the ship which did not explode. *Hull* opened fire on the attacking aircraft but as the vessel entered Irish waters the plane halted its attack and withdrew, showing an awareness of the geographical limits to offensive action by some Luftwaffe crews. This was not so immediately evident when the British trader *Skerries* was attacked off the Waterford coast three miles south of Ram Head LOP. Though nearing Irish territorial waters the aircraft did not call off its attack, only ceasing when *Skerries* replied with machine-gun fire. Volunteer Thomas Monsell who was on duty outside Ram Head LOP reported that he

> heard the noise of [a] plane coming from the south, a few minutes later I saw a plane about 100 feet high and about ½ mile south-east of steamer. I then heard noise of ships serine [*sic*]. The plane was then turning west. A few seconds later the first bomb fell about 50 feet on the starboard side of the ship, the second fell 50 feet further west. I then heard the noise of machine-gun fire coming from the ship, and saw the splash of buletts [*sic*] in the water behind the plane as she was going west. The ship at this time was slowed down and keeping on her coarse [*sic*], the plane went on west.[171]

Such sporadic attacks continued through the summer and early autumn but it was not until October that the level of attacks rose again off the south-east coast. The Norwegian vessel *Rask* departed Cork alone bound for Newport, Wales on the afternoon of 19 October. That evening off Tuskar Rock three German aircraft attacked the vessel with bombs, all of which missed the ship. *Rask* was armed with machine-guns and returned fire, dispersing the aircraft. Two of the aircraft were believed hit. The third aircraft returned about twenty minutes later and while it was flying low over the ship a powerful explosion occurred underneath the bridge, causing the engine to stop and *Rask* turned over to port and sank. Five survivors landed at Ballyconnigar. Five, in the ship's second lifeboat with the bodies of seven dead, were rescued by the British vessel *Wallace Rose*, which also picked up three bodies from the sea, landing them at Rosslare.[172] On the evening of 25 October *Glenageary*, carrying a cargo of coal, was attacked at low-level to the north of Rosslare by a single German aircraft. The damage to the ship was slight and there were no casualties. Bryan considered it 'extremely difficult – if not impossible' for the attacking aircraft to have recognized the Irish markings on the ship which was lit only with side-lights.[173] The Master of the ship later stated that he zig-zagged the ship before it was attacked, an un-neutral action which Walshe considered to be 'only

171 Ibid., Monsell to IO Southern Command, 23 June 1941. 172 NAI DFA 206/79, Butler to Garvin, 20 Oct. 1941. 173 NAI DFA Secretary's Files P18, The recent bombing of our ships, 12 Nov. 1941.

looking for trouble'.[174] Greenore LOP witnessed an attack at close range the following day when the 398-ton British freighter *Empire Daffodil* opened fire on a German He-111 while within Irish territorial waters. Volunteers Butler and O'Gorman saw the vessel 'open fire on [the] plane with tracer bullets and [the] plane return fire with light green tracers' whilst simultaneously dropping bombs, but *Empire Daffodil* escaped undamaged.[175] The Limerick Steamship Company's *Lanahrone* was attacked, but not hit, one-and-a-half miles north-west of the Saltee Islands on 29 October. She had full illuminated Irish markings, though her lights were switched off at the commencement of the attack. When Walshe contacted Hempel in the aftermath of further attacks on the Irish vessels *Glencree* and *Glenageary* he was told that Germany had 'never given any guarantee that Irish ships plying between England and Ireland would be free from attack'.[176] Dolefully Walshe concluded: 'no doubt, as the war gets nearer to its crisis, the Irish Sea will be come as dangerous for our shipping as the French and Dutch Waters are for German shipping'.[177]

Coastwatchers' reports on these attacks showed G2 that they had identified a limited area of operations where German forces attacked coastal shipping located roughly between Waterford Harbour and Tuskar Rock. Despite these attacks, by the autumn of 1941 a small number of convoys had returned to southern routes, being visible from the LOPs on the Cork and Kerry coastlines and to a lesser extent those around Wexford and Waterford. Aware of attacks on shipping off the Wexford and Waterford coast, convoys spotted by LOPs along the Cork and Kerry coast were rarely seen by LOPs in Curragh Command, indicating that they kept further south from the Irish coast for reasons other than the St George's Channel minefield.

CONCLUSION

The battle of the Atlantic off Ireland settled into an established pattern through 1941 and so too did the work of the coastwatchers monitoring its course. The main centre of conflict had moved from the north-western Irish coast into the mid-Atlantic gap, leaving a more localized scenario close to Ireland that did not always reflect the trend of the wider battle. Eastern Command coastwatchers concentrated on co-operation with ADC to augment the defence of Dublin against air attack, Curragh Command kept a look out for aircraft operating against local shipping and Southern Command coastwatchers sought to record Luftwaffe overflights and Coastal Command reconnaissance along the Cork and Kerry coast. The focus of coast watching remained in Western Command which recorded substantial air and marine activity off the Inishowen peninsula and the

174 Ibid., Walshe to Ferguson, 6 Jan. 1942.   175 MA G2/X/423 Pt II, Butler to Mackey, 27 Oct. 1941.   176 NAI DFA Secretary's Files P18, The recent bombing of our ships, 12 Nov. 1941.   177 Ibid.

north Donegal coast and from Donegal Bay west around the 'north-Mayo corner' to Achill Island, an area that by the end of the year was largely associated with the landfall of ferry flights. G2 were now reasonably certain that they could estimate what could, or indeed should, happen at any given point around the Irish coastline. With this overview in place, it was easier for G2 to establish strategic changes to Allied and German plans, such as occurred when coastal flights declined in the second half of 1941 and ferry flights began.

As far as British-Irish relations were concerned, 1941 saw the last attempt by London to use the southern Irish ports. The increased use of Lough Foyle and Derry and the nearby Northern Irish air bases reflect the focus of battle off the north-west coast and in the mid-Atlantic. Berehaven became strategically redundant and the Shannon estuary lost its attraction as the Derry bases rose in importance. The deliberately understated purpose of the Donegal air corridor shows the increased role air power was playing in the Atlantic theatre. Allied aircraft were transiting Irish airspace with de Valera's agreement. Through the air corridor from Lough Erne Britain had obtained the access to Irish territory for her air forces that de Valera would never allow for British naval forces through the treaty ports. Arguably, the war in the Atlantic might have been very different had it not been for the existence of the air corridor.

By autumn 1941 Britain was more optimistic about the course of the war in the Atlantic. G2 learned from a conversation between intelligence officers at Foynes and Conor Carrigan of the public relations branch of the Dominions Office, and from its MI5 connections, that 'the Battle of the Atlantic has now taken a definite turn for the better, and the pessimism of six months ago has almost entirely disappeared'.[178] Winston Churchill, writing after the end of the war, described July 1940 to July 1941 as the year 'when we could claim the British Battle of the Atlantic was won'.[179] That was an optimistic position written in retrospect; there were still almost four years of conflict remaining.

178 NAI DFA Secretary's Files A8, report from Carrigan, attached to Bryan to Walshe, 21 Oct. 1941.   179 Allen, *Storm*, p. 90.

CHAPTER SIX

Coast Watching Service operations with Air Defence Command

BY 1941 THE MAJORITY of incidents reported by coastwatchers along the Irish east coast were overflights of belligerent aircraft. In these cases, coastwatchers reported directly to ADC headquarters in Dublin. LOPs from Ballagan Point south to Ram Head in Waterford were linked into ADC's early warning and air observer system. Their reports enabled ADC to order Air Corps fighters to scramble to intercept incoming aircraft. When, on 13 April 1940, Kilmichael, Dalkey and Rush LOPs sighted unidentified aircraft off the east coast, aircraft from Baldonnell sent to investigate concluded that the incoming aircraft were escorting a convoy rather than posing a threat to Irish neutrality.[1] As fuel supplies grew scarce, such patrols grew less frequent and instead the coastwatchers warned ADC to ready the few anti-aircraft guns ringed around Dublin to defend the capital against attack from the air. Before looking in detail at the role of the Coast Watching Service in assisting ADC, it is helpful to set the context by examining Irish air defence planning in the run up to the Second World War.

PLANNING IRISH AIR DEFENCE, 1938–41

On 21 September 1938, spurred by the Sudeten crisis, a meeting presided over by the Taoiseach and Acting Minister for Defence, Eamon de Valera, discussed the glaring inadequacies in Irish air defence, particularly the lack of defences for Dublin city. De Valera was 'anxious to put Irish defences into a good state, as he did not want to be "caught napping" if there was trouble in Europe.'[2] He referred to the need to buy sixteen 3.7-inch anti-aircraft guns with ammunition at a cost of £340,000 and forty-four searchlights at an additional cost of £96,000 for the defence of central Dublin. The separate purchase of sixty-four Bofors light anti-aircraft guns for airfield defence and the defence of other strategic sites would cost an additional £300,000.[3] These were, for the time, plans to purchase state of the art equipment and de Valera deserves credit for initiating a far-sighted debate. But he did not take any further initiative to develop the plan. A

1 MA DRS 183, 15 Apr. 1940.   2 TNA DO 35/894/10, memorandum by MacDonald of meeting with Walshe and Dulanty, 12 Oct. 1938.   3 £340,992 was sanctioned on 10 Mar. 1939 for sixty-four Bofors guns. The War Office in London told the Department of Defence to order immediately to expedite delivery.

further meeting on 21 September degenerated into a discussion on 'the wisdom of taking a decision now to spend all this money on anti-aircraft guns which might leave us short as regards other essential items of defence'.[4] The full order for anti-aircraft equipment was not placed.

The plans to purchase large numbers of anti-aircraft weapons show that de Valera envisaged a policy of armed neutrality. The failure to follow through on this decision meant that Dublin was inadequately defended during the Second World War. While much of the blame should be laid with the Department of Defence because of the sheer ineptitude of their handling of the Army re-organization scheme, the Department of Finance should also share the blame for Ireland's weak defences on the outbreak of the Second World War. In light of the apparent success of the Munich agreement, the Secretary of the Department of Finance, James J. McElligott, advocated that 'Defence should revise their plans with a view to curtailing expenditure and that they should try as far as possible to spread the expenditure over a period of years in order to ease the burden on the Exchequer'.[5] McElligott told his colleague Walter Doolin that he had

> reiterated the plea so often made from this Department for a clear statement of defence policy and a full estimate of the cost of giving effect to that policy. I feel we must keep hammering at this if we are to get anywhere with the Department of Defence.[6]

By Christmas 1938 the Defence Forces possessed only four obsolete 3-inch anti-aircraft guns of 1914-vintage. The delivery of more modern weapons was not expected until March 1939, leaving a deficiency of sixteen guns on the number deemed necessary for effective defence. A total of 4,899 rounds were in stock for the 3-inch guns, with a further 3,842 on order, creating a potential stock of 8,741 and leaving a deficiency of 21,259 rounds. Procuring anti-aircraft weaponry now took on the highest priority for the Defence Forces. In January 1939 when Finance began examining the Army Re-organisation Scheme, a change in that Department's thinking was evident. McElligott's colleague C.S. Almond took the steps that Defence was incapable of taking and drew up the rudiments of an Irish defence policy. Almond began that 'the possibility of our taking the offensive against any other country may, I take it, be ruled out'.[7] He concluded that the 'immediate problem' was to devise 'a scheme of defence against air attacks'.[8] While 'attack from the air would probably be infrequent and spasmodic' as aircraft attacking Ireland would first have to pass over British territory and seas, Ireland still required 'an adequate air force, adequate anti-

4 NAI DF S4/7/39, minute by McElligott, 21 Sept. 1938.   5 Ibid.   6 Ibid., continuation of minute.   7 Ibid., Almond to Doolin, 2 Jan. 1939.   8 Ibid., Defence Estimates, 16 Jan. 1939, a revise of Almond to Doolin, 2 Jan. 1939.

aircraft armaments with ancillary services such as searchlights, and a full development of ARP'.[9] Almond condemned Defence for being unable to prepare such a scheme and criticized the department for instead demanding 'a miniature army ... equipped in all its branches'. He wanted the re-organization scheme to be 'completely revised so that it will concentrate mainly on air defence'. This did not please Defence who demanded 'a proper balance between the energy and money we spend on the development of land forces, coastal forces, air forces, and ARP'.[10] This fundamental disagreement further contributed to the slow pace of rearmament.

Though the required equipment was lacking, a reasonably detailed air defence and air observation system for Dublin existed on paper from just prior to the outbreak of the Second World War. Vulnerable areas had been identified but the plan to defend them assumed the availability of an adequate number of anti-aircraft guns and searchlights. If orders for anti-aircraft guns had been placed with British firms in 1938 they would have been completed before the summer of 1940. After the fall of France, Britain refused supplies of arms and equipment to Ireland. Four months of procrastination following the Munich agreement and three months of wrangling between the Department of Finance and the Department of Defence slowed Ireland's rearmament policy to a snail's pace. When orders for 3.7-inch guns and Bofors guns were finally submitted in the late spring of 1939 the orders were caught up in the outbreak of war and the equipment was diverted to the British war effort. Thus, Ireland entered the war poorly armed and with 'puny resources' to defend herself from air attack.[11]

Eighty-four anti-aircraft guns and seventy-four searchlights were finally ordered but their full complement was never delivered. Attempts to purchase equivalent weapons in the United States failed. When defence plans were put into operation, ADC knew it had only four 3-inch anti-aircraft guns and four searchlights. De Valera's July 1939 comment that 'in this country we had delayed too long in making adequate defence plans' was now proven correct.[12] The fear of aerial attack on Irish cities was very real in the minds of senior Irish foreign policy makers in August 1939. When Walshe formally informed Hempel of Ireland's desire to remain neutral, it was a bombing raid on Dublin or Cork that Walshe had in mind as the event that would bring Ireland into the war. He told the German Minister that 'a definite attack, for example dropping bombs on Irish towns' would see Ireland abandon its neutral position.[13] Ireland's limited air defences concentrated on defending Dublin and the region surrounding the Foynes seaplane base, Rineanna airport, Limerick port and the Ardnacrusha power station. For the first months of the Second World War Ireland had no

9 Ibid.   10 Ibid., memorandum by the Department of Defence, Defence Estimate, 21 Jan. 1939.   11 MA G2/X/293, Rooney to Archer, undated, but April 1940.   12 NAI DF S4/7/39, minute by Almond, 18 July 1939.   13 *DGFP D: VII*, p. 311, Hempel to Foreign Ministry, Berlin, 26 Aug 1939.

force capable of meeting any form of aerial attack. Matters would only improve slightly through 1940.

An invasion of Ireland looked likely in the weeks following the German invasion of France. When the Cabinet met on 17 May 1940 in a two-and-a-quarter hour session it ordered the Anti-Aircraft Brigade of the Army to be put on its war establishment. This was little enough and looked much better on paper than in reality. In a further attempt to bolster anti-aircraft defences, authority was given for 'the immediate procurement, so far as practicable' of sixty Bofors-40 light anti-aircraft guns with 100,000 rounds of ammunition and sixteen 3.7-inch heavy anti-aircraft guns with 10,000 rounds of ammunition.[14] Bofors guns for airfield defence were the more important of the two, being seventh in a list of sixteen items urgently required by the Defence Forces in May 1940. Bren guns, radio equipment and anti-tank rifles were the highest priority, with 3.7-inch guns and searchlights in tenth and eleventh position.[15] De Valera and Dulanty pleaded with limited success for Britain to release these weapons to Ireland.

The Defence Forces mounted extensive anti-aircraft artillery training during the early summer of 1940 with what equipment they had available. The air-defence situation did improve somewhat over the next few months. On 26 July 1940 Britain released a limited amount of military equipment to Ireland, including anti-aircraft guns and searchlights. The War Office delivered 8,502 rounds of ammunition for the 3.7-inch guns on 22 and 23 August along with a mere 1,006 rounds of Bofors ammunition. Four 3.7-inch guns arrived on 6 September and a request for further 3.7-inch guns with ammunition and search-lights appeared on a list given to Maffey on 16 September. Between May and November 1940 Dublin had fourteen guns of all types in use. Swansea in Wales, by comparison, had by February 1941 eighteen guns and by the spring of 1941 Belfast had twenty-four heavy guns and fourteen light guns, half of its approved strength. As these comparisons show, Dublin remained seriously under-defended from aerial attack and, as one British source put it, 'thinking people visualise uneasily what would be the effect of a serious air raid on the city'.[16]

The control of Irish air defence evolved in a piecemeal manner. By January 1941 ADC covered the entirety of Eastern Command and Curragh Command and the sections of Western Command in Longford and Westmeath. No definite terms of reference on status, responsibility or control were issued. This caused difficulties when the OC Eastern Command decided that for operations within

14 NAI DT CAB 2/3 (G.C. 2/169), 17 May 1940. Seven infantry battalions (1st, 2nd, 3rd, 4th, 5th, 7th, and 9th) as well as the 1st and 2nd Field Companies of Engineers, the 1st and 2nd Field Ambulances and all drivers were also mobilized. Two thousand men were to be mobilized and a further 3,000 men, to be called up subject to further consultation with the government, were added to this figure at a meeting on 18 May. 15 NAI DFA Secretary's Files A1, list attached to Boland to Beary, 1 May 1940. 16 TNA ADM 223/486, Irish

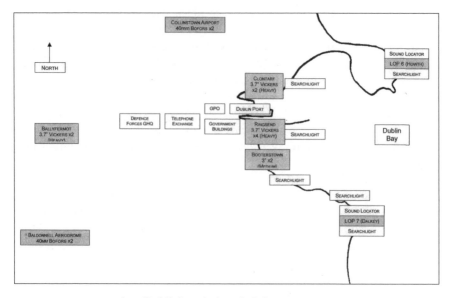

6.1: Dublin's anti-aircraft defences, 1940–1

the Eastern Command area ADC was responsible to him, but that as ADC boundaries ran outside the Eastern Command area general air defence policy was a matter for GHQ. A memorandum from January 1941 revealed further confusion as 'no plan for the co-ordination of air defence, air intelligence or passive air measures was ever sanctioned'.[17] The Air Corps and the Dublin Anti-Aircraft Battalion co-ordinated operations 'through mutual arrangement'; it was a situation that, while workable, was 'not the sort of organisation that would stand up to active service conditions'.[18] Indeed, on several occasions gunners had opened fire on Air Corps aircraft. Not until early May 1941 was an attempt made to develop air defence on a nationwide basis from the Eastern Sector to the remainder of the country by establishing reporting centres at Cork, Limerick, Waterford and Athlone, though this would take time to come into operation.

Colonel Delamere, OC ADC, also had differences of opinion with Archer over the role of ADC. Delamere was annoyed that by December 1940 ADC was 'mainly concerned with collecting and tabulating air intelligence for the G2 branch'.[19] G2, Delamere scathingly continued, were 'concerned with the collection of air information for External Affairs and government purposes generally, operational deductions do not appear to be made by any branch of the general staff'. A volunteer observer corps system had been turned down as to establish special posts would have been costly and would necessitate the installation of many new phone lines. The air observer system was instead built

Affairs, 13 Oct. 1940.   **17** MA ADC 1/2, Air Defence Command, 18 Jan. 1941.   **18** Ibid.
19 Ibid., Notes for conference with Assistant Chief of Staff by Commandant Delamere, 16

around the LOPs of the Coast Watching Service and Garda stations. It relied 'solely on what can be seen and heard by the observers'.[20] They were an organized body with the required skills and their involvement in air observation would cost nothing. To Delamere it was 'the best organised net that could at short notice, give night and day service'.[21]

ANTI-AIRCRAFT WEAPONS AND THE DEFENCE OF DUBLIN CITY

Before moving on to look at the role of the Coast Watching Service in this piecemeal air defence system, this section looks at the types of equipment in use by ADC. This is necessary in order to explain in later sections how the Coast Watching Service operated in conjunction with ADC. There were heavy and medium guns in operation around Dublin city as well as heavy and light machine-guns. The heavy guns were the modern Vickers 3.7-inch, delivered in September 1940, though with only 4,500 rounds, compared to the required 10,000. The medium guns were obsolete First World War vintage 3-inch weapons. These defended against high-level attack from targets at or above 10,000 feet. The modern Bofors-40 defended against low-level attack from targets at or below 500 feet. The problem was not this equipment, which with the exception of the 3-inch guns was modern, but the low numbers of each gun at the disposal of the Defence Forces, a situation which had arisen because of the slow procurement process.

The Vickers 3.7-inch heavy anti-aircraft gun, a British design of which Ireland initially possessed six, entered production in 1937, with the first guns being delivered for British use in January 1938. The gun became the backbone of Britain's defences during the battle of Britain; 'extremely advanced for their time ... by the middle of the war, [the 3.7 inch gun] was one of the best guns of its type in the world'.[22] Firing up to eight rounds a minute it had an effective ceiling of between 25,000 and 32,000 feet. In Dublin the few 3.7-inch guns available were deployed at Ringsend Park in a half-battery of four guns, divided into two sections, and in a pair at Clontarf in a patch of waste ground behind Brian Boru Street and Conquer Hill, beside the tram depot. Together the two sites protected Dublin's port and docks from aerial attack. The port area, the oil depot on the North Wall and the Pigeon House electricity generating station were vulnerable points judged to be in need of protection. These were also the facilities that the British would use to resupply their forces in the event of their being called in to assist the Irish Defence Forces in resisting a German invasion of Ireland.[23] The guns also protected strategic sites in central Dublin such as

Dec. 1940. **20** TNA AIR 2/7233, extract from RAF Wireless Intelligence Service Summary No. 14, 21 Apr. 1941. **21** MA ADC 1/2, memorandum by Delamere, Air Defence Observation System, 5 Feb. 1941. **22** See www.hypospace.net/equipment/AA%Guns.htm (accessed 3 Aug. 2004). **23** From May 1941 Britain had detailed maps and information on

Government Buildings, Defence Forces GHQ at Parkgate Street, the telegraph and broadcasting station at the GPO, the Bank of Ireland on College Green and Crown Alley telephone exchange.[24] The positioning of the guns suggests that an air attack was expected across Dublin Bay using the line of the River Liffey as the landmark for a bombing run.

The 3.7-inch guns were placed about a mile away from the strategic points they were defending. They were not necessarily expected to shoot down attacking planes, 'their main effect was to disrupt attacks and thereby reduce their accuracy'.[25] During the battle of Britain anti-aircraft-gunners rarely shot down planes and protection against accurate attack was their main task. Anti-aircraft fire aimed to 'disturb the aim and deter the faint hearted. The number of planes shot down is by no means the only measure of anti-aircraft efficiency and value'.[26] The placing of four guns in a half-battery at Ringsend, as opposed to Clontarf, indicates that the attack on Dublin was expected from a southerly direction. In December 1940 Delamere considered 'that the most likely direction of approach to our coast will be from the South East, South and South West'.[27] In other words, it would come from the Luftwaffe.

When establishing the Ringsend battery the Army took over a considerable portion of Ringsend Park and turned the area into a small barracks. While the gun position was surrounded by barbed wire, the park area was not out of bounds to civilians. In addition to the four guns, the range and height finder and the predictor set, there was an L-shaped group of Nissen huts in which the regular soldiers attached to the battery lived. John Donnelly, who lived in the Coastguard Station on Pigeon House Road and later served in the Irish Navy, remembered being on the way to school one morning and hearing the guns in Ringsend Park being fired for the first time as an unidentified plane passed overhead. There was panic and he and others were herded into a house on the outskirts of the park and sent downstairs into a basement air raid shelter.[28] But when a British Spitfire and an unidentified German aircraft came tumbling and turning 'just like seagulls' in a dogfight over Ringsend and down the line of the River Liffey the guns stayed silent. Donnelly recalled hearing only the machine-guns of the aircraft as they fired at each other as they flew back out to sea. Bob Donaldson, an LDF Volunteer who lived on Cambridge Avenue near to Ringsend Park, remembered the guns always being synchronized and ready for

the main ports in Ireland. It had been provided with the agreement of de Valera on the grounds that 'if they wanted to go to the trouble, the British could get all the information without having recourse to us' (NAI DFA Secretary's Files, A8, Walshe to Archer, 14 May 1941).   **24** NAI DT S11403, List of guards on vulnerable points in the Eastern Command area, 13 Apr. 1940.   **25** Alfred Price and Darko Pavlovic, *Britain's air defences 1939–45* (Oxford, 2004), p. 9. The technical data in this section comes from this source.   **26** Ministry of Information, *Roof over Britain: the official story of Britain's anti-aircraft defences, 1939–1942* (London, 1943), p. 7.   **27** MA ADC 1/2, memorandum by Delamere, 12 Dec. 1940. **28** Phone conversation with John Donnelly, Dublin, 9 Dec. 2004.

action. But even when the predictor, of which he was the operator, tracked a target, the order would not always be given by the gunnery officer to open fire. Donaldson recalled a British Coastal Command Sunderland flying boat which, as a slow moving aircraft he had little difficulty targeting, being within their zone of fire but being left to proceed unhindered as it was clear that the pilot had lost his bearings on return from an Atlantic patrol.[29]

An air attack on a specific target such as Dublin's port and docks would be through a pattern bombing attack where the aircraft entered their bombing run straight and level at between 8,000 and 16,000 feet. At least two miles from the target they would close formation, with the bomb aimer in the lead aircraft dropping his bombs and leading the other aircraft to the target zone. ARP exercises in 1941 anticipated that Dublin would be 'attacked by a large number of aircraft flying over the city in successive waves' over a one hour period. The raid would be 'widespread' though 'the main weight of the attack' would be 'directed at certain selected points', dropping a possible 77,000 pounds of high explosive and 9,500 pounds of incendiary bombs.[30] Two thousand casualties were anticipated in this exercise, with the core of the attack being 'directed at the port and central city area'. Though few in number and unlikely to put up sustained resistance against waves of aircraft (the 1941 exercise anticipated that of the fifty aircraft attacking Dublin, two would be shot down), the 3.7-inch guns could engage with a target up to six-and-a-half miles away. In Dublin, this was approximately between Howth Head to the north-east and Killiney Hill in Dalkey to the south-east, the eastern limits of the no-fly zone over the city. On each of these headlands was, as will be described below, the capital's short-range early warning system of a LOP, a sound locator and a searchlight. These would visually and electronically track the target while it was outside gun range while the gun crews would train their weapons on a predicted aiming point ahead of the target aircraft.[31] When the attacking aircraft crossed into the six-and-a-half mile radius of the gun's engagement, roughly by flying over Dublin Bay, the gun crews could open fire, the troops being trained that they would have thirty seconds to engage the aircraft. As bombs had a 'forward throw', to strike Dublin's port and docks they would have to be released up to a mile and a half from their target.[32] As their bombing run would be at least two miles, the aircraft attacking Dublin would be in formation when they were over Dublin Bay or had passed the coast over Howth or Dalkey. By this time they would, if all went to plan on the defending Irish side, have been tracked by LOPs along the coast and gun crews would be ready to meet them.

29 Phone conversation with Bob Donaldson, Dublin, 13 Dec. 2004. **30** NAI 97/9/208, Report on Combined Exercise, Dublin ARP Service-Sunday, 6th July, 1941. **31** Price and Pavlovic, *Britain's air defences*, p. 10. The measurements and tactical descriptions used are taken from this source, in particular the section entitled 'Principles of siting heavy anti-aircraft guns'. **32** Ibid. Defined as 'the distance they [the bombs] travelled forward, between release

Supporting the 3.7-inch heavy guns were the four medium 3-inch guns which were deployed at Ballyfermot Hill, in the Trimleston Estate at Booterstown and later at Stillorgan. They were over twenty-five years old and in Britain were regarded by 1940 as being 'quite unfit to be employed'.[33] Ireland could not be so choosey. These old guns had rapid rates of traverse and elevation. Light and mobile they had good rates of fire at 20 to 25 rounds per minute. Depending on the charge, which was usually high explosive or shrapnel, their effective ceiling was between 14,000 feet and 23,500 feet. These guns remained in Ballyfermot until the late spring of 1942 when they were transferred to Dublin airport. Ballyfermot then received a battery of four 3.7-inch guns housed in concrete emplacements but by this date the danger of aerial attack on Dublin had diminished greatly.

The most modern weapons at the disposal of ADC were four Swedish-designed Bofors-40s. Initial plans had been to order sixty-four of these guns and to make them automatic firing from 'remote control power from predictors'.[34] Two of the four guns eventually delivered were deployed at Baldonnell aerodrome and two at the newly constructed Collinstown airport. Both were fire-controlled by manual sights. With a ceiling of 10,000 feet they were quick firing, delivering 120 rounds per minute. Light and mobile, they had the power to knock down aircraft of any size but were especially effective against dive bombers. The objective of these guns was to disrupt an attacker during their bombing run.

Less effective, but used in short-range anti-aircraft and airfield defence, were the Hotchkiss and Vickers heavy machine-guns and the Lewis light machine-gun. With this final category of weapons it was necessary to hit the pilot, the engine or a control surface. The most famous aerial casualty of the Lewis gun was Manfred von Richtofen, the Red Baron. The French-made Hotchkiss first entered use in 1909. It had design flaws, in particular the use of a magazine strip instead of a belt feed in early models. Even with a belt feed the gun was unable to meet its maximum rate of fire of 600 rounds per minute. Although a First World War vintage, the Hotchkiss was used by the French until the end of the Second World War and variations of the design were used by Britain and the United States. The Vickers gun was the standard British machine-gun in the early years of World War One. It could fire 600 rounds of .303 ammunition per minute with a range of 4,500 yards. Being water-cooled it could fire continuously for long periods of time. The United States-made Lewis gun was first developed in 1911 and, firing .303 ammunition, was the standard British infantry support weapon on the Western Front in the First World War. It was air-cooled and could fire 500–600 rounds a minute to a range of 600 yards. Light and easy to handle, mounted on a tripod it was available for rapid use in anti-aircraft defence. By 1943 it was still judged effective and had 'brought down many low-flying raiders who sought by diving from the cloud to surprise the defences'.[35]

and impact.'   **33** Gilbert, *Churchill war papers*, p. 705, Churchill to Admiral Phillips, 30 Jan. 1940.   **34** NAI DF S4/7/39, MacMahon to McElligott, 31 July 1939.   **35** Ministry of

This motley array of equipment of varying age, reliability and effectiveness was not ideal defence against the Dorniers and Heinkels of the Luftwaffe. As the war progressed it was not augmented by add-on new technology. This was particularly true for the 3.7-inch guns, which were adapted by Britain for automatic firing and radar control. Had the finances been available for the purchase of such technology by Dublin, it is unlikely that the Allies would have parted with such resources to Ireland. It was not until the 1950s that the Irish Defence Forces obtained gun-laying radar with automatic fire control.[36] This paucity of equipment meant that ADC had to be smart when allocating its anti-aircraft weapons. Delamere sought to defend Dublin by integrating the meagre stock of weapons available with an early warning system, making the best use of the terrain around Dublin and gambling that an attack would come from the south. He could also rely on his men, who used hold 'sweeps' to bet 'who would shoot down something first'.[37]

LOPS, SEARCHLIGHTS AND SOUND DETECTORS

If ADC in Dublin had little chance of successfully downing enemy aircraft over the city, there was at least a system in place to anticipate a potential attack and to provide a ten to twenty minute warning of attacking aircraft crossing into Irish airspace. In this system the LOPs of the Coast Watching Service played a vital role. Before turning to the LOPs, the other elements in this unified system of air defence require a brief description. Six searchlights located in a ring around the coast of Dublin each provided a 90cm, 210-million candle watt beam to illuminate the night sky. Two on the north side of the city were located at Howth Head and Clontarf while the four along the southern coastline of the city were at Ringsend, Blackrock, Sandycove and Dalkey. The Sandycove light, however, was essentially a naval fighting light for use with port control gun batteries and only secondarily an anti-aircraft searchlight. The primary task for searchlights was to search for incoming aircraft and to illuminate targets allowing anti-aircraft guns to engage. The searchlight could be 'an effective form of air defence in its own right' if by catching a bomber in its beam it blinded the crew and obscured the aircraft's target.[38]

To alert searchlight and anti-aircraft gun crews around Dublin sound locators were located on Howth Head and at Sorrento Park in Dalkey, both in the vicinity of the local LOP. Sound locators were little more than giant electronic ears directing searchlights towards incoming aircraft. Intended to give a searchlight or gun crew an indication of the direction and altitude of approaching aircraft, they gave an imprecise indication of the location of an enemy plane and could

Information, *Roof over Britain*, p. 24.   **36** Two sets of No. 3 Mark 7 anti-aircraft radar were purchased.   **37** UCDA P71/98, manuscript notes by Bryan.   **38** Price and Pavlovic, *Britain's air defences*, p. 9.

easily be swamped by background noise close to their own position. Additionally, 'if several planes were present in the area, the engine noises swamped the locators'.[39] Though by 1940 Ireland had 'the latest type of sound locators', with a maximum range of about three-and-a-half miles, they were never effective and were quickly rendered obsolete by advances in radar.[40]

For estimating the altitude of approaching aircraft, vital information for anti-aircraft gun crews and fighter aircraft, there was the 'observer instrument'. A February 1941 memorandum on air observation by Delamere noted that 'we have none of these instruments', adding that field glasses were in short supply and a public appeal for them might be necessary.[41] Such an appeal was later made for binoculars for the LSF. However, the AA battalion at Ringsend Park was equipped with two up-to-date pieces of optical and electronic equipment essential for effective air defence. Photographs of the park show that the battery operated with a height and range finder. Bob Donaldson, who served in the LDF at the Ringsend Park battery for the duration of the Emergency, added that his unit also had a predictor instrument. This allowed gunfire to be placed in the vicinity of an attacking aircraft with greater accuracy and allowed the AA battalion to deploy continuously pointed fire. The predictor had a crew of three and Donaldson was the main gun layer. He would call out bearings of approaching aircraft that would also be electrically transmitted to the height and range finder and to the gun crew. Photographs of Ringsend Park show the guns and the predictor linked by thick electrical cabling. When Donaldson took up his post at Ringsend all the equipment was in position and he was emphatically told that the equipment was paid for, that it belonged to the Irish Defence Forces and that the force were not beholden onto any country when operating it.

Beyond this apparatus, the most sophisticated command and control equipment in the possession of ADC was the telephone. Through a system of open and closed circuits connecting groups of LOPs and observer posts on a single line to each other and ADC headquarters in Dublin Castle the network led to a

> telephone report centre ... capable of handling about 30 posts situated over a radius of about 25 miles. The report centre contains a plotting table where the information on the movement of aircraft from the posts is plotted instantaneously. Each report centre plotter is capable of dealing with 3 or 4 posts.[42]

The ADC telephone control system appeared effective on paper and it operated tolerably well during normal working conditions. However Luftwaffe raids on

---

39 Ibid., p. 23.   40 TNA DO 35/1008/8, Hope to Pritchard, 27 Feb. 1940.   41 MA ADC 1/2, Air Defence Command, 18 Jan. 1941.   42 MA ADC 3/1, Organisation of the Air Observer Corps, undated, but Sept. 1939.

Belfast on the night of 15–16 April 1941 led to the telephone system in Belfast being so seriously damaged that when the Northern Ireland cabinet met the following day at noon the Minister for Public Safety could not provide accurate reports on casualties and damage.[43] A simulated collapse of the telephone system was included during an ARP exercise in Dublin in July 1941. The collapse occurred fifty-two minutes into the simulated raid after five waves of bombers were deemed to have attacked the city. The use of the telephone in conditions where lines could easily be damaged by explosions during air raids was extremely problematic. Short-range radio equipment was largely unavailable to the Irish Army. It was not until well into 1941 that plans for using short-wave radio 'to transmit reports of infringements of neutrality and [the] progress of belligerent aircraft over Irish territory or territorial waters' were first considered, this system coming into operation in 1942.[44]

The nine LOPs between Howth Head and Carnsore Point bore the heaviest responsibility for reporting infringements of airspace. It was from these posts that the first notice of an air attack on Dublin from the south would be received. Though the anti-aircraft defences around Dublin were weak, the tactical use of the LOPs ensured that that the aerial attacker would lose the element of surprise. Through a series of colour-coded alerts ADC could ensure that the guns around the city were ready to engage. LOP No. 7 at Sorrento Park near Vico Road in Dalkey was the key link in this ADC coastal chain. Strategically, it was vital for the defence of the central Dublin area from the south. To the north it commanded a view of the entrance to Dublin Bay and to the neighbouring post at Howth Head. To the south it overlooked Killiney Bay with a view as far south as Bray Head and, on a good day, Wicklow Head. The LOP at Dalkey was itself part of a larger military establishment in the secluded suburban park. This included a searchlight platform (code-named LAMP), a bank of sound detectors and a light anti-aircraft position. This latter was intended for use in defence of the position against a low-flying attack. Howth Head LOP (No. 6), which like Dalkey was also located in close proximity to a searchlight position (code-named CANDLE), also held a commanding view to the south and could, in good visibility, see down the coast to Wicklow Head.[45]

GERMANY AIR ACTIVITY OVER IRELAND, JULY 1940–MAY 1941

The bombing of the North Strand in Dublin by the Luftwaffe on the night of 30–1 May 1941 provides the most important example of the twenty LOPs linked into ADC in simultaneous operation. LOP logbooks collectively show that as the

---

43 Public Record Office of Northern Ireland (hereafter PRONI), CAB4/469b, cabinet conclusions, 16 Apr. 1941.   **44** MA ADC 1/2, Meeting at the COS Office, 5 May 1941.
45 A final fixed searchlight was located in Blackrock Park Dublin (Code-named MATCH). The three posts ceased operation in Feb. 1944.

German aircraft passed up the east coast of Ireland their progress was accurately reported to ADC. This information allowed the capital's anti-aircraft defences to be readied for action. The logbooks also show that the North Strand bombing was part of much wider German air activity over the east coast of Ireland during the twelve months since May 1940, when German aircraft were first sighted heading into Irish airspace and a German invasion of Ireland was still a strong possibility.

At 2350 on 5 May 1940 G2 received reports of the arrival of German aircraft off Ireland from 'a British source', which stated simply: 'Hostile aircraft approaching Irish coast. One heading for Ireland. No additional details were ascertained.'[46] It was a typical low-key incursion for this period of the war. Though air activity from May 1940 was on an increased scale compared to the final months of 1939, it was not until the middle of August 1940 that belligerent air activity near Ireland really began to rise. That rise was to have fatal consequences. At 1340 on 26 August Carnsore Point LOP spotted two He-111 aircraft five miles off the coast coming in from the south-east: 'The sound of the aircraft came in waves and was of the heavy drone type.' On seeing the aircraft, Volunteer Nicholas Redmond passed his telescope to Volunteer James Brown and set to reporting the incursion.[47] As he was telephoning ADC the aircraft passed directly overhead and Brown 'had to use the glass vertically to see them'.[48] Greenore Point, north-east of Carnsore, 'at 1341 hours observed two low-winged monoplanes 3 miles west of post travelling over land from south to north-west. Nationality unknown. Height about 10,000 feet'.[49] This was nothing unusual: between 20 and 31 August forty aircraft entered Irish airspace between Dungarvan and Wexford.[50] Volunteer Green at Greenore Point would later tell G2 he saw the aircraft through breaks in the cloud and though he used binoculars he 'could not distinguish any markings. Colour of the aircraft browny grey.'[51] Significantly, he added 'I am satisfied both planes were the same type, i.e. wing tips drawn backwards, fin shaped tail. They looked like Heinkel 111 type.' Others had, mistaking the Heinkel's front facing machine-gun for a propeller, identified the aircraft as having three propellers, like a Ju-52, but Green stuck to his story, and his colleagues at Greenore and the neighbouring post at Carnsore Point corroborated his facts. Green told his debriefing officer Commandant Murphy, who tested Green's ability to identify aircraft with silhouettes and photographs, that he had 'not previously seen aircraft during my LOP duties that I could identify as German aircraft'.[52] However, immediately the aircraft passed over his post he 'compared their appearance with the chart and concluded

---

46 MA DRS 201, 6 May 1940.   47 NAI DFA 221/147, Archer to Walshe, 11 Sept. 1940.
48 Ibid., statement by Volunteer James Brown (206392), 3 Sept. 1940.   49 Ibid., Archer to Walshe, 11 Sept. 1940.   50 NAI DFA Secretary's Files A29, Summary of aerial activity on our south-eastern sector from Aug., 1940 to June, 1941.   51 NAI DFA 221/147, Archer to Walshe, 11 Sept. 1940.   52 Ibid., statement by Volunteer P. Green (207682), 2 Sept. 1940.

they were like the German Heinkel 111. This was before I heard any explosions or before I had any idea of trouble.'

The two planes flew lower in the early autumn sunshine, the first plane immediately in front of and about fifty feet higher than the second. They passed over Carnsore LOP 'side by side below the clouds' and continued to the north-west.[53] Turning west, they flew north of and parallel to the Rosslare to Waterford railway line. Twelve local witnesses saw aircraft with 'two black crosses edged with white on the under surface of the wing', one adding that 'the black cross is a distinctive marking of German military aeroplanes'.[54] Agnes Nolan of Campile saw one of the aircraft as it circled overhead her brother's house where she was visiting. The experience terrified her and she told the investigation into the bombing that 'it was a very dark plane: very big … I could see the marks very plainly. I took it to be the Swastika … I got frightened when I saw it was a German plane.'[55] The aircraft separated, one circled Duncormick railway station and dropped four 250kg high-explosive bombs near Ambrosetown, and the other circled over Campile. This was an initial run over the target, which continued with 'a timed descent and a wide turn calculated to bring the aircraft back over the target'.[56] At 1350, using the Schleighflug method of 'a gradual descent' to 'a low altitude with the engines throttled back', the Heinkel glided in to attack and dropped delayed action high-explosive bombs on the creamery in Campile village, killing three girls. Joseph O'Connor, the son of the sergeant at Campile Garda station, who added to his statement that 'I am ten years and three months old', and who 'often saw a photograph of a German plane in the paper', 'saw three bombs coming out' of one plane, 'they were like black stout bottles'.[57] At Ambrosetown the aircraft appeared to have targeted the railway viaduct with bombs fused to explode on impact but missed by about 1,700 feet, hitting a nearby cottage, but killing no one.[58]

To the Irish investigators both bombings were deliberate acts that could not be put down to poor visibility or navigational error. It was a fine early autumn day and visibility was exceptionally good, over eighty to one-hundred miles from the altitude the planes were flying. There were no clouds over the sea and a few thick white clouds over the land. The investigators considered that with clear skies 'an elementary knowledge of geography would be sufficient for the pilots to know that they were approaching Ireland'. Air Corps pilots flying over the area within an hour of the bombings agreed. The low altitude of the Campile

---

53 NAI DFA Secretary's Files A8, Investigation into the bombing of Ambrosetown and Campile on 26 Aug. 1940, 17 Sept. 1940.   54 Ibid.   55 NAI DFA 221/147, statement by Nolan to F. M. O'Connor, Wexford County Coroner, 27 Aug. 1940.   56 Allen, *Storm*, p. 109. 57 NAI DFA 221/147, Statement made by Joseph O'Connor, Garda Station, Campile, Co. Waterford, 29 Aug. 1940.   58 The military investigators made their analysis from an unexploded bomb found at Campile and from an analysis of bomb craters and fragments of bombs found at the scene.

bombing showed the pilot realized his location and further realized he 'would not be met with any ground defensive fire [and] would not have acted thus if he believed that he were over England or Wales'.[59] The method of attack and the manoeuvre adopted were deliberate Luftwaffe tactics: these were not bombs dropped by accident but through a deliberate attack.

The Defence Forces felt that Campile had been attacked because the creamery and its export trade to Britain was known from before the war to German commercial agents. They further considered the attack on the railway line, like attacks on the Rosslare to Fishguard mail boat, to be an attempt to prevent trade with Britain – in particular cattle exports. This is somewhat far-fetched. The raid was likely to have been deliberate but the location the result of pilot error. The American Minister to Ireland, David Gray, commented to the State Department that 'although there continues to be no attempt to dismiss the actual dropping of the bombs as an accident, there is a disposition to accept the theory that the German pilot, through a navigational error, mistook his target as being in enemy territory'.[60] The German government later paid £12,000 to Ireland in compensation for the attack. Until September 1940 Luftwaffe pilots were under orders only to attack targets of military value, but this included factories and communications infrastructure. To a lost pilot, Campile appeared to be a legitimate military target.

A Defence Forces memorandum from September 1940, the month in which a German invasion of Britain was thought to be imminent and in which the London Blitz began, anticipated that Ireland's future air defence position would worsen. It argued that 'the longer the war lasts, the more intense the air effort is likely to become; and the harder pressed either of the belligerents become, the less regard will be paid to our neutrality'.[61] Late on 5 September, as Britain braced itself for invasion, an incursion over Dublin was expected and Dalkey LOP was instructed to 'keep a sharp look out for aircraft, searchlight station to stand by'.[62] Would German forces launch diversionary raids on Ireland? The alert was called off after an hour. Through September, as London suffered under the Blitz, German aircraft regularly crossed into Irish airspace between Waterford and Wexford and flew along the east coast, though they seemed to make a specific effort to avoid Dublin. One former anti-aircraft artillery officer remembered how 'nightly from midnight, German squadrons droned by Dublin on bombing missions over Britain. These were so regular, in fact, that time-pieces could be checked and set by them.'[63] During periods of such activity the Irish authorities temporarily suspended transmissions from the Athlone Radio

59 NAI DFA Secretary's Files A8, Investigation into the bombing of Ambrosetown and Campile on 26 Aug. 1940, 17 Sept. 1940. 60 NARA RG 84 Dublin Legation, General, Box 7 (1940), Gray to Hull, 28 Aug. 1940. 61 MA ADC 1/2, Report on air operations and intelligence, 17 Sept. 1940. 62 MA LOP 7, 5 Sept. 1940. 63 Captain Brian F. Maguire (Retd.), 'Life in an A.A. Outpost 1939–1946', *An Cosantóir*, 24: 1 (Jan. 1974), 23–6, at 23.

Eireann broadcasting station 'by request' in case its transmissions acted as a direction finding beacon for German aircraft.[64] On the night of 18 September activity was heavy as bombers passed over Dublin city; there were nightly alerts over the following days as more heavy bombers were heard over the capital.[65] When the OC RAF Northern Ireland, Air Commodore C.N. Carr, visited Colonel P.A. Mulcahy in Dublin in October 1940 to 'establish a personal liaison with him' he was 'able to examine briefly the daily charts showing tracks of German aircraft over Eire and establish without doubt that considerable numbers of German aircraft fly over Eire at night from the South to Dublin before turning East to Liverpool and other targets'.[66] Aerial activity over the Irish Sea lasted up to Christmas 1940. On two further occasions bombs were dropped. On 25 October four high-explosive bombs and over 100 incendiary bombs were dropped in open countryside near Rathdrum in Wicklow and military posts around Dublin city sighted a German aircraft with 'Swastika on fin and numbers 57 on fuselage, black cross with white surround on wings'.[67] During a Luftwaffe raid on Liverpool on 20 December two bombs were dropped on the Dublin suburb of Sandycove and bombs were also dropped on Carrickmacross in Louth. On the same night German aircraft dropped bombs in Northern Ireland at Dromore in Down and at Larne in Antrim.

At 1926 on 20 December Howth LOP spotted an aircraft flying south and moving inland. The aircraft was next sighted at Sandycove at 1930, where 'blinding flares' were seen and bombs were dropped which landed in the vicinity of the local railway station.[68] Some damage was done but a train entering the station was undamaged. Despite damage to infrastructure and local houses there were only three minor injuries, all suffered by men walking on the street where the bomb landed.[69] There was a suggestion, largely conjecture, that the plane was coming from the direction of the Kish lightship and 'seemed to be following the direction of the mail boat at an estimated height of 400–500 feet'.[70] Accurate reporting was difficult as few in Sandycove and Dún Laoghaire saw the plane 'owing to the darkness of the night'.[71] However, Captain Jones, who was berthing the mail boat, *Hibernia*, as the plane passed overhead and dropped its bombs, told Gardaí that 'on the voyage from Holyhead he received a wireless message from the British Admiralty to be on the look out for enemy aircraft.'[72] However he saw no aircraft until he was about to berth. That night a large force

64 MA DRS 314, 17 Sept. 1940.   65 MA LOP 7, 18 Sept. 1940.   66 TNA AIR 2/5130, Carr to Under-Secretary of State, Air Ministry, 14 Oct. 1940.   67 MA DRS 347, 25 Oct. 1940.   68 Allen, *Storm*, p. 63, quoting a Defence Forces report on the incident from Military Archives.   69 At the junction of Summerhill Road and Rosmeen Gardens, with the second bomb falling into the garden at the rear of number 17 Rosmeen Gardens.   70 NAI DFA 221/147C, Extract from daily reports summary No. 396, 20 Dec. 1940.   71 Ibid., report by Superintendent Wolfe to Assistant Commissioner Dublin Metropolitan Division, 23 Dec. 1940.   72 Ibid., report by Superintendent Wolfe to Assistant Commissioner Dublin Metropolitan Division, 21 Dec. 1940.

from Luftflotte 3 had flown up the Irish Sea bound for targets in Liverpool. A navigational error by one of these aircraft, perhaps due to incorrect forecasting of high altitude winds, could have brought it over Dublin. A later report added that the ship's lights had been put on when it was berthing in Dún Laoghaire and that 'a bomber aeroplane immediately swooped down on the ship and the lights had to be extinguished'.[73]

To Walshe this was a sign 'that Germany was apparently ceasing to have regard for Irish susceptibilities ... the events revealed a new attitude of indifference'.[74] On the night of 21 December German aircraft bound for Liverpool were again spotted by LOPs on the east coast. Maffey reported that Hempel was beginning to defend actions by Germany over Irish territory that 'previously he was wont to regret' and Karl Petersen, his Press Attaché, was 'increasingly boastful in his cups' of the Luftwaffe's actions.[75] Walshe told Maffey that the German line seemed to be 'To hell with everybody. Those who don't like the New Order must stomach it'.[76] There was, a British intelligence source reported, 'the greatest anxiety ... manifest in official circles' in Dublin as to German intentions towards Ireland.[77]

A German invasion of Ireland was in fact unlikely at this point in the war. At a meeting with Admiral Raeder, Generals Keitel and Jodl, and Commander von Puttkamer on 3 December 1940 where an invasion of Ireland was discussed, Hitler stated that 'a landing in Ireland' could 'only be attempted if Ireland requests help'.[78] He continued that 'the occupation of Ireland might lead to the end of the war'. While this remark hints at interest in Ireland, the discussion took place in a specific wider context, that of an aggressive speech to the House of Commons on 3 November by Churchill where the Prime Minister hinted that a tougher attitude towards Ireland might soon be necessary. Though the meeting in Berlin agreed that 'investigations' were to be made into an invasion of Ireland, Raeder considered that, even if Ireland requested help, British naval supremacy in the waters surrounding Ireland meant that no transport operation of troops to Ireland could succeed.[79] It would be impossible to maintain adequate supply lines to the invading forces. An airborne invasion could not be expected to succeed because 'every attempt at transporting troops by Ju-52s would be in great danger from British fighters'.[80] Raeder concluded that 'it would not be possible to follow up an Irish request for help by sending an expeditionary force'. Such views were, of course, unknown in Dublin where fear of a German invasion remained high through Christmas 1940. However, they show that at the

73 UCDA P104/3534, minutes, Defence Conference, twenty-eighth meeting, 31 Dec. 1941.
74 TNA DO 130/12, Maffey to Secretary of State for Dominion Affairs, 22 Dec. 1940.
75 Ibid.   76 Ibid., quoting Walshe directly.   77 TNA ADM 223/486, Irish Affairs, 7 Jan. 1941.   78 Mallmann Showell, *Fuehrer conferences*, p. 157, 'Report of the C.-in-C., Navy, to the Fuehrer on December 3, 1940, at 1630'.   79 Ibid., p. 158, The Question of supporting Ireland against Britain, undated, but discussed with Hitler and others on 3 Dec. 1940.
80 Ibid.

highest levels of German command a successful invasion of Ireland was considered impossible, even if such forces intervened at the request of Dublin.

On 19 December Hempel informed Walshe of Berlin's wish that four extra civilian staff for the German legation be flown into Rineanna in a civilian Ju-52 airliner (registration D-AGAK) on 22 December. The four were serving members of the German army being sent to Dublin as military attachés to the legation who were to observe British marine and aerial activity. Hempel insisted that 'the German Government would regard a refusal in a most serious light'.[81] In 'one of the sharpest crises' in wartime Irish-German relations, de Valera refused to allow the increase in staff stating that it would undermine neutrality.[82] Dublin, being unaware that German high command thought an invasion of Ireland impossible, expected the worst. German forces had shown that they could land a well-equipped attacking force at a captured aerodrome in no more than an hour. All military leave was cancelled and the civil defence and fire brigades in Dublin were put on alert to expect air raids. Northern Ireland officials at the border customs post outside Dundalk noticed how 'troops at Dundalk and Carrickmacross were on the alert during the night 20–21 December and the LSF was very active.'[83] Hempel realized the Irish probably knew that the alleged civilian staff were military and that they feared it was the commencement of an invasion. But he followed orders from foreign minister Joachim von Ribbentrop 'not to reveal the *real* mission of the new personnel'.[84] Ultimately Hempel's understanding of affairs in Dublin prevailed over Ribbentrop's desire to force the issue and it was dropped after Hempel told Ribbentrop that the Irish stance would only harden if Berlin continued to demand their way. Hempel later told Boland that a few days after de Valera's refusal to allow the staff to land the head of the German Foreign Office, Ernst von Weizaecker, sent a telegram to Hempel indicating that he 'was personally not sorry that he request had been turned down. It was apparently an instance of the Abwehr trying to push a scheme against the opposition of the German Foreign Office.'[85]

There was particularly heavy air activity over eastern Ireland in the days after the attempt to land the officials, G2 putting it down to heavy raids on west coast cities and towns in Britain. Then, on Hitler's order, the Luftwaffe halted air raids on Britain for Christmas 1940. Raids began again on 28 December and the following day another incursion over Dublin took place. At 1530 on 29 December ADC issued the air raid warning 'RED'. A daylight air attack on Dublin appeared imminent. A German Ju-88, a fast medium-range daylight bomber and reconnaissance aircraft, flew in from the north-west of the city. The

81 NAI DFA Secretary's Files A47, Boland to Nunan, 10 July 1953. 82 Ibid. 83 TNA WO 106/6045, Pryce to HQ BTNI, 23 Dec. 1940. 84 Allen, *Storm*, p. 66, paraphrasing an unnumbered telegram sent to Hempel by Ribbentrop on 25 Dec. 1940. 85 NAI DFA Secretary's Files A47, Boland to Nunan, 10 July 1953.

aircraft had been spotted twenty-five minutes earlier flying north over Tramore. It flew inland as far as Navan where it turned. At an estimated height of 4,800 feet it passed directly over the Ballyfermot anti-aircraft battery, low enough to see that 'the German black cross marking was clearly discernible on the wings'.[86] Clearly a reconnaissance flight, captured German documents showed that the aircraft had photographed Baldonnell aerodrome this routing would also have given the aircraft a well-defined view of the low-level approaches to Dublin required for a bombing run from the east. All German aircraft passing over Ireland were regarded by Dublin as combat flights and as such were open to being fired upon. As Walshe told Hempel, 'a German plane appearing over Irish territory was essentially an operational plane since it had come hundreds of miles right into an actively belligerent area and must therefore be ready at any moment for combat'.[87] Ballyfermot AA battery fired three rounds at the Ju-88 and was then instructed to cease firing by the Gun Position Officer who commanded the post as, in a potentially suicidal move, 'two interceptor aircraft of the Air Corps entered the zone of fire'.[88] Though scrambled 'to intercept the [German] aircraft when it was travelling south',[89] the slow rates of climb of the fighters meant that – not surprisingly – the Irish aircraft 'could not make contact' with the Ju-88 which then flew south towards Wicklow and crossed the coast out over the Irish Sea.[90] At the very least, it shows a level of integration between ADC and the Air Corps in an operational situation. The engagement also bears out the view of the Department of External Affairs that 'we still recognize a general obligation to prevent belligerents from over-flying Irish territory, and, from time to time, demonstrate our sincerity of purpose by firing on planes which persist in hovering over posts where anti-aircraft guns are in position'.[91] The three rounds fired from the Ballyfermot guns were considered to have burst near the target aircraft and it was 'reported to have taken avoiding action as a result of the fire, i.e. change of course, speed and height'.[92] To destroy an aircraft an anti-aircraft shell must burst between 50 and 100 feet from the target. The guns were not close enough but Delamere could regard this as a success. Such a 'jinking' manoeuvre would cause an aircraft on a bombing run or, possibly in this case, taking reconnaissance photographs, to break off its straight and level approach to its target. With black lumps of flak appearing around it and the explosions rocking the aircraft the German plane was forced to change height, speed and direction by the guns at Ballyfermot.

86 MA ADC 4/1, AA Action against Belligerent aircraft 29 Dec. 1940.   87 NAI DFA Secretary's Files A2, Walshe to de Valera, referring to a conversation with Hempel noted in memorandum 'Release of German planes', 15 Dec. 1943.   88 MA ADC 4/1, AA Action against Belligerent aircraft 29 Dec. 1940. I would like to thank Simon Nolan for his helpful discussion of these points.   89 MA DRS 403, 30 Dec. 1940.   90 NAI JUS 8/756, Inspector Nangle to Commissioner C Division, 30 Dec. 1940.   91 NAI DFA Secretary's Files A26, Rynne to Walshe, 30 Nov. 1942.   92 MA ADC 4/1, AA Action against Belligerent aircraft 29 Dec. 1940.

The first three days of 1941 saw bombs dropped on locations in Leinster. On 1 January bombs fell at Duleek and Drogheda in Meath. In Drogheda, it was thought that the Boyne railway viaduct was a possible target as the attacking aircraft circled over it before dropping its five high-explosive bombs. The following morning high-explosive bombs were dropped near the Curragh Racecourse and incendiary bombs were dropped nearby at Walshestown, destroying many tons of hay. Also on the morning of 2 January an unidentified aircraft dropped high-explosive bombs on Knockroe, Borris, in Carlow. The bombs hit one house and Kathleen Shannon, aged 16, Mary Ellen Shannon, aged 50 and Bridget Shannon, aged 40, were killed, with Michael and James Shannon being seriously injured. G2 reported that at the Curragh and at Knockroe 'the parts of H.E. Bombs and Incendiary have been identified as of German Manufacture'.[93] On 3 January a further bomb fell at Donore Terrace off the South Circular Road in Dublin. Walshe officially protested to Hempel on 3 January at the bombings which were 'causing the greatest perturbation to the Government and amongst our people'.[94] He attacked Hempel for the careless-ness shown, remarking that if the bombings continued 'both the Government and the people would be obliged to conclude that they were due to a deliberate policy on the part of the German government'. Privately, External Affairs felt that the intentional bombing of Ireland was 'most unlikely', but they cannot have had far from their minds that they had refused German requests to increase staff at the Dublin legation before Christmas 1940.[95] Frank Aiken told the Defence Conference that he 'hoped, and believed personally' that the three days of bombing incidents had been 'mistakes due to weather conditions in conjunction with concentrated raids on British west coast towns'.[96] Hempel tried to blame Britain for the bombing but Walshe would have none of it, replying that 'it would be quite impossible for the British authorities to give an order for the bombing of any part of Ireland without it coming to the knowledge of some Irishman in the British forces'. British intelligence, from information gained from interrogation of captured Luftwaffe airmen, considered it unlikely that the raids had been deliberate, putting one of the bombing incidents in the Dublin area down to 'one of the more inexperienced KG40 crews ... apparently they flew over the town, which was brightly lighted, and thought it was Liverpool'.[97]

When, during a conversation with a G2 officer, Henning Thomsen, second-in-command of the German legation in Dublin, commented on these attacks, he said that 'there were no German targets north of Cardiff on the second night', that is to say 3 January.[98] The attack had been a mistake, and the German

93 MA G2/X/315 Pt II, Curragh Command, Monthly Report C.W.S. – Month of Jan. 1941. 94 NAI DFA 221/147A, secret memorandum by Walshe, 3 Jan. 1941.   95 Ibid., telegram Dublin to Irish foreign missions, 4 Jan. 1941.   96 UCDA P104/3534, Defence Conference, 29th Meeting, 3 Jan. 1941.   97 TNA AIR 40/154, Further report on F.W. Condor of KG40 brought down 200 miles north-west of Ireland on 10 Jan. 1941.   98 NAI DFA Secretary's

legation would of course not say otherwise. Indeed when the G2 officer commented that 'we in Ireland were fortunate not to have more' bombing attacks,
Thomsen continued ominously that the country had 'been "very lucky in this
respect so far"', adding that

> with more intensive aerial activity over England as was bound to come
> shortly, there were bound to be mistakes. It was easy to lose the way ...
> with aircraft engaged in combat the airmen saw nothing but the fight,
> speed factor, etc., being taken into consideration, fifty miles meant so
> little.[99]

A British intelligence assessment considered that the bombings led to 'a radical
change in the attitude of the Irish government towards the war'.[100] Hitherto,
there had been minor crises viewed in a 'detached manner' but over Christmas
1940 there had developed 'a state of acute anxiety'. In light of these German
attacks and with increased worries about Dublin's poorly defended position,
Dulanty approached Viscount Cranborne in January 1941 to seek further anti-
aircraft weapons. Britain refused, Churchill telling Cranborne that if 'we were
assured that it was Southern Ireland's intention to enter the war, we would of
course, if possible, beforehand share out anti-aircraft weapons with them'.[101]
The policy was part of a wider move by Churchill to show 'the depth and
intensity of feeling against the policy of Irish neutrality'.[102] Evidence found by
Trevor Allen suggests that in January 1941 Dublin did have real cause to worry.
On 11 January at 1720 BST a He-111 from KGr126 left Nantes with, according
to the log of pilot Unteroffizier Thomas Hammerl, a LMB 1000kg mine
destined 'for the Dublin area'.[103] No mines or bombs were recorded as having
dropped in the vicinity of Dublin that night and the aircraft returned to Nantes
with its mission completed at 0036 on 12 January. The incident was never known
in Dublin but coming after the new legation staff incident and after a period of
sporadic pinprick bombing, in particular the incident at Sandycove and attacks
on the mail boat, it adds a menacing postscript to Walshe's fears of Germany's
intentions as 1941 began.

Evidence of increased German flights along the east coast of Ireland appears
regularly in LOP logbooks from spring 1941. These flights were heading north
to attack convoys docked at Liverpool, the Clyde and Bangor Bay. Their routes
were radioed en-clair from the four Command areas to GHQ in Dublin in the
expectation that the transmissions would be picked up by the British who knew

Files A8, undated and untitled memo attached to Archer to Walshe, 13 Mar. 1941.   **99** Ibid.
100 TNA ADM 223/483, Irish Affairs, 7 Jan. 1941.   **101** Martin Gilbert (ed.), *The Churchill
war papers, volume III. The ever widening war: 1941* (London, 2000), pp 161–2, Churchill to
Cranborne, 31 Jan. 1941.   **102** Ibid., p. 162.   **103** Allen, *Storm*, p. 66, footnoted as
'information from Flt-Lt. C.H. Goss'.

that 'important plots of unidentified or alien aircraft are passed by telephone to the Army controlled W/T station at Dublin from where they are re-broadcast'.[104] The chosen frequencies were in a crowded area of the radio band occupied by many beacons and, depending on atmospheric conditions, could often not be picked up by the British. The reports were of considerable importance to the British and after being intercepted by the RAF Wireless Intelligence Section were immediately passed on to Air Intelligence (A.I. 3A). G2 were surprised to learn later that the British seemed to have trouble picking up the reports. When offered four British radio sets to replace Irish equipment the Irish politely refused, arguing that this was more than even Irish neutrality allowed.

British activity off the Irish east coast was well catalogued in these months but unlike obvious German operational flights, British flights were 'of an aimless and confused character' as aircraft 'seemed to be "milling around" and have no definite mission'.[105] The flights being put down to pilots undergoing training. Maffey called on Walshe in late March and informed him that the RAF felt that 'the lighting of our main towns in the vicinity of the coast [was] a navigational help to the Germans'.[106] In an attempt to outflank British radar, attacking aircraft would stay well clear of radar stations in Cornwall and Wales, bringing them close to and over Irish territory. Maffey explained that the British authorities would be grateful if lighting, in particular neon lighting and trade and private lighting, could be restricted. Despite a period of 'considerable and confused activity out to sea off Hook Head and Carnsore Point' in early April 1941, flights from the Wexford coast were making a habit of approaching Dublin, circling and turning east.[107] The Department of Defence noted that 'it was apparent that the lights on the South Coast and of Dublin were used as points of arrival and departure on synchronized timing'. More usually, flights arriving from the south flew this route, suggesting that 'accurate position checks for aircraft proceeding to targets could be obtained'.[108]

An increase in the German air presence off the Irish coast linked in with the beginning of Luftwaffe raids on Belfast. The first raid took place on the night of 7–8 April when 'a small squadron of German bombers, led by a pathfinder He-111 from Kampfgruppe 26' destroyed the Harland and Wolff fuselage factory and seriously damaged the docks.[109] That night reports of aircraft along the border between Cavan and Tyrone were transmitted from the Irish observers to British air defence services. German reconnaissance aircraft had been spotted crossing into Irish territory on the afternoon of Easter Monday, 15 April, by

104 TNA AIR 2/7233, extract from RAF Wireless Intelligence Service Summary No. 14, 21 Apr. 1941.   105 NAI DFA Secretary's Files A29, Summary of aerial activity on our south-eastern sector from Aug. 1940 to June 1941.   106 NAI DFA Secretary's Files A2, secret untitled memorandum by Walshe, 29 Mar. 1941.   107 NAI DFA Secretary's Files A29, Summary of aerial activity on our south-eastern sector from Aug. 1940 to June 1941. 108 Ibid.   109 Jonathan Bardon, *A history of Ulster* (Belfast, 1992), p. 564.

Hook Head LOP in Waterford. A He-111 was engaged by air defences in Belfast just before 1330 that day and a similar aircraft left Irish airspace at 1426 after being spotted by Forlorn Point LOP in Wexford. Belfast was being photographed by the Luftwaffe and was moving up the list of German targets. The second, and much larger, raid on the city by about 160 aircraft took place during a period of full moon on the night of Easter Tuesday, 15–16 April.[110] The participating aircraft were warned by Hermann Göring to stay clear of neutral Irish territory but coastwatchers and observers along the east Irish coast spotted several aircraft.[111]

By 0200 on 16 April Belfast had sustained a heavy raid and the last attack took place at 0345. Fires raged, water mains were ruptured and phone lines were down. Minister of Public Security John McDermott rang Minister of Commerce Sir Basil Brooke at 0415 asking for his 'authority to order fire engines from Eire'. Brooke recorded in his diary that 'I gave him authority as it is obviously a question of expediency ... I am afraid there has been serious damage in Belfast, and there are bound to be many casualties.'[112] Roused from sleep, de Valera agreed to McDermott's request and thirteen fire brigades from Dún Laoghaire, Dublin, Drogheda and Dundalk sped to Belfast. In total 745 people were killed and 430 seriously injured.[113] Maffey, returning through Belfast from a visit to London where he himself had been bombed, told Walshe that the situation in Belfast 'was more horrifying than London because of the small dwelling houses of poor people which were destroyed'.[114] Refugees streamed out of Belfast, many crossing the border to stay with relatives in the South or to 'various communal centres under Red Cross arrangements [where they] were being fed and housed'.[115] Some days later Maffey told Walshe that the Northern Ireland government 'were extremely appreciative of the measures [Dublin] had taken to help them'.[116]

On 23 April, between 0910 and 0915, the medium anti-aircraft guns at Blackrock and the heavy anti-aircraft guns at Ringsend fired on a Condor which had been spotted thirty minutes previously over Carlow heading towards Dublin. This action followed a standard procedure. From July 1940 'all aircraft with the exception of aircraft identified as Irish [would] be fired on without warning' if they entered a prohibited zone stretching in a rectangle from Howth Head to Killiney Hill to Tallaght, to Blanchardstown and back to Howth Head.[117] At between 10,000 and 15,000 feet the Condor flew in a north-easterly direction over Dublin in patchy cloud and poor visibility and 'it was noted that [the]

---

110 Allen, *Storm*, pp 123–42. 111 Ibid., pp 116–18 and p. 121. 112 PRONI D/3004/D/32, typescript of Brooke diaries, 1941, entry for 16 Apr. 1941. 113 Figures from Bardon, *Ulster*, p. 568. 114 NAI DFA Secretary's Files A2, Walshe to de Valera, 21 Apr. 1941. 115 PRONI CAB/9/CD/217/1, notes of a meeting in the Law Courts, Belfast, 19 Apr. 1941. 116 NAI DFA Secretary's Files A2, Walshe to de Valera, 21 Apr. 1941. 117 MA ADC 43, memorandum by Commandant Mulcahy, OC Air Corps, 16 July 1940.

height and speed' of the aircraft 'was increased as a result of [the] action taken by [the] defences'.[118] The ten rounds fired by the two sets of anti-aircraft guns did not hit the aircraft but the change of speed and height indicated that the crew had definitely noticed that they were being fired on. Four of the rounds were 'reliably reported as bursting close to the aircraft', a suggestion that this was not simply a warning to the intruder to leave Irish territory. It was only the limited visibility that prevented the guns from opening greater fire.[119]

Such states of emergency were regular as Carnsore and Greenore LOPs spotted aircraft heading north along the south-east coast and relayed the information to ADC in Dublin. While reconnaissance aircraft could be expected at any time, the daylight peak of flights being between 1000 to 1500, aircraft on bombing missions were expected during the night-time peak of 2300 to 0100. Standard procedure was to make landfall at Tuskar Rock or Hook Head lighthouse, fly along the east coast to Bray about five miles off shore – outside Irish territorial waters – turn east, checking position by the lights of Dublin, and return to the east coast north of Dublin by turning west at the Rockabill lighthouse off Skerries. This lighthouse was visible to aircraft from as far south as Wicklow Head when they were flying at altitudes of 10,000 feet. The aircraft knew where they were. The route used 'distinctive lights' for accurate navigation and was 'too regular to be coincidence'.[120]

A number of the over 200 Luftwaffe aircraft flying north to bomb Belfast, 'the only objective of military importance in Northern Ireland', on the night of 4–5 May 1941 were recorded in the Ballagan Point logbook.[121] During this third raid there were too many aircraft to count and there was 'continuous air activity over [the] LOP from 0005 until 0248. All aircraft came from a southerly direction and proceeded north. Flying high. Nationality unknown'.[122] Visibility that night was moderate and some of the aircraft were seen at low altitude dropping flares which 'remained alight for three minutes', while the others moved north at higher altitudes.[123] Colonel John Reynolds, the Military Attaché at the American legation in Dublin, sent a confidential despatch to the War Department in Washington on the afternoon of 5 May that 'unidentified planes flew over Dublin at eleven o'clock PM last night. Belfast was bombed shortly after midnight. Every indication is that this route is being used by German flyers on the way to north Ireland'.[124] One German pilot remembered that 'visibility was wonderful, I could make out my targets perfectly'.[125] That night 150 people were killed in Belfast and considerable damage was done to the shipyard and the harbour area. Fires burned along the densely inhabited Newtownards Road from

118 Ibid., Commandant McCarthy to Director of Artillery, 23 Apr. 1941. 119 Ibid. 120 NAI DFA Secretary's Files A29, Summary of aerial activity on our south-eastern sector from Aug. 1940 to June 1941. 121 PRONI CAB9/CD/33/1, report by Commander Pim on general defence matters, 31 Mar. 1939. 122 MA LOP 2, 5 May 1941. 123 Ibid. 124 NARA RG 319 Box 459, Reynolds to War Department, 5 May 1941. 125 Bardon,

the 95,992 incendiary bombs and 237 tons of high explosives which were dropped on the city.[126] Again, fire brigades from across the border were sent to Belfast.

Over the following nights LOPs on the east coast remained on a heightened state of alert. This was the beginning of seventeen nights when 'more intense activity occurred than had been previously experienced'.[127] Belfast was bombed again on the night of 5–6 May. At 0143 on the morning of 6 May Bray Head LOP in Wicklow noted the sound of aircraft six miles north east of the post travelling south-east. Further aircraft, out to sea to the east of the post, were logged at 0213. The raids of 5–6 May on Belfast turned out to be the final raid on the city by the Luftwaffe. But nocturnal flights of unidentified aircraft continued along Ireland's east coast. Bray Head and Wicklow Head LOPs heard numerous aircraft over their posts on the night of 6–7 May and there was a further emergency on the night of 8 May. In these latter cases the Irish suspicion was that at least some of the aircraft were British fighters sent up in anticipation of the return of the Luftwaffe but there were no engagements between British and German aircraft in Irish airspace. German aircraft continued to probe Irish territory. What appeared to be a He-111 was spotted one-and-a-half miles east of Wicklow Head just after midday on 26 May flying north at about 500 feet. At 1245 it returned and sighted one mile west of Wicklow Head heading south at 700 feet. The plane may have been lost and flying low to escape the overcast conditions.[128] Two unidentified aircraft were spotted later that evening; there was always a passing RAF presence in the area and nothing conclusive could be drawn about the nationality of these planes. However, at 0547 the following morning, 27 May, two German planes were definitely identified by Wicklow Head LOP in good visibility five miles east of the post heading south. At the same time, further north along the coast, Bray Head LOP sighted a 'heavy bomber type' aircraft of unknown nationality south west of their position, travelling east, presumably the same aircraft.[129] Later in the day the defences at Rosslare Harbour fired on and hit a He-111 that appeared to be on a reconnaissance flight.

On the night of 28 May the Luftwaffe were again off the Irish coast in strength. A force of fifty heavy bombers flew north along the south-east coast in three identifiable waves. It seemed they were heading for Dublin. They passed east of the city, over Dalkey and on to Rush. One aircraft reached Cootehill in Cavan before turning back and was heard returning over Mountmellick. Searching for Cardiff or Liverpool and confused when the land below them no longer matched their bomb aimers' maps, they almost bombed Dublin in error. When they realized their mistake, several aircraft jettisoned their bombs off the east coast of Ireland. Major J.W. Wofford, the newly appointed Military Attaché at the United States legation in Dublin, reported this increased air activity to

Ulster, p. 569.   **126** Ibid., p. 570.   **127** NAI DFA Secretary's Files A29, Summary of aerial activity on our south-eastern sector from Aug. 1940 to June 1941.   **128** MA LOP 9, 25 May 1941.   **129** MA LOP 8, 27 May 1941.

Washington, adding that at about eight o'clock on the morning of 29 May 'two British Hurricances engaged a German bomber just east of Dublin. [They] flew over the city at no more than three hundred feet [and] were fired on by anti-aircraft'.[130]

Bray Head LOP noted continual heavy explosions and bright flashes between midnight and 0200 on the night of 28–29 May. At 0107 the post 'heard [the] sound [of] two heavy explosions north-east of [the] post and numerous others [,] some did not sound very distant'.[131] Eight minutes later there were four 'very heavy explosions' to the north-east of the post which seemed 'very near'.[132] Through the night ADC worked frantically to provide a picture of what was taking place along the east coast. Bray Head attempted to contact ADC on numerous occasions from midnight but each time ADC was engaged. When at 0120 they did get through they found that ADC were 'too busy' and simply 'took time and direction of travel [of the aircraft] in each case'.[133] In retrospect, we know that this was a sign of things to come. With this in mind it is well to note Bray Head's timings. They record an almost continual series of explosions between 0030 and 0130: an almost exact precursor of what would happen in two night's time as German bombs fell on Dublin city.

AN OVERVIEW OF THE EVENTS OF 30–31 MAY 1941 OVER
DUBLIN AND THE IRISH EAST COAST

The night of 29 May was quiet with no alerts along the east coast. Visibility was poor in rain with an overcast sky.[134] The Luftwaffe stayed away. The thirtieth of May began quietly. Bray Head LOP put in a routine order of coal for the post. Dublin was getting ready for a bank holiday weekend and the weather looked promising. Though the day started cloudy, it later became clear and sunny but a sea fog fell as night began. The Luftwaffe returned. LOPs along the east coast reported the first of three waves of incoming aircraft off Carnsore Point just before midnight on 30 May. They flew north along the coastline, probably heading for Belfast. Aircraft were also reported inland over Kildare, Meath and Westmeath, all flying north. Poor visibility on the night was commented upon by both Irish and German sources. It was a murky night, visibility was moderate to poor and the sky was cloudy. The wind was light but its direction changed through the night; initially coming from the north-west, it swung east, backing north-east by morning.[135] At approximately 0130 the first wave of aircraft turned over Northern Irish territory and flew back south along the coast. Between 0130 and 0230 aircraft flying from the north to the south-east were seen to jettison bombs out to sea along the Irish coast. They were lightening their weight after

130 NARA RG 319 Box 459, telegram from Wofford to War Department, 29 May 1941.   131 MA LOP 8, 29 May 1941.   132 Ibid.   133 Ibid.   134 Ibid. Weather report for 2100 hours 29 May 1941.   135 These weather details are compiled from weather observations in LOP logbooks.

the abortive raid on Belfast, just as they had done two nights previously. It was on this return leg that Dublin was bombed.

It is of course not impossible that a small number of aircraft in the groups heading for Belfast had Dublin as a target. Sketchy evidence of such a plan was published in the *Irish Times* of 19 June 1997. Research by Leo Sheridan suggested that the Luftwaffe bombing of Dublin was 'not accidental'. Sheridan claimed to have discovered evidence while researching in a Munich army base that the Dublin raid was code-named Roman Helmet and 'was aimed at intimidating the government after a number of neutrality breaches'. A Dornier Do-17 bomber carrying six bombs, with three primed, targeted North Strand Fire Station, then Dorset St Fire Station and finally Aras an Uachtaráin, the residence of the President of Ireland. A plan to bomb Dublin such as that described in 'Roman Helmet' may have existed in theory or on paper, such is the purpose of military planning, but there is nothing to suggest that the events on the night of 30–31 May 1941 over Dublin were part of a pre-ordained plan. The events of the night will be examined in detail below, but Sheridan's story as reproduced in the *Irish Times* lacks important details. Firstly, there were many aircraft over Dublin, and indeed over the length of the eastern Irish coast on the night of 30–31 May, not just one single aircraft. Secondly, it is unlikely that the Luftwaffe would send just one aircraft to bomb three small targets. Precision bombing of the kind suggested in Sheridan's report was not possible during the Second World War. Finally, the two or more aircraft that were identified as having dropped bombs on the Phoenix Park and on the North Strand came over the city from the north-west. Aircraft deliberately targeting Dublin would not waste fuel by flying north, turning eighty or so miles beyond their intended targets and flying south again to release their bombs along an indefinite line of attack. However, some of Sheridan's evidence does tally with events on the night. He notes that 'an artillery gunnery, having heard the plane, released some rounds and tailed its wing, forcing it to turn'. Sheridan continues that the plane sent a signal to a German submarine ten miles south of the Kish Lightship indicating that it had been interfered with by ground fire; however it never returned to base. It is certain that at 0130 the Bofors-40 guns at Collinstown Airport opened fire on an aircraft coming from the south, forcing it to turn and fly south-east over Dublin Bay.

Just before Christmas 1998 the *Irish Times* ran an article entitled 'German flier asks for forgiveness for bombing'.[136] The previous day a former Luftwaffe pilot, now living in Canada and identified only as 'Heinrich', had told the Gay Byrne Show on RTÉ Radio One that 'the attack was a mistake'; Belfast was the intended target. 'Heinrich', in the lead plane, was to drop flares for the guidance of the following bombers, two squadrons of thirty planes. The flares were

136 *Irish Times*, 23 Dec. 1998, p. 8.

ineffective and 'either a fault in the guiding beam system or the bad weather that night led them astray'.[137] This would suggest that the bombs were dropped deliberately, though by mistake, on Dublin and that it was the only target. But this does not take account of aircraft dropping bombs into the sea along the east coast at the same time. When 'Heinrich' and his colleagues realized their error there was 'quite a bit of excitement' and an inquiry was held.[138] The crews blamed the meteorological services; the German foreign office expressed regret and blamed high altitude winds blowing the bombers off course. Hempel, after his initial shock, tried to blame the British. Germany maintained there was no conclusive proof that German planes dropped the bombs. However, markings on the bomb fragments identified them as German.

THE NORTH STRAND BOMBING FROM LOP LOGBOOKS

Sheridan's argument and 'Heinrich's' tale contribute to over sixty years of speculation as to why bombs were dropped on Dublin on the night of 30–31 May 1941. These have ranged from suggestions that Britain deliberately interfered with German radio navigation to ensure bombs were dropped on Dublin to suggestions that Germany bombed Dublin in response for de Valera's despatch of fire-engines to Belfast. Yet there has been no attempt to piece together the events of 30–31 May from Irish primary sources. In most accounts aircraft simply appear over Dublin and the argument revolves around the rationale for the 'air raid'. An examination of LOP logbooks and reports from ADC puts the bombing of the North Strand in a wider context and suggest that, in a tragic accident, the bombs were dropped by aircraft running low on fuel seeking to reduce their weight. Dublin was not the intended target, nor was Dublin mistaken for Belfast.

At 2340 Forlorn Point LOP reported unidentified aircraft entering Irish territory. Three minutes later aircraft passed south-west of Ballyconnigar Hill LOP travelling north.[139] The air raid alarm was sounded at 2348 as ADC received information that an unknown number of unauthorized aircraft were east of Carnsore Point.[140] The origin of this report is unclear. Perhaps it was passed on by British sources, as warnings in respect of German aircraft passing over the English midlands and the west coast of Britain 'were passed automatically' to the Irish.[141] It is also possible that reports came from the Tuskar Rock lighthouse. In any case, no such details appear in the Carnsore

137 Ibid.   138 Ibid.   139 MA LOP 12, 30 May 1941.   140 MA ADC 43, A/Commandant M.P. McCarthy to Director of Artillery, 10 June 1941. Another Department of Defence document states that aircraft were first heard flying northwards at 2240 GMT, or 2340 IST, over the Wexford coast, but this does not tally exactly with logbooks, a common problem due to the lack of synchronization of clocks.   141 NAI DFA Secretary's Files A3, minutes of a meeting between representatives of the government of Eire and representatives of the Dominions Office and service departments of the United Kingdom, 24 May 1940.

Point LOP logbook. Code 'YELLOW', the preliminary air raid warning, was issued as the unidentified aircraft entered the fighter zone around Dublin. The guns and searchlights around Dublin went on standby and men were 'stood to'. This had happened on previous nights and so far there was nothing out of the ordinary. A second wave of aircraft passed over Carnsore Point at 0034. They were flying north at high altitude, passing directly over the post, poor visibility preventing detailed observation by the LOP. The weather report taken to the north at Ballyconnigar Hill at midnight was of a fine night with a calm sea and a light easterly wind. Although the sky was clear, the report also noted that visibility was poor. The course of individual aircraft over the country now became unclear. Ballyconnigar Hill heard aircraft at approximately fifteen-minute intervals at 0012, 0026 and 0041. They came from the south-east and south-west, travelling north-east in line with the coast at about 8,000 feet. Inland, aircraft were heard over Mullingar at 0113, Portarlington at 0140 and Mountrath at 0156.[142] At 0130 Ballyconnigar Hill heard one aircraft five miles south of the post and travelling north passing out to sea half a mile east.

The first wave of aircraft continued north, tracked by the LOPs at Cahore Point, Kilmichael Head and Wicklow Head. Wicklow Head reported the 'continuous sound of aircraft going north from 00.00 to 01.45'.[143] Air raid warning 'RED' was given to gun crews in Dublin. Hostile aircraft were approaching and entering the anti-aircraft artillery zone. Gun crews now 'realised that there was something very different happening ... [T]he reports from Air Defence Control carried information that seemed to indicate a developing threat to the city, ... coolly, calmly, the Ack-Ack defences of Dublin, undoubtedly limited, prepared for action.'[144] At 0002 Bray Head LOP picked up the trail from Wicklow Head. The German bombers were estimated to be eight miles south-east and three miles south-west, travelling north towards Dublin. The sound detectors at Sorrento Park in Dalkey picked up the approaching first wave at 0004 and the Dalkey and Sandycove searchlights unsuccessfully attempted to illuminate them. No targets were spotted. A searchlight battery made an easy target and standard practice was to illuminate only for as long as absolutely required and then douse. In classic blitz film footage searchlights are seen sweeping the sky but this was merely a public relations exercise. The Irish practice was to use searchlights as and when required and they 'were exposed and doused intermittently until 02.13 hours'.[145]

As the first wave of aircraft headed north from Dublin, Dunany Point LOP picked them up at 0018. To the south of Dublin, Ballyconnigar Hill picked up another incoming wave at 0026. For the next two hours and nine minutes aircraft

142 NAI DFA 221/147E, undated and untitled memorandum with Bryan to Boland, 29 July 1941. Times were originally given in GMT, but have been reproduced here as summer time (that is, +1 hour).   143 MA LOP 9, 31 May 1941.   144 Maguire, 'Life in an A.A. Outpost 1939–1946', p. 25.   145 NAI DFA 221/147E, memorandum by G2, Bombing Incidents:

were regularly seen over Dublin, first from the south and south-east and then from the north and north-west as they returned after failing to find their targets in Northern Ireland. These aircraft were successfully illuminated for anti-aircraft gun action on three occasions and all the city's batteries opened fire on at least one occasion each during the night. The *Irish Times* of 31 May reported that aircraft 'were first heard over Dublin shortly after midnight'. This tallies with the LOP and ADC reports that anti-aircraft defences and searchlights 'immediately went into action'.[146] Patrick Maloney recorded in his diary that 'as we walked across O'Connell Bridge we heard planes in overhead. Anti-aircraft fire burst overhead. Red Flares shone bright, fireworks in the sky. There were four searchlights visible in the sky. The planes moved away.'[147] At 0035 Clontarf Battery was the first of the Dublin defences to open fire, firing four rounds when it locked on to an aircraft caught in a searchlight beam moving north to the east at about 7,000 feet. The direction of this flight shows that it did not have Dublin as its intended target. The aircraft dodged the beam and the four rounds; 'the proximity of the bursts in relation to the target could not be estimated'.[148] The report suggests that the gun crew were attempting 'continuously pointed fire' – a tactic described as 'the most dangerous type of AA fire', an AA-gun tracked an aircraft, in this case one illuminated by a searchlight, and fired at a maximum rate at a predicted distance in the sky in front of it.[149] The aircraft jinked out of the beam and when the rounds exploded there was no aircraft visible for the searchlight to illuminate. During the first engagement and the interval following, aircraft continued to fly along the coast over Dublin towards Belfast. At 0018 and 0027 Dunany Point heard aircraft to the south-east flying north. The last of the three waves of aircraft to pass north along the Irish coast came in over Carnsore Point LOP at 0034. There followed what the *Irish Times* described as 'an interval' of just over and hour before 'the anti-aircraft defences opened up with greater intensity'.[150]

Between 0128 and 0131 the batteries at Ringsend (0128), Clontarf (0128), Stillorgan (0130) and Ballyfermot (0131) opened fire almost simultaneously on two 'large twin-engined monoplanes' coming from the north. The Bofors battery at Collinstown Airport fired twice, at 0130 and at 0145 at a similar aircraft illuminated in the sky over the city. In the first of these two engagements by Collinstown the target aircraft was flying north, but on being fired upon it turned and flew south-east toward Dublin Bay. *Irish Times* journalist Tony Gray vividly described the guns in action as a bomb dropped:

21.5.'41, 3 June 1941.   **146** *Irish Times*, 31 May 1941.   **147** Diary extract, reprinted in Benjamin Grob-Fitzgibbon, *The Irish experience during the Second World War: an oral history* (Dublin, 2004), p. 29.   **148** MA ADC 43, A/Commandant M.P. McCarthy to Director of Artillery, 10 June 1941.   **149** Price and Pavlovic, *Britain's air defences*, p. 23.   **150** *Irish Times*, 31 May 1941.

Suddenly the throb of engines sounded, presently growing into a savage crescendo. Pencils of searchlights slowly plotted arcs in the night converging now as, like a callipers they seemed to hold that humming menace in their grip. Now anti aircraft fire split the skies in solemn peals and sharp cracks, and the aeroplane hum arose, and then there was a blinding flash and a deafening smash, followed by silence.[151]

To Patrick Maloney, now sitting on his bed in his digs talking to friends, 'the rounds of anti-aircraft fire became insistent and powerful. The room was lighted up time and time again as shells burst in the black sky.'[152] The aircraft fired upon by Ringsend and Clontarf was caught in searchlight beams. Of the eight rounds fired (four by each battery), two from Ringsend were observed to be 'in the centre of the beams and close to the target' and those from Clontarf 'very close'. However, the aircraft jinked to escape the searchlight beams and explosions. Searchlights also illuminated the target engaged by Ballyfermot and Stillorgan from 0130 to 0131. Seven rounds were fired but the pilot took evasive action before the shell bursts and 'no observations for effect [were] possible'.[153] As with the engagement at 0035, the evidence suggests continuously pointed fire.

Against popular images of continually firing box barrages used during the London blitz, the action of the Irish crews firing four rounds each seems conservative and parsimonious. However, the box barrage involved guns firing into a box of sky without adequate information as to the location of the target. It wasted ammunition though, as with images of constantly weaving searchlights, it was good for public morale. Such a response would have been inappropriate from the Dublin batteries as at all times reasonable information regarding the targets was available and, as with 'continuously pointed fire', targets were engaged by heavy guns only after first being successfully illuminated by searchlights. Operationally, this was a successful engagement as LOPs, sound locators, searchlights and guns all worked together to engage the target. When the Defence Conference met in Leinster House on 5 June it discussed the bombing of Dublin, with Minister for Defence Oscar Traynor reading out a report on the events of 30–31 May. In the following discussion 'agreement was expressed with the action taken by the Army in firing on planes illuminated by searchlights'.[154] There had been, however, 'an unfavourable reaction of the general public to the bringing into operation of the ground defences', but the meeting agreed that the engagement by the anti-aircraft defences had been 'necessary in order to protect the integrity of our territory … against belligerent aircraft'.[155]

---

151 Ibid., 2 June 1941.   152 Diary extract, reprinted in Grob-Fitzgibbon, *Oral history*, p. 29.
153 MA ADC 43, A/Commandant M.P. McCarthy to Director of Artillery, 10 June 1941.
154 UCDA P104/3534, Defence Conference, 44th meeting, minutes, 5 June 1941.   155 Ibid.

Four high-explosive bombs were, in the words of the Military Attaché at the United States legation in Dublin, 'indiscriminately' dropped on Dublin on the night of 30–31 May 1941.[156] Three landed within a half a mile of each other close to the Royal Canal between North Strand and Summerhill in the northeast inner city. The fourth landed in the Phoenix Park on the west side of the city. The first bomb, estimated to have weighed 250lbs, fell at 0130, landing on the North Circular Road near the junction with North Richmond Street, close to O'Connell Christian Brothers Schools. In an area with a high concentration of flats and tenements it was remarkable that there were no casualties, but the explosion demolished a shop and set a house on fire. The fire was quickly extinguished but water, gas and electricity mains were damaged. The location tallies roughly with the track of the aircraft fired upon by the Ringsend and Clontarf batteries. A second bomb of similar weight fell almost at the same time, within a couple of hundred yards of the first, at the junction of Richmond Cottages and Summerhill Parade. Damage was also caused to infrastructure in the area. Two houses were demolished and one woman was seriously injured, dying two weeks later in hospital. Two hundred persons were treated on the spot for minor injuries and fourteen more serious cases were treated in hospital.

A smaller explosion from an unknown device, possibly a flare, followed shortly after 0130 and a third 250lb bomb fell in the Phoenix Park at 0132. It is possible that a bomb dropped from the aircraft fired upon by Ballyfermot and Stillorgan at 0131 caused this smaller explosion which shattered windows in Aras an Uachtaráin and in the American Minister's residence. Commandant Maurice P. McCarthy who reported on the anti-aircraft operation was of this opinion, reporting that 'two objects alleged to be green flares were seen dropping from the aircraft which coincided with and probably were the bombs dropped in Phoenix Park'. McCarthy concluded that 'the pilot of this aircraft, being unable to avoid the beams, thought it safer to jettison his bombload rather than risk it being detonated as a result of a hit by AA shell'. This suggests that the bombs were dropped on Dublin after, and possibly as a result of, the city's defences opening fire.

At 0205 a 500lb bomb exploded on the street on tram tracks on the North Strand opposite the junction with North William Street. No anti-aircraft battery is recorded as having opened fire on an aircraft at this time. The explosion was heard across the city. A survivor described the blast of hot air following the explosion 'having the effect of a grizzly bear squeezing the air from your lungs, then flinging you away'.[157] A contemporary G2 report argued that the first three bombs were dropped by one aircraft and 'since this plane was heard to circle the sky for some time afterwards, it is also possible that the fourth bomb was dropped from the same aircraft'.[158] This came from the suggestion that an

---

156 NARA RG 319, Box 459, telegram (confidential), Wofford to War Department, 2 June 1941.   **157** Colin Scudds, 'The North Strand bombing – 1941', *Dún Laoghaire Journal*, 11 (2002), 6–11 at 9.   **158** NAI DFA 221/147E, memorandum by G2, Bombing Incidents:

aircraft came inland at Dun Laoghaire at 0140, skirted the west side of the city, flew west and north west as far as Kilcock, circled here at 0156 and flew due east over Dublin city 'dropping [a] large bomb at 0202 on the site of fires started by [the] first of [the] two previous bombs'.[159] This aircraft passed Wicklow Head heading south at 0215.

Twenty-five houses were demolished in the explosion and forty-five were damaged beyond repair and had to be demolished. Three hundred houses were rendered 'temporarily unfit for use' and minor damage was caused to a further one thousand houses.[160] Widespread destruction was also caused to public utilities by this bomb as electricity, gas, public lighting and sewers were all damaged in the vicinity of the blast. The explosion started fires but these were brought under control within half an hour. Photographs from the area the following morning show the intense destruction in this small area of Dublin's north inner city.

Seventeen bodies were recovered by 2200 on the day of the bombing but the search was not completed until almost a week later, by which time a further six bodies had been recovered. Trapped injured were given morphine by the rescue services and some of those trapped were fed through funnels and long tubing. Forty-five people had been seriously injured and there were an estimated 300 minor casualties. When the Department of Defence reported on the attack on 8 July, eight men, ten women, seven children and two unidentified individuals had been 'killed outright or died from injuries as a result of this bomb'. One man was still missing, presumed dead. He was, the Department of Defence noted, 'believed to have been on the street when the bombs fell and if this is so there is little chance of his body being found'.[161] Thom's Dublin street directory shows that many of the houses in the vicinity of the North Strand blast had been vacant and many had been demolished in the 1930s. While evidence of the poverty and run down nature of Dublin's inner city in the 1940s, the casualties would have been greater had these houses been occupied. Twelve of the dead were given a public funeral by Dublin Corporation on 5 June, with de Valera and cabinet ministers attending.[162]

As the two aircraft released their bombs over Dublin, German aircraft were present in the skies along Ireland's entire east coast. At 0130 Dunany Point spotted red and white flares dropped from an aircraft to the south-west of the post that was still heading north. Reports from Ballagan Point and Dunany Point LOPs suggest that the first waves of German aircraft by this time had moved

31.5.'41, 3 June 1941.   **159** Ibid., undated and untitled memorandum with Bryan to Boland, 29 July 1941. Times were originally given in GMT, but have been reproduced here as summer time (that is, +1 hour).   **160** NAI DT S12405A, memorandum by the Department of Defence, Air Raid Precautions: Report on Bombing Incident – 31st May 1941, 8 July 1941. **161** Ibid.   **162** The other victims were given private funerals by their relatives. A representative of the Department of Defence attended all the private funerals.

north into Northern Ireland. Unable to locate their targets they were turning back. There were stragglers, but the majority of the aircraft logged by LOPs along the coast for the remainder of the emergency period that night were returning south from approximately 0130.

Dunany Head logged two explosions to the south-west at 0103 and four heavy explosions out to sea to the south-east at 0128, actions indicative of aircraft low on fuel dropping bombs. Wicklow Head LOP logged two heavy explosions at 0105 and 0154. At 0144 Ballyconnigar Hill, to the south of Wicklow Head, heard an aircraft eight miles to the west of the post travelling south east and passing out over the sea to the south of the post. At 0210 Wicklow Head heard an aircraft six miles north-east of the post tracking south-east. At 0230 the emergency was called off. A straggler from the waves of bombers was observed by Bray Head at 0350, having been shot at with machine-gun fire at Dalkey LOP as it passed by. It was definitely identified as a Junkers, flying down the coast at 5,000 feet heading south.

On de Valera's instructions, Walshe summoned Hempel to see him at midday on 31 May at Government Buildings to explain the actions of the previous night. Hempel arrived swiftly, 'clearly moved and disturbed ... he realized what a terrible position it was for him ... he did not believe the bombing could have been deliberate'.[163] He conveyed to Walshe his deepest sympathy with the relatives of those killed, put the bombing down to 'some tragic error' and 'wanted to do everything to make reparation for the tragedy'. Hempel had already contacted Berlin, warning them 'to be extremely careful not to make any cheap propaganda use of the bombing'. Walshe told Hempel in definite terms that overflying of Ireland by Germans had 'done nothing but harm to our relations ... [H]e should emphasise that point with all his strength.' The Irish Chargé d'Affaires in Berlin, William Warnock, protested to the German government expressing 'the strength and depth of indignation caused among the Irish people by the tragic loss of life and injury to persons and property following the bombing of this neutral country. No neutral country has suffered a single catastrophe from air bombing involving such extensive loss of life.'[164] The aide mémoire Warnock handed to the German Foreign Ministry was forcefully worded, its final paragraph beginning that Dublin could not emphasise 'too strongly that the strain imposed on Irish-German relations by such tragic events might well become insupportable.'[165] Walshe had after all told Hempel in 1939 that just such an incident might bring Ireland into the global conflict. Under-Secretary of State Dr Ernst Woermann told Warnock that he was 'deeply concerned at the incident, which he described as terrible'; all authorities concerned were undertaking investigations. If Germany were responsible,

163 NAI DFA 221/147E, secret memorandum by Walshe, 31 May 1941.   164 Ibid., telegram, Dublin to Warnock, 2 June 1941.   165 NAI DFA Berlin Embassy 48/17, Aide Mémoire, 3 June 1941.

reparations would be paid and 'there was absolutely no question of German aircraft having bombed Dublin on purpose'.[166]

An Air Corps reconnaissance flight over Dublin on the night of 5–6 July 1941 sought to recreate the conditions experienced by belligerent aircraft flying over the east coast of Ireland. The moon was almost full and it was a clear night. In his report, the pilot considered the night to be too bright for his mission as 'the brightness of the night [had] a considerable dimming effect on the ground lights'.[167] At 3,000 feet 'every road and important centre could be identified with ease ... [T]he lighting was regular and well defined,' house lighting could be seen and the effect of the cowling of street lighting to prevent upward glare was noticeable. By 0030 the Air Corps aircraft was at 10,000 feet over Wicklow Head and returning to Baldonnell. The pilot recorded that lighting in suburban streets had been extinguished. There was little difficulty recognizing Dublin, the lights of the city within the Royal Canal to the north and the Grand Canal to the south were cowled, but left on until half an hour before dawn. However, he added that 'when the suburban lights were extinguished, it was difficult to locate exactly the limits of the "built-up" area of the city generally'.[168] Nevertheless, on the night Dublin was bombed the pilot could see the ground, and 'any pilot, provided that he is below cloud and making any effort to check his position from ground features and lights, would have no difficulty in locating his position from the lights of the east coast and Dublin City'.[169] There may have been something in this analysis, as Michael Rynne at External Affairs noted that 'in all previous cases the bombs were dropped either at the canals or outside them – never inside the O'Connell Street – d'Olier Street area'.[170]

EVENTS AFTER 30–31 MAY 1941

On the night following the North Strand bombings there was a further air raid alert over Dublin. It seemed that the Luftwaffe was returning. Inland observer posts reported aircraft over counties Wexford, Waterford, Kilkenny, Carlow, Offaly, Laois, Kildare and Westmeath. Aircraft also passed along the east coast. At 2357 the emergency line from Wicklow Head LOP was opened to ADC in Dublin. Aircraft were passing ten miles to the south-east heading north. The alert followed the same pattern as the previous night. Continuous waves of aircraft passed north by Wicklow Head between midnight and 0042.[171] The lines to ADC were jammed by reports. The German planes flew north past Dublin. Dunany Point reported a series of heavy explosion to the north, east and south-east between 0008 and 0158 as aircraft were heard passing north and then south

166 NAI DFA 221/147E, telegram, Warnock to Dublin, 5 May 1945.   167 NAI DFA Secretary's Files, A29, Night reconnaissance of the city of Dublin – 23.30 to 01.00 hours on the 5th–6th July, '41.   168 Ibid.   169 Ibid.   170 Ibid., minute from Rynne to Walshe, 24 Oct. 1941.   171 MA LOP 9, 1 June 1941.

by Dunany Point, suggesting that they were again turning and dumping bombs after failing to locate targets in Northern Ireland.[172] At 0102 Wicklow Head saw 'one bright flash' and heard 'a loud explosion in the direction of Arklow' as two bombs were dropped near the town.[173] There was no damage to property beyond some smashed windows. The emergency ended at just after 0400. On inspection, bomb fragments were found bearing German markings.

There were continual 'RED' air raid warnings over Dublin through June 1941. At 1035 on the morning of 19 June Dalkey LOP received a 'RED' warning and the searchlight battery was informed. Aircraft, estimated at an altitude of 4,000 feet, were heard near the post 45 minutes later but the emergency passed and the all clear was sounded at midday. High alerts were to continue, sometimes at hourly intervals, through late June and early July 1941. One of the more serious took place on the afternoon of 13 July. At 1405 a code 'YELLOW' warning was received, with the state of alert increasing to 'RED' five minutes later at 1410. Two minutes later an aircraft, identified in poor visibility as a British flying boat, was spotted over Killiney Bay heading north towards Dublin from Bray.[174] The aircraft closed in on the Dalkey position, being estimated to be at a range of three miles at 1415 and at an altitude of 500 feet. The post logbook recorded that at 1415 the 'searchlight battery went into action with machine-gun and rifle fire on an unknown aircraft'.[175] The aircraft came in over the coast 300 yards south east from the post at a low-level attacking position and altitude. The light anti-aircraft guns 'maintained fire until [the] aircraft [was] out of range flying N. West' towards Dublin city. One hundred and eighty-one rounds were fired but none were thought to have hit their target. The alert continued until 1600.

ADC reported 'large formations of foreign aircraft' heading north in waves along the east coast of Ireland and over counties immediately inland between 2350 on 23 July and 0130 on 24 July.[176] Most of the aircraft appeared, by turning east in the south Dublin to north Wicklow area, to be engaged on bombing raids on Liverpool and Merseyside. Dalkey LOP logged one aircraft seven miles east of the post going north at 0045, changing direction and flying east. A few aircraft continued north to bomb areas in Northern Ireland. Bombs, including one large high-explosive bomb, were dropped at George's Quay, Dundalk between 0130 and 0132 on 24 July. There were no casualties and only minor damage to property. The Dublin defences did not go into action that night but 'five searchlights were exposed at intervals between the period of 0034 and 0138 hrs'.[177] Dalkey also heard heavy explosions to the east of the post in the Irish Sea at 0200 on 24 July. G2 reports on the progress of the bombers identified the

---

172 MA LOP 2, 1 June 1941.   173 MA LOP 9, 1 June 1941.   174 Bray estimated that the flying boat was at an altitude of 200 feet.   175 MA LOP 7, 13 July 1940.   176 NAI JUS 90/119/297, Barrett to Murphy, 24 July 1941.   177 NAI DFA 221/147F, G2 memorandum, Bombing incident in the vicinity of Dundalk, Co. Louth, on morning of 24th July 1941, 27 July 1941.

standard flight path of a German bombing mission. But in addition to these flights, as activity decreased in the Eastern Sector, aircraft were heard moving westwards and north-westwards along the south coast from Waterford to Kerry. This activity continued until 0630. Two hours later, a large number of British Hudsons began skirting the coast in small groups from Dursey Head in Cork to Wexford and north to the border with Northern Ireland in Louth. Three Hudsons were sighted over Rosslare Harbour at 1007 and reported to ADC by Greenore LOP. The aircraft came in from the south-west and flew north-east at between 1,000 and 1,500 feet. As they passed Rosslare Harbour village, the 'Military at Rosslare Harbour opened fire on the leading plane'; they also fired on two aircraft that followed the first three ten minutes later.[178] Garda Sergeant Patrick McGrath 'had the planes under observation and as far as he could see the fire did not affect any of the planes'.

Air raid warnings continued through the autumn and winter of 1941 until the spring of 1942. Thereafter entries for enemy aircraft sighted over Dublin are much less frequent in LOP logbooks. G2 knew from Delamere's visits to RAF Control and Fighter Headquarters at Aldergrove that 'a considerable amount of night flying navigational training' took place over the Irish Sea.[179] A night time report from November 1944 of 'approximately 28 aircraft showing navigation lights' sighted by Rush, Howth and Dalkey LOPs '5–8 miles E moving North and South' was 'presumed Allied [aircraft] engaged on squadron night exercises.'[180] British aircraft also continued to buzz Dublin and to circle around known landmarks such as the Kish lightship. They kept up patrols against the Luftwaffe along the eastern Irish coast but the Germans did not return. By early autumn 1943 the anti-aircraft post at Dalkey had been mothballed. On 20 August an inspecting officer noted that the door locks and seals were in position. The position was formally closed on 20 February 1944. Through 1944 and early 1945 Dalkey LOP noted passing patrolling Irish and Allied aircraft and there were occasional air raid warnings over the capital but never anything like the warnings of the summer of 1941. Regular inspections continued until March 1945 when the complex was dismantled, leaving only the LOP. The LOP logbook notes that a cookhouse, medical post, lock-up stores and a lean-to shelter were removed by Army engineers on the day the war ended in Europe. Over the following months 'AA personnel completed the removal of barbed wire defences from [the] LOP'.[181]

CONCLUSION

The Department of Defence noted that towards the end of May 1941 German flights along the east coast 'became confused and aimless and it was impossible

178 NAI JUS 90/119/297, Farrell to Murphy, 27 July 1941.   179 NAI DFA Secretary's Files A3, Archer to Traynor, 27 Mar. 1941, copy sent to Walshe.   180 MA DRS 1599, 21 Nov. 1944.   181 MA LOP 7, 9 May 1945.

to plot the course of these aircraft'.[182] Defence considered it significant that it was during January and May 1941, two periods of particularly confused and aimless flying, that bombs were dropped on Ireland. In both cases these periods of confusion ended following nights when bombs were dropped.

The combined reports from LOPs 1 to 20 explain the events of May bank holiday weekend 1941 in a detail that no other source can provide. They show that the bombing of the North Strand was a mistake. They place the bombing in the wider context of events off the east coast of Ireland and show a scattered force of bombers having failed to find their assigned target doing what Allied and Axis crews across the theatres of war did when they were lost and low on fuel. They dropped excess weight to improve flight time, speed and altitude. In this case it was their bomb load. Most aircraft dropped their bombs out to sea, as LOP reports indicate, but two aircraft over Dublin did not, with tragic consequences for the residents of the North Strand. While it can be argued that had the German aircraft not been fired upon by the Dublin defences they would not have dropped their bombs to make a faster getaway at a higher altitude, the corollary is that the flak must have burst near enough to them to cause concern, suggesting a reasonable level of efficiency and training in the gun crews involved. The German aircrews simply wished to get back to their bases and so they jettisoned their bombloads along the Irish east coast.

As far as the Irish defences were concerned, the enemy force was identified, followed and engaged. Quite how Germany might have reacted to one of her aircraft being shot down by the Defence Forces is a matter that does not arise – doubtless the gunners continued to hold their lotteries. The overall ADC framework held up reasonably well, though it is apparent that the phone system was unable to cope with the amount of traffic generated by the German incursion. Though LOPs, searchlight and sound operator crews, and AA-gunners were marshalled by ADC in a manner which could at least be described as respectable, the lack of defences around Dublin was thrown into sharp relief. The North Strand bombing was a mistake and engaging single aircraft was relatively straightforward. It would have been another matter altogether if the Luftwaffe had arrived over Dublin in force and with a mission objective in the area. The LOPs might well have signalled their imminent arrival but the city's meagre defences would have soon been overwhelmed and perhaps have run out of ammunition. The Defence Forces and the authorities knew this and it was in this context that ARP exercises undertaken in July 1941 in the aftermath of the North Strand bombing expected two thousand deaths and the widespread breakdown of communications within the city should the Luftwaffe return. Despite further alerts, they did not return as the war in Europe turned to the east.

182 NAI DFA Secretary's Files, A29, Summary of aerial activity on our south-eastern sector from Aug. 1940 to June 1941.

CHAPTER SEVEN

The United States enters the Second World War: Operation BOLERO

FROM JANUARY TO JUNE 1942 U-boats sank almost 3.5 million tons of shipping in the western North Atlantic, the Caribbean and the Gulf of Mexico. This 'Second Happy Time' was Dönitz's response to the United States' entry into the Second World War and to Washington's refusal to institute a convoy system along the American east coast. From Berlin, Warnock informed Dublin that in Germany these successes came 'at [the] right moment to counteract [the] influence of reverses in Russia'.[1] In contrast to the slaughter in the western Atlantic and, from later in the year, in the mid-Atlantic, where U-boats returned to full-scale attacks on convoys, submarines were absent from the waters around Ireland during 1942.[2] The year instead saw rising convoy traffic off the north Irish coast as, soon after the entry of the United States into the war in December 1941, the deployment of American forces to Europe began. Through 1942 the waters around Ireland became important supply routes for Operation BOLERO, the massive movement of American military personnel and equipment to Britain to assemble the invasion force destined for the Operation TORCH landings in North Africa in November 1942 and Operation OVERLORD in June 1944. G2 learned through their intelligence officers at Foynes that as this deployment was underway 'U. Boat activity ... intensified to check the A[merican] E[xpeditionary] F[orce] flow to Europe.'[3] Information from Foynes and Shannon and from Garda sources in Derry further suggested that 'in spite of heavy shipping losses, sufficient tonnage can be made available should or when a 2nd Front is decided on'.[4] The deployment of United States air power to Europe also gained momentum through 1942 and 'Ferry flights' of American aircraft became a regular feature in the skies over Mayo. Concerns about their safety brought the Coast Watching Service to the attention of David Gray, the United States Minister to Ireland. Via Gray, from 1942, coastwatchers' reports had a ready audience in Washington when they concerned American aircraft missing off Ireland and the recovery of the bodies of American crewmen killed in crashes on Irish territory. Coastal Command reconnaissance and convoy escort

1 NAI DFA Secretaries Files P12/3, Warnock to Walshe, 28 Jan. 1942. 2 Garda C3 Branch provided External Affairs with reports of these mid-Atlantic sinkings from information gained from sources in the British and American dockyards in Derry. 3 NAI DFA Secretary's Files A8, Précis of reports from IO Shannon Airport, Foynes. Period to 8th June, 1942. 4 Ibid., Reports from IO Shannon Airport, Foynes. Period August 2nd till 8th

operations off Ireland increased to protect the United States forces deploying to Europe. Still short of VLR aircraft, but operating with new equipment, improved radar and weapons such as the Leigh Light and more powerful depth charges, Coastal Command was 'born again' in 1942; 'bidding definite farewell to its "Scarecrow" phase' and being resurrected 'as a killer'.[5] Its aircraft routinely flew through Irish skies. Taking one month's figures for RAF flights around Ireland, in January 1942 there were between 102 and 132 flights each day off the north coast and up to twenty-nine flights daily along the southern coast, the majority being Coastal Command aircraft escorting convoys or on routine patrols.[6]

The most important zones of belligerent activity around Ireland during 1942 remained off the north and west coasts. Allied operations increased from Lough Foyle and the airbases around Derry which were 'in constant use by the RAF'.[7] A secondary zone of belligerent activity existed along the south and south-west coast where Coastal Command patrolling continued and where, from late 1942, with U-boat activity in the area reduced, convoys returned to the seas off Cork and Wexford. Between these zones, from Brandon Point in Kerry to Slyne Head in Galway, the west coast remained generally quiet. There was little naval activity along the east coast, though air incursions continued. As in previous years, Western Command LOPs remained the most active through 1942. Incident reports from Western Command peaked in June at almost 5,000, declining in the autumn, possibly due to the deployment of forces for Operation TORCH, rising again towards the year's end before again declining in December due to the ferocious winter storms hitting the Irish Atlantic coast. The LOPs on Inishowen remained central to Western Command coast watching and a visit to Malin Head LOP by General McKenna on 22 October underlined the significance of these most northerly posts. Allied destroyers and submarines exercised off north Donegal and Coastal Command aircraft from Limavady and Ballykelly trained off the northern coast, firing rockets and guns and dropping depth charges in view of the LOPs along Inishowen. These LOPs also sighted convoys assembling, destroyer escorts forming from forces operating out of Derry and liners converted into troopships passing at speed, many disembarking American GIs on the dockside in Derry.

With the growing importance of the naval and air bases around Derry the heat went out of Britain's desire to retake the southern Irish ports. When Lord Cranborne advised Churchill in February 1942 to 'refrain from reopening' the ports question, Churchill agreed with his Dominions Secretary.[8] By the summer of 1942 London had lost interest in facilities in neutral Ireland. Dulanty told Walshe of a meeting with Malcolm MacDonald where MacDonald remarked

inclusive. 5 Terraine, *Business*, p. 434. 6 TNA AIR 2/4735, minute, Director General of Air Safety to Lord Rossmore, 27 Jan. 1942. 7 NAI DFA Secretary's Files P43/1, Special Observations re Derry Area, undated, but Jan. 1942. 8 TNA PREM 3/127/3A, Cranborne to Churchill, 4 Feb. 1942.

that 'in none of his conversations with Cabinet Ministers had "the question of Eire in any form" at all been mentioned'.[9] The War Cabinet no longer thought Germany had designs on Ireland, Churchill informing a meeting in July that the situation had 'changed as compared [to] 2 years ago', there was 'no risk now of invasion of Ireland'.[10] Britain made a limited amount of military equipment available Ireland in September 1942 in order to facilitate 'a general working liaison ... especially with the Air Force'.[11] In a further sign of improved British–Irish relations, a British military mission visited Ireland in December. Co-operation between Dublin and London had developed and Dublin was placing at British disposal 'through the coastal watch and ward ... a system of intelligence which', as Maffey told the War Cabinet in London, 'works for our purposes.'[12]

Now two and a half years in existence the Coast Watching Service was well established. District Officers reported 'very favourably' on personnel and during 'surprise visits of inspection' to LOPs NCOs and men 'were found to be alert, properly dressed, and well acquainted with their duties'.[13] Inspecting officers singled out the NCOs and men of Ballycotton LOP for particular praise. District Officer Lieutenant Barrett reported that the post was 'very clean due to the interest' in their work taken by Corporal Roche and Volunteer O'Driscoll and the efficiency of the post was 'outstanding'.[14] Also praised were Galley Head and Bray Head (Valentia) LOPs. Commandant Donegan expressed 'great satisfaction at the manner in which personnel carried out their duties' at Galley Head and District Officer O'Carroll reported that Bray Head was 'kept in excellent condition' reflecting 'great credit on Corporal J[ohn] Dore, NCO in charge'.[15] To ensure high standards prevailed at all posts, from late May 1942 fourteen-day refresher courses for coastwatchers took place at Haulbowline. Special courses for NCOs in charge of LOPs began in July 1943.

Two significant developments in the organization of the Coast Watching Service occurred in 1942. The Irish air observer network expanded during the year with the opening of a countrywide system of reporting centres staffed on a twenty-four-hour basis. The Coast Watching Service integrated into this wider network. Coastwatchers reported to new Air and Marine Intelligence reporting centres in Dublin (Eastern Sector), Mallow (Southern Sector), Limerick (Shannon Sector) and Athlone (Western Sector), thereby reducing the pressure on intelligence staff at Command level. The new reporting centres were commanded by Central Control, operating from St Joseph's monastery at Clondalkin to the west of Dublin. Radio transmitters for communication between reporting

9 NAI DFA Secretary's Files P12/14(1), Dulanty to Walshe, 7 May 1942.   10 TNA CAB 195/1, W.M. (42) 96th Meeting, 27 July 1942.   11 TNA DO 35/1109/8, Maffey to Machtig, 18 May 1942.   12 TNA DO 35/1109/7, Irish Policy, 2 Feb. 1942.   13 MA G2/X/315 Pt II, Monthly Report Marine Service Depot, Haulbowline, Southern Command, Feb. 1942.   14 Ibid., May 1942.   15 Ibid., July 1942.

centres and Central Control began operation in February 1942. This new system enabled aircraft spotted at any point over Irish territory to be tracked the entire length and breadth of the country rather than, as previously, just over the eastern and south-eastern counties. The second development took place on 17 July when overall control of the Coast Watching Service was removed from the Marine Service. The Marine Service had proposed this move from October 1940, claiming there was 'no possibility of linking two forces of such totally different characters. The fact they have received a common name has not brought unity – and can never bring it'.[16] The creation of the Maritime Inscription second-line reserve naval force in September 1940 had made the need to create a separate Marine Service 'all the more necessary'.[17] The former M&CWS became the Marine Service, and the Coast Watching Service became an Army controlled and administered operation, though co-operation between the Army and the Marine Service on coastal defence and observation continued. In day-to-day terms, the separation made no difference to the operation of LOPs.

CHANGING TRENDS OFF THE NORTH AND
WEST COASTS OF IRELAND

Coastwatchers' reports from the most important area of Coast Watching Service operations through 1942, the coast from Clew Bay north to Lough Foyle, covered six areas. They identified the increasing level of naval operations off Inishowen, including the large rise in training off the peninsula and in destroyer traffic from Lough Foyle protecting the rising number of convoys sighted off the north coast. Increased Coastal Command air patrols from Northern Irish bases were also linked to the protection of these convoys, though the overall level of air operations off Ireland declined in 1942 compared to 1941. Instead, 1942 saw a more defined pattern of air operations related to specific tasks such as convoy escorts. The final area was the rise in Ferry Command delivery flights transiting Irish territory along the North Mayo Corner, the precursor to a massive increase in delivery flights that would occur in 1943. The trend through 1942 was for operations off the north and west coast to rise month on month, though with a slight dip in August and September, until poor weather in November and December led levels to decrease. The one exception to this trend was the rising number of delivery flights making European landfall off North Mayo. Western Command coastwatchers showed G2 that through 1942 the Allied war machine was increasing in momentum and size as United States forces deployed to Europe.

There was no hint of these future developments in January 1942 when the low level of activity off western and northern coasts was 'the same as last month'

16 MA EDP 20/5, Memorandum, 1 Oct. 1940. 17 Ibid.

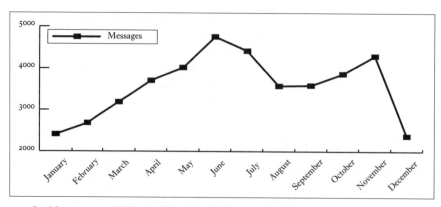

7.1: Incident reports (Western Command/Western Sector LOPs): January–December
1942 (Source: MA G2/X/315 part II)

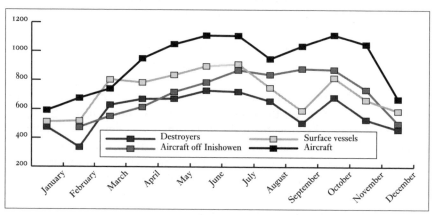

7.2: Aircraft and surface vessels sighted (Western Command): 1942
(Source: MA G2/X/315 part II)

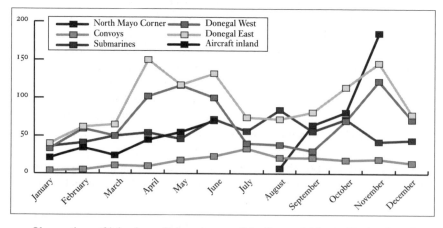

7.3: Observations of inland overflights, the use of the Donegal 'air corridor', submarines,
convoys and ferry flights (over the 'Mayo Corner'): 1942 (Source: MA G2/X/315 part II)

with only a slight increase in numbers of aircraft spotted as the 'usual reconnaissance flights' passed on routine patrols and aircraft en-route to escort convoys
were reported.[18] Air activity remained 'spasmodic'[19] and through February
flying remained at a 'low-level'.[20] Seasonal factors, particularly weather, were
responsible. Both months saw days of activity interspersed with days where few
flights were observed. Searching for an explanation, intelligence officers noticed
that 'the days of activity' along the north Donegal coast 'coincide with convoys
approaching or leaving our shores'.[21] Inishowen LOPs reported a large increase
in convoy escort operations in mid-February as the 'Mid-Ocean Escort Force'
began taking convoys the entire distance from Newfoundland to Derry; 'the
famous "Newfy–Derry" run'.[22] North coast convoy traffic increased substantially through the first half of 1942, from four convoys in January to thirty-three
in July. Often containing upwards of forty vessels, convoys took a standard form;
freighters accompanied by a handful of oil tankers and always flanked by a
moderate to heavy escort of destroyers and corvettes. The sighting of rising
numbers of tankers in convoys indicated an increase in Allied fuel consumption
and growing pressure on stocks held in Britain. Notable sightings included the
British battle cruiser *Renown* in the escort to a convoy of twelve oil tankers
passing north coast LOPs on 11 March. Later in 1942, Malin Head reported the
presence of 'aircraft carriers' in convoys. These were escort carriers, giving
localized anti-submarine protection to convoys. They became a regular feature
of observations off Donegal from 1942. On 27 May Glengad Head observed a
battleship escorted by two destroyers joining an aircraft carrier moving east.
Horn Head LOP, following the progress of another convoy, 'observed 3 Aircraft
taking off from Carrier and circling over Convoy'.[23] Through such reports G2's
knowledge of convoys developed from simply knowing of the passage and size
of convoys to analyzing their routes, structure, patterns of assembly and the air
and naval escorts allocated to them. When Malin Head LOP reported a stationary
convoy of thirty ships twenty miles north-west of the post, coastwatchers added
that the convoy waited for three hours for ten other ships to join before the
combined force departed, leading G2 to conclude that 'westbound convoy[s]
apparently have an assembly point "somewhere" north of Malin Head'.[24] While
it added another piece to the intelligence picture, the vague conclusion showed
the limits of what G2 could achieve with the resources at its disposal.

Troopships carrying United States soldiers passed in full view of north
Donegal LOPs through 1942. A significant sighting in the early stages of these
deployments occurred on 25 January when Malin Head sighted two large liners
seven miles to the east, one of which appeared to be *Queen Elizabeth*. Liners of
the 'Queen Mary type' would often be spotted off Donegal. Converted to

18 MA G2/X/315 Pt II, Western Sector, Monthly Report, Jan. 1942. 19 Ibid. 20 Ibid.,
Feb. 1942. 21 Ibid. 22 Terraine, *Business*, p. 435. 23 MA G2/X/315 Pt II, Western
Sector, Monthly Report, Nov. 1942. 24 Ibid., May 1942.

troopships and each carrying almost 15,000 troops, they were daily evidence of the movement of United States forces to Britain 'as an essential preliminary to the opening of the "Second Front"'.[25] American forces landing in Derry trained in the area. One report of particularly heavy gunfire on 24 March 'was established to be artillery practice by U.S. Marines' at McGilligan Point.[26] This area was 'very heavily fortified by the British' and with 'a large garrison' of British forces stationed there, the Marines had taken over and were using British guns in exercises that were expected to continue into the summer.[27] G2 learned that American forces in Northern Ireland included 'armoured units', concluding that 'as these are not needed for defensive action, they are probably for the "invasion army"'.[28] Reports arriving with G2 that the Chief of the Imperial General Staff, Field Marshal Sir Alan Brooke, had told the United States troops in Northern Ireland that 'they would "certainly see action against the Nazis"' were a further 'pointer to the early formation of the 2nd Front'.[29]

Through March and April reports of naval exercises off the north coast – 'gunfire, explosions and flares' – arrived daily at Western Command headquarters in Athlone.[30] The manoeuvring of vessels engaged in target practice came to be regarded as normal. Fighter aircraft staging mock battles was a new development, as was a report from Fort Dunree of 'a Spitfire stunt flying over the Fort'.[31] Spitfires were also spotted over Donegal Bay and around Melmore and Fanad headlands. As spring turned into summer their training flights became routine. There was a 'marked increase' over north Donegal in 'fighter activity' from airfields in Derry.[32] No sustained German air or marine activity was reported to Western Command in the first months of 1942. The Luftwaffe was almost completely absent from Irish skies, a trend noticeable as the war on the Russian front intensified. Conscious of this development, Boland later wrote to Walshe that 'German aircraft have been very infrequent in this part of the world within the last twelve months.'[33] From Berlin, Warnock reported that 'the main strength of the German Air Force had been removed from the western European seaboard, and Ireland benefited indirectly from the fact that German operations against Great Britain were on a reduced scale.'[34] Only one positively identified German aircraft was seen by coastwatchers in March, heading from Western into Southern Command and passing out to sea off the Cork coast. Given the regularity of Condor flights through 1940 and 1941 it was also

25 Patrick Beesly, *Very special intelligence: the story of the Admiralty's operational intelligence centre 1939–1945* (London, 2000 edition), p. 148.   26 MA G2/X/315 Pt II, Western Sector, Monthly Report, Mar. 1942.   27 NAI DFA Secretary's Files P43/1, Air and Naval Bases in N.I., undated, but Aug. 1941.   28 NAI DFA Secretary's Files A8, Précis of reports from IO Shannon Airport, Foynes. Period to 8th June, 1942.   29 Ibid.   30 MA G2/X/315 Pt II, Western Sector, Monthly Report, Apr. 1942.   31 Ibid., July 1942.   32 Ibid., July 1942. 33 NAI DFA Secretary's Files P18, minute, Boland to Walshe, 29 Oct. 1942.   34 NAI DFA Berlin Embassy 19/3, Irish Legation at Berlin. Annual Report, 1942.

something of an oddity when Rossan Point LOP in Donegal sighted a Ju-88 flying north-westerly six miles west of the post on 18 June. The two Blohm and Voss flying boats reported by Letterkenny Garda station, Fort Dunree and Inishowen Head LOP on 21 July were also unusual. They did not go unnoticed, as minutes later two RAF Spitfires were seen in pursuit.

The body of a German airman, Leutnant Werner Bornefeld, washed ashore at Lunnagh Strand, Bunbeg, Donegal on 14 February. Among the effects found on his body were the grim trophies of war: 'five photographs of burning ships and of German aircraft'.[35] Bornefeld's body had not been long in the water, though no aircraft had been reported shot down in the area. Through 1942 only thirteen bodies were recovered along the Irish coastline, a notable change from 1940 and 1941. The nature of the flotsam also changed: most appeared to have been in the water for some time. Typical were a 'badly damaged lifeboat' that came ashore near Annagh Head, Belmullet and various barrels and tanks, including a curious 'cylindrical metal object (36" x 2½" with aerial 14) containing automatic wireless transmitting apparatus of German origin' brought ashore by fishermen at Clifden and which was possibly a German automatic meteorological buoy.[36] The equipment was the subject of a special G2 report. Such equipment was also seen by agencies beyond Ireland. A contemporaneous British Air Ministry intelligence report on similar equipment found off Milford Haven compared it to 'the buoy examined in Ireland'.[37] Altogether, these were nothing like the levels of human remains and flotsam recovered in the preceding years as the battle of the Atlantic for the time being moved away from Irish shores.

Routine patrols by 'British and "presumed" British aircraft' were 'observed daily' along north and north-west coasts during March, particularly around the North Mayo Corner.[38] A British Blenheim bomber on a training flight crashed near Crossmolina, Mayo, on 13 March. Ground defences at Rathmullen, Donegal, had opened fire on the aircraft earlier in the same day. Three of the crew of four were injured in the crash and were taken to Castlebar Hospital. Their ultimate destination was 'governed by a special message from G.H.Q.', which suggests that they were released over the border into Northern Ireland. After 'days of considerable activity … followed by days of abnormal quietness', the second half of April brought 'intensifications of coastal patrols and numerous overland flights' across Western Sector which accompanied 'the fine weather at this time of year'.[39] Flight Sergeant B.F. Snell of 58 Squadron, 19 Group, Coastal Command, based at St Eval in Cornwall took part in these patrols. On 27 April he flew a Whitley V off the west coast of Ireland on what his logbook records as a seven-hour and forty-minute 'anti-aircraft escort'

---

35 MA G2/X/446 Pt. II, minute on file, 23 Feb. 1942.   36 MA G2/X/315 Pt II, Western Sector, Monthly Report, Nov. 1942.   37 TNA AIR 40/41, German automatic floating transmitter controlled by meteorological unit, 29 Oct. 1942.   38 MA G2/X/315 Pt II, Western Sector, Monthly Report, Mar. 1942.   39 Ibid., Apr. 1942.

patrol.[40] Continuing good weather in May saw further increases in patrolling but with a return to the same 'inconsistent irregularity' seen earlier in the year.[41] Aircraft from 15 Group Coastal Command sought out submarines close to Ireland. Wellington 'A' of 304 Squadron based at Tiree in Scotland mounted a low-level attack with depth charges on 'a possible U-boat' ten miles north west of Downpatrick Head, Mayo, at 1940 on 9 June.[42] The LOP on Downpatrick Head reported considerable British air activity in the vicinity of the post through the afternoon of 9 June but it did not report the attempted attack by A/304. By early evening visibility at the headland was reported as moderate and, with a cloudy sky, did not exceed five miles.

By the summer of 1942 vessels carrying United States troops were a regular sight off Donegal. Three unescorted troopships entered and left Lough Foyle on 14 May, having disembarked troops and equipment in Derry, a large party of troops arriving in Belfast the same day. Sixteen liners converted into troopships were spotted through June as troop movements continued. A convoy sighted on 9 June off Malin Head comprised four liners, six destroyers, one battleship (estimated at 35,000 tons) and one 10,000-ton merchant vessel. A similar convoy of thirteen liners accompanied by eight destroyers and one cruiser passed west by Glengad Head and Malin Head on 30 July. Hunting such targets, U-boats returned to the North Atlantic in late August 1942 and large convoy battles took place in the mid-Atlantic in early autumn. Sightings by coastwatchers of naval surface vessels, particularly destroyers, fell for the remainder of 1942. Convoy traffic declined from a summer high of thirty-three convoys in July to fourteen in December. However, the size of individual convoys rose: there was security in numbers. In late August Defence Forces intelligence officers at Foynes overheard a conversation that 'one of the largest convoys ever known, has successfully crossed the Atlantic. Some of the new precautions are proving effective'.[43]

Garda C3 Branch maintained surveillance of the movements of United States troops arriving in and stationed in Derry and the coastwatchers watched their onward deployment from Derry in smaller vessels. In September 'Passenger Boats of the Mail Boat type – the "BENNYCHREE" of 2,000 tons and the "PRINCESS MAUD" of 1,500 tons' entered Lough Foyle carrying American troops and 'two slightly smaller vessels, the "NORTHLAND" and the "NAUGHTON"' were sighted later in the month taking troops out of Derry 'believed to be British troops bound for the Near East'.[44] Activity in the docks in Derry reduced temporarily with the launching of Operation TORCH on 8 November, though large liners converted into troopships continued to pass the north coast. Five liners, escorted by a cruiser and four destroyers, were sighted east of Malin Head

40 TNA AIR 4/94.   41 MA G2/X/315 Pt II, Western Sector, Monthly Report, May 1942. 42 TNA AIR 25/254, 15 Group Operations Record Book, 9 June 1942.   43 NAI DFA Secretary's Files A8, Reports of IO Shannon Airport, Foynes. Period 23rd to 29th Aug. inclusive, 30 Aug. 1942.   44 MA G2/X/315 Pt II, Western Sector, Monthly Report, Sept.

on 16 December and Western Sector drew the attention of G2 to the 'large percentage of Troop Transports' in the fourteen convoys seen by north Donegal LOPs that month.[45]

FERRY FLIGHTS DURING 1942

In January 1942 coastwatchers reported 591 aircraft off the north-west coast. Sightings rose to 1,100 in June. Before June almost all aircraft sighted were British, the observation in May of 'a single American Flying Fortress' off Inishowen was significant and it made it into the Western Sector report for the month.[46] Then, suddenly, in June American aircraft began to be 'observed frequently', particularly off Inishowen, beginning a trend that continued through the summer.[47] The summer brought Western Sector its busiest month to date in 1942 with 4,755 incidents reported in June alone as aerial activity 'maintained a greater regularity'[48] due to 'increased activity off North Donegal and in Donegal Bay'.[49] Donegal Bay LOPs logged regular training flights where British aircraft circled 'for long periods in the Bay', and dropped 'Depth Charges and Smoke Bombs'.[50] But it was delivery flights that caught G2's attention during the summer. From dawn until mid-morning coastwatchers from Mayo to Donegal reported American aircraft coming in from the Atlantic flying towards Northern Ireland.

A number of crashes earlier in 1942 had proved the G2 hypothesis that these were aircraft on delivery flights. On 15 April at 0945 an unarmed Hudson (FH263) being ferried from Canada to Scotland made a forced landing near Blacksod LOP after encountering severe weather. The crew of three were uninjured and the aircraft 'which was slightly damaged, was subsequently repaired and was disposed of in accordance with instructions received'.[51] This translated into 'a British Salvage Party with four large vehicles, a portable crane and a Hillman private saloon car' arriving at the scene four days after the crash, dismantling the aircraft and, with an Irish Defence Forces escort, taking it by road to Northern Ireland.[52] Three weeks later on 4 May a second unarmed Hudson (FH376) landed at 0730 at Pollnagreen 1 mile north-east of Ballyliffen, Inishowen. The crew of three, dressed in civilian clothing, were unhurt and were taken to Fort Lenan. The aircraft was also on a delivery flight. It had run out of fuel and was refuelled from stocks sent from Northern Ireland. It left in accordance with orders received from GHQ in Dublin.[53] G2 were quick to link the two flights, noting the closeness of the registration numbers of the aircraft. Garda sources reported that the second aircraft was one of '150 squadrons of bombers, each squadron consisting of 15 machines' which had arrived from

1942.   45 Ibid., Dec. 1942.   46 Ibid., May 1942.   47 Ibid., June 1942.   48 Ibid.   49 Ibid.
50 Ibid.   51 Ibid., Apr. 1942.   52 NAI JUS 90/119/297, Burns to Murphy, 27 Apr. 1942.
53 NAI DFA Secretary's Files A26, Bryan to Walshe, 5 May 1942.

America that week. Whatever the truth of the numbers, the report continued that 'this may be taken as an indication of the rate at which aeroplanes will arrive in England in future'.[54] A further Ferry Command Hudson (42–66130) made a forced landing on a beach at Dunfanaghy in Donegal at 1230 on 16 June. When it appeared that the aircraft would be lost with the incoming tide '200 local men volunteered to haul it to safety' over the soft sand.[55] Fuel sent in five-gallon drums from an RAF base near Derry was passed by a human chain to the aircraft and poured in by hand. A cooler welcome awaited two Spitfires sent from Northern Ireland to view the grounded aircraft. As the fighters circled over Malin Head 'the Ground Defences went into action [and] 27 rounds were fired'.[56] The aircraft circled again and flew west towards Dunfanaghy.

One ferry pilot described his and his co-pilots impressions of arriving at dawn over the Irish coast en-route to Scotland: 'We soon saw the purple line … [W]e flew over neutral Ireland as we homed right in on [the] UU7 [beacon]. To hell with the Irish.'[57] One special flight followed this course on the night of 25–6 June 1942. Field Marshal Sir Alan Brooke recorded in his diary the last hours of a transatlantic crossing with Winston Churchill:

> I went up to sit in the second pilot's seat where I found the P.M. Beautiful moon shining on a sea of clouds, as the moon was nearly full the scene was beyond words. Shortly afterwards the clouds began to break and the sea became visible, with only patches of cloud lying about. Then out of the darkness dark patches loomed up out of the horizon, which turned out to be the north coast of Mayo! We soon struck the coast, only just visible in the moonlight. P.M. was as thrilled as I was! We skirted the north coast of Mayo and sailed in just south of the mouth of the Erne, and on right over the middle of Lough Erne, hitting the north coast [of Lough Erne] at about Killadeas. On over Armagh, north corner of Lough Neagh, and just north of Belfast. Then across the channel and back to Stranraer, where we made a perfect landing at 11.10 pm by American time but 5.10 am by British time.[58]

Brooke also recorded

> staring into the darkness trying to make out if we could see land, the pilot saying that if our landfall was correct we should soon see a lighthouse. And then suddenly flicking out of the darkness was a small spark of light! We had crossed that vast expanse of water and struck the exact spot we hoped for.[59]

54 NAI DFA Secretary's Files P43/1, MacMághnuis to Murphy, 5 May 1942. 55 TNA DO 121/87, Irish Affairs, 4 July 1942. 56 MA G2/X/315 Pt II, Western Sector, Monthly Report, June 1942. 57 Don McVicar, *North Atlantic cat* (Shrewsbury, 1983), p. 99. 58 Alex Danchev and Daniel Todman (eds), *War diaries 1939–1945: Field Marshal Lord Alanbrooke* (London, 2001), p. 273. 59 Ibid., p. 274.

It was either Eagle Island or Black Rock lighthouse off the north Mayo coast and it is not clear from logbooks whether the coastwatchers saw or heard this particular flight. What is evident is that the aircraft followed the usual transatlantic track, skirting Erris Head and passing along the Donegal air corridor into Northern Ireland airspace.

Like the three Hudsons mentioned above, loss of bearing and lack of fuel were almost always the cause of aircraft on delivery flights landing on Irish territory. An American B-25 Mitchell on a delivery flight to Prestwick landed near Strokestown, Roscommon on 4 July 1942. The aircraft was first sighted by coastwatchers at Kilcreadun and Loop Head coming in from the Atlantic. It passed over Kilkee heading north before making its unplanned descent. Low on fuel and with the port engine out of action, it made a forced landing, damaging a propeller and its landing gear before coming to a halt. The crew of four, three civilians and a RCAF Sergeant in uniform were arrested by the military at Boyle, released the following day and crossed the border at Swanlinbar.

In July the number of inland flights over Mayo, Sligo and north Galway was fifty-two, the highest yet recorded in 1942. Among these flights, thirty-one unidentified aircraft were 'observed to move overland across Connaught in a North-Easterly direction towards the Border'.[60] The majority of these flights occurred before noon and were 'aircraft being ferried from America to Northern Ireland'.[61] Some landed at Castle Archdale, explaining why more aircraft crossed from the Atlantic east over the Donegal Corridor than were seen to leave Lough Erne and fly west. Other ferry flights made for airfields in Northern Ireland, Scotland and England. G2 was now 'certain' that flights observed over north Mayo in the early to mid-morning 'were of aircraft being ferried from Newfoundland to Northern Ireland and England'.[62] All used Achill Head and Clare Island at the mouth of Clew Bay as landfall points. Delivery flights increased to such an extent that by the autumn of 1942 Ferry Command flights vied with Coastal Command flights to become the main aerial activity observed by coastwatchers over north Mayo. On the morning of 30 September during a period of 'intense air activity by British aircraft moving north eastwards over Mayo and adjoining counties', Lockheed Ventura AJ-460, caught in bad weather and low on fuel, made a wheels-up landing at Emlagh, two miles south of Roonagh Point LOP, on the southern entrance to Clew Bay. It was the very point G2 had already identified as the most likely position for a ferry flight to make landfall. The Ventura was on a delivery flight from Newfoundland. The crew, uninjured, were allowed to leave Irish territory. Coastwatchers at Roonagh were informed that 'three Englishmen' would arrive by car to visit the scene and inspect the aircraft, which was then salvaged.[63] The morning of Sunday 25 October stood out as a period of 'intense overland activity' with flights 'moving

60 MA G2/X/315 Pt II, Western Sector, Monthly Report, July 1942.   61 Ibid.   62 Ibid., Sept. 1942.   63 MA LOP 57, 7 Oct. 1942.

towards the border from the Galway/Mayo coastline'. Twenty aircraft were observed that morning, five of them definitely identified as American. Later that day Ferry Command Boston bomber BZ200 came down at Tulladooly, north-west of Crossmolina. One crewman was killed when the aircraft overturned on landing in a bog. The aircraft was wrecked and the two surviving crew were released across the border. Ferry flights over North Mayo rose further from eighty-one in October to 185 in November and crashes and forced landings continued as weather declined with the onset of winter. At dusk on 17 November a Catalina made a forced landing on Lough Gill. The aircraft, being ferried from Bermuda to Scotland, was undamaged and the crew were uninjured. The pilot reported to the Irish authorities that he thought he was landing on Lough Erne but had confused Sligo and Donegal Bays. Wing Commander Begg wrote some days after this incident that 'with the increase of trans-Atlantic ferrying and the expansion of training around our coasts' the number of forced landings in Ireland would increase.[64] He added that he had learned from Boland and Archer that Dublin was 'getting somewhat perturbed' at the number of emergency landings as 'reports as to the fate of the crew and machines will certainly attract the attention of the German Legation.'

PATTERNS OF ACTIVITY IN LATE 1942

Excluding ferry flights, from July to December 1942 there was a noticeable change in the scope of Allied operations off the north and north-west coasts. As air operations off Inishowen were steady, a decline in flights from Lough Erne was responsible for a decrease in Coastal Command operations. The decline in air activity along the west coast continued into September with a return to the irregular patterns of flying seen earlier in the year. Days of 'considerable activity coincided with the arrival or departure of Convoys off our Northern Shores and the arrival of aircraft being ferried from America'. They contrasted with days of 'slight activity mainly coinciding with the periods of abnormal weather'.[65] Perhaps a further reason for the decline in observed Coastal Command activity was that from late July to late August the area south-east of Iceland became 'an active one for aircraft sightings and attacks' on U-boats.[66] Coastal Command aircraft were heading north from the Derry bases and not passing LOPs along the Irish coast.

To counter U-boats and protect convoys, flights from Lough Erne began to rise through October. The number of United States aircraft taking part in these patrols observed by coastwatchers increased as Coastal Command received long-

64 TNA DO 35/1109/14, Begg to Assistant Chief of the Air Staff, 26 Nov. 1942.   65 MA G2/X/315 Pt II, Western Sector, Monthly Report, Sept. 1942.   66 David Syrett (ed.), *The battle of the Atlantic and signals intelligence: U-boat situations and trends, 1941–1945* (Aldershot, 1998), p. 64, U-boat Situation. Week ending 27/7/42.

needed reinforcements to replace their ageing aircraft. American aircraft training for anti-U-boat missions practised over Donegal Bay and circled near Finner Camp. Further north Garda sources reported that United States Flying Fortresses were 'training hard and performing flight exercises' off Inishowen.[67] The increase in activity was particularly noticeable during the last ten days of October. After weeks when aerial activity 'varied considerably', the end of the month saw 'a sharp increase in all areas' with 1,144 flights reported, the highest number seen in the area for the year, though 'an exceptionally large number' were training flights of short duration.[68] Intense coastal patrolling from Castle Archdale also commenced towards the end of October. An explanation in the rise may lie in a British intelligence report indicating 'U-boats much closer to Ireland than is normal'.[69] British forces considered that 'timely air cover can effectively break down the shadowing routine and enable convoys to draw clear' of U-boats.[70] By November 'the majority of the 90 U-Boats now in the Atlantic [were] working in [the] North-western Approaches between 20°–40° West'.[71] Operations from Lough Erne rose again in November with 'more frequent' and 'well maintained' Coastal Command patrols from Lough Erne 'down along the Mayo/Galway coastline' in a period where aerial activity elsewhere in Western Command decreased.[72] Lough Erne flights were now more numerous than coastwatchers had seen for fifteen months. Off Mayo and Galway Catalina and Sunderland flying boats were 'especially active during periods when troop transport convoys were observed'.[73] More flights led to more landings on Irish territory. A Catalina first observed over Boyle on the evening of 18 November flew south-west, crossing into the Atlantic at Aughris Point, Galway. Heard some time later circling off the west coast of Galway, the seaplane made a forced landing on the Shannon near the mouth of the River Fergus. The flying boat had engine trouble and the aircraft and its crew of nine were permitted to leave when the problem was rectified.

SAFEGUARDING AMERICAN INTERESTS, 1942–3

Until 1942 American interest in the Coast Watching Service was limited. The American Minister to Ireland, David Gray, knew of the existence of the service and the Military Attaché at the American legation, Major J.W. Wofford, visited Malin Head LOP in June 1941 shortly after he arrived in Ireland.[74] With the

---

67 NAI DFA Secretary's Files P43/1, Ua Ceallaigh to Murphy, 14 Sept. 1942. 68 MA G2/X/315 Pt II, Western Sector, Monthly Report, Oct. 1942. 69 Syrett, *Signals intelligence*, p. 91, U-boat Situation. Week ending 19/10/42. 70 Ibid., p. 89, U-boat Situation. Week ending 12/10/42. 71 Ibid., p. 85, U-boat Situation. Week ending 28/9/42. 72 MA G2/X/315 Pt II, Western Sector, Monthly Report, Nov. 1942. 73 Ibid. 74 Military attachés were directly responsible to the War Department through the Assistant Chief of Staff, G2, and were members of embassy staff advising their ambassador/minister on military matters.

entry of the United States into the war and the increase through 1942 in the number of aircraft flown by United States crews crossing the Atlantic entering Irish airspace, American interest in the coastwatchers rose. An American Douglas DC3 flown by Lieutenant Bernard Sauer and Lieutenant Jack Goudy, en-route from Iceland to Prestwick, lost and short on fuel, 'effected a perfect landing' at the newly completed Shannon airport just before 1800 on 6 July 1942.[75] The fifteen passengers were in United States army uniform and some were carrying side arms. United States Vice-Consul at Foynes Willard Calder received an anonymous phone call that the plane was under Irish military guard at Shannon. Calder informed Gray who telephoned Walshe. In the meantime, Calder drove to Shannon and made contact with the grounded crew who were 'under technical arrest'.[76] The DC3 was on a transport flight and with no offensive weapons or military equipment on board the Irish authorities took a 'lenient view'. The guard was lifted and the crew released. GHQ in Dublin wanted Sauer's aircraft to leave immediately, but Sauer was reluctant to depart as his crew were 'tired' and 'he was not happy about the behavior of one of his engines'.[77] Captain Paget MacCormack, the Air Corps officer liasing with Sauer, agreed that 'it would be most unfair to force a tired crew off the ground that night'.[78] The Americans were 'given everything they wanted to eat and drink and were entertained most lavishly' at the various messes in Shannon.[79] After a trial flight to check the engines, the aircraft left Shannon just before midday on 7 July and 'was routed to a Six County Aerodrome at St Angelo via Loop Head and territorial waters to Mullaghmore, Co. Sligo, thence to Border and Aerodrome'.[80] Before he left, Sauer thanked the Irish authorities for 'the wonderful hospitality which had been shown to him, his crew and his passengers'.[81] Calder minuted that 'our officers and men had obviously made themselves extremely popular with the Military at Rineanna'.[82]

David Gray was increasingly concerned about the fate of American crews who might make emergency landings on Irish territory. He wrote to Hull that though American planes such as Sauer's had landed in Ireland and had 'been secretly helped to safety', 'sixteen bombers on their arrival over Eire were, for some time, lost, but a safe landing was made after a time in Northern Ireland'.[83] Paying no attention to the evidence before him, such as Sauer's case, Gray argued that American crews would soon be forced down in neutral Ireland and 'when that happens their planes will be seized and the pilots interned'. This was a ludicrous suggestion as G2 records show that Ireland interned no United

75 NAI JUS 90/119/298, Casey to Murphy, 7 July 1942. The aircraft was from the 12th Air Force-62nd Troop Carrier Group, moving from Florence, SC to Keevil, Wiltshire. 76 NARA RG 84 Dublin legation, SSF, Box 4 (1942), Calder to Gray, 8 July 1942.   77 Ibid. 78 Ibid.   79 Ibid.   80 NAI DFA Secretary's Files A26, Landing of troop-carrying aircraft at Rynana on 6/7/1942.   81 Ibid.   82 NARA RG 84 Dublin legation, SSF, Box 4 (1942), Calder to Gray, 8 July 1942.   83 NARA RG 84 Dublin legation, SSF, Box 5 (1942), Gray to

States aircrews through the war. Gray then told Hull that whereas the British agreed that their airmen should be interned 'so that the same treatment will be accorded [to] German crews', Washington should take a stronger line because 'almost all of Ireland's supplies shipped by sea are receiving the protection of the air patrols of the United Nations'.[84] It would be an unfriendly act for Dublin to intern downed crews and Gray felt that Washington should protest to Dublin and make news of internments known, something London had refused to do, to embarrass de Valera and create bad press for Ireland in the United States. It was a definite indication of Walshe's strongly held opinion that Gray was 'a source of bitter poison in all our relations with the U.S.'[85]

On instruction from the State Department Gray met Walshe on 30 November and pointed out the 'inevitability of mistakes occurring which would result in American planes landing in Southern Ireland, especially as it [was] probable that the number of American forces in the North will be increased'.[86] Though no United States crews had been interned, Gray continued that the internment of American aircrews was unacceptable. He highlighted the difference between training flights and combat military flights, arguing that internment should not result from landings made during the former. Gray held that United States aircraft operating from Northern Ireland bases would only be on non-combat training flights. Quite why Gray expected Dublin to refuse to accept this point is unclear, the explanation appears to have been that Gray, a victim of his own rhetoric, had worked himself up to expect that Dublin would intern all United States pilots, whatever their missions. The American Minister desired an agreement 'in accord with natural justice and American interests'.[87] An explanation of his behaviour lies in his assertion to Hull that

> my experience with Mr de Valera has been that the less one claims, the less one is likely to obtain and that it is wise to even ask for more than one wants in order to obtain what one wants. He is a grudging and adroit negotiator.[88]

Walshe replied that the difference between flights would 'in all probability be recognised by the Irish government'.

Moving to combat flights, Gray became more aggressive but Walshe calmly replied that the Irish government would 'look at the matter from the United States point of view'. Gray did not pick up this obvious reference to helping the Allies and to American interests. Walshe continued that he preferred the terms 'operational' and 'non-operational', to 'combat' and 'training' and added that the

Hull, 16 Oct. 1942. 84 Ibid. 85 NAI DFA Washington Embassy file 148, Walshe to Brennan, 6 June 1942. 86 NARA RG 84 Dublin legation, General, Box 10 (1942), paraphrase of telegram no. 239, 1 Dec. 1942. 87 Ibid., SSF, Box 6 (1943), Gray to Hull, 9 Jan. 1943. 88 Ibid.

Irish government would 'be much better able to construe landings as having occurred during non-combat flights' if press announcements were suppressed. Owing to his intense dislike of de Valera and of Irish neutrality, Gray did not realize that American and Irish interests were working in tandem over the release of downed United States pilots. Indeed Walshe specifically told Gray that 'in practice our attitude of friendly neutrality towards the United Nations results normally ... in the internment only of crews on operational flights'.[89] Walshe agreed with Gray's suggestion that the conditions surrounding the release of downed airmen be put down on paper. This was what Gray really wanted, later telling Hull that

> it was therefore really with the aim of obtaining assent in writing to the principle of releasing planes grounded during non-combat flights ... that I opened the negotiations with the emphasis upon the reluctance of the American Government to assent to internment as a course for combatant, that is, operational flights.

Walshe hoped that Gray would advise the State Department that 'the status quo, whatever its defects, is, in the circumstances, the best for all concerned'.[90] Gray relished playing hardball with Walshe, now concentrating on operational combat flights – which Walshe said he would have to refer to de Valera – while agreeing 'to recognise, in principle that internment should not return from groundings from non-operational flights'. This was, Gray felt, 'the crux of the matter'.[91]

Gray rejoiced that Ireland and America were undergoing a new period in their relations, turning the meeting with Walshe over the 'grounded aeroplane situation' into a moment of great significance.[92] The meeting was evidence to Gray of a strengthening of relations between the two states that had weakened following de Valera's protests against the stationing of American troops in Derry. As Gray put it, 'the first fruits of this rebirth' were that he was able to 'get the release' of a Flying Fortress and its crew which had come down at Mullaghmore, Sligo, on 5 December. In euphoric terms he continued 'it was all handled very adroitly and pleasantly ... [T]hey have accepted the release of all groundings during non-operation[al] flights and the reservations on our part as to acceptance of internment on operational flights. In other words everything is fine thus far.'

The forced landing of a P-38F Lockheed Lightning on the strand at Ballyvaughan, Clare on 23 December 1942 tested Gray's agreement. Garda and military intelligence showed great interest in the Lightning, in particular its great speed. One Garda Special Branch report commented that the Lightning 'can overtake, rather easily, the British Spitfire. Its speed is well over 400 m.p.h. –

89 Ibid., General, Box 10 (1942), Walshe to Gray, 11 Dec. 1942.   90 Ibid.   91 Ibid., SSF, Box 6 (1943), Gray to Hull, 9 Jan. 1943.   92 Ibid., General, Box 10 (1942), Gray to Winant, 7 Dec. 1942.

probably around 430 m.p.h.'[93] The Lightning that came down at Ballyvaughan was from the 82nd fighter group which had relocated to Northern Ireland in November 1942. Lieutenant Colonel Pincus Taback of the Group's 97th Fighter Squadron recorded in his diary that aircraft from his squadron 'took off in mass for Oran, North Africa' from St Eval in England on 23 December 1942. The squadron was attacked over the Bay of Biscay and its aircraft dispersed. Taback lost the formation and made the trip alone, landing in Gibraltar late in the evening of 23 December. His diary entry for 23 December ended: 'Lt. Green shot down by JU 88[.] Broadhead?'[94] Second Lieutenant Arthur Broadhead had turned back to St Eval, but lost and without his long-range drop tanks, jettisoned during his encounter with the Luftwaffe, was low on fuel. Spotting land below he landed his Lightning on a sandbank close to the shore at Ballyvaughan, and was safe in Irish military custody. The American legation in Dublin had arranged his release but were 'unable to send for him or to inspect his aircraft for salvage purposes'.[95] Having seen his aircraft land, LDF and coastwatchers from nearby Black Head LOP had gone to Broadhead's assistance. They waded out to the downed aircraft and helped Broadhead ashore. After being put up over Christmas by the local LDF Group Leader at his home, Broadhead was taken to the border outside Dundalk by one of the clerks at the American legation and handed over to the British military.

Broadhead's treatment led Gray to conclude that the Dublin legation showed an 'inability to take care of our people and material'.[96] Gray copperfastened his agreement on the return of airmen from non-operational flights in a conversation with Walshe on 6 January 1943. A new Military Attaché, Lieutenant Colonel James L. Hathaway ('a young officer of exceptional intelligence and industry, combined with a very pleasing personality'),[97] took over 'the detail of co-operating with the Irish military authorities and with our own air forces in Northern Ireland to facilitate the disposition of grounded men and material'.[98] Gray now felt that he had the situation under control. It had been on the brink of disaster as Walshe asked Gray to ensure 'that American air personnel in Northern Ireland be carefully instructed so that in case of accident the pilot and crew would make statements which would warrant the Irish authorities in construing the flights as non-operational'. Walshe added that 'on at least one occasion friendly Irish officers were obliged to withdraw and invent a story to give to the American pilot in order to establish grounds for his release'.[99] With this in mind, Gray concluded that 'the results of the negotiations were much more easily achieved than I may have led you to believe'.[100] Gray was deluding

93 NAI DFA Secretary's Files P43/1, Ua Ceallaigh to Murphy, 14 Dec. 1942.   94 Diary at www.82ndfightergroup.com/tabackdiary.htm (accessed 5 July 2005).   95 NARA RG 319 Records of the Army Staff, Box 459, Military Attaché Dublin, Incoming and Outgoing messages 1942–1945, telegram, Gray to War Department, 24 Dec. 1942.   96 Ibid.   97 NARA RG 84 Dublin legation, General, Box 13 (1943), Gray to Hartle, 27 Jan. 1943.   98 Ibid., SSF, Box 6 (1943), Gray to Hull, 9 Jan. 1943.   99 Ibid.   100 Ibid.

himself; the Irish had all along wished to help the United States. Walshe later wondered why any 'government in the world would leave their affairs in the hands of a frustrated old man who has been so demonstrably hostile' to Irish-American relations.[101]

SOUTHERN COMMAND AND CURRAGH COMMAND DURING 1942

Ferry flights and downed American airmen were not a problem along the south and south-west coast of Ireland during 1942. Compared to those of their colleagues in Western Command, the observations from LOPs in Southern Command were stable through the spring and summer of 1942. Despite increased RAF fighter activity along the Wexford coast, observations from LOPs in Curragh Command, with their routine reports of beached mines and drifting barrage balloons show a similar stability. There were no events in either command equivalent to the great activity seen off Inishowen and Connacht. But there was a distinct difference in the nature of reports from Southern Command. Unlike other command OCs, Colonel James O'Hanrahan, OC Southern Command, paid careful attention in his reports to the relationship between military activity and weather conditions. He set Irish and belligerent operations within the climatic conditions prevalent along the south and south-west coast through 1942. Poor weather in January greatly reduced activity, with strong south-westerly winds, rain and fog preventing flying. Operations were reduced and in low visibility coastwatchers could not observe those that did take place. The only positive effect of the poor weather was that it led to an absence of drifting mines and runaway barrage balloons in Curragh Command. As conditions improved, aircraft were seen passing the south coast 'a considerable distance outside territorial waters'. Normally these were single aircraft at high-altitude, their route and altitude suggesting that they were 'not concentrating on shipping activity off our coastline, but rather on objectives much further westwards'.[102] O'Hanrahan concluded that these were 'long-distance reconnaissance' patrols. By contrast, the few aircraft observed just outside Irish territorial waters flying at between 100 and 1,000 feet had local objectives. With a 'sharp and well maintained' improvement in the weather in February O'Hanrahan anticipated more high-altitude flights. Activity remained light until the second half of February as reported flights barely rose, from eighty-five to eighty-seven, from January to February, suggesting that coastwatchers had been reporting fairly accurately during the poor weather in January. Of twelve flights over south-west Cork and west Kerry during February 'nothing of importance' was noted.[103] These aircraft, the usual single aircraft on routine high-level

101 NAI DFA Washington Embassy, file 73, telegram, Estero to Hibernia, 6 Apr. 1944.
102 MA G2/X/315 Pt II, Southern Command, Monthly Report on Coastal Intelligence, Jan. 1942.   103 Ibid., Southern Command, Monthly Report on Coastal Intelligence, Feb. 1942.

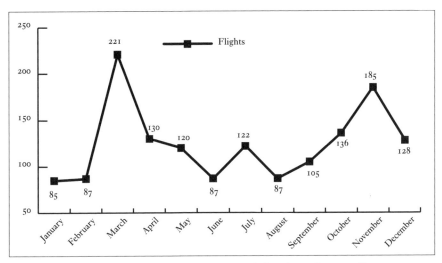

7.4: Monthly totals of overflights observed (Southern Command): 1942
(Source: MA, G2/X/315)

reconnaissance flights, had deliberately flown over Ireland 'shortening their route to objectives in the Atlantic'.[104]

With the arrival of spring, there was a change in weather along the south coast. Poor conditions in the first half of March gave way to sunshine interspersed with fog and O'Hanrahan's prediction came to pass as belligerent activity was 'on a much increased scale'. Long-range flights increased, coastwatchers finding it difficult to identify the nationality of these high-altitude flights. Despite this difficulty, the change in trends was clear as the 221 aircraft seen or heard by Southern Command coastwatchers in March 1942 (a rise from 87 in February) indicated a sizeable increase in Coastal Command activity off the southern coast. When these flights flew over Irish territory, it was again 'obvious [that] their motives were none other than either a check on their courses or a curtailment of their flights'.[105] The rise in flights during March was temporary, only 130 flights were observed in April, the majority again being unidentified high altitude flights. A reduction to 120 flights observed during May was due to poor flying conditions as the summer began with heavy hail and strong south to south-west winds. Most flights 'were so distant from L.O.P.s or at high altitudes that detection of their nationality was not possible'.[106] Identified flights were mainly British (thirty-eight flights), but seven German aircraft were also identified. Southern Command saw more German aircraft activity through 1942 than Western Command, though the overall number of German flights remained low, never more than eight a month, the average being four. A Ju-88 crashed on

104 Ibid.   105 Ibid.   106 Ibid., May 1942.

Mount Gabriel north of Schull in Cork on 3 March. The aircraft exploded and was completely destroyed with the crew of four being killed in the crash. Dursey Head LOP reported that four of the crew of a German aircraft, which was destroyed at sea, had landed on the Bull Rock lighthouse on 22 March. An Irish Lights tender took them to Berehaven the following day and they were later interned.[107]

Low-level aircraft sighted were generally German, seeking shipping targets off the south coast, though attacks on shipping were greatly reduced during 1942. The British trawler *Crag an Eran* was machine-gunned and bombed by two German seaplanes fifteen miles south-west of the Old Head of Kinsale on 7 January and had to dock in Kinsale for repairs. That day three other trawlers were bombed twenty-five miles south of Kinsale. The S.S. *Great Western* had been machine-gunned the previous day by a German Do-215 inside Irish waters off the Saltee Islands, though the information before Commandant Mackey, Curragh Command IO, suggested that there was no damage or casualties from the attack. These attacks in January were isolated cases. There were no reported attacks for the remainder of the month, nor in February, 'nor were there on the few vessels that continue to trade between our Ports and England's, a feature that would indicate that aerial activity was not concentrating on targets or objectives within an appreciable distance of our coastal limits'.[108] Attacks faded out during the year. On the high seas attacks by German aircraft on Irish ships continued. On 2 June a Ju-88 sank the Dublin-bound *City of Bremen* of the Palgrave-Murphy line 130 miles south-west of Mizen Head. Later that month Captain William Henderson of Irish Shipping's *Irish Elm*, returning on a voyage from America, reported that

> when about 600 miles off the Irish coast ... [he] was circled by two German bombers, probably Condors. They circled him for a considerable time and inspected him closely but didn't molest him. The incident had given the crew great confidence in the protection afforded by the neutral markings. Captain Henderson himself thought the planes photographed him and he said that probably the German naval and air forces knew the Irish shipping companies' vessels well by this time.[109]

The sinking of *City of Bremen* suggested otherwise.

O'Hanrahan was exasperated when he submitted his coastal intelligence report for June; flying conditions were 'seldom so favourable', but activity was on an 'even more reduced scale than during May or for any other month since October [1941]'.[110] Other than patrols following the coastline, flights during June

107 Ibid., Monthly Report Marine Service Depot, Haulbowline, Southern Command, Mar. 1942.   108 Ibid., Southern Command, Monthly Report on Coastal Intelligence, Feb. 1942. 109 NAI DFA Secretary's Files P18, memorandum by Walshe, 4 June 1942.   110 MA

were concentrated west of a line from Mount Brandon in Kerry to Skibbereen in Cork. Only eighty-seven aircraft were recorded during June; four were German and ten British. O'Hanrahan devoted much space to analysing why these figures were so low. Noting that the decline was common to each belligerent, he felt it suggested 'a priority of demand elsewhere for aircraft, a possible change in aerial tactics'.[111] The lack of German aircraft was also considered to result from 'the proximity of British aerodromes based on that country's S.W. territory' ensuring 'the speedy arrival of sufficient aircraft to turn the scales against a heavy and sustained [German] attack from the air'. O'Hanrahan had a point. To the east of Southern Command, in Curragh Command, coastwatchers at Greenore Point noticed how the RAF provided a low-level 'fighter-bomber' escort to vessels trading between Fishguard and Rosslare and how 'the plane kept in proximity to the ship by circling her and in this way appeared to come over the Village of Rosslare Pier'.[112] Fighters from RAF 10 Group were increasingly active off the south and east Irish coast. Their Commanding Officer informed the Air Ministry that

> on average Fighters of this Group are engaged in chasing hostile aircraft three or four times a week. Activity extends to within three miles of the Irish coast off Cork to off Wicklow and it is anticipated that such activity will tend to increase rather than to decrease.[113]

In July aerial activity increased slightly, though the majority of flights remained outside territorial waters. Despite generally good conditions, as in June, the distance of flights from the shore and their high altitude made it difficult for coastwatchers to establish their nationality. Flights during August were 'on a much reduced scale'.[114] Even so, O'Hanrahan emphasized that during August 'there was no day without some form of activity which had not heretofore been a regular monthly feature'. During August, Spitfires shot down a Ju-88 off Wexford. The pilot, Hauptmann Bernt, and his crew of three made a forced landing at Tramore, Waterford. Aware that captured Allied pilots were normally released, Hempel protested to Walshe when Bernt and his colleagues were interned in the Curragh.

Naval activity off the south coast remained slight to June 1942. Coastwatchers saw four small convoys in January, the largest consisting of eleven vessels escorted by two destroyers, a torpedo boat and an escort ship. The two convoys seen in February had single aircraft escorts. This 'negligible aerial umbrella' suggested to O'Hanrahan that the convoys were in little danger of aerial

G2/X/315 Pt II, Southern Command, Monthly Report on Coastal Intelligence, June 1942. 111 Ibid. 112 NAI JUS 90/119/295, Carr to Murphy, 15 Jan. 1942. 113 TNA AIR 2/4735, Orlebar to Air Ministry, 1 Oct. 1942. 114 MA G2/X/315 Pt II, Southern Command, Monthly Report on Coastal Intelligence, Aug. 1942.

attack.[115] The single aircraft was in fact mounting a dedicated anti-submarine escort for the convoy. By late August a change was evident in naval activity due to a 'greater tendency than before to move convoys – undoubtedly British – along the southern route'.[116] First noted in the early summer months, these small heavily escorted convoys had continuous aerial protection. On 20 September one of the largest convoys to pass within sight of the south coast, twenty-five vessels including corvettes and destroyers, was spotted moving west between twelve and twenty miles offshore. Towards the end of the month a force of twelve vessels reinforced by four cruisers and eight torpedo boats passed west about eighteen miles to the south. O'Hanrahan speculated that 'it may have been moving to meet the troop convoy referred to in German communiqués'.[117]

O'Hanrahan did not put much store by the rise in the number of flights from eighty-seven in August to 105 in September, as 'it does not follow that this slight increase portents to greater activity uniformly distributed'.[118] However, from September air and marine activity off the south coast began to rise; the beginning of a sustained increase in Coastal Command activity that lasted until the end of the year. Good flying weather in October and November, bright, dry and calm, saw conditions off southern Ireland not seen since February and were 'to a certain extent availed of'.[119] By October 1942 O'Hanrahan, having analyzed the trend for the previous two months, concluded that the increase in activity first seen in September was

> in great part attributable to a form of activity off the south coast that is becoming more apparent each month viz: the gradually increasing use of the southern sea lanes by British convoys. The form and time of increased activity suggests that those convoys are picked up at a given location several hundred miles west of our territory and escorted for the remainder of their eastern journey by continuous relays of aircraft.[120]

The 136 flights reported by south coast LOPs in October, the Sunderlands, Wellingtons and Whitleys of Coastal Command, were the greatest number seen since the unusually high figure of 221 in March. The increase matched a concurrent rise in British naval activity in the area, with a mix of corvettes and destroyers now regularly passing the south coast. Through November flying conditions 'were never so good', the absence of cloud aided visibility and the wind was so light that 'little movement on the surface could escape detection by the naked eye'.[121] The gradual increase in operations since August had now reached a level where 'the jump between any two consecutive months has not been so high as that between October and November'.[122] This was not seasonal

---

115 Ibid., Southern Command, Monthly Report on Coastal Intelligence, June 1942.
116 Ibid. 117 Ibid., Sept. 1942. 118 Ibid. 119 Ibid., Oct. 1942. 120 Ibid. 121 Ibid., Nov. 1942. 122 Ibid.

activity, precisely the opposite had occurred for the same months of 1941 when activity reached 'its almost rock-bottom point in November'. Daylight operations outside territorial waters, but near enough to the shore to be spotted from LOPs, had risen considerably since August.

While the usual types of Coastal Command aircraft were observed, three Liberators were sighted in November, the first mention of these American aircraft off the south coast. The Liberator was, in late 1942, 'by far the most complicated and expensive combat aircraft the world had seen'.[123] 'Essential instruments of long-range air war', they would become a fixture in the skies off Cork and Kerry for the remainder of the war as Coastal Command took the offensive.[124] Though the number of flights observed had increased there was no corresponding increase in the violation of Irish territory or waters, 'the comparatively few infringements being of no military importance'.[125] One infringement over Waterville was 'outside the range of our ground defences and its speed too high and movement so unswerving as to assume that its penetration had no military significance'.[126] O'Hanrahan concluded that the increase in flights was connected with American and British convoy traffic patterns prior to the Allied landings in North Africa.

The sea-lanes off the south coast, 'discarded by belligerent shipping and naval craft since September, 1939', were as 1942 ended 'more generally in use on a gradually increasing scale'.[127] On 9 November, after five days where no activity had been reported, a westbound convoy of approximately forty vessels escorted by a cruiser, four destroyers and a vessel described as a monitor, accompanied by an aerial escort, was reported as the largest convoy yet observed off the south coast. Baltimore LOP heard heavy gunfire and explosions as it followed the convoy. Convoy traffic was down in December, but the four convoys observed were large, such as that seen by Seven Heads LOP on 21 December of twenty vessels accompanied by three corvettes and two escort vessels.

With a return to poor weather in December 'flying should have been negligible', though flight numbers fell during the month it was 'not possible to conclude that this is an indication of a lull in aerial activity or evidence of one in the immediate future'.[128] Aircraft were regularly seen near to the south coast but overall activity was low. Through the poor visibility, Sunderlands, Wellingtons and Whitleys were seen on patrol and convoy escort. Although only one Liberator was sighted, it received little attention in O'Hanrahan's report, suggesting that that type of aircraft, previously considered unusual, was now a standard sight off the south coast. Flying through 1942 had been almost always in daylight hours and the short period of daylight in December led O'Hanrahan to return to interpret seasonal factors and weather affecting flights so that

---

123 Terraine, *Business*, p. 539, quoting Bill Gunston, *Encyclopaedia of the world's combat aircraft* (1976), p. 42. 124 Ibid. 125 MA G2/X/315 Pt II, Southern Command, Monthly Report on Coastal Intelligence, Nov. 1942. 126 Ibid. 127 Ibid. 128 Ibid., Dec. 1942.

'increased activity is to be expected with the longer flying hours that shall in future operate progressively until June'.[129] O'Hanrahan cannot have known how true his words would be. The Allies were planning major operations in the Bay of Biscay up to southern Irish coastal waters for 1943.

CONCLUSION

The year ended with Western Sector reporting that operations off the northern coast of Ireland were declining due to poor weather conditions. On 9 December Coastal Command was forced to cancel all flights due to bad weather. It was the beginning of a very poor winter across the North Atlantic. Due to this weather, Western Sector incident reports were down considerably on November from 4,297 to 2,374 in December. Though coastal patrols were observed almost every day, westbound flights from Lough Erne were reduced by half to a mere seventy-one as, 'weather permitting, Atlantic Patrols were still maintained from Lough Erne and Derry Bases'.[130] The monthly total of 669 aircraft observed was the lowest number for sixteen months. As seen above, it was a similar picture for Southern Command, where rain, drizzle and fog 'with strong winds occasionally reaching storm pitch made December the worst flying month for a long period and probably the most testing one for aircraft in 1942'.[131]

Through 1942 the coastwatchers and G2 had followed increasing Allied air and naval power around Ireland as American forces arrived in Europe. Less obvious to G2, Dönitz's U-boat force had now grown to its greatest strength and in January 1943 Germany would 'fling into the Atlantic struggle the greatest possible strength'.[132] December 1942, the point at which this chapter ends, marks the half-way stage in a period often seen as leading to the culmination of the battle of the Atlantic. The ten months from July 1942 to May 1943 were when 'the battle was to be fought out to a decisive conclusion'.[133] There was by the end of 1942 a definite air of change in the nature of belligerent operations in the Atlantic theatre. Strategically the Allies were stronger around Ireland and German forces were noticeably absent, though further out to sea 'the German submarine campaign in the North Atlantic' was judged 'very strong'.[134] The growth in Allied strength was predominantly due to the deployment of American forces. The related United States interest in securing Irish co-operation to release downed airmen and aircraft was the most significant development of belligerent interest in the operations of the coastwatchers since 1939. Overall, there was little evidence to the Irish, with their small air and marine intelligence service, of a turning point in the battle of the Atlantic by the

---

129 Ibid.　130 Ibid., Western Sector, Monthly Report, Dec. 1942.　131 Ibid., Southern Command, Monthly Report on Coastal Intelligence, Dec. 1942.　132 Terraine, *Business*, p. 514, quoting S.W. Roskill, *The war at sea* (London, 1951–4), vol. ii, p. 355.　133 MacIntyre, *Atlantic*, p. 131.　134 NAI DFA Secretary's Files P43/1, Ua Ceallaigh to Murphy, 14 Dec.

end of 1942. All G2 could conclude was that new types of weaponry were in place and that there was a rising tempo in operations as the Allies sought to tackle a conflict that remained far to the west of Ireland by defending convoys bringing greater and greater amounts of men and equipment to Britain for the final showdown with Nazi Germany. All information showed that 'production has got into full stride in the United States'.[135] Above all, in December 1942 the Irish intelligence services and the coastwatchers knew that 'the Atlantic convoy was still the heartbeat of the war'.[136] Nineteen-forty-three would see Allied and Axis forces in the Atlantic 'locked in a deadly, ruthless series of fights, in which no mercy would be expected and little shown'.[137]

1942.   **135** Ibid., MacMághnuis to Murphy, 5 May 1942.   **136** Terraine, *Business*, p. 514, quoting Roskill, *The war at sea*, vol. ii, p. 218.   **137** Ibid., quoting Roskill, *The war at sea*, vol. ii, p. 355.

CHAPTER EIGHT

'The War in its culminating and greatest phase is moving nearer to our territory'[1]

IN JANUARY 1943 THE WAR Cabinet agreed that 'the possibility of the enemy attempting [an] invasion of Great Britain' could be 'disregarded'.[2] The Admiralty was informed that, due to this reduced threat, further supplies of naval equipment need not be given to Ireland. Also in January, at the Casablanca Conference, the Allies agreed that only the unconditional surrender of Germany would achieve their war aims in Europe. The expectation in Ireland and elsewhere was that the Allied second front on the continent would soon be opened. In preparation, United States forces were deploying onwards from Derry in large numbers to bases in Britain. Garda reports from the city indicated that there was 'much talk in Derry about the opening of a second front in Europe'.[3] The feeling in American circles was that 'big moves will be made in many directions at an early date'.[4] Bryan's sources also suggested this and he circulated a limited issue 'Intelligence Note' in which he maintained that

> it can safely be assumed that the Allied powers will open operations on a large scale in Europe in the near future. This will be the culminating point of the war there ... [S]hould any or all of these operations take place along the French coasts vast naval, air and shipping movements will take place adjacent to Irish territory ... [I]t cannot be assumed, however, that the Germans will wait passively whilst the Allied convoys and naval and air forces are moving to the attack ... [C]ounter action will automatically lead to an intensified state of incidents ... near or over our territory ... [W]hen the war reaches areas adjacent to Ireland the country must be prepared for any eventuality.[5]

The need to maintain 'readiness for possible contingencies' required 'increased vigilance and alertness on the part of all members of the Defence Forces'. Bryan forecast that for G2 the 'intelligence battle will intensify', while the Coast

---

1 NAI DFA Secretary's Files A8 (1), Ireland and operations in Western Europe, secret and limited issue intelligence note, no date, but received by External Affairs, Jan. 1943. 2 TNA ADM 1/13032, Admiralty to Horton, 20 Jan. 1943. 3 NAI DFA Secretary's Files P43/1, Ó Coileáin to Murphy, 8 Mar. 1943. 4 Ibid., Ó Coileáin to Murphy, 5 Jan. 1943. 5 NAI DFA Secretary's Files A8 (1), Ireland and operations in Western Europe, secret and limited issue intelligence note, no date, but received by External Affairs, Jan. 1943.

Watching Service 'must be ready to deal with the increased duties which will ensue from intensified air and marine activity' around Ireland. Reinforcing his message Bryan added that attempts to use Ireland 'as a base for secret agents or as a channel for communications for secret or underground activities' could only be countered by 'continuous vigilance on the part of all civil and military agents'.

Bryan did not know that at Casablanca the Allies delayed the invasion of Europe to 1944. Instead, 1943 saw the Allied build-up for the invasion of Europe continue. Garda sources reported from Derry that 'the Americans are very confident that they have reached the point in production of all types of war machines when they will be able to meet and defeat all opposition'.[6] Proving this point coastwatchers reported increasing numbers of convoys and delivery flights passing Ireland through 1943 and saw Coastal Command pursue the war against the U-boat with renewed vigour off the Irish coast, its forces augmented by fresh United States aircraft and crews. The growing involvement of United States forces in the Atlantic theatre close to Ireland further increased United States interest in the work of the coastwatchers. Through 1943 American interests had a direct influence on the operations of the service as further USAAF aircraft came down in Ireland and Gray prevailed upon the Irish government to construct basic navigation aids along the Irish coast to assist American aircrews operating near Ireland.

WINTER STORMS

Along the south coast of Ireland January 1943 brought 'extremely wet and stormy weather' and LOPs 'were in a very wet condition whereby maps, charts, etc., suffered damage'.[7] The worst storms in fifty years disrupted communications between LOPs and Southern Command headquarters in Cork, Power Head LOP reporting that the post telephone was out of order 'owing to short circuiting of wires due to dampness'.[8] Conditions were as bad along the west coast and a 'strong Atlantic gale, which blew during the last week of the month, necessitated an intensive search by British aircraft for missing naval units and their survivors and rafts off the western shores of Connaught'.[9] Damaged lifeboats and flotsam washed ashore and, though LOPs were instructed 'to keep a sharp lookout and render any aid possible', no reports of survivors reached Western Command headquarters. Some weeks later the bodies of Able Seaman Charles Walmsley and Stoker Vincent Lavery were found on the Donegal coast. They were two of the crew of Royal Navy minelayer HMS *Corncrake* which foundered off Ireland in the Atlantic storms on 25 January with the loss of all hands while escorting Gibraltar-bound convoy KMS8.

6 NAI DFA Secretary's Files P43/1, Ó Coileáin to Murphy, 5 Jan. 1943.   7 MA G2/X/315 Pt II, Monthly Report – Sub/Depot, Marine Service, Southern Command, Jan. 1943. 8 Ibid.   9 Ibid., Western Command, AMI, Monthly Report, Jan. 1943.

Coastwatchers from Wexford to Kerry reported that January's bad weather reduced air activity off the south coast. Patrols were confined to the most remote coasts of Cork and Kerry and represented no threat to Irish neutrality. Further north coastwatchers in Donegal and Sligo reported increased training by aircraft over Donegal Bay. LOPs sighted aircraft towing

> aerial targets out into Donegal Bay for machine-gun and bombing practice, in which Catalinas and Sunderlands were also reported taking part. Long distance patrol aircraft circling in the Bay and dropping depth charges [were] observed on average three or four times weekly.[10]

For Commandant James Power, OC AMI Western Command, Donegal Bay was 'the theatre of target practice' through 1943 as the skies above the bay were home to aircraft shooting and bombing imaginary targets in the sea only a matter of miles from Irish territory.[11] German aircraft now rarely appeared off Ireland's north-west coast, and Donegal Bay, close to the airbases on Lough Erne and around Derry, was an ideal training ground for Allied aircrews. It was a safe one too, as the rescue vessel *Robert Hastie* could deploy from Killybegs if any training flight came down offshore. The safety of locals was a lower priority for the RAF. Patrick Brady of Inishmurray Island off the Sligo coast nearly became the victim of the 'intense target practice' carried out by flying boats on 20 May. When fishing off Bowmore and Sheddan Rocks 'a hail of machine-gun fire from a Sunderland Flying Boat burst around him, luckily without doing any injury'.[12] As the intensity of training increased over Donegal Bay Power warned that 'continued activity of this nature may lead to loss of life amongst fishermen and islanders'.[13] Although regular training continued until the following winter, no injuries or fatalities occurred. This despite continuing reports from LOPs, such as that from St John's Point of 'a British aircraft 5 miles SW moving W … circled, dropped two (2) smoke bombs and when 3 miles W of LOP fired bursts of machine gun fire.'[14]

Captain Maurice Daly, OC Mallow Sector AMI, took over responsibility for air and marine intelligence in Southern Command from Colonel O'Hanrahan in February. He reported to Bryan that though weather for flying during the month was 'somewhat better' towards the south of Ireland, nevertheless 'an increase in aerial activity was not evident' along the south coast.[15] By the end of February Western Command noted a similar 'lack of operational work' along the Connacht coast.[16] During this lull, the regular arrival of American aircraft around dawn off the North Mayo Corner moving north-east overland towards

10 Ibid.   11 Ibid., Western Sector, AMI, Monthly Report, Feb. 1943.   12 Ibid., Western Command, AMI, Monthly Report, May 1943.   13 Ibid., June 1943.   14 MA DRS 1307, 6 Dec. 1943.   15 MA G2/X/315 Pt II, Mallow Sector, Monthly Report on Coastal Intelligence, Feb. 1943.   16 Ibid., Western Sector, AMI, Monthly Report, Feb. 1943.

the border heralded the return of delivery flights to Irish skies and was a sign of things to come during the second half of 1943. One American aircraft, first sighted by LOPs along the Galway coast, moved south-east, reported by Gardaí at Galway and Gort, before it 'circled Shannon Airport and made one attempt to land' and then moved south-east. Later picked up by military observers at Limerick and Kilmacthomas, the aircraft was last seen flying out to sea by coastwatchers at Dunabrattin Head LOP.[17] Beyond such lost American delivery flights, military air activity was conspicuous by its low profile off the south and west coasts of Ireland in the first months of 1943.

The winter storms also reduced naval activity around Ireland. Off the south coast convoy traffic was slight and groups of patrolling destroyers passed LOPs only every few days. Seven Heads LOP added to one convoy report 'that a plane was observed circling over the convoy'.[18] This provided G2 with continuing evidence of Allied resolve to use air power to counter U-boats. On 17 February Mizen Head LOP reported an unusually large and well-protected convoy of forty-seven vessels, eleven of which were a naval escort, which was 'staggered out for protection purposes' sixteen miles off the coast.[19] Such large convoys had begun returning to the seas off Ireland's southern coast from late 1942. Convoy traffic remained sparse along the more popular north coast routes. Nonetheless, the few convoys sighted in these waters provided important intelligence for G2. They showed the continuing movement of American military power to Europe as the Allied invasion force assembled in Britain and Northern Ireland. Comprising large numbers of liners and tankers, these well-escorted convoys carried troops, military equipment and – most vitally – oil. As weather improved through March and April, sightings of convoys off Donegal began to rise, their escorts 'firing flares and shots' as they passed by LOPs.[20] Also rising were the numbers of the associated air patrols protecting the convoys, which were 'well-maintained from Northern Ireland bases'.[21]

Through the coastwatchers, G2 could explain most air and marine movements off the Irish coast in early 1943. The tenor of Power's reports from Western Command was similar to those of O'Hanrahan and Daly in Southern Command. With the winter storms subsiding, all showed increasing Allied operations off Ireland from March 1943. However, in these months the centre of naval action in the Atlantic was far to the west of Ireland in the mid-Atlantic, where the outlook for the Allies remained bleak as U-boats continued their attacks on convoys to interrupt Allied supply lines.

---

17 MA DRS 1065, 22 Feb. 1943.   18 MA G2/X/315 Pt II, Mallow Sector, Monthly Report on Coastal Intelligence, Feb. 1943.   19 Ibid.   20 MA DRS 1087, 18 Mar. 1943.   21 MA G2/X/315 Pt II, Western Command, AMI, Monthly Report, Mar. 1943.

THE CLIMAX OF THE BATTLE OF THE ATLANTIC

Coastal Command maintained that in the first months of 1943 the U-boat 'menace' in the Atlantic 'bade fair to strangle our strategy in Europe and held out to the Axis their last remaining hope of avoiding decisive defeat'.[22] The Allies agreed at Casablanca that for 1943 the defeat of the U-boat 'would be the first charge on our combined resources'.[23] They chose to strike over the Bay of Biscay, which three out of four U-boats had to cross to get to their oceanic operational areas. In February 1943 Coastal Command began Operation GONDOLA, the first in a series of offensives against U-boats transiting the Bay. Sixty-seven U-boats were deployed against Atlantic convoys in February, but only U-211 was damaged and U-519 sunk due to GONDOLA. The operation had been 'an expensive and uneconomical means' of attacking U-boats.[24] Coastwatchers reporting to Daly, unaware of GONDOLA, saw nothing to indicate that the operation was underway as it took place well to the south of Irish waters.

The reality was that in early 1943 an Allied victory in the North Atlantic seemed far away. Shipping losses escalated to a dangerous level and the combined U-boat attack in mid-March on eastbound convoys SC122[25] and HX229[26] became the greatest convoy battle of the war. Due to a lack of escort protection, both convoys merged and were attacked in the mid-Atlantic by a combined force of thirty-eight U-boats on 16 and 17 March. Twenty-two ships were sunk in the attack. The view held in the immediate post-war years that in March 1943 Germany came near to disrupting communications between the USA and Britain has been questioned by more recent scholarship.[27] John Terraine argues that 'there was nothing in the actual performance of the SC122/HX229 battle by itself to warrant such a degree of pessimism'.[28] In fact 'assuming forty U-boats participated, the confirmed sinkings came to an average of about one-half ship per U-boat, no greater success rate than usual'.[29] However with the SC122/HX229 battle coming after three and a half years of war, the battle of the Atlantic reached a psychological crisis in March 1943 and war weariness turned the attack on the two convoys into a greater catastrophe than it was. In the words of Clay Blair, 'there never was a defining "turning point" in the battle of the Atlantic, only a gradually accelerating German defeat from 1942 onward'.[30] The same conclusion is apparent from G2 analysis of the conflict off Ireland as the evidence provided by coastwatchers from 1942 onwards was of a continual rise in the tempo and power of dedicated Allied operations against an ever-dwindling German presence.

22 NARA RG84 London Embassy, Ambassador's Files, Box 3, file 'Ireland', *Coastal Command Review (Dec. 1943)*, p. 1.   23 Ibid.   24 TNA AIR 15/349, The value of the Bay of Biscay Patrols, memo by Slessor, 23 Mar. 1943.   25 Comprising fifty vessels, guarded by Escort Group B-5, and departing New York on 5 Mar.   26 Comprising thirty-eight vessels, guarded by Escort Group B-4, and departing New York on 8 Mar.   27 Clay Blair, *Hitler's U-boat war: The hunted 1942-1945* (London, 2001), p. 169.   28 Terraine, *Business*, p. 571.   29 Ibid., p. 266.   30 Blair,

Coastal Command followed GONDOLA with Operation ENCLOSE I, during which aircraft sighted twenty-six U-boats and attacked fifteen, though they sank only U-665. VLR aircraft were nonetheless achieving successes by their presence over the Bay and the deployment of Liberators further out over the Atlantic to close the mid-Atlantic gap led to 'an enormous advance in the lethal efficiency of Coastal Command'.[31] British naval intelligence noted 'the growing tendency' of U-boats 'to terminate offensive operations against convoys as soon as they come into effective range of aircraft from Ireland or Iceland'.[32] Operation ENCLOSE II from 6 to 13 April clocked up eleven sightings of U-boats, four attacks and one kill (U-376). As with GONDOLA, there were few signs of ENCLOSE I or II off the southern Irish coast. But despite rain, low cloud and poor coastal visibility during the first half of April, Coastal Command aircraft were seen in greater numbers off the south Irish coast, with 'a considerable increase in activity inside territorial waters' as aircraft, including many unfamiliar with the region, passed over Ireland.[33]

One aircraft unfamiliar with its surroundings was sighted just before 1300 on 7 April when Galley Head LOP reported a 'four engined mid-winged one rudder monoplane with a white star on fuselage 4 miles East of post moving North'.[34] The aircraft was flying at 200 feet and appeared to be American. When 'about 4 miles north east of [the] post [the aircraft] circled and moved off in an easterly direction'. At 1257, the aircraft was '6 miles north-east [and] remained circling in that vicinity for 8 minutes ... and moved off to east'. B-17F Flying Fortress (42-3090) *t'Ain't a Bird*, from the 351st Bomber Group based at Polebrook, Northhamptonshire, England, was running dangerously low on fuel as it passed over the Cork coast searching for a place to land. The pilot believed he was in Norway and landed shortly after 1300 to the north-east of Galley Head LOP on marshy ground outside Clonakilty. The crew of eleven were entertained at O'Donovan's Hotel in the town and after three days left for Northern Ireland, though navigator Second Lieutenant Haynes remained in Cork hospital due to injuries.[35] Following repairs, on 2 May a replacement Allied crew flew the aircraft to Northern Ireland via Rineanna, taking off from a temporary 800-yard runway constructed by Defence Forces engineers using railway sleepers.

Coastal Command continued its Biscay operations through April, launching Operation DERANGE with a force of 120 Wellingtons, Liberators and Halifaxes armed with the Leigh Light and the new ASV III centimetric radar. The operation centred on the southern sector of Biscay and so remained out of sight of coastwatchers. Yet through May south coast LOPs continually heard gunfire and explosions from beyond the horizon. A further sign of increased operations

Hunted, p. 293. **31** NARA RG84 London Embassy, Ambassador's Files, Box 3, file 'Ireland', *Coastal Command Review (Dec. 1943)*, p. 1. **32** Syrett, *Signals intelligence*, p. 167, U-boat Situation. Week ending 19/4/43. **33** MA G2/X/315 Pt II, Mallow Sector, Monthly Report on Coastal Intelligence, Apr. 1943. **34** MA LOP 27, 7 Apr. 1943. **35** The crew's mascot,

off the south coast was the rise in the number of spent smoke floats, used by aircraft for positioning and to calculate wind direction, which were washed ashore. Through May Coastal Command 'counter measures against U-boat activity resulted in the heaviest toll on these craft since hostilities commenced, and a marked decline in shipping losses'.[36] By the end of May, the U-boats were on the defensive, an intelligence source suggesting that 'morale and efficiency' were 'flagging and growing apprehension is clearly felt of air attack'.[37] On 24 May, after the sinking of U-752, Dönitz instructed his U-boats to quit the North Atlantic and reposition south-west of the Azores. Aware of a change in German submarine operations, an American liaison officer with Coastal Command commented that 'in May 1943 U-boat sightings in the Bay of Biscay reached a peak. Since that time there has been a steady decrease in enemy submarine sightings'.[38] By the end of May, Germany had lost the battle of the Atlantic and British signals intelligence noticed 'a remarkable reduction in the number of U-boats operating in the North Atlantic'.[39] From Berlin, Warnock reported to Dublin that on the German side the 'fall in U-Boat sinkings [was] disappointing though it is confidently hoped to find [a] means of combating improved British defences'.[40] The RAF 'Y-Service' war diary triumphantly concluded that 'new and successful countermeasures indicate further Allied successes in the unrelenting campaign against Germany's No. 1 weapon, and foreshadows complete supremacy in the not far distant future'.[41] Irish intelligence agencies were not long picking up information through sources in Derry. The Garda Chief Superintendent in Letterkenny reported in the first week of July that during the six weeks prior to 1 July

> not a single ship was lost from Convoys crossing the Atlantic. It is believed that the Atlantic is, at the moment, almost free from German under-water craft … while it is believed that the danger from U-Boats will never again assume its former magnitude or anything approaching it, it is expected that there will be a renewal of activity on a much smaller scale in a few months time.[42]

SUMMER 1943

Off northern and western coasts American overflights mixed with Coastal Command patrols escorting the still rising number of convoys passing through the north-west approaches. Power was unequivocal in his summer 1943 reports

a monkey named 'Tojo', died in Clonakilty and is buried at O'Donovan's Hotel.   36 TNA HW 2/3, Cheadle War Diary Oct. 1942-Mar. 1944, p. 552.   37 Syrett, *Signals intelligence*, p. 185, U-boat Situation. Week ending 24/5/43.   38 NARA RG 38 Box 332, log of liaison officer FAW7 at 19 Group Coastal Command, May 1943.   39 Syrett, *Signals intelligence*, p. 187, U-boat trend. Replacing report delivered 24/5/43.   40 NAI DFA Secretary's Files P12/3, telegram, Hibernia to Estero, 13 July 1943.   41 TNA HW 2/3, Cheadle War Diary Oct. 1942-Mar. 1944, p. 564. 42 NAI DFA Secretary's Files P43/1, Ua Ceallaigh to Murphy, 7 July 1943.

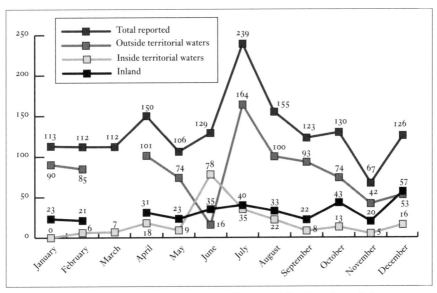

8.1: Overflights and incursions (Southern Command/Mallow Sector): January–December 1943 (Source: MA G2/X/315 pt II (no March 1943 report located))

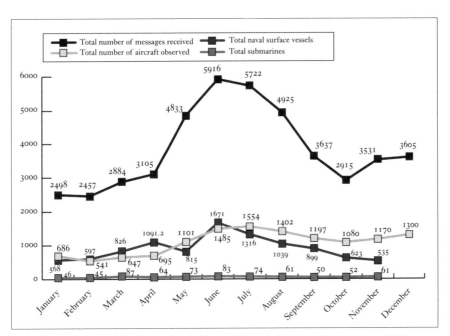

8.2: Messages received, air, naval and submarine activity (Western Command/Western Sector): January–December 1943 (Source: MA G2/X/315 pt II (partial December 1943 report located))

that the reason for the increase in American overflights was 'due to delivery flights from USA to British Air bases'.[43] The growth in the number and frequency of delivery flights had been apparent from early in the year. For example on 16 and 17 April 'intensive inland activity' occurred between 0700 and 1200 as 'at least' twenty Flying Fortresses flew 'across N. Mayo and Sligo in the direction of Lough Erne'. Visibility on both days was poor and Power speculated that 'a considerably larger number [of aircraft] could quite possibly have passed over'. Incidents reported from Western Command rose to a yearly high of 4,833 in May because of rising air activity. On 28 May 'between 07.00 hours and 14.00 hours 45 Fortress Bombers were reported moving Eastwards into Northern Ireland' through Irish airspace. They took a route 'not customary heretofore', arriving off Rossan Point in Donegal and flying the coastline south to Mullaghmore. Lost, on making landfall they followed the Irish coast south to the Donegal air corridor, flying it into Northern Ireland, navigating the route using the signal from the Killadeas beacon beside Lough Erne. The growth in air activity continued through June with 'increased activity in [the] Inishowen Peninsula and north Donegal areas'.[44] Fifty American aircraft flew east over Lough Erne between 0620 and 0940 on 6 June, twenty-eight positively identified as Flying Fortresses on delivery flights. Coastwatchers' reports showed that the navigation of delivery flights, which could make their landfall at any point along the western seaboard, had 'improved considerably' by June 'as over 90% came in directly over Donegal Bay' and used the air corridor into Northern Ireland.[45] Delivery flights were now the most prominent form of Allied air activity over Western Command.

A slight increase in air operations off the south coast followed in June as DERANGE ended. Coastal Command saturated the Bay of Biscay, mounting 'an all-out series of intense hunter-killer operations', code-named MUSKETRY, SEASLUG and PERCUSSION, against U-boats.[46] To the north, Liberators and Sunderlands flew off the southern Irish coast and the sound of gunfire and explosions from air attacks on suspected submarines remained a daily phenomenon for coastwatchers. Weather in June was good, and flights followed the route between Mizen Head and Valentia Island 'that now appears to be a settled course principally used as a more direct approach to the Objective'.[47] Galley Head LOP reported regular sightings of RAF-liveried Liberators, one being seen in good visibility on 14 June at 1330 six miles to the south flying west at 2,000 feet towards Baltimore. These low-level patrols operated in conjunction with naval escort groups and searched the waters immediately off the Irish coast for U-boats. As the patrolling Liberator was sighted on 14 June, the LOP three posts to the east of Galley Head at Flat Head and the military posts at Fort Carlisle and Fort Templebreedy in Cork harbour reported 'seven destroyers

43 MA G2/X/315 Pt II, Western Sector, AMI, Monthly Report, Apr. 1943.   44 Ibid., Western Command, AMI, Monthly Report, June 1943.   45 Ibid.   46 Blair, *Hunted*, p. 307.
47 MA G2/X/315 Pt II, Mallow Sector, Monthly Report on Coastal Intelligence, June 1943.

13–18 miles S. moving W'. The destroyers 'altered course and moved east as far as Ram Head'.[48] Subsequent overflights, explosions and gunfire indicated that Allied forces were hunting U-boats off the south Irish coast.

It remained busy on the sea-lanes off north Donegal through the high summer months. LOPs along the north coast followed the continuing passage of troopships, freighters and tankers. These convoys were now larger and more heavily defended than before. Heavy troop movements took place through June and July, including the observation by Malin Head on 18 June of a liner estimated at 18,000 tons 'with troops on board', though the LOP 'could not give any indication of number on board or dress'.[49] A consequence of this convoy traffic was a rise in destroyer and corvette activity out of Lough Foyle. On 29 July LOPs from Glengad to Aranmore Island followed the progress west of a convoy of forty ships escorted by four destroyers which had assembled north of Malin Head. The following day five large liners escorted by four frigates passed east by Malin Head and Glengad Head. Considerable naval traffic also passed off the south coast through summer 1943, including the usual groups of patrolling destroyers. These destroyers were often accompanied by aircraft, however on 29 and 30 July eight destroyers were joined by four submarines as they moved east about twenty miles offshore by Power Head, Ballycotton and Helvick Head LOPs. Sightings of submarines training off the Foyle and Inishowen were normal during 1943, but surfaced submarines off the south coast were an unusual sight, making an earlier unconfirmed sighting by Ballycotton LOP on 8 July of 'the conning tower of a submarine 9 miles south' and moving west worthy of a section of its own in Mallow Sector's July report.[50] A further section in the report noted the appearance off the south coast of hospital ships. They became regular sightings from early July, possibly linked to the evacuation of casualties following the Allied landings in Sicily.

Daly reported to Bryan that July 1943 had seen 'a considerable increase in activity' off the south coast in 'very favourable flying conditions'.[51] The number of coastal patrols (239 flights) sighted by southern coastwatchers now reached numbers not seen since March 1942. Flights were usually from the east to the west, indicating a specific patrol pattern, a trademark of Coastal Command anti-submarine patrols. Daly reported that the increase was due to 'the improved British method of convoy protection in the Atlantic from home bases, bombers being used against submarine packs', a reference to the rising numbers of Liberators operating with Coastal Command through 1943. Of the eighty-three aircraft identified in July, nearly one third were British; only two were American and two were German. On 23 July one of the German aircraft, a Ju-88 on a weather reconnaissance flight, following a regular track known to coastwatchers, was sighted by Dursey Head LOP and crashed 300 yards west of the post at Ballinacarriga, killing the crew of four. Daly drew Bryan's attention to 'the

48 Ibid.   49 Ibid.   50 Ibid., July 1943.   51 Ibid.

short-cut complex' shown by these pilots who chose to pass over the extremities of Cork and Kerry and in doing so flew dangerously near to the mountains in the area. Showing the dangers inherent in the 'short-cut complex', a Liberator initially identified as American, though flown by RAF Coastal Command, crashed in 'extremely bad weather' on the mountain-side near Kilkmackowen, five miles north of Castletownbere, at 2000 on 27 August.[52] A military force from Bere Island arrived on the site just after midnight. The Air Corps speculated that the 'aircraft was probably on Atlantic Patrol, and coming down through cloud struck the side of [the] mountain', where it skidded approximately 400 yards before exploding.[53] The crew died in the crash and the aircraft was destroyed. Ordnance officers destroyed armaments, including aerial torpedoes, depth charges and bombs. They removed loose equipment and handed it over to the British.

FERRY FLIGHTS, AUTUMN–WINTER 1943

During July 183 United States aircraft were identified crossing Western Sector, 'the highest total of American Aircraft yet reported in any month', over 90 per cent were on delivery flights.[54] Attention along the west coast through August concentrated on Mayo 'where an increase of 80 flights was noted', assumed to be delivery flights, bringing the monthly total of aircraft sightings to 243. Then an unexplained 'falling off in the deliveries of American bombers' occurred in September. Power suggested that 'small deliveries may have taken place but it was impossible to isolate them from the routine work of the main bases in Northern Ireland'.[55] Air activity over Southern Command was also low through September and October, the majority of the flights reported being coastal patrols outside territorial waters. The small number of territorial infringements were 'of no military significance'.[56] There was little change also in Western Command as Captain J.K. 'Joe' Birthistle, OC Western Sector Report Centre in Athlone, who had replaced Power, suggested that reductions were due to seasonal factors 'which occur yearly at the approach of winter'.[57]

The only unseasonable matter was the return in October of ferry flights of Flying Fortresses off north Mayo transiting the air corridor towards Lough Erne. It was the beginning of a massive movement of aircraft from the United States to Britain. At External Affairs Walshe told de Valera that, according to Maffey, there was 'inevitably coming a time in the near future when there would be an "enormous" increase of aircraft, British and American, flying over us'.[58] Maffey's prediction was swiftly fulfilled. Showing how the Defence Forces were

52 NAI DF S4/48/43, MacMahon to McElligott, 22 Apr. 1944. 53 Ibid., Quinn to MacMahon, 21 Sept. 1943. 54 MA G2/X/315 Pt II, Western Sector, AMI, Monthly Report, July 1943. 55 Ibid., Sept. 1943. 56 Ibid., Mallow Sector, Monthly Report on Coastal Intelligence, Sept. 1943. 57 Ibid., Western Command, AMI, Monthly Report, Oct. 1943. 58 NAI DFA Secretary's Files A2, remark by Maffey, quoted in Walshe to de Valera,

now making increased use of inter-Sector radio communications in air observations, Daly in Mallow Sector reported in November that 'incoming radio reports show heavy activity mainly in the Athlone Sector'. Ferry flights increased during November with 350 four-engined bombers crossing the Atlantic during the month. Incident reports in Western Command rose accordingly as LOPs and Garda Stations south of Donegal Bay reported an increase in 'aircraft ferried from America ... many of which flew overland from the west coast to the border'.[59] They sighted one hundred and seventy seven delivery flights, identifying seventy-five as Flying Fortresses. The majority of flights occurring between 16 and 24 November, all taking place 'between the hours of 08.00 and 15.00 – 80% being recorded before 12.00 hours'.[60] As a result of 'the extraordinarily heavy and somewhat unprecedented aerial activity over the entire north-west area' on 22 November, when over one hundred 'large four-engined bombers' flew over Galway and Mayo to the border, 'the extensive Army use' of the telephone network in the west of Ireland 'led to the curtailment of telephone services to the public', placing great strain on the entire telephone system.[61] As a result of this 'very large increase' in overland activity in November, 169 aircraft were sighted overland, compared to forty-one for October.

Due to poor weather and reduced daylight, December was normally a quiet month for coastwatchers, but not in Western Command in December 1943 as delivery flights continued to cross Ireland. Aircraft reported totalled 1,300, 'a very high figure for the season' compared to the 669 in December 1942. In December 295 aircraft made delivery flights across the Atlantic and coast-watchers and Gardaí reported sightings of 175 delivery flights. This was only two less than the November total of 177, but the pattern of arrivals was now different as there were 'more frequent deliveries with lower numbers' and it was 'believed that the number of aircraft ferried from America is far greater than recorded'.[62]

AMERICAN FORCED LANDINGS DURING 1943

Up to January 1943 Gray had negotiated successfully the departure from Ireland of all grounded American aircraft and their crews. His contacts with Walshe were to prove vital when, due to navigational errors, a United States B-17F Flying Fortress (41–9045) *Stinky*, flown by Captain Thomas Heulings, crash-landed at the Nursery Field at Mellowes Agricultural College outside Athenry, Galway at 1150 on 15 January 1943, sustaining 'considerable damage to wings, undercarriage and propellers'.[63] The aircraft had departed from Gibraltar en-route to England ten hours earlier. It was first sighted by coastwatchers as it

14 Oct. 1943. **59** MA G2/X/315 Pt II, Western Sector, AMI, Monthly Report, Nov. 1943. **60** Ibid. **61** MA EDP 20/5, McKenna to MacMahon, Jan. 1944. **62** MA G2/X/315 Pt II, Western Sector, AMI, Monthly Report, Dec. 1943. **63** Ibid., Western Command, AMI,

passed over Brandon Head and Kerry Head, flying up the west coast before turning inland over Galway. *Stinky*, converted into a VIP transport, was carrying sixteen passengers and crew. With Captain Heulings, his co-pilot Lieutenant James McLaughlin, his navigator Lieutenant C.B. Collins and seven enlisted men, were Lieutenant General Jacob Devers,[64] General Gladeon Barnes,[65] Major General Edward Brooks,[66] Brigadier General Williston Palmer,[67] Colonel William Sexton[68] and Major Earle Hormell.[69] Devers and his staff had been returning from a fact-finding tour of North Africa when their aircraft strayed off course over the Bay of Biscay. They were the highest-ranking United States officers grounded in Ireland during the Second World War and it was the most serious and politically sensitive case of an American plane making a forced landing on Irish territory. Met by a group from the LDF and then by regular troops (who very much impressed Devers by their 'smart appearance and apparent efficiency'), the Americans surrendered their weapons and were brought to a local hotel where they were given a lunch in their honour.[70] Within hours Gray made arrangements for their release and transit to the border. The Americans crossed the border near Sligo at 0200 on 16 January. *Stinky* was dismantled and transported to Langford Lodge airfield in Northern Ireland, but the aircraft was beyond repair and was scrapped.

Stinky had come down beside the Dublin to Galway railway line and it was impossible to keep the landing a secret. Hempel protested to External Affairs when he heard that the crew had been released whereas German airmen were interned. Walshe maintained that the aircraft was on a non-operational flight and was technically a transport aircraft. The message from the American legation in Dublin to aircrews liable to land in neutral Ireland was that 'regardless of the facts' their flight was non-operational.[71] The legation added that this was emphasized by the actions of the crew of a British bomber who landed in Ireland and who were interned after making 'a statement that they were returning from a bombing raid on the continent'.[72]

Since Gray's agreement with Dublin on the treatment of American airmen and aircraft on non-operational flights that landed in Ireland six American aircraft had landed and all crews and aircraft had been released. Hathaway and

Monthly Report, Jan. 1943. **64** Eisenhower's Chief of Staff, Commander in Chief of the Mediterranean Theatre and later Commander in Chief of United States Ground Forces. **65** Later Chief of the Research and Development Service, Office Chief of Ordnance at the White Sands Missile Range, New Mexico. **66** Led the 2nd Armoured Division from Omaha Beach on D-Day through the St Lo breakthrough until the surrender of German forces; later served in the Korean War. **67** Brigadier General commanding the VII Corps artillery, Vice Chief of Staff of the United States Army, first Director of Military Assistance at the Department of Defense. **68** Assistant Secretary, War Department General Staff. **69** Personal Assistant to General Devers. **70** NAI DFA Secretaries Files A8 (1), Bryan to Walshe, 8 May 1943. **71** NARA RG 84 Dublin legation, SSF, Box 6 (1943), Gray to Hull, 10 Apr. 1943. **72** Ibid., Brown to Matthews, 19 Feb. 1943.

Gray ensured that the crew and aircraft, where not too badly damaged, left neutral Ireland quickly and any media interest in the downed airmen was suppressed. Gray praised the

> energy, resourcefulness and tact ... of Lieutenant Colonel James L. Hathaway who has been able to represent the flight in all these cases as non-operational and to the co-operative attitude of the British and American Military Commands in Northern Ireland which have established and maintained cordial relations with the Military Authorities of Eire.[73]

Particular praise was also lavished on the former commander of United States forces in Northern Ireland Major General Russell Hartle and his successor Brigadier General Edmund Hill, as through them 'the unofficial liaison and co-operation between our Forces in Northern Ireland and the Military Authorities in Eire depend'.[74] Walshe and de Valera were not mentioned. When Hill and Hathaway met de Valera, the Taoiseach reiterated Irish policy towards the landing and release of planes and their crews, informing both officers that 'there was no passage in international law that applied and that the present modus operandi in Ireland obviously worked out in favour of the Allies'.[75]

A dangerous incident took place on 17 April. During a period of heavy American air activity over Ireland, a lost B-17F Flying Fortress (42–29755), *The Last Straw*, was fired upon by anti-aircraft defences while over Dublin, the aircraft having been tracked by ADC for over an hour since it was first sighted over Cavan. Dalkey LOP heard 'four heavy explosions' to the north at 1213 as the guns opened fire and saw the aircraft 'moving north east' at 2,000 feet. Shortly afterwards they sighted the aircraft again along with 'Ack-Ack fire 5 miles North of Post'.[76] After this welcome, First Lieutenant Cecil Walters landed the aircraft, which was low on fuel, at Dublin airport. The aircraft was quickly refuelled and left for Langford Lodge in Northern Ireland, Defence Forces GHQ thereafter issuing instructions that Allied Aircraft were not to be fired upon unless their intentions were undoubtedly hostile. Gray was furious, not at the Irish opening fire on the aircraft, but because the crew had not received instructions to stress on landing that they were on a non-operational flight. It transpired from a telegram sent by Gray to Hull, for onward trans-mission to President Roosevelt, that 'non-operational status' had been claimed by the crew 'of only one of the six planes' for which Gray and Hathaway had obtained release.[77] 'Internment', Gray continued, 'is certain to result should this continue'. Covering himself and his staff, Gray felt that 'the responsibility will rest not on this Legation but on the Air Command in the event that the

73 Ibid., Gray to Hull, 10 Apr. 1943.   74 Ibid.   75 Ibid., Hathaway to Gray, 19 Apr. 1943.
76 MA LOP 7, 17 Apr. 1943.   77 NARA RG 84 Dublin legation, SSF, Box 6 (1943), Hathaway to Gray, 19 Apr. 1943.

Government of Eire finds it necessary to seize a $350,000 aircraft and to intern trained crews'. Gray did not make it clear what he thought the Irish authorities would do with a solitary Flying Fortress. Yet writing to Hull on 21 April he felt that his policy to secure the release of crews whether they were on operational or non-operational flights had 'borne fruit'. It was accepted by the Irish authorities, and in particular by de Valera, that

> our claim that the missions of the various American combat aircraft grounded on Eire territory were to be considered non-operational, although what evidence was available appeared to indicate that the opposite was indeed the fact.[78]

It was not until 12 May that another landing occurred. At 0945 a B-17F Flying Fortress entering the Donegal corridor and running short of fuel landed on a beach just north of Bundoran. None of the crew was injured and all were released, 'loose equipment [was] salvaged and handed over, [and the] remainder of the aircraft was demolished'.[79] On 4 June a B-26 Marauder observed by Ballagan Head and Clogher Head LOPs made a wheels-up landing on the beach at Termonfeckin in Louth, three miles north of Drogheda. The aircraft was salvaged and the crew were handed over to the military in Northern Ireland. The evacuation and salvage process was running very smoothly. Just over a month later, on the morning of 10 July, Liberator *Travelin' Trollop* was seen circling over Lahinch through dark cloud and drizzle. The aircraft had flown from Gander for Prestwick on a delivery flight. Low on fuel and without radio contact to ascertain his location, Second Lieutenant Max Beuthuysen landed the aircraft on Lahinch beach. Martin Skerritt, the first local to reach the downed aircraft remembered that 'I was only fourteen years old, and in awe of the plane. I'd never seen one before. Then I saw the crew and became a bit nervous.'[80] Soon afterwards Gardaí and LDF arrived and the crew were taken to the local Army camp. The aircraft was guarded, equipment salvaged and the eleven-man crew entertained locally before being sent over the border from where they flew to Prestwick. The treatment of these three aircraft and their crews showed that Gray had in reality little to be worried about.

THE CONTINUING WAR AGAINST THE U-BOAT AND THE CONDOR

During the summer of 1943 the United States Navy reluctantly provided the RAF with VLR Liberators equipped with centimetric radar to assist Coastal Command mount increased operations against U-boats crossing the Bay of Biscay. Two bombing squadrons, VB-103 and VB-105, advance elements of

78 Ibid., Gray to Hull, 21 Apr. 1943.   79 NAI DFA Secretary's Files A26, secret G2 memorandum, Chronological list of forced landings or crashes of belligerent aircraft on Irish territory waters since the outbreak of the war to the 31st Mar. 1944.   80 *Irish Examiner*, 27

Fleet Air Wing 7 (FAW7) of the United States Navy Twelfth Fleet, later joined by VB-110, arrived in England in August 1943 under the command of Commodore William T. Hamilton and established their headquarters at Plymouth.[81] Under the operational control of the RAF, FAW7 were assigned to 19 Group Coastal Command which undertook the protection of convoys in the seas south of Ireland. FAW7's aircraft flew search and destroy missions against U-boats attacking convoys in the western approaches and they battled Ju-88s in the skies over Biscay. The Americans replaced weary Coastal Command aircrews and 'began to assume greater and greater responsibility for air patrols over the Bay of Biscay'.[82] Their 'Battle of the Bay' was unglamorous and unspectacular, as Liberator pilot Lieutenant Robert F. Duffy put it:

> you have to go out there, fly for hours and hours, week in week out, and never see anything. Then maybe, after a month, or even years, you sight a submarine which is visible for perhaps 30 seconds. If you hit it, fine. If you miss it, you will give yourself hell for the next 20 years.[83]

As the Allies gained air superiority over the Bay of Biscay with these new forces, U-boat crews christened it the 'Valley of Death'. Allied aircraft sank sixty-five U-boats in Biscay waters from 1943 to 1944. From an Irish perspective, the FAW7 air patrols over Biscay had a specific significance. For FAW7, the 'Bay Area' extended up to the limits of Irish territorial waters. This had the knock-on effect of increasing the number of United States aircraft seen by coastwatchers in Irish skies from the autumn of 1943.

Coastal Command operations during autumn 1943 inflicted 'horrendous losses' on U-boats, leaving the force 'hard-pressed to carry on'.[84] An RAF source scoffed that heavy losses were 'depriving the Hun of the initiative'.[85] The Admiralty politely concluded that the Germans were 'bewildered'.[86] There were few Allied sightings of U-boats through August; coastwatchers noticed a consequent reduction in naval patrols off the north coast, despite heavy convoy traffic then passing northern and western LOPs. De Valera visited Malin Head LOP on 3 August, signing the LOP logbook. During the visit Lieutenant Fitzsimmons lent the LOP binoculars 'to two lady visitors to look at [a] convoy' comprising 'eight freighters (5000 tons), one tanker (10,000 tons), one destroyer and two corvettes' that passed at 1715 twelve miles to the north heading west in good visibility.[87] Convoy traffic off the north coast was heavy in early August and 'six heavily escorted aircraft carriers were reported moving rapidly westwards

Sept. 2000.   81 VB-111 joined FAW7 temporarily in October 1943 but was redeployed to Morocco.   82 Blair, *Hunted*, p. 419.   83 Quoted in Gene S. McIntyre, 'Fleet Air Wing-7 History', www.vpnavy.com/faw7_1943.html, (accessed 7 July 2005).   84 Blair, *Hunted*, p. 418.   85 TNA HW 2/3, Cheadle War Diary Oct. 1942–Mar. 1944, p. 624.   86 TNA AIR 20/1243, Historical Outline.   87 MA LOP 80, 3 Aug. 1943.

along the northern coast of Donegal' at a time when 'the Germans claimed considerable damage to an Atlantic convoy'.[88] German forces regrouped and attacks on convoys increased in September. Dönitz knew it would be 'a hard fight in spite of our new weapons'.[89] Garda sources in Derry reported renewed attacks on convoys in late September and referred to one of the new German weapons, the acoustic torpedo, 'which is operated by the rotation or swerve of the propellers of the target ship ... it is stated that on one occasion a torpedo of this type actually circled a ship and eventually struck it astern'.[90] These attacks, praised by Hitler as 'the only bright spot at present in an otherwise dark war situation', soon petered out.[91] By October it was

> very difficult to resist the conclusion that the primary pre-occupation of the U-boat crews is now not to kill but to avoid being killed – and that is the beginning of the end in a service which must rely entirely for its effect on a bold offensive spirit.[92]

Despite this reckoning of the demise of the U-boats, the level of aerial protection of convoys by Coastal Command rose again in response to the regrouping of German forces. Through October Donegal LOPs recorded renewed 'heavy activity' in the air 'to coincide with the arrival and departure of convoys off our Northern shores'. However, despite German efforts, convoys were getting through unmolested and through October the passage of fourteen eastbound convoys, mainly tankers and freighters, and eight westbound convoys was reported to G2.

The Kriegsmarine and the Luftwaffe began co-ordinated air reconnaissance patrols to search out Britain to Gibraltar convoys. Almost absent since 1941, 'German 4-engined monoplanes' were again seen over the Mayo/Galway coastline on 5 and 13 December 1943. One passed north-west out over the Atlantic, while on 13 December the second 'appeared to be returning from a reconnaissance patrol', flying southwards over Mace Head LOP and Roundstone. It crashed at Portroe, Dromineer, Tipperary. The crew abandoned and destroyed the aircraft 'sending different coloured lights and portions of the Plane high into the air'.[93] First on the scene was Nenagh LDF Section Leader, John Loughnane, with local LSF and LDF members. Loughnane was injured by shrapnel from the exploding aircraft and had his wounds dressed by a German airman. As the

88 MA G2/X/315 Pt II, Western Sector, AMI, Monthly Report, Aug. 1943. 89 Mallmann Showell, *Fuehrer conferences*, p. 367, Minutes of Conferences at the Fuehrer's Headquarters from September 10 to 12, 1943, 15 Sept. 1943. 90 NAI DFA Secretary's Files P43/1, Ua Ceallaigh to Murphy, 28 Sept. 1943. 91 Mallmann Showell, *Fuehrer conferences*, p. 369, Conference Minutes of the C.-in-C., Navy at the Fuehrer's Headquarters on September 24, 1943, 25 Sept. 1943. 92 NARA RG84 London Embassy, Ambassador's Files, Box 3, file Ireland, *Coastal Command Review (Dec. 1943)*, p. 2. 93 NAI JUS 90/119/298, statement by Thomas Meara to Gardaí, 21 Dec. 1943.

aircraft caught fire, Loughnane saw that the eight crewmen 'stood to attention and gave the Nazi salute'.[94] One approached Loughnane's LDF colleague Patrick Morrissey who recalled that he 'touched his chest and said "German" and pointed at me. I said "Eire". He then reached out his hand and shook hands with me.'[95] Though by now seriously wounded, Loughnane helped take the German airmen into custody, the crew ending up interned in the Curragh.[96] Hempel demanded their release, arguing that they were on a training flight. Walshe did not believe him:

> I told him we had no evidence that the plane was in effect a training plane, since the crew had blown it up after landing. Indeed the explosion was so great that it was heard fifty miles away, and I could not imagine a training plane having so much explosives on board.[97]

He added that the Irish authorities

> never accepted the word of the British or the Americans as to the character, operational or otherwise, of a plane. We always had to examine the plane and see for ourselves. We could not do in his case what we could not do for the British and American representatives ... it could not be conceived that a German plane could come into such a highly belligerent area as the waters immediately beyond our territorial area without being fully armed. Geography itself was a decisive factor in the character of the planes which overflew our territory.[98]

The belated co-operation between the Luftwaffe and the Kriegsmarine could not alter the course of the war in the Atlantic. Convoys were getting through unharmed; during December Western Command sighted nine eastbound convoys and one westbound. 'Every square yard of the ocean' had become 'a potential death trap for the unwary U-boat' and submarine activity against convoys was 'considerably reduced'.[99] Churchill declared that 'the back of the U-boats is broken'.[100] By the end of December 1943, the defeat of the U-boat was 'an accomplished fact'.[101] Dönitz knew that 'because of the enemy's superiority, our submarines are limited more and more to underwater operations'.[102] To ensure victory Coastal Command planned to intensify its anti-U-boat

94 Ibid., statement by Loughnane to Gardaí, 21 Dec. 1943. 95 Ibid., statement by Morrissey to Gardaí, 15 Dec. 1943. 96 Loughnane lost his right eye through shrapnel injuries. 97 NAI DFA Secretary's Files A2, Walshe to de Valera, 15 Dec. 1943. 98 Ibid. 99 TNA HW 2/3, Cheadle War Diary Oct. 1942–Mar. 1944, p. 643. 100 Ibid. 101 NARA RG84 London Embassy, Ambassador's Files, Box 3, file Ireland, *Coastal Command Review (Dec. 1943)* vol. II, no. 8, p. 2. 102 Mallmann Showell, *Fuehrer conferences*, p. 373, Minutes of the Conference of the C.-in-C., Navy, with the Fuehrer on December 19 and 20, 1943, at Headquarters Wolfsschanze, 8 Jan. 1944.

operations in the first months of 1944, a move which would lead to a further and very noticeable increase in the number of American aircraft flying off Ireland's south and south-west coast.

AIDS TO NAVIGATION: (I) 'EIRE SIGNS'

From April 1943 to March 1944 21,000 military aircraft were reported near or over Ireland. Overflights rose from 778 for 1942–3 to 1,600 in 1943–4. Of the 21,000 aircraft, 12,180 were identified, 99.65 per cent of these were Allied aircraft; the figure being roughly evenly divided between British and American. There were forty forced landings. In response to the huge increase in flights crossing Irish territory (especially delivery flights), increased Coastal Command operations around Ireland and the landing of greater numbers of military aircraft on Irish territory, the Defence Forces took one simple step. As General McKenna told the Minister for Defence, 'in order to warn belligerent aircraft of their position, the word "EIRE" has been prominently displayed close to the LOPs' of the Coast Watching Service.[103] From the summer of 1943 these aerial identification signs were constructed 'as a matter of the greatest urgency' at or near most posts.[104] It was a way 'to reduce the number of aircraft landing because their crews had lost their bearings'.[105] The decision to construct the signs was taken in a rather secret manner. The Minister for Finance simply gave oral sanction and the matter was not minuted as having been discussed by the Cabinet. Perhaps this was not secrecy but merely a routine transaction. However, American sources show a different picture. Gray informed Hull that the 'plainly marked signs' had 'been erected as a result, at least partially, of the efforts of' the American legation in Dublin.[106] He asked the Irish authorities to construct markers to indicate to aircrews that they were passing over neutral territory. It was one thing to ensure that United States aircraft that landed in Ireland were returned to operational service and their crews released, but it would be much better if these aircraft, if lost and not short on fuel, did not have to land in Ireland.

The signs were cheap visual aids to navigation, reading simply 'EIRE' in block capital letters. At the further request of the United States air force, the number of the nearby LOP was added to the signs during or shortly after construction and this action turned the aerial markers into aerial navigation aids. On 19 June Malin Head LOP received a call 'from DO to have the letters 80 placed 30 feet from the top of Eire and in the centre. Each letter to be between 15 and 20 feet by 2 feet'.[107] The evidence from Malin Head LOP thus suggests

103 MA General Report on the Army for year 1 Apr. 1943–1 Mar. 44.   **104** NAI DF S7/2/40, MacMahon to McElligott, 8 Jan. 1946.   **105** MA General Report on the Army for year 1 Apr. 1943 – 1 Mar. 44.   **106** NARA RG 319 Records of the Army Staff Assistant Chief of Staff, G-2, Box 460, telegram No. 171, Gray to Hull, 21 Dec. 1943.   **107** MA LOP 80,

that the numbers were added in June 1943, shortly after construction of the 'Eire signs' began. According to Joseph Carroll, 'General Hill who commanded the American air force in Northern Ireland then flew around the coast in a Flying Fortress with General McKenna noting every sign and its identification number and this information proved to be an invaluable navigation aid for the inexperienced American pilots'.[108]

Two types of 'Eire sign' were constructed. The initial signs from summer 1943 were of simple construction. The coastwatchers at Malin Head were told merely 'to collect flat stones to make letters'.[109] No explicit orders were given as to shape, size or orientation of the sign. Most were approximately four metres long and two metres high. In many cases, such as at Baltimore and at Galley Head in Cork and at Lenadoon in Sligo, these signs were found to be too small. To replace the 1943 signs, larger signs built to a standard format of twelve metres long by six metres high and surrounded by a wide rectangular stone border, were constructed during the summer of 1944. The 1944 signs were sizeable constructions as 'in some cases up to 150 tons of stone were used' with the structure then being embedded in concrete and whitewashed to increase visibility.[110] Being conspicuously coloured against the landscape, the signs were designed to be seen from the air. An aerial photograph of Cahore Point LOP taken after the war shows two separate 'Eire signs', one not more than a couple of metres long built during 1943, the other the standard sign of 1944 dimensions. Both signs were constructed by the coastwatchers. At Ballagan Point construction of the post's 'Eire sign' began on 12 June 1943. Construction took thirteen days and, ultimately, an order from District Officer Lieutenant McCabe to have the sign completed 'at once'. Then on 25 June the LOP logbook simply noted: 'sign completed'.[111] Further south at Wicklow Head LOP the sign and number were constructed at the same time but over only eight days. Three days after the sign was completed an RAF Coastal Command Liberator passed south half-a-mile west of the post at 1,000 feet. Possibly this was just a coincidence, but perhaps not: later that day Wicklow Head LOP was ordered to put a border around the sign and to extend the size of the number '9' next to the sign.

All available personnel at each post were ordered to report for duty to have the signs completed as quickly as possible. A move to twelve-hour watches at Malin Head LOP during the construction of the post's 'Eire sign' almost led to a mutiny, leaving the corporal in charge no alternative but to ring the local district officer 'intimating that the men refused to work at EIRE under the twelve hour duty system'.[112] When District Officer Lieutenant McGinley arrived at the post the following day he was in no mood to put up with the state of affairs, scrawling in the LOP logbook that there was 'no [...] word in the

16 Apr. 1943.   **108** Carroll, *War years*, p. 121.   **109** MA LOP 81, 10 Apr. 1943.   **110** NAI DF S7/2/40, MacMahon to McElligott, 31 Oct. 1945.   **111** MA LOP 1, entries from 12 to 25 June 1943.   **112** MA LOP 80, 20 May 1944.

Army' as refuse, the missing word since having been carefully cut out of the logbook. There was no further complaint by the men at Malin Head. All except those on rest were put on duty to complete the sign and number by 29 May when a Hudson carrying the Chief of Staff would 'leave Baldonnell at 11.15 for Loop Head and then coast wise to Inishowen' on a flight inspecting the signs.[113] Unfortunately for the men at Malin Head, McKenna was not impressed with their work. He noted 'site poor letters appeared thin – not painted generally unsatisfactory'.[114] Following the inspection flight a second sign was begun which was completed without a hitch by 9 June. Both signs can still be seen on the headland.

Senior officers often visited LOPs to view the progress of work on the signs and their number markers. OC Western Command, Colonel Felix McCorley, inspected Black Head LOP on the south side of Galway Bay on 11 August 1943 and 'also inspected the "Eire" signs at the LOP'.[115] The logbook for Lamb's Head LOP in Kerry noted on 8 January 1944 that the 'Eire sign to be finished off and whitewashed early next week. Ready to be photographed by the Chief of Staff'.[116] Malin Head was informed on 6 January 1944 by a 'call from No. 2 Sub-depot. Have the word EIRE whitewashed and kept clean and tidy.'[117] Ongoing inspections of signs were carried out for the remainder of the war, Galley Head LOP noting an 'inspection of "Eire" sign' on 23 May 1944 by OC Southern Command, Colonel O'Hanrahan.[118] The inspection resulted in further alterations to the sign, the work being carried out with all available men so that the NCO in charge reported on 29 May that he 'could not effect a relief for watch keeper at 16.00 hours. All hands employed on sign.'[119] The sign was completed just in time for the aerial inspection by the Chief of Staff. McKenna's interest in the signs underlines their strategic significance and his report following a coastal inspection flight revealed vastly differing qualities of construction around the country. Flying by Corraun, Mayo, at 1,500 feet, McKenna saw that the sign had 'clear and distinct letters' while the 'figures appeared a bit thin'.[120] Further north at Erris Head the site was satisfactory and 'party seen at work', though the sign was not yet painted. McKenna concluded 'many of the figures were narrower and not as well made as the letters. Well made thick letters showed up much better than thin lettering'. Following a further inspection at the end of June 'the signs were found to be clearly visible from the air', but certain improvements were suggested. At Melmore Head in Donegal, the sign was on a low-lying area and was 'nearly hidden from an aircraft flying parallel with the coast', another sign was required.[121]

113 Ibid. 114 MA EDP 20/5, untitled memorandum, 30 May 1944. 115 MA G2/X/315 Pt II, M&CWS, Southern Command, sub-depot report, Aug. 1943. 116 MA LOP 33, 8 Jan. 1944. 117 MA LOP 80, 6 Jan. 1944. 118 MA LOP 27, 23 May 1944. 119 Ibid., 29 May 1944. 120 MA EDP 20/5, untitled memorandum, 30 May 1944. 121 Ibid., Childers to

Initially the 'Eire signs' were intended to warn belligerent aircraft of their location over neutral Irish territory. A Western Sector air and marine intelligence report for October 1943 commented on this important function that

> since the beginning of August [1943] no crashes or forced landings occurred on our territory[,] this constitutes a record for the Western Sector; the neutrality signs along the coast may account for this improvement, which is very marked.[122]

The explicit reference to 'neutrality signs' shows that the signs were working and that they were intended primarily to warn aircraft that they were over Irish territory. It was one thing for a flight crew to know that they were over Irish territory; they also had to know where exactly they were over that territory. Gray explained to Hull that 'all along the coast of Eire there have been erected conspicuous signs marked Eire and numbered. Any pilot with the aid of the key map can find his location.'[123] To Gray the existence of the numbers was more important than the location signs, and of course 'any pilot' really meant any Allied pilot (the Germans were not told of the existence of the signs). The signs allowed navigators to plot their position along the Irish coast and alter or maintain their course as appropriate. A secret document from March 1944, 'Flying Bulletin Number 5', from the Office of the Commanding General of the Headquarters of the United States Strategic Air Forces in Europe and entitled 'Briefing instructions: Northern Ireland and Eire' explained how

> 1. A system of marking the coastline of Eire to orient pilots flying in that district as to their location has been put into effect as follows:
> a. The word 'EIRE' is spelled out in six (6) foot or larger block letters at eighty-three (83) points on the Eire coastline. These selected points are spaced between eight (8) and ten (10) miles apart and have been visibly numbered consecutively, running clockwise from Ballagan Point (1) on the East coast, South and around the coastline to Inishowen-Head (82), with the exception of point 83 which is located at Foileye.[124]

This information was included in the briefings for all air crews 'who will possibly fly in the vicinity of Ireland'.[125] With the aid of this information, and a bearing from the Derrynacross Beacon in Northern Ireland, they could set course for Nutts Corner near Belfast or their chosen landing ground. On the last leg of the Atlantic crossing navigators were told that this was where they 'needed

McCorley, 3 July 1944.   122 MA G2/X/315 Pt II, Western Command, AMI, Monthly Report, Oct. 1943.   123 NARA RG 319 Records of the Army Staff Assistant Chief of Staff, G-2, Box 460, telegram No. 171, Gray to Hull, 21 Dec. 1943.   124 TNA AIR 2/4735, 16 Mar. 1944.   125 Ibid.

to be really sharp … [I]f we landed in Southern Ireland, we'd be delayed for about six months. If we landed in Northern Ireland, we'd be okay.'[126] Writing in *An Cosantóir* in 1988, Owen Quinn observed that 'grounded foreign pilots were heard to admit that these signs were unmistakable aids to navigation'.[127] The Irish government could argue that the signs and numbers would enable belligerent aircraft to leave Irish territory immediately, but the numbers enabled aircraft to plot their course deviation and return to their planned route. Commandant Quinn later told an interviewer that 'if a pilot got in any way in trouble with his navigation or with fog or anything like that he had a list of these look out posts and a little map of the area he was travelling in and if he spotted number 6, he could say "Ah, sure, I'm over Dublin, I've only to turn right for home, that's it".'[128] A pilot suffering compass failure or damage to navigational equipment could easily use the EIRE signs and their associated numbers to navigate by dead reckoning.

The construction of the signs did not always prevent American aircraft landing on Irish territory, but it was noticeable that following the introduction of the signs those United States aircraft that did land on Irish territory tended to do so at Shannon airport. On 5 November 1943 two C-47 Dakota transport aircraft landed at Shannon in close succession after making landfall off Dursey Island in Cork.[129] They told the Irish authorities that they were lost due to bad weather and low on fuel. Both aircraft and the fourteen passengers and crew they carried left that day following an improvement in the weather and refuelling from the stocks now held at the airport earmarked for United States aircraft. Not all aircraft were able to benefit from the EIRE signs. Flying Fortress B-17G (42–34120) *Bella Donna* bound for Northern Ireland and flown by Second Lieutenant Richard C. Walch crashed in poor weather eight miles north-east of Sligo on Truskmore Mountain, Cliffoney, just to the east of Benbulbin at 1800 on 9 December 1943. In the crash Second Lieutenants Wallace and Fox were killed, Staff Sergeant Mendoza and Sergeant Latecki were seriously injured and received hospital treatment in Sligo. When Hathaway reported to Washington on the crash the following day, Latecki was not expected to live; by 13 December he was dead. Wallace, Fox and Latecki were the first fatalities from an American aircraft crash-landing on Irish territory. The six remaining crew, all of whom were injured, the bodies of the dead crewmen and all 'classified equipment' were moved to Northern Ireland by the time Hathaway sent his first report on the crash on 10 December.[130] Gray augmented Hathaway's report, commenting on

126 Bert Hallum (as told to Jerry Hoffman Sr.), 'Reflections on being a pilot in WWII', www.303rdbg.com/relections-hallum.html (accessed 12 July 2005).   127 Owen Quinn, 'Coastwatch', *An Cosantóir*, Jan. 1988, 23-7 at 26.   128 Grob-Fitzgibbon, *Oral history*, p. 199. 129 C-47 42–24074, flown by Lieutenant L.J. Harrison and C-47 42–24098, flown by H. Krauss.   130 NARA RG 319 Records of the Army Staff Assistant Chief of Staff, G-2, Box 460, Hathaway to War Department, 10 Dec. 1943.

the 'excellent liaison' between the American legation in Dublin, 'the Irish Air Command' and Brigadier General Hill and his forces in Northern Ireland. He informed the State Department that 'arrangements to salvage the secret apparatus, remove the bodies to Northern Ireland, and hospitalise the wounded were made without friction'.[131] The American legation in Dublin wrote to McKenna to convey its thanks 'for the great kindness and consideration which your officers in the Sligo area have manifested on the occasion of the recent crash of a B-17 plane bound for Northern Ireland'.[132] Gray added that 'we appreciate more deeply the goodwill and kindness accorded to our dead and injured'. This expression of goodwill was necessary because, in a potentially serious blunder, uniformed United States troops had crossed the border from Northern Ireland to rush medical aid to the injured personnel. Then, the morning following the crash, a United States army medical officer arrived at Sligo hospital in uniform to consult with the Irish authorities. He should have been wearing civilian clothes. 'Fortunately', Gray pointed out to Hill, 'the attitude of the Irish Army officers who were first in contact with the situation and subsequently of the Chief of Staff of the Irish Army was so generous and friendly that no friction occurred.'[133] Gray knew that the American forces' actions were 'praiseworthy and innocent of any design to infringe the neutrality of Eire', but reminded Hill that United States forces crossing the border for rescue or salvage work must do so out of uniform. He warned Hill that though 'the great majority' of Irish people were well-disposed 'to our war effort', there was a minority who would use this incident to embarrass the Irish government. He added his usual refrain that, if the incident had 'been formally reported to the Irish government', the internment of the crew would have been likely and 'the American Government would have been under obligations to make apologies and amends to the Irish Government'. To Gray, this would have been the worst of all outcomes.

While there was an element of diplomacy to these remarks to Hill, Gray brought up an operational matter that provides significant information on the importance of the 'Eire signs'. In December there was at best 'only six hours of daylight in Ireland'.[134] Gray asked that this be 'pointed out' to the War Department because 'in fading light it is impossible to read the coastal signs put up by the Eire Government'. Accordingly, Gray asked that 'to allow a margin of safety planes bound for Northern Ireland should not be routed on schedules which contemplate passage after 2pm along the coast of Eire'. Clearly the signs were not lit at night and functioned as a navigational aid only in daylight. However the records of LOP 26 at Seven Heads in Cork contain reference to a

131 Ibid., Gray to State Department (No. 166), 13 Dec. 1943.   132 NARA RG 84 Dublin Legation, Box 13 (1943), Gray to McKenna, 13 Dec. 1943.   133 Ibid., Gray to Hill, 23 Dec. 1943.   134 NARA RG 319 Records of the Army Staff Assistant Chief of Staff, G-2, Box 460, paraphrase of Gray to State Department (No. 166 Secret), 13 Dec. 1943.

'fire signal'[135] and those of the neighbouring LOP at Galley Head include a curt entry that the 'Signal fire [is] to be erected to its original size. Above to be completed within 24 hours failure to carry out this instruction will entail disciplinary action.'[136] Visits to sites of LOPs, contemporary photographs and present-day photographs provide no outright evidence as to whether the signs were illuminated at night as these entries suggest.

Gray was personally affected by the crash at Truskmore and the deaths of his three young fellow-countrymen. His raw emotion surfaced in letter to Dr Evelyn Connolly, Dispensary Doctor of Cliffoney, Sligo. On her way to a dinner party when hearing of the plane crash, she immediately made for the scene:

> You were the only medical officer in this area and without waiting to change into suitable clothing you set out with the first rescue party, in the cold and rain, up the formidable mountain. There were places where the ascent could only be made on hands and knees, where the men who accompanied you, had to drag you up steep rocks, but you never faltered. On arriving at the scene of the accident, you directed the removal of the dead and wounded, administered first surgical aid, assuaged pain, and materially contributed to the chance of survival in the case of several of the seriously injured.
>
> For this devoted service notably beyond what may reasonably be demanded of a civilian physician I now thank you in the name of the Commander in Chief of the United States Army and Navy, the President of the United States.[137]

A week after the Sligo crash, following the safe landing of another Flying Fortress (42–37985) at Shannon, Gray sent an angry telegram to Hull on air crew behaviour. After reminding the Secretary of State of the purpose of the chain of EIRE marker signs, and that Hathaway had passed information on their existence to the War Department, Gray continued:

> In the cases of the two Fortresses which recently crash-landed in Eire, the pilots had not been given this information. In addition, they were given a map which incorrectly had Phoenix Park marked as an airfield ... [O]ur military attaché has provided full and accurate information about airfields. This mission is felt to be blameless for the American lives and valuable equipment lost here.[138]

135 MA LOP 26, 3 Nov. 1943.   136 MA LOP 27, 4 Apr. 1944.   137 NARA RG 84 Dublin Legation, Box 13 (1943), Gray to Connolly, 23 Dec. 1943.   138 NARA RG 319 Records of the Army Staff Assistant Chief of Staff, G-2, Box 460 (No. 171), Gray to Hull, 21 Dec. 1943.

Further proof of the importance of the signs to Allied airmen came from documents handed over to Gardaí following the crash landing of an American Flying Fortress at Foulkescourt, Johnstown, Kilkenny on 23 January 1944. The crew had baled out over Northern Ireland, leaving the Flying Fortress to fly on automatic pilot until it crashed. One confidential document recovered advised aircrews: 'Do not land in Eire except in emergency. If possible try and make one of the nineteen (19) serviceable airports in North Ireland. However, land at airport in Eire rather than crash land in North Ireland.'[139] It continued, 'How to tell you are over neutral Ireland (Eire)[.] The word "EIRE" has been spelled out in six (6) foot block letters at eighty three (83) places along the Eire coast line observer posts and at airports and along the border between North Ireland and Ireland.'

Despite the presence of the 'Eire signs', sixteen United States aircraft landed or crashed on Irish territory from January to 6 June 1944.[140] At least one of these aircraft devised an opportunity to land at Shannon. A C-47 flown by Captain C.B. Anderson, with eight others on board, flying from Marrakech in Morocco to England, landed at Shannon on 6 March 1944. Anderson could have reached England with the fuel on board but he told Hathaway that 'he was briefed at Marrakech that landing at Rineanna would be [a] "lark", with food, rest, drinks and [a] speedy release'. Hathaway requested that Marrakech be at once 'enlightened' that 'serious repercussions [were] possible from such a briefing'.[141] There was, he considered, a 'pronounced deficiency' in the briefings being given at the base.[142] Whatever its actual status really was, Anderson did not know to tell the Irish authorities that his flight was non-operational. He and his crew had not been advised on the need for 'discretion in conduct, speech and manner' and got rather a rude welcome being '"surprised" and alarmed when two armoured cars met them and armed soldiers surrounded their plane. From what they had been told at Marrakech, they expected to be welcomed with open arms'.[143] In Hathaway's opinion crews from North African bases were usually poorly briefed and 'this was the worst yet'.

Anderson had not been told that Eire was neutral and Northern Ireland was at war and that there was an international border between the two areas. He did not know that internment possibly awaited him and his crew for admitting to landing in Ireland while on an operational mission. This was an outcome Gray had been able to avoid to date. Further, the crew had no information on the Donegal Air Corridor, the radio frequencies for using the corridor, and had no

139 NAI DFA Secretary's Files A26, extract from confidential memorandum attached to O'Reilly to Murphy, undated, but Jan. 1944.   140 Five B-17s, 3 B-24s, 1 Liberator, 3 DC-3s, 2 B-26s, 1 'Lockheed fighter' and 2 'army co-operation aircraft' (details from NAI DFA A26 and NARA RG 84).   141 NARA RG 319 Records of the Army Chief of Staff, Box 459, telegram, Hathaway to War Department, 8 Mar. 1944.   142 NARA RG 84 Dublin Legation, SSF, Box 7 (1944), Hathaway to Gray, 8 Mar. 1944.   143 Ibid.

information on the location of USAAF bases in Northern Ireland. They had no map of Ireland and had only 'a mimeographed copy of a sketch of the Irish coastline with the numbered shore markers and three major aerodromes, only, indicated on it'. This map, Hathaway sarcastically observed, 'helped them to orient themselves when they made a landfall'.

The construction of the 'Eire signs' was seized on by farmers as an opportunity for seeking compensation from the Department of Finance. One farmer from Whitegate, Cork, claimed compensation for loss of crops from the field at Power Head where one sign was constructed. He dolefully informed the Department of Defence that

> his intention in 1944 was to set a crop of turnips in the field in which the Sign was constructed, but as the setting season was then far advanced he could not set the turnips elsewhere so that he lost the crop; in 1945 he would have set a crop of barley.[144]

He claimed £50 compensation for loss of crops and £12 for use by the Defence Forces of the right of way across his lands to the LOP on Power Head. At the end of the war farmers seeking stone for walls removed many of the signs. In other cases, the Department of Defence removed the signs. Few of the 'Eire signs' now remain or are visible. They required constant maintenance throughout their operational life and when unattended were soon reclaimed by nature. Only on the most remote and inaccessible headlands have the signs survived the sixty years since they were constructed. Most remaining signs are on the west Mayo coast, in particular on Achill at Corraun and at Moyteogue Head, at Erris Head and at Portacloy. A handful of examples also still remain visible in Donegal, at Carrigan Head, at Malin Head and, just visible through the grass, at Bloody Foreland. One of the signs at Malin Head, the construction of which caused a near mutiny at the headland LOP, has become something of a tourist attraction. Unlike the coastwatchers stationed there in 1943, tourists have been willing to work with local stone and add their own names in imitation of a sign of which few of them probably know the origins.

THE ATTACK ON THE MV KERLOGUE, 23 OCTOBER 1943

While on patrol over Biscay FAW7 aircraft regularly saw vessels belonging to Irish shipping companies. On the morning of 23 October 1943 at 0728 a patrol flown by Lieutenant 'Dutch' de Hahn and Ensign Gail Burkey closed on a radar contact with a surface vessel.[145] Twenty-six miles distant they sighted the Wexford Steamship Company's 335-ton MV *Kerlogue* approximately eighty miles off the Cork coast and bound for Lisbon with a cargo of coal. It was

144 NAI DF S7/2/40, MacMahon to McElligott, 4 July 1946. 145 At 50.13´N 08.40´W.

'typical to head for a "blip" in the Bay of Biscay only to find that there below ... was a dirty little cargo boat with "EIRE" written in big letters on its hull', but this encounter with *Kerlogue* has added significance.[146] *Kerlogue* was well off its prescribed course; a fact borne out by the ship's log, and this was to have tragic consequences.

At 1600 *Kerlogue* was subject to a twenty-five minute cannon attack by two unidentified aircraft roughly 120 miles off Kinsale. Gray reported to Washington that a 'confidential source' advised him that it was 'probably a British air patrol' which attacked the Irish vessel. He added that *Kerlogue* was 'believed to have been one hundred miles off the course prescribed for her by the British Admiralty and hence was believed to be a hostile ship'.[147] The aircraft were later identified as Mosquitoes from RAF 307 Polish Squadron, flying patrols as part of 'Operation INSTEP'. They claimed that the Irish vessel was French, that it had returned fire and that they left *Kerlogue* 'circling with smoke issuing from it'.[148] Gray told Hull that the Irish were willing to co-operate to suppress this news, but added that 'it is impossible to keep a secret in Ireland'.

With four casualties on board, including the Ship's Master, 30-year-old Captain Desmond Fortune,[149] Chief Officer Denis Valencie turned the ship around and headed for Cork harbour. Just after 1800, *Kerlogue* was spotted by a patrolling Sunderland, 'L' of 10 Squadron of 19 Group Coastal Command, flown by Flight Officer Clark and Flight Officer Stansfield.[150] Clarke and Stansfield circled the Irish ship, which signalled S.O.S. and requested an escort as it had been attacked, had injured crew onboard and required medical assistance. Under orders to complete its patrol, the Sunderland signalled that it could not comply with *Kerlogue*'s request but that it would send a message reporting the position of the stricken ship. The Admiralty later said that the Sunderland assumed the damage had been caused by a German aircraft and that the ship was in communication by radio with its home port.

The British were reluctant to pay compensation to the crew of *Kerlogue*. One Admiralty official noted that the 'Dominions Secretary does not want compensation given lest it be said that we are being soft on the Irish; he would not mind it being given if a special reason can be made'.[151] But that same official felt that some compensation 'might be given' as the attack took place outside

---

146 First Engineer Paddy Watson, quoted in Norman Franks, *Dark sky, deep water: first hand experiences of the anti-U-boat war in World War Two* (London, 2004 edition), p. 73. 147 NARA RG 319 Box 460, Records of the Army Staff, Assistant Chief of Staff, G-2, Gray to Hull, 1 Dec. 1943.   148 TNA AIR 25/487, 19 Group narrative for 23 Oct. 1943. The aircraft were S/307 and D/307.   149 The British Naval Attaché in Dublin reported to the DNI that it was 'unfortunate from the British point of view' that Fortune had been involved in the *Kerlogue* incident as he was 'always ready to pass on any information in his possession' (TNA ADM 1/15817, Naval attaché to DNI, 8 Dec. 1943).   150 At 49°49′N, 09°11′W, on a course of 315° (true) at a speed of about 5 knots. See AIR 27/152.   151 TNA ADM 1/15817, minute, Waldock to DNI, 25 Jan. 1944.

declared danger areas to shipping in the Bay of Biscay where they were liable to be attacked on sight, even though the vessel was well off its prescribed route. In a damning indictment of the men of 307 Squadron, he concluded 'there was nothing very suspicious about the ship and anyone but Polish pilots would have hesitated to attack without inquiring at base'. Officially the RAF would apportion no blame to the Poles. They had been warned to expect *Kerlogue*, they knew she was at sea the day of the attack, but they had not expected to find her 'east of 12 degrees west'.[152] Following a 'full and careful investigation', and despite various discrepancies over the exact position of the attack and whether it was in fact in the prohibited area, the British were willing only to make private 'ex gratia payments' to those injured in the attack due to the discrepancy of the ship's position when attacked. They would accept no responsibility for the attack. The War Cabinet agreed that there was no reason why Britain 'should not make ex-gratia grants openly in this case, seeing that the matter arose out of a mistake, and that the ship had been engaged in carrying a British cargo at the time'.[153] Maffey hoped that these payments would be granted as they would facilitate his ongoing negotiations for the release of the remaining British airmen interned in Ireland.

CONCLUSION

In addition to monitoring routine Coastal Command patrols and forces training off the north coast, the coastwatchers reported on two very different operations off the Irish coast through 1943. The information they collected fed into the ongoing intelligence battle facing Bryan and his colleagues as they analyzed coastwatchers' reports to anticipate trends in the battle of the Atlantic and the development of Allied plans for the invasion of occupied Europe. Firstly, through 1943 the coastwatchers on the south coast gave G2 a glimpse into the unrelenting 'Battle of the Bay' which, though focussed centrally on Biscay, stretched further north to Ireland's southern coast. Second, and of much more immediate concern, was the impact of the massive rise in delivery flights from North America on air traffic over Ireland. The war in the air had become the principal focus of the Coast Watching Service. Aiding crash-landed airmen had always been part of coast watching operations, but the 'Eire signs' stretched the limits of neutrality to unexplored areas. Such co-operation was perhaps made possible by the growing likelihood of an Allied victory and the almost complete absence of German forces from the seas and skies off Ireland. But, more importantly, it was necessitated by the practical matter of the phenomenal increase in Allied air operations close to Ireland, either over Biscay, over Galway and north Mayo, or off Donegal. The Irish had established the Coast Watching

152 Ibid., Admiralty telegram to Archer, 22 Nov. 1943.   153 Ibid., extract from War Cabinet conclusions (162 (43)), 26 Nov. 1943.

Service using advice from Britain, but in 1943 the United States had directly intervened in the structure and operation of the service through the installation of the 'Eire signs' and identification numbers along the coastline. Established in 1939 to protect neutrality, 1943 saw the Coast Watching Service become an adjunct to the massive operation to move forces to Europe to participate in OVERLORD which up to now it had only observed. The practicalities of war, in particular adapting to the huge increase in delivery flights and the rising levels of anti-submarine operations and convoy escorts, taken with Ireland's 'certain consideration' for the Allies, were the defining factors. By the end of 1943 the coastwatchers were effectively assisting Allied air operations over the Atlantic leading to the opening of the second front in Europe. From the Irish legation at Vichy, Seán Murphy reported that while the 'occupying authorities fear invasion', the 'vast majority of the French population ... eagerly await it'.[154] Convoys crossing the Atlantic were now 'from five to ten times as big as in previous years. Very big escorts, including battleships, accompany the convoys'.[155] Walshe told Hempel in December 1943 that 'the whole world was talking about a Second Front ... it was obvious to everybody that the supreme crisis of the war was at hand'.[156]

154 NAI DFA Secretary's Files P12/1, Murphy to Walshe, 23 Aug. 1943.   155 NAI DFA Secretary's Files P43/1, Ó Coileáin to Murphy, 27 Oct. 1943.   156 NAI DFA Secretary's Files A25, Walshe to de Valera, 15 Dec. 1943.

CHAPTER NINE

D-Day and after

BY JANUARY 1944 THE LOPs of the Coast Watching Service, now four years in operation, were beginning to show signs of their hasty wartime construction. Despite continual repairs, the majority of posts along the south coast were in an 'unsatisfactory condition'.[1] Captain O'Riordan, OC M&CWS sub-depot, Southern Command, reported that

> unless repairs are affected during the coming months it will not be possible to carry out repairs in bad weather, with the results that the men's health will be seriously affected by dampness, and the efficiency of the posts concerned considerably reduced through absences of men on sick leave.[2]

Inspections showed that despite these difficult working conditions coast-watchers' morale remained high, disciplinary offences were few and District Officers commented 'very favourably on personnel'.[3]

Along the south coast, coastwatchers entered a period of increased activity in January 1944 as FAW7 redeployed to the area following intelligence that U-boats had begun 'to creep towards Ireland'.[4] Sightings of FAW7's United States-liveried Liberators rose, with their '4-engined high winged monoplane' silhouette a distinctive shape in the winter sky. By the end of January there had been 'a steep rise in aerial activity' along the south and south-west coast as weather improved and 'further increased activity' was anticipated 'as the zero hour for the invasion of Europe approaches'.[5] The rise in activity was brought to the attention of Minister for Defence Oscar Traynor. Unusually, the daily report summary for 21 January is marked 'seen by Minister.'[6] At the same time, G2 officers at Foynes reported that United States consular staff 'appear hourly to expect the European Invasion, and keep close to Radios at news-times'.[7]

1 MA G2/X/315 Pt II, Monthly report, Sub-depot, M&CWS, Southern Command, Jan. 1944. 2 Ibid., Monthly report, M&CWS, Southern Command, July 1944. 3 Ibid., Monthly report, Sub-depot, M&CWS, Southern Command, Feb. 1944. 4 NARA RG 38 Box 332, FAW7 liaison officer, Headquarters, Coastal Command, 17 Mar. 1944. 5 MA G2/X/315 Pt II, Mallow Sector AMI, Monthly Report on Coastal Intelligence, Jan. 1945. 6 MA DRS 1346, 21 Jan. 1944. 7 NAI DFA Secretary's Files A8(1), Reports from IO Shannon Airport, Foynes, 9 Jan 1944.

AIR AND NAVAL OPERATIONS OFF IRELAND,
DECEMBER 1943–FEBRUARY 1944

'Enemy submarines' were now 'nearer to the British Isles than at any time in the past three years'.[8] Admiralty Intelligence concluded that 'the main concentration' of U-boats had 'closed in to about 350 miles from Slyne Head in an endeavour to locate our convoys'.[9] Observed convoy traffic off the north-west Irish coast fell in January 1944 due to poor visibility, yet of note was a 'large Troop Transport Convoy of 380,000 tons' of nineteen liners (estimated at 20,000 tons each) with a heavy escort, reported eastbound off Malin Head by coastwatchers on 7 January. As they closed on the west coast of Ireland in search of these convoys, fifteen U-boats were lost in January and twenty in February. Surface escort groups sank seven U-boats in five days and aircraft sank a further five: 'the U/Boats just "couldn't take it"'.[10] By February FAW7 were operating further west around Ireland and 'an unprecedented number' of aircraft engaged U-boats in locations identified from enigma decrypts.[11] FAW7's operations summary for 11 February included references to 'anti-submarine patrols in the Bay area and to westward of Ireland'.[12] Also on 11 February, illustrating the increase in Coastal Command operations off the south coast, Galley Head LOP reported five aircraft passing on low-level anti-submarine patrols over a five hour period, commencing at 1037 when a United States Liberator passed west over the LOP at 2,000 feet.

The week of 18 to 24 February 1944 was a poor one for the squadrons of FAW7. Despite 816 hours of flying, 'no U-boat attacks or enemy aircraft combats took place'.[13] Intelligence indicated that U-boats were in an area 'so far west of Ireland that it was not covered by Coastal Command's routine anti-submarine patrols'. Watching these anti-U-boat operations, Western Sector coastwatchers reported that during February 'coastal patrols and routine activity … broke all records for the past two years in the Inishowen Peninsula, and Donegal Bay Areas'.[14] Activity also rose off the south coast. A special note attached to G2's Daily Report Summary for 18 February recorded that 'during the period 11.18 – 16.55 hours 38 aircraft (36 USA, 2 Unknown) flew East from LOP BALTIMORE to CARNSORE POINT, thence NE being last reported by LOP BALLYCONNIGAR.'[15] Subsequent summaries for the south coast contained a similar special note – 'activity continuing' – though G2 incorrectly attributed it to ferry flights rather than anti-U-boat patrols.[16] South coast coastwatchers

---

8 NARA RG 38, Box 332, FAW7, War Diary, 1–31 Jan. 1944. 9 TNA AIR 20/1243, Historical Outline. 10 Ibid. 11 Blair, *Hunted*, p. 497. 12 NARA RG 38 Box 332, Daily Operations Summary, 11 Feb. 1944. 13 Ibid., memorandum, Commander FAW7 to Commander Air Force, Atlantic Fleet, 14 Mar. 1944. 14 MA G2/X/315 Pt II, Western Sector AMI, Monthly Report, Feb. 1944. 15 MA DRS 1370, 18 Feb. 1944. 16 MA DRS 1373, 22 Feb. 1944.

reported 22, 24 and 25 February as the busiest days of Allied air activity in their region as increased numbers of anti-U-boat air patrols passed.

At 0105 on 27 February Lamb's Head LOP 'sighted [a] big flare of light at the back of the great Skellig's rock' and phoned the neighbouring Bolus Head and Bray Head LOPs.[17] Bolus Head 'heard a flash, and heard three explosions'.[18] Bray Head saw 'flames as those from a burning ship'.[19] The keeper of the lighthouse on the Great Skellig rock heard 'a crash, three explosions and saw a flash of light in the sea'.[20] Seven and a half hours into an anti-submarine patrol Liberator H/110 from squadron VB-110 based at Dunkeswell in Devon and flown by 28-year-old Lieutenant John L. 'Lou' Williams, on his fifth mission, had hit the north side of Skellig, crashing into the sea below.[21] Fire burned on the water for four minutes. There were no survivors.

The following afternoon Lamb's Head received a message 'to report any information we have about the plane that crashed at the Skellig's Rock'.[22] A search by the Skellig lighthouse keeper revealed only a long streak of white paint on the rock. He later recovered a life jacket from the water with the squadron number of the aircraft on it. A search by small craft, including a British tug given permission to search the area, and the Valentia lifeboat, and an aerial search by the RAF, found no trace of the aircraft. The weather was so severe that the lifeboat had to return to port. By 3 March, when Lieutenant Commander James Reedy, the officer commanding squadron VB-110, visited Dublin to discuss the crash with United States diplomats, 'no material trace' of H/110 had been found. Reedy was satisfied that 'no purpose would be served by making a journey to the scene of the accident'.[23] Several pieces of debris and wreckage were later picked up but, writing to Gray on 6 May 1944, Reedy considered that 'the possibility of finding more evidence of the crash is rather remote'.[24]

The background to the crash of H/110 lies in the practice of anti-U-boat patrols of flying below 150 metres (500 feet) to avoid contact with U-boat radar. In January 1944 FAW7 crews had been instructed by intelligence officers to fly at 500 feet at night to carry out attacks.[25] When Coastal Command squadron leaders later met they discussed low-altitude attacks and opinion divided over

17 MA LOP 33, 27 Feb. 1944. The Bolus Head and Bray Head logbooks covering the period have not survived.   18 NAI JUS 90/119/299, Ó Séaghdha to Murphy, 28 Feb. 1944. 19 MA G2/X/315 Pt II, Monthly Report-Sub-depot, M&CWS, Southern Command, Feb. 1944.   20 NARA RG 84 Dublin legation, SSF Box 7 (1944), Gray to Winant, 29 Feb. 1944. 21 The crew were: Lt. Williams (Pilot), Lt. Charles Quigle (Co-pilot), Ensign Lee Bowan (Navigator), Acmm. Elijah Willis (Crew Captain), Amm2c. Gordon Davidson (Second Mechanic), Rm2c. John Huffman (First Radio Officer), Rm3c. Herbert Crow (Radioman), Amm3c. John McLaughlin (Ordnance Officer), Amm3c. Ernest Libby (Gunner), Sea2c. Jack Flener (Waist Gunner) and Sea2c. Morris Olson (Gunner).   22 MA LOP 33, 27 Feb. 1944. 23 NARA RG 84 Dublin Legation, SSF, Box 7 (1944), Gray to Miller, 3 Mar. 1944.   24 Ibid., Reedy to Gray, 6 May 1944.   25 NARA RG 38 Box 332, liaison office FAW7, HQ 19 Group Coastal Command, Feb. 1943.

the matter. One officer liked to be able to see the water; another considered that a fully laden Liberator should not be flown at altitudes under 1,000 feet. The high points of the Great Skellig rock are to the north-east of the island at 185 metres (607 feet) high and to the south-west at 214 metres (705 feet). If Williams' H/110, as seems likely, mistook the radar return from the Great Skellig rock for a submarine and flew towards it to attack at low altitude, the aircraft and crew did not stand a chance.

Airborne at 1656, H/110 commenced its patrol forty kilometres south-east of the Old Head of Kinsale[26] at 1830 and began a zig-zag patrol, flying west for 185 kilometres, south for twenty-one kilometres and back east for 185 kilometres until it reached a position seventy-six kilometres south of its original start point. H/110 was to repeat the pattern until it reached its fuel endurance limit and then return to base. The daily Coastal Command narrative merely recorded that 'no messages [were] received from this aircraft and it failed to return'.[27] Initial reports suggested that H/110 had crashed due to bad weather as a force eight 'north-easterly gale accompanied by sleet and rain was blowing' off Skellig and could certainly have put H/110 off course into the rock.[28] What no document makes clear, but which a comparison of the routing in the Coastal Command daily narrative for 26–27 February with the location of the crash shows, is that H/110 was twenty four miles off course when it crashed, and, since the aircraft hit the back of the Great Skellig rock, Williams was flying in the wrong direction. The most likely explanation remains that fatigued after flying for many hours in bad weather and with positive submarine sightings rare, the crew of H/110 mistook the radar returns from Skellig for a U-boat with fatal results. The scattered remains of Williams' aircraft were located many years later in 10 to 25 metres of water and are 'reputed to lie 100m west of Blue Cove under the cliffs'.[29]

AIDS TO NAVIGATION: (II) THE VALENTIA ISLAND BEACON

The crash of H/110 highlighted the need to develop Allied air navigation aids over the Bay of Biscay, adding another level of complexity to Irish co-operation with the Allies in the run up to D-Day. In 1943 the Dominions Office felt that 'Eire could assist substantially in rescue work without the slightest breach of neutrality and with good hope of doing something to diminish the risk of forced landings in Eire' by agreeing to the installation of additional navigation equipment at the Valentia Island telegraph and radio station.[30] This would improve 'direction finding facilities to the south over the Bay of Biscay', an area

---

26 At 51°28′N, 8°00′W.   **27** TNA AIR 25/491.   **28** MA G2/X/315 Pt II, Mallow Sector AMI, Monthly Report on Coastal Intelligence, Feb. 1944.   **29** www.irishwrecksonline.net/details/PB4Y653b.htm (accessed 8 July 2005).   **30** NAI DFA Secretary's Files A30, aide memoire, Maffey to Walshe, 7 Feb. 1944.

inadequately covered by British RDF stations.[31] By 1944 the necessity for improved RDF was 'even greater ... because of our increased air traffic across the Bay'.[32] Using equipment provided by the Air Ministry, the Valentia station would keep watch on the international distress frequency of 500 kilocycles and 'take the bearing of any aircraft transmitting a distress signal' using the RDF equipment. Maffey added that 'these arrangements would help us more than they would help the enemy, since the latter can obtain excellent cross findings by using his own stations in France'. He considered that as the 500-kilocycle distress frequency was internationally regulated, the additions to Valentia would 'not amount to an un-neutral service'. Pre-war Valentia had been 'a busy Coast Station handling a large volume of ship-shore general traffic'. By 1944 war conditions meant that the station was 'almost exclusively restricted to the listening-in watch for SOS and distress messages'.[33] The proposed additions to the station would merely mean extending the existing provisions and would be 'intended for rescue purposes exclusively'. De Valera agreed with Maffey that there could be 'no objection based on the policy of neutrality'.[34]

There had been previous attempts during the war to reconfigure the equipment at Valentia but political considerations had halted them. Bryan minuted that 'outside authorities were very interested in the care and control of Radio Stations here prior to the Second Front opening and still are.'[35] In April 1944, following discussions between the Department of Posts and Telegraphs and the British Post Office, arrangements were made for the extension of the navigation equipment at Valentia. British engineers supervised the installation of the Adcock Direction Finding apparatus and four-antenna array provided by the British Air Ministry. It was

> a war requirement to facilitate air-sea rescue operations off the south-west of Ireland and in the Bay of Biscay during a very difficult period of the war. The difficulties of arranging for the installation of this equipment in a neutral country were well appreciated here ... [T]here can be no doubt that the Eire authorities were well aware at the time that they were carrying out an 'un-neutral act', but closed their eyes to the real need for the special DF facility.[36]

Land's End and Valentia would fix transmissions from aircraft in distress by RDF. Valentia would then transmit to the aircraft its bearing from Valentia. Land's End would hear Valentia's signal to the aircraft and would plot a fix for

---

31 TNA ADM 1/21542, visit to Malin Head and Valentia stations, 9 May 1949.   32 Ibid., Direction finding W/T facilities at Valencia, undated.   33 MA G2/X/399, report by Guilfoyle, 19 May 1944.   34 NAI DFA Secretary's Files A30, Walshe to Cremins, 6 Mar. 1944.   35 MA G2/X/399, Bryan to Whelan, 17 July 1944.   36 TNA ADM 1/21542, memorandum on visit to Malin Head and Valentia stations, 9 May 1949.

the aircraft's position using a bearing from Land's End. The information so obtained would be passed to Coastal Command by Land's End. The system was ready in time for D-Day on 6 June 1944 to assist with operations over Biscay on the western flank of operation OVERLORD.

'THE APPROACHING CLIMAX OF THE WAR', THE RUN UP TO D-DAY[37]

German High Command expected the invasion of Europe to take place from the spring of 1944. The Allied military build-up for the invasion continued through winter 1943 into 1944. The number of delivery flights sighted by coastwatchers remained high through the early months of the year and convoy traffic off the north coast rose. Writing in retrospect to Oscar Traynor, McKenna summarized that 'owing to the invasion of France there was an increase in air and marine activity' off the Irish coast.[38] Five thousand aircraft crossed the Atlantic in 1944, marking the peak of delivery operations; 280 aircraft made the crossing in January. Athlone Sector reported rising air activity through January; 157 delivery flights, out of which ninety-two were definitely American, though the number of delivery flights was known to be 'far greater than those actually sighted'.[39] Due to 'a change in the system of ferrying', aircraft were now being delivered 'daily in small numbers – usually five or six, occasionally ten or fifteen … instead of large deliveries on an average of once weekly'.[40] It became difficult for coastwatchers to separate delivery flights from routine activity. However there was no doubt about the trend. By February 1944 numbers of Flying Fortresses moving 'in a North/Easterly direction from the West Coast to the Border' had risen for the fourth successive month.[41]

In mid-February a G2 officer at Foynes overheard passengers talking about 'the immense convoys of troops sailing to Europe' to take part in the invasion.[42] From further overheard conversations between American government officials, G2 learned that '200,000 U.S. troops have either landed or are in transit to N. Ireland. The UK is so crowded that there is no further room, and the North is therefore being used.'[43] Coastwatchers reported a further 'large increase in the Convoy tonnage' as '12 Eastbound Convoys … 230 ships of 1,467,000 tons' were sighted off the north coast during February. This was an increase in eastbound tonnage of 'almost half a million; Freight and Merchant Vessels accounted for over 50% while tankers … accounted for the balance'.[44] By March the number

---

37 NAI DFA Secretary's Files, file Memoranda etc., submitted to Taoiseach, 1944, Suggestions for increased precautions on the Border, Walshe to de Valera, 2 Mar. 1944. 38 MA General report on the Army for the year 1/4/44–31/3/45. 39 MA G2/X/315 Pt II, Western Sector, AMI, Monthly Report, Jan. 1944. 40 Ibid., Western Sector AMI, Monthly Report, Feb. 1944. 41 Ibid. 42 NAI DFA Secretary's Files A8(1), Reports from IO Shannon Airport, Foynes: 12th–29th Feb. 1944. 43 Ibid., 9 Jan. 1944. 44 Ibid., 12th–29th Feb. 1944.

of 'Landing Barges' stationed in Derry was rising and they were seen 'moving in and out of the Foyle almost daily'. Further evidence of the impending invasion of Europe was the arrival of a large troopship convoy seen by Horn Head and Glengad Head on 15 March and the arrival the previous day in Lough Foyle of 'a Troopship of 8,000 tons ... with Americans aboard'.[45] It was one of the 238 ships making up the seven eastbound convoys sighted through March, in total an estimated 2,053,000 tons of shipping, their passage accompanied by 'numerous flares and flashing lights' as their escorting naval vessels signalled to each other and to patrolling Coastal Command aircraft.[46]

Coastal Command were concerned that new types of German submarine would be deployed as the invasion of Europe drew near and that 'the enemy planned to bring out these submarines against the invasion fleet'.[47] By 17 March U-boats had retired towards twenty five degrees west and FAW7 returned to their usual Bay of Biscay and Celtic Sea patrols. In most cases they flew far out to sea, well out of sight of the coastwatchers, but Mallow Sector reported that during March Coastal Command aircraft remained present off the Irish coast and flights were 'mainly in a general easterly direction' and during daylight hours.[48] Between 0845 and 1042 on 5 March Galley Head LOP reported ten Liberators flying east at altitudes between 1,000 and 5,000 feet. From 1215 to 1447 a further seven Liberators were sighted, also moving east. These flights were normal anti-submarine patrolling but Mallow Sector incorrectly reported them as delivery flights, though the altitude, separation of flights and timing indicates otherwise. The ten busiest days of the month saw between 15 and 41 aircraft pass daily off the south coast, the average being 21 aircraft. Again, Captain Daly at Mallow Sector AMI misinterpreted the intentions and flight paths of these aircraft. He relied too heavily on information from Athlone Sector, which reported 'an abnormally high' level of air activity during March and April. In March 'for the first time since September 1941 more than 2,000 aircraft were reported'.[49] In April, though delivery flights were 'spasmodic and somewhat irregular ... approximately 350 A/C were ferried from America'.[50] Daly continued to mistake coastal flights in Mallow Sector for delivery flights, though Western Sector reports showed that delivery flights tended to arrive together in early morning waves. For example, on 5 May air 'activity started N.E. over counties MAYO, SLIGO, GALWAY at 07.46 [and was] still continuing' at 0900.[51] By contrast, the single aircraft patrolling off the south coast arrived at approximately forty-minute intervals and were sighted during all daylight hours, morning and afternoon. Captain O'Brien in Limerick Sector AMI, covering the

---

45 MA G2/X/315 Pt II, Western Sector AMI, Monthly Report, Mar. 1944.   46 Ibid.
47 NARA RG 38 Box 332, liaison officer FAW7, 19 Group Coastal Command, Feb. 1944.
48 MA G2/X/315 Pt II, Mallow Sector AMI, Monthly Report on Coastal Intelligence, Mar.
1944.   49 Ibid., Western Sector AMI, Monthly Report, Mar. 1944.   50 Ibid., Apr. 1944.
51 MA DRS 1433, 5 May 1944.

coast from Dingle north to Black Head on the south side of Galway Bay, understood the difference between delivery and patrol flights. He divided traffic into coastal patrols where aircraft flew 'inland occasionally in periods of bad weather or having lost their bearings' and delivery flights which 'ferry aircraft en-route to and from the North'.[52]

In the run up to OVERLORD the Allies flew patrols close to the coast of Kerry, Cork and Waterford on the extended right-flank of the D-Day landing zone. With the invasion imminent, squadron commanders of FAW7 and RAF Coastal Command discussed countering 'the U/Boat concentration west of Ireland' and offensive operations against U-boats in the Bay of Biscay.[53] They planned for 'heavy combined anti-submarine operations by ships and planes' during the invasion, expecting that the 'U/Boats probably will come in close. Hunting groups will probably operate west of the Channel, Land's End and Brest'.[54] As a countermeasure, naval escort groups operating west of Ireland were to relocate off Brest and Land's End and operate in co-ordination with Coastal Command aircraft. U-boats were expected to behave 'recklessly' during the invasion; there would be 'increased rather than decreased opportunities for work' for Coastal Command crews.[55] They anticipated a great battle between combined Allied air and naval assets and U-boats on the right-flank of the invasion zone in an area including the waters off the south coast of Ireland. In April 1944 19 Group Coastal Command, now increased to twenty-five squadrons, commenced 'Operation CORK' in the Irish Sea, Celtic Sea and the western approaches to 'preclude U/Boats breaking through undetected' from the Atlantic Ocean to the landing beaches.[56] The operation saw aircraft patrol from the Waterford, Cork and Kerry coast south through the western approaches to the English Channel, into the mid-Channel area and down the west coast of France. CORK enabled thirty aircraft to patrol 20,000 square miles of water and make complete radar sweeps of the entire area every thirty minutes. Coastwatchers saw and reported these aircraft but G2 failed to understand their true purpose: daily report summaries referred to them as 'apparently [a] portion of "Ferry flight" from North Africa to British bases.'[57]

Numbers of aircraft sighted off the south coast by coastwatchers were down in April, beginning a decline that would spread to all AMI sectors and continue past D-Day to August. Initially this decline appeared due to low visibility through April so 'aircraft flying even a few miles outside territorial waters could not be seen'.[58] The poor visibility hid much of CORK from southern

52 MA G2/X/315 Pt III, Limerick Sector AMI, Coastal Intelligence Report, July 1944. 53 NARA RG 38 Box 332, excerpts from log of FAW7 liaison officer at Headquarters, Coastal Command, 17 Mar. 1944. 54 Ibid. 55 Ibid., excerpts from log of FAW7 liaison officer at Headquarters, Coastal Command, 22 Mar. 1944. 56 Ibid., FAW7 War Diary, 1–30 June 1944. 57 MA DRS 1412, 11 Apr. 1944. 58 MA G2/X/315 Pt III, Mallow Sector AMI, Monthly Report on Coastal Intelligence, Apr. 1944.

coastwatchers but Daly reported to Bryan that positive identifications of aircraft were up through the month and 'the majority of aircraft observed were American'.[59] Through CORK 19 Group shouldered the main burden of Coastal Command anti-submarine operations in the run-up to D-Day. The operation was supposed to represent an enormous airborne cork sealing up the approaches to the English Channel to prevent U-boats from entering the invasion zone; in practice, it had only minor success harassing U-boats.

D-DAY, THE COAST WATCHING SERVICE AND NATIONAL SECURITY

Writing before D-Day but after the 'American Note' incident of 21 February 1944, McKenna argued that

> any large-scale operations in Western Europe would again focus attention on the neutral status of this country, positioned as it is in such close proximity to England and north-west France. Some development such as the delivery of the American note to our government demanding the expulsion of the remaining Axis diplomatic staffs was not therefore altogether unexpected.[60]

London and Washington agreed that '100 per cent security could not be guaranteed so long as the Axis Missions were in Dublin'.[61] The American Note had been sent so as 'the responsibility would be on you [Dublin] in case any leak should be traced to Ireland'.[62] Walshe felt the Allies were using the situation in Dublin to 'prepare a scapegoat for possible heavy casualties in forthcoming operations.'[63] In a softer move, on 28 March Maffey presented de Valera with a memorandum outlining 'all possible means of strengthening existing arrangements with other countries to ensure that information as to military activities does not reach the enemy'.[64] As far as Ireland was concerned this related to the suspension of certain shipping and air services, the curtailment of telephone links and precautions concerning diplomatic communications. Walshe travelled to London on 30 March and suggested to the Dominions Secretary, Lord Cranborne, and to Sir Eric Machtig and Sir John Stephenson at the Dominions Office that Ireland was 'ready ... to accept further suggestions for the period immediately ahead'.[65] All three 'expressed their appreciation of what had already been done'.[66] Walshe

59 Ibid. **60** MA General Report on the Army for the year 1943–44. **61** TNA KV 4/280, telegram from Dominions Office to Maffey, 25 Apr. 1944. **62** NAI DFA Secretary's Files A53, telegram 63, Irish Legation Washington to Dublin, 27 Feb. 1944. **63** NAI DFA Berlin Embassy 18/2, telegram 52, Estero to Cremin, 12 Mar. 1944. **64** NAI DFA Secretary's Files A59, untitled secret memorandum, 28 Mar. 1944. **65** Ibid., Walshe to de Valera, 3 Apr. 1944. **66** Ibid.

went one step further when he met with Ervine 'Spike' Marlin of the OSS and two of Marlin's senior officers. On de Valera's instructions, he explained to the Americans that the Taoiseach was ready to be 'even more helpful in the sphere of Intelligence during the critical months ahead'. He requested talks on security matters and the appointment of 'some suitable person' as British and American security liaison officers in Dublin in the run up to the invasion of Europe. A meeting in London on 4 April between senior figures in the British and American security and intelligence services was told by Colonel Valentine Vivian of MI6 that, due to contact of 'the greatest possible value' with the Irish authorities, 'everything possible was being done to prevent the use of Eire as a base by enemy agents'. The meeting was also told by the Director of MI5, Sir David Petrie, that 'broadly speaking we were convinced that, short of a decision to discard neutrality, nothing more could be done to improve the existing arrangements' for intelligence co-operation between Dublin and London.[67] An MI5 minute considered the Irish proposal 'a very clever one ... they rather had us in a cleft stick. It might be difficult to refuse as the Eire government could then say, if anything went wrong with "Overlord", that they had made us an offer to station officers in Dublin but that we had turned it down.'[68] In Cecil Liddell's view, Dublin alone was 'in a position to take any executive action in the interests of security' in Ireland as D-Day drew near.[69] At a press conference in New York, in reply to a question on the possibility of U-boats making contact with individuals on the Irish coast, Robert Brennan had categorically stated that

> it would be virtually impossible to conduct any espionage service by this means, firstly because of the vigilance of our coast-watching service, secondly because of the wholehearted co-operation that service receives from longshoremen and fishermen, and thirdly because it presupposes an efficient and widespread organisation which we know does not exist.[70]

Using the Coast Watching Service, security around the Irish coast intensified as the final preparations for OVERLORD were put in place. A confidential message to all LOPs on 5 April 1944 showed how close Irish contact with the Allies had become. To ensure that there were no leakages concerning OVERLORD, Dublin took the executive action required. Coastwatchers at all posts were informed that

> A period of particular emergency due to probable opening of the <u>Second Front</u> appears to be imminent. From now onwards personnel of the <u>Marine Service</u> particularly the <u>Coast Watching Service</u> should be

67 TNA KV 4/280, 'OVERLORD' Security-contact with the Eire Authorities on Security Matters, 5 Apr. 1944. 68 Ibid., Minute No. 145, Cecil Liddell to Guy Liddell. 69 Ibid., Note on Conference Held on 21.4.44 at O.S.S., 22 Apr. 1944. 70 NAI DFA Secretary's Files A53, telegram 108, Washington to Dublin, 19 Mar. 1944.

specially on the alert for unusual activities at sea or in the air. Unusual or suspicious activities of boats or attempts made to contact between vessels or aircraft on land should receive special and close attention and must be immediately reported to this sector and to local Garda barracks.[71]

Eastern Sector LOPs were informed by ADC to be 'alert and watchful for any unusual activity in the air and at sea and to report same to Eastern Sector and local Guards without delay'.[72] Dalkey LOP only saw local traffic, trawlers, rowing boats on fishing trips and the odd yacht. Conscious that they should report correctly they reported all these craft and were swiftly told by Eastern Sector that there was no need to report 'rowing boats and pleasure craft ... until further notice but all fishery vessels and trading craft are to be reported'.[73] Traffic between Britain and Ireland was already very much reduced and all Irish shipping with European ports was, by agreement with the Allies, to cease. Walshe briefed officials from Supplies and Industry and Commerce in the last fortnight of March that it had been 'hinted' to Dublin that all British–owned shipping between Britain and Ireland would be withdrawn 'presumably for British second-front operations' and 'as a military security step preparatory to the opening of the promised second front in Europe'.[74] As expected, through April few vessels were seen off the Irish coast, though this also seemed to be due to poor visibility. With traffic so low, the sighting of the 'remarkably high' number of seventy-five tankers off Inishowen was indicative of continuing stockpiling for the imminent Allied invasion of Europe.[75]

The role of coastwatchers in preventing the 'transmission to the enemy' of information from Northern Ireland and Britain was the first topic on a list prepared by MI5 for tripartite security discussions between Irish, British and American officials.[76] Anglo-American concerns included 'the control and security of trawlers, motor boats, and other small craft', a matter already covered by the instructions issued to the coastwatchers on 5 April and which would be reinforced in early May.[77] Bryan and Assistant Garda Commissioner Patrick Carroll met with Cecil Liddell of MI5 and Spike Marlin and Hugh Will of OSS on 2, 3 and 4 May in Dublin to agree measures to ensure that no leakage occurred from Ireland of information that could compromise OVERLORD. While the Allies maintained that there could be no 'satisfactory guarantee of security'[78] so long as the Axis missions remained open in Dublin, Cecil Liddell felt that 'it was obvious that the Irish representatives were anxious to do what they could. In most cases it was found possible to agree that what was required was an

71 MA LOP 38, 5 Apr. 1944. 72 MA LOP 7, 5 Apr. 1944. 73 Ibid., 10 May 1944.
74 NAI DFA Secretary's Files P162, Conference on shipping, 21 Mar. 1944. 75 MA
G2/X/315 Pt II, Western Sector AMI, Monthly Report, Apr. 1944. 76 TNA KV 4/280,
Agenda for Security Discussions, 24 Apr. 1944. 77 Ibid. 78 Ibid., Cecil Liddell to Costar,
19 May 1944.

intensification of the measures already in force'.[79] Coastwatchers would continue to prevent 'illicit landings or communications with the enemy from the coast or by coastal craft'.[80] On 3 May a confidential message to all LOPs indicated that the Irish authorities were under increased pressure from the Allies to ensure that no information on the opening of the second front escaped through Irish channels:

> From this day on all LOPs will keep a record of the movement of all Irish boats, they will record the time they go out, where they go to and when they are returning. This information will be passed on to Limerick 710 every morning at 09.00. In the event of anything really serious the LOPs will communicate with Limerick 710 immediately. The LOP will report unknown trawlers or cargo boats as usual, they will report every morning whether they have a report or not.[81]

Western Sector reported 'spasmodic' air activity through May interspersed with 'periods of continuous activity' as 'the arrival and departure of convoys off our Northern Shores' was 'followed by periods of minimum patrols'.[82] A few large eastbound convoys 'brought very large numbers of aircraft out on Atlantic patrols – mainly from Derry bases'. Sixteen heavily escorted eastbound convoys were seen during May, the combined tonnage of 4,777,000 tons was 'remarkably high', as was the freighter tonnage of 3,493,000 tons – 'practically three times greater than any previous month'. South coast LOPs reported increased naval activity through May. As groups of destroyers passed along the Cork coast outside territorial waters, coastwatchers saw white flares and heard gunfire and explosions. Typical was the simultaneous report by Helvick Head LOP and Fort Carlisle and Fort Templebreedy in Cork harbour at 0013 on 1 June of 'four loud explosions' ten to fifteen miles out to sea.[83] In the air, activity off the south and south-west coast was down during May. Flights had been 'fairly evenly distributed' through the month, and though the weather had been 'fine' for almost the entire month, visibility off the south-west coast had been 'moderate occasionally dropping to poor'. This certainly reduced the number of aircraft sighted. Yet Captain Daly felt that something was in the offing, concluding that the 'reduction in aerial activity has nothing to do with weather conditions'.[84]

79 Ibid., Notes of meeting of American, British and Eire Security Officers, Held in Dublin on 2nd, 3rd, 4th May 1944.   80 Ibid., Points for communication with Colonel Archer. 81 MA LOP 38, 3 May 1944.   82 MA G2/X/315 Pt II, Western Sector AMI, Monthly Report, May 1944.   83 Ibid., Mallow Sector AMI, Monthly Report on Coastal Intelligence, May 1944.   84 Ibid.

IRELAND AND WEATHER FORECASTING FOR
THE D-DAY LANDINGS

On the evening of 2 June 1944 the weather for the Allied invasion of Europe 'looked reasonable'.[85] However, Supreme Allied Commander General Dwight Eisenhower's weather experts 'were worried about a depression over Iceland' that was moving south towards Ireland putting the launch of the operation in doubt.[86] The commanding officers agreed that Operation NEPTUNE, the amphibious phase of Operation OVERLORD, would commence on the early morning of 5 June. Nevertheless, they agreed to consult their meteorological advisers on 3 June in case conditions changed. Through 3 June Allied meteorologists grew concerned about falling pressure off the west coast of Ireland as the depression over Iceland moved south-east, pushing back a high-pressure area coming up from the Azores. A 'long period of settled conditions was breaking up and the outlook for D-Day and the succeeding days was now most unpromising'.[87] Forecasters expected that the cold front would bring high winds and clouds over the Normandy beaches on 5 June, conditions far from suitable for amphibious operations requiring low winds and high visibility. When the commanders met at 2130 on 3 June there was a 'grave gloom over the place'.[88] They agreed that the invasion fleet would make ready to sail, realizing that 'a final decision regarding postponement must be taken early on the 4th June'.[89] At 0430 on 4 June 'weather reports were discouraging … [T]he landing was possible but would be difficult … [W]eighing all the factors, Eisenhower decided to postpone D-Day for 24 hours.'[90]

Group Captain J.M. Stagg, Chief Meteorological Officer to SHAEF, knew that 'if the sea and the beaches are open to the direction from … swell produced by high winds up to hundreds of miles away … then the force and direction of winds hundreds of miles away from the operational area has to be taken into account'.[91] The weather report from one of Europe's most westerly points, Blacksod lighthouse at the end of the Belmullet Peninsula in north Mayo, now became crucial as Eisenhower's forecasters sought to track and forecast the duration of an approaching fair spell behind the low pressure area to see if it allowed a window within which to launch OVERLORD. Coded weather telegrams of conditions at the lighthouse at 1300 hours on 4 June sent by Blacksod lighthouse keeper Ted Sweeney to Dublin showed conditions on the west coast of Ireland to be far from favourable for the invasion as the front from Iceland passed in from the Atlantic Ocean towards France.[92] Blacksod lighthouse was

85 Viscount Montgomery of Alamein, *The memoirs of Field-Marshal Montgomery of Alamein* (Barnsley, 2005 edition), p. 248.   86 Ibid.   87 TNA AIR 37/1124A, 'Operation OVERLORD'. The decision to launch the operation.   88 Ibid., Overlord Weather.   89 Montgomery, *Memoirs*, p. 248.   90 Ibid.   91 TNA AIR 37/1124A, Extracts from Group Captain Stagg's report on the meteorological implications in the selection of the day for the Allied invasion of France, 6th June, 1944.   92 *Irish Times*, 6 June 1994, p. 7.

buffeted by continuous rain and a force four 17-miles-per-hour south-west wind which at times gusted to a 42-miles-per-hour force eight gale. The pressure was a far from reassuring 999 millibars. Sweeney's weather reports were sent from Dublin to London with onward transmission to SHAEF. Allied forecasters anticipated that the low-pressure area passing over western Ireland would arrive over the British Channel coast on 5 June. If the invasion went ahead on 5 June, the low-pressure area would bring strong south-westerly winds and heavy cloud cover as Eisenhower's forces embarked for occupied Europe. The army needed dry ground and the navy needed winds of force three (twelve miles-per-hour) or less for OVERLORD to proceed. The tide, phase of the moon and the time of sunrise were in a favourable combination for the invasion on 5, 6 and 7 June when there would be clear skies, good moonlight, light winds and low tide at dawn. Eisenhower again postponed OVERLORD for twenty-four hours.

By the evening of 4 June there had 'been some rapid and unexpected developments in the situation over the Atlantic'.[93] The front had swept further south than expected and would pass down the English Channel overnight. The low-pressure area was now expected to be short-lived and with the area of high pressure coming in behind it came 'the probability of a good fair period with reduced winds and little cloud from early hours Monday morning to Tuesday dawn'.[94] Meteorologists advised the invasion commanders at 2130 on 4 June that that evening there was the 'prospect of a fair spell setting in after the passage of the cold front'.[95] They advised the invasion commanders to use 'the good interval starting overnight'.[96] The 'vital decision' was taken, and OVERLORD was on again.[97] As Sunday gave way to Monday strong winds, rain and low cloud passed over the SHAEF headquarters at Portsmouth. A British weather ship anchored south of Iceland reported that pressure was rising in the north Atlantic as the front 'suddenly cut down south and swept through Ireland'.[98] At 0200 on 5 June 'the Irish reports were not considered to be disconcerting ... [T]he picture for 6th June looked rather promising considering the unsettled nature of the weather.'[99] The clearance following the front reached the west coast of Ireland by the early morning on 5 June and was over Portsmouth by 0400, but then there was another change as wind speed rose and low cloud passed over Portsmouth. 'What the mischief was going wrong', Stagg privately committed to his diary.[100]

Extracts from another private log kept by US army meteorologists Colonel Holzman and Colonel Krick show just how central the reports from Blacksod had now become to Allied weather planning. During their morning briefing on 5 June

---

93 TNA AIR 37/1124A, Overlord Weather.   **94** Ibid.   **95** Ibid.   **96** Ibid.   **97** Ibid., Air Marshal to Wilmot, 12 Aug. 1948.   **98** Ibid.   **99** Ibid. Extract from a report by Allied Naval C-IN-C, AEF on 'Operation NEPTUNE'.   **100** Ibid., Overlord Weather.

Captain Smith entered the conference room with the last report from Blacksod. It had indicated a cold front passing through there near 1200 hours. This front had been expected by Colonels Krick and Holzman but had been given up because of the lack of substantiating evidence over the Atlantic. With the verification of the report that the front was passing through Ireland, complete confidence was then restored in the subsequent development of the basic process anticipated by Widewing for the past week.[101]

Reports from Blacksod for 1300 GMT on 5 June showed the high-pressure area following the cold front passing over Ireland and heading towards the Normandy coast, allowing Allied planners to verify their weather projections for the coming days. The Permanent Secretary at the Foreign Office, Sir Alexander Cadogan, seemed uncertain: in London it was 'grey, overcast and w. wind. But pundits say it is going to be beautiful, so the expedition is on.'[102] By the afternoon of 5 June the improvement in the weather was apparent at Erris Head LOP. At 1210, when a trawler passed from the north-west, visibility was moderate and the rain had cleared. By 1600 visibility was good, a Flying Fortress was sighted passing north-east over the post at 5,000 feet. Allied notes for 1800 on 5 June show that

> Pressure in IRELAND was still showing slight rises only and the weakness of the ridge, with isobars on its eastern side cyclonically curved, was still apparent. Cloudy or overcast conditions with the cloud base at 1,000 ft to 2,000 ft persisted over the Channel area, and as far to the west and north-west as Valentia and Blacksod. The wind was still west to west-north-west force 4–5 and visibility 10–15 miles.[103]

New charts were prepared. The meteorologists disagreed on the speed the front would travel across Ireland and Britain to France. At Blacksod the wind was west to south-westerly at a more moderate force five, approximately 20 miles-per-hour, with clear spells and pressure 1014 millibars and rising.[104] By the early evening of 5 June weather reports showed that, though there was low cloud and westerly winds over the channel, this would be followed by the clear skies and more moderate south westerly winds then passing over Ireland. These calmer conditions would reach the channel and the landing beaches by the early morning of 6 June as the invasion fleet arrived off the French coast, giving a

101 Ibid., Extracts from the private log kept by Colonel Holzman and Colonel Krick US Army. Widewing was the code-name given to the United Kingdom HQ of USAAF weather service.   102 David Dilks (ed.), *The diaries of Sir Alexander Cadogan 1938–1945* (London, 1971), p. 634. Cadogan's italics.   103 TNA AIR 37/1124A, Overlord Weather, Extract from a report by Allied Naval C-IN-C, AEF on 'Operation NEPTUNE'.   104 See www.met.ie/aboutus/weatherobservingstations/claremorris_history.asp (accessed 8 May 2004).

favourable weather window for the landings. When asked on the late evening of 5 June by Eisenhower to prophesy on the weather outlook Stagg replied 'I hold my forecast, Sir, breaks after dark tonight'. Eisenhower clapped Stagg on the shoulder, replying '"Good, Stagg, hold to it," and went out smiling'.[105]

At 0100 on 6 June 'the Irish stations still showed no sign of rising pressure and the ridge remained well to the Westward' and 'the cloud was now more broken than previously'.[106] On the early morning of 6 June, as the Allied landing craft were nearing the French coast, Erris Head reported the beginning of a change in the weather. At 0500 Volunteers Lavelle and Moloney sighted a Flying Fortress half a mile east of their post heading north-east at 7,000 feet. Three more delivery flights were spotted by 0800, reported at distances up to four miles and at altitudes of up to 7,000 feet. On each occasion visibility was good, despite a cloudy sky, showers and a heavy swell on the sea in a strong west to north-west wind. Allied reports stated that 'the pressure rises at Valentia and Blacksod were still very slight'.[107] The weather window for the invasion was closing over western Ireland but NEPTUNE and OVERLORD were underway in the fair spell forecast. Photographs show low cloud over the invasion beaches on 6 June as the landings began but it had cleared by early afternoon as forecast. A captured German meteorological officer later told Stagg that he and his colleagues had 'failed to catch the significance of a "weather front" which passed through the Channel area on the 5th June with a relatively good interlude behind it'.[108] Thanks to the Blacksod report, Stagg and his colleagues did not make the same mistake as the Germans who were 'completely taken by surprise when the Allied Invasion started ... both because of their weather forecast and because the Allied Forces went in on low tide with all the under water obstacles exposed'.[109]

A 1944 memorandum in the archives of the Department of Foreign Affairs explained that the supply of meteorological data to Britain was a long-term component of British-Irish wartime co-operation:

> Since the outbreak of the war, the Irish Meteorological Service has continued to supply to the British Meteorological Service weather reports and meteorological data generally. These are not being supplied to any other country. They are of course extremely important as a basis for weather forecasts.[110]

These facts remained hidden to the 1980s and the significance of Ted Sweeney's reports remained unknown for almost forty years. Neutral Ireland had significantly reduced the odds for Eisenhower's D-Day meteorologists and by

105 TNA AIR 37/1124A, Overlord Weather. 106 Ibid. 107 Ibid. 108 Ibid., Stagg to Chief, Ops Section, G-3 Division, Forward SHAEF, 17 Aug. 1944. 109 Ibid., Extract from a report by Allied Naval C-IN-C, AEF on 'Operation NEPTUNE'. 110 NAI DFA Secretary's Files, Files, Memoranda etc., submitted to Taoiseach, 1944, Co-operation with British

extension for the entire invasion force depending on their forecasts. Meteorologists concluded that June 1944 was 'the worst June of the century'.[111] Conditions had been 'so unsettled and developments so abnormal that it was possible only on rare occasions to predict the weather with detailed accuracy for more than 24 hours ahead'.[112] The Germans had assumed that weather conditions were likely to be such that no invasion would be possible on 5 or 6 June and 'the tactical surprise achieved in the Allied landings was to a large extent due to the decision to launch the assault on the forecast of a brief fair interval in a very unsettled period'.[113] When in 2004 a plaque was unveiled at Blacksod lighthouse commemorating the significance of the reports from the station in the success of the D-Day landings, the main Irish television news report on the unveiling failed to mention that Ireland had remained neutral in the Second World War.

THE CALM AFTER D-DAY

Gray had suggested to Hull that 'when the invasion starts' there would be 'numerous cases of forced landings on Eire soil' by American aircraft which had 'lost their bearings in returning from operational flights over the continent'.[114] He wondered how the Irish would react when crews said they were on non-operational flights though their aircraft carried 'unmistakable evidence of combat damage and wounded or dead personnel'. Dublin might intern the survivors. The Defence Forces had anticipated Gray's thoughts, McKenna writing to MacMahon six months before D-Day that with 'the opening of large scale operations by the Allied powers expected to occur in the near future' there would 'almost certainly' be 'an increase in the number of incidents due to belligerent aircraft on or near our territory'.[115] On 6 June, as OVERLORD began, McKenna issued instructions for the rescue of 'naval craft which may land in combat damaged condition on the coasts of Eire'.[116] The orders applied specifically to the southern and south-eastern coasts and referred to damaged belligerent craft inside and outside territorial waters. They identified no specific belligerent but the implication was that they applied to the Allied invasion force. Survivors from craft which had gone adrift in the landings and ended up 'shipwrecked' on Irish territory were to be told only that they were on neutral territory and were 'being taken under escort to a military post pending instructions from higher authority'. Hathaway and Gray interpreted this as 'a desire if not an intention on the part of the Eire Government not to intern but to facilitate a secret release' of such soldiers.

Government, undated.   111 TNA AIR 37/1124A, Extract from a report by Allied Naval C-IN-C, AEF on 'Operation NEPTUNE'.   112 Ibid.   113 Ibid.   114 NARA RG 84 Dublin Legation, SSF, Box 7 (1944), Gray to Hull, 2 June 1944.   115 MA EDP 20/5, McKenna to MacMahon, Jan. 1944.   116 NARA RG 84 Dublin Legation, SSF, Box 7 (1944), Gray to

Using McKenna's instructions, the Coast Watching Service was briefed to expect the arrival of damaged air and naval craft on Irish shores during the Allied invasion of Europe. Coastwatchers were to report the condition of downed aircraft or shipwrecked vessels and any attempt at landing made by men onboard. The NCO at Galley Head LOP was instructed by his district officer, Lieutenant Barrett, that the LOP was to 'report all sea craft to Message Centre immediately, owing to possibility of shipwrecked crews'.[117] Message Centres would then inform the Gardaí, the Coast Life Saving Service, the Lifeboat Service and the Command Intelligence Officer. LOPs were to remain in contact with their Message Centre, informing them of the condition of shipwrecked vessels and the progress of rescue operations. Though the circumstances forecast never materialized, the plans are a further example of Irish co-operation with the Allies during the Second World War.

In the week after D-Day forty U-boats were mustered to attack the Allied landing force and shipping off the coast of Devon and Cornwall. The response of these U-boats to the invasion was 'prompt, energetic but remarkably confused'.[118] FAW7 counterattacked with 'an intensive operational effort' against 'the threat of enemy submarines to the troop and supply convoys to the Allied beachheads'.[119] In response to the invasion, Germany also launched its Vergeltungswaffen (retaliation weapons). Known to the Allies since early 1943, the V-weapons first became known to Ireland later in that year. William Warnock, the Irish Chargé d'Affaires in Berlin, reported rumours of a secret weapon 'which is said to be so phenomenal that it will change the whole course of the war ... [I]t has range of 300 kilometres ... Southern England will be laid waste in short time.'[120] The first V-1 flying bombs landed on London on 13 June 1944. Four days later all LOPs received information about 'a new type of aircraft' that had 'No pilot. Direct course. A drone like an aircraft which is out of order. Smaller than a Spitfire and [the] same appearance. At night shows a light appears like [a] yellow globe.'[121] This was the V-1's petrol burning pulsejet which gave the rocket a cruise speed of 400 miles an hour. To convince unwary coastwatchers that they were dealing with weapons of some speed, Limerick Sector added that the V-1 could be easily identified as it 'Goes like an Express Train'.[122] This was all useful information but it was extremely unlikely that a V-1 rocket would have the range to reach any area guarded by the coastwatchers.

Not surprisingly, V-1's did not materialize off Ireland. The skies and waters around Ireland were relatively quiet in the months immediately after D-Day. Off the south-west coast the expected increase in 'aerial activity after the invasion of Europe has not been materialized ... [I]nstead there has been a steady decline in

Hull, 12 June 1944.   **117** MA LOP 27, 7 June 1944.   **118** Syrett, *Signals intelligence*, p. 393, U-boat Situation. Week ending 12/6/44.   **119** NARA RG 38, FAW7, War Diary, 1–31 Dec. 1944.   **120** NAI DFA Secretary's Files P12/3, Hibernia to Estero, 8 Oct. 1943.   **121** MA LOP 38, 17 June 1944.   **122** Ibid.

the number of flights reported.'[123] Despite air activity every day, daily totals rarely went over fifteen flights in June. With overflights also down in July Captain Daly in Mallow Sector, continuing to misinterpret anti-submarine patrols as delivery flights, deduced that 'a sufficiency of aircraft, at least to carry out the initial landings, had already been delivered'. In Western Sector, with reduced activity from the Derry air bases, flights declined off Inishowen. They increased in the 'Donegal Bay and Mayo coastal Areas' with the passage of 'over 400 delivery flights' during June and in July of over 500 deliveries of 'heavy Four-Engined Bombers' over Western Command.[124] Contrary to Daly's assertions, enough aircraft had not been delivered to the Allied expeditionary force in Europe. Along the east coast increasing numbers of aircraft which appeared to have experienced navigational difficulties were cited in daily report summaries, these aircraft were 'presumed to be Allied and were probably returning to British bases from missions on the Western Front.'[125]

Off the north coast the impact of OVERLORD was evident in a great reduction in naval activity. 'Since the beginning of June only skeleton Naval forces' were based in Lough Foyle and convoy tonnage off the north coast during June, 'especially Eastbound, was scarcely 50% of the May figures – which were of course abnormally high'.[126] The 'advance in France' was expected to be 'very rapid in the near future', and with it the Northern Ireland bases would 'be of little use for any purpose' as shipping was expected to sail direct to England and France.[127] Off the south coast, naval activity through June and July remained low: a handful of convoys, hospital ships and regular patrols of groups of destroyers. Heavy explosions, thought to be depth charges, were heard as the destroyers passed and the usual flashes and flares were reported well out to sea. The overall picture was of an unexpected calm in Irish seas and skies after D-Day.

U-BOATS RETURN TO IRISH WATERS, AUGUST–DECEMBER 1944

Through early August military activity off the Irish coast continued to fall, reinforcing the 'steady decline since the invasion of France'.[128] Coastwatchers in Mallow Sector reported only eighty-nine sightings of aircraft through August and Limerick Sector reported 'a decrease in the amount of aircraft on coastal patrol' with only a handful of delivery flights 'at very high altitudes and at great speeds'.[129] In Athlone Sector delivery flights, estimated at 300 aircraft in August, were down by 50 per cent on July. At sea, other than the usual destroyer patrols,

123 MA G2/X/315 Pt III, Mallow Sector AMI, Monthly Report on Coastal Intelligence, June 1944.   124 Ibid., Western Sector AMI, Monthly Report, June 1944.   125 MA DRS 1501, 27 July 1944.   126 MA G2/X/315 Pt III, Western Sector AMI, Monthly Report, June 1944.   127 NAI DFA Secretary's Files P43/1, Ua Ceallaigh to Murphy, 24 June 1944. 128 MA G2/X/315 Pt III, Western Sector AMI, Monthly Report, Aug. 1944.   129 Ibid., Limerick Sector AMI, Coastal Intelligence Report, Aug. 1944.

all Mallow could report as out of the ordinary was a large convoy of thirty ships, '1 aircraft carrier, 5 destroyers and the remainder transports and oil tankers', sighted sailing east outside territorial waters off the south coast on 21 August.[130] This convoy caught Bryan's attention. Naval activity 'since D-Day [had] been on a greatly reduced scale along our Northern Shores' and this single large convoy suggested the beginning of a change in Allied tactics: to instead route convoys off the south coast. The reason behind this change was that U-boat activity off the south coast of Ireland had 'ceased, for all practical purposes' with the capture of the U-boat bases along the French Atlantic coast.[131] With these waters rid of German submarines, the trend identified in August developed and by September 1944 'practically all the transatlantic shipping' was being 'routed south of Ireland'.[132]

Allied signals intelligence reported in early September that Germany had responded to the change in Allied convoy routes by ordering U-boats into waters south of Cork. Coastal Command countered by strengthening anti-submarine patrols in the area as 'the most profitable place to look for the U-boat is close to the U-boat's target'.[133] Captain Daly, knowing nothing of Coastal Command's plans, reported 'an abnormal increase' in flights off the south coast in September.[134] To G2, this 'heavy aerial activity off the South Coast [was] no doubt connected with naval activity in the same area.'[135] By the middle of the month '70% of aircraft activity outside territorial waters on [the] South coast [was] due to [the] presence of naval craft.'[136] These flights did not extend west into Limerick Sector as Daly's colleague in Limerick, Captain O'Brien, saw little change in flight numbers through September, with only 'a steady coastal patrol being executed'.[137] Though Daly also knew nothing of the renewed submarine threat, he did know from coastwatchers' reports that the increase in air activity was 'due to the presence of convoys and naval craft reported almost every day off the south coast' and he deduced that these aircraft were protecting the convoys.[138] Some of these convoys were the largest seen off the south coast; Baltimore and Old Head LOPs reporting 'a large convoy, of between 80 and 90 ships, comprising of destroyers, cargo boats and escorts' moving east on 15 September.[139] By mid-September the Allies discounted the earlier intelligence reports of U-boat activity off Cork as 'so much shipping of all classes has recently passed through this area without stimulating any reaction'.[140] Coastal

130 Ibid., Mallow Sector AMI, Monthly Report on Coastal Intelligence, Aug. 1944. 131 TNA AIR 2/586, The employment of A/U Squadrons at present in 19 Group, 26 Sept. 1944.   132 Ibid.   133 Ibid., Alternative Plan for Convoy Escort and U/Boat Hunt in North Western Approaches, Sept. 1944.   134 MA G2/X/315 Pt III, Mallow Sector AMI, Monthly Report on Coastal Intelligence, Sept. 1944.   135 MA DRS 1536, 8 Sept. 1944.   136 MA DRS 1544, 18 Sept. 1944.   137 MA G2/X/315 Pt III, Limerick Sector AMI, Coastal Intelligence Report, Sept. 1944.   138 Ibid., Mallow Sector AMI, Monthly Report on Coastal Intelligence, Sept. 1944.   139 Ibid.   140 Syrett, *Signals intelligence*, p. 454, U-boat Situation. Week ending 18/9/44.

Command accordingly redeployed off north-west Ireland and Scotland. Mallow Sector identified this development, reporting that during October air traffic off the south coast had declined. Sightings of convoys off the south coast continued to rise through October and November as merchant shipping, well protected by destroyers, passed in numbers not seen since 1940.

With convoys switched to southern routes, coastwatchers on Inishowen reported 'abnormally low' traffic through September, Birthistle deducing that 'supply convoys for the War Theatre [were] following the Southern route and moving direct to European ports'.[141] Chief Superintendent O'Coileáin in Letterkenny reported that his sources in Derry told him that 'the United States Naval Base at Derry is to be decommissioned … [T]he base is regarded as having fulfilled its mission in that it took a notable part in winning the "Battle of the Atlantic" against the U-Boats.'[142] Despite this development, there was in August and September 1944 still a very real U-boat threat off Donegal. Coastwatchers on Inishowen reported 'a considerable amount of patrolling and manoeuvring' as Coastal Command and naval Escort Groups hunted suspected submarines.[143] Senior Coastal Command officers proposed twenty-four hour 'Air Swept Channel Patrols' or 'air flooding' in the north-western approaches, using the two Sunderland squadrons from Castle Archdale by day and the two squadrons of Leigh light equipped Wellingtons based at Limavady by night, to counter U-boats equipped with the newly introduced schnorkel breathing system.[144]

The Allies anticipated a considerable threat from the schnorkel as it allowed submarines to stay submerged and ventilate while running their diesel engines to recharge their batteries. Rumours of the new system filtered through to the Department of External Affairs via Cremin in Berlin who reported on 'a new type of submarine', one of a number of weapons being developed which could 'make the tide turn' in Germany's favour.[145] If U-boats could stay submerged for greater periods they could more easily evade detection. The effectiveness of schnorkel-equipped U-boats was seen on the afternoon of 30 August when Malin Head 'observed [a] portion of an Eastbound Convoy covered with smoke' fifteen miles to the north.[146] The convoy of twenty-eight vessels and ten escorts was shrouded in what coastwatchers thought was 'apparently a smokescreen'.[147] When the smoke cleared 'two fiercely burning wrecks' were sighted and frigates were 'patrolling in the vicinity'.[148] Gardaí were alerted, the Malin lifeboat was despatched and Malin Head LOP received calls from local military and neighbouring LOPs about the burning wrecks, culminating in a call from

141 MA G2/X/315 Pt III, Western Sector AMI, Monthly Report, Oct. 1944.   142 NAI DFA Secretary's Files P43/1, O Coileáin to Murphy, 12 Aug. 1944.   143 MA G2/X/315 Pt III, Western Sector AMI, Monthly Report, Aug. 1944.   144 TNA AIR 2/586, Air Swept Channel Patrols, 7 Sept. 1944.   145 NAI DFA Secretary's Files P12/3, Iverna to Estero, 29 Aug. 1944.   146 TNA AIR 2/586, Air Swept Channel Patrols, 7 Sept. 1944.   147 MA LOP 80, 30 Aug. 1944.   148 MA G2/X/315 Pt III, Western Sector AMI, Monthly Report, Aug.

Western Command headquarters in Athlone 'to give a report on everything that was done at LOP from time smoke was first seen until fires extinguished'.[149] Coastwatchers along Inishowen reported that 'no explosions were heard – only a vivid flash and immediate flames'. 'For two subsequent days' LOPs from Horn Head to Glengad Head 'observed continuous patrolling all along the coast'.[150] Schnorkel-equipped U-482 had attacked Liverpool-bound tanker convoy CU36 and torpedoed the American turbine tanker *Jacksonville* which had exploded and broken in two. The U-boat then attacked the nearby ONS251 and HX205 convoys Naval Intelligence subsequently intercepted reports from U-482 claiming 'to have sunk 2 large tankers, a freighter and an escort'.[151] The Donegal coast was a perfect hunting ground for U-boats. A situation report from Kapitänleutnant Hans-Joachim von Morstein of U-483 mentioned that the nearby 'area in front of Lough Swilly' was 'especially good for "schnorkelling"' ('Besonders gute Schnorchelemöglichkeiten') day and night, concluding that 'location [was] hardly possible, absolutely no interference.'[152] Von Morstein also pointed to an area between Tory Island and Rinrawros on the Donegal coast as suitable for schnorkelling 'if necessary after being spotted'.

Despite the apparent Allied victory in the Atlantic in 1943, the attacks by U-482 off Ireland showed that there was still 'plenty of fight left in the U-boats'.[153] A 'surprise appearance' courtesy of the schnorkel and the 'courageous exploitation of opportunities' could prove costly to Allied shipping.[154] Signals intelligence suggested that two U-boats were active between Malin Head and Barra Head in Scotland. Using 'air flooding', with seven aircraft in the air twenty-four hours a day, Coastal Command saturated the area to flush them out. The gap of one hour between each patrolling aircraft made 'the area so hot that submarines will be forced to withdraw to seaward and operate away from the focal point of our convoy routes'.[155] The introduction of 'air flooding' did not go unnoticed by coastwatchers who through September reported 'very heavy activity off the Northern shores of Donegal' due to 'intensified Atlantic patrols from the Derry Bases' as Coastal Command attempted to rid the north-western approaches of schnorkel-equipped U-boats.[156]

Naval operations from Lough Foyle, 'on a very limited scale' since D-Day, increased as U-boats returned to the seas off the north coast. Patrols by frigates and corvettes took place 'off the Northern shores of Donegal on numerous occasions' during September and claimed early successes in countering U-boats, with U-743 and U-484 sunk on 9 September. British naval intelligence estimated

1944. 149 MA LOP 80, 31 Aug. 1944. 150 MA G2/X/315 Pt III, Western Sector AMI, Monthly Report, Aug. 1944. 151 Syrett, *Signals intelligence*, p. 450, U-boat Situation. Week ending 11/9/44. 152 MA U-260 papers, File 7, translation of 'Situation Report Nr. 13 for Type VIIc', original on File 2 'Lagemeldung Nr 13 für Typ VIIc' (no date). 153 Syrett, *Signals intelligence*, p. 452, U-boat Trend. Period 4/9/44–13/9/44. 154 Ibid. 155 TNA AIR 2/586, Anti-Submarine operations – North Channel Area, 17 Sept. 1944. 156 MA G2/X/315 Pt III, Western Sector AMI, Monthly Report, Sept. 1944.

that by mid-September six U-boats were operating north of Ireland. Evidence appeared mid-afternoon on 20 September when Liberator 38825 of 110 Squadron FAW7 picked up a 'disappearing radar contact' thirty miles north west of Rossan Point, Donegal.[157] After sighting an oil slick, 'a sono-buoy pattern was laid from which doubtful contacts were obtained'.[158] Surface vessels went to the scene and the air patrol continued to the 'prudent limit of endurance'. After almost nine hours patrolling, no submarine was located. What the airmen and sailors did not know, but Admiralty Intelligence did, was that at least one U-boat close to the north coast had been 'impressed by the strength of the defences and having encountered strong air patrols and A/S groups considered that inshore operations in the North Ireland area were very difficult'.[159] A second submarine failed to enter the area. Despite this report, as September ended three U-boats remained active off north-west Ireland and air patrols accompanied 'by frigate flotillas ... off our Northern shores' operated against these vessels well into October.[160] Despite this increase in patrolling, U-boats continued to lurk off Donegal with success. A 'bright glow, apparently a ship on fire' fifteen miles to the north of Malin Head at 0345 on 14 October which burned for over two hours revealed the 'hulk of a ship' by daylight, the vessel soon sinking.[161] Frigates countered, patrolling the area in search of the attacking U-boat.

On 23 October Dönitz broadcast a special message to his U-boat crews that the Western Front off the British and Irish coasts was the decisive front as Britain remained vulnerable to maritime blockade. In his October report to Bryan, submitted after Dönitz's broadcast, Birthistle echoed these views: 'the war zone is daily moving slowly Eastwards, nevertheless the Atlantic still remains an important theatre where active operations are yet essential'.[162] Coastal Command expected Dönitz's message to herald an immediate renewal of the submarine campaign in the approaches to the Channel. The damaging of a U-boat off south-west Ireland on 25 October confirmed these suspicions; signals intelligence maintained that 'this U-boat would not have been sent out alone'.[163] They concluded that 'the U-boat arm is rallying'.[164] The situation 'remained quiet but [was] gradually becoming more difficult'.[165] Submarines had become elusive through use of the schnorkel and there was 'no doubt any longer that the anticipated effect on the war against U-boats of this device has been realized in

157 NARA RG 38, FAW7, War Diary, 1–30 Sept. 1944.   158 The sono-buoy was an electronic device which listened for the noise from the propellers of a submerged U-boat. A pattern of five sono-buoys was dropped near a suspected U-boat and by comparing signals from the units estimates of position and course of the U-boat could be made.   159 Syrett, *Signals intelligence*, p. 461, U-boat Trend. Period 18/9/44–27/9/44.   160 MA G2/X/315 Pt III, Western Sector AMI, Monthly Report, Oct. 1944.   161 MA LOP 80, 14 Oct. 1944. 162 MA G2/X/315 Pt III, Western Sector AMI, Monthly Report, Oct. 1944.   163 Syrett, *Signals intelligence*, p. 480, U-boat Trend. Period 23/10/44–1/11/44.   164 Ibid., p. 471, U-boat Situation. Week ending 23/10/44.   165 Ibid., p. 485, U-boat Trend. Period 30/10/44–6/11/44.

at least the degree which was feared'.[166] With U-boats beginning to blockade Britain from within her coastal waters Dönitz's fleet, augmented by new technology, remained a threat to the end of the war. As a response to Dönitz's message FAW7 flew increased sorties through all Irish coastal waters but by November they had returned to concentrate on the western approaches as the new U-boat campaign in the area was in its early stages. Signals intelligence had anticipated this since October when it argued that the failure of U-boats to find substantial targets to the north of Ireland 'may result in a new disposition in the approaches to St George's Channel on an appreciation that our shipping is using this route'.[167] Sustained attacks by Escort Group 30 on 11 November south of Ireland on what appeared to be a bottomed U-boat and a subsequent attack on the night of 14–15 November on a U-boat off Bantry Bay, apparently heading for the Channel, sought to eradicate the U-boat threat in the area as a convoy was due to pass. This movement of naval forces caught G2's attention. Reports from Greenore and Carnsore Point LOPs between 1108 and 1136 on 10 November of '7 unknown naval craft 7–12 miles SE moving SW' and reports at the same time from Mizen Head, Sheep's Head and Dursey Head LOPs of '5 unknown destroyers 3–18 miles SW manoeuvring and moving SW' fit the pattern of an anti-submarine operation in progress.[168] A note to Bryan specifically pointed out that 'this activity may have been connected with a westbound convoy which was subsequently observed off the south coast.'[169] Escort Group 30 operated with considerable success south of Ireland through November, notching up another 'promising attack' on an unidentified U-boat on 26 November.[170] Its destroyers were regularly spotted from the shore by coastwatchers.

Aircraft from FAW7 patrolled off Ireland's south coast seeking out German submarines heading for the English Channel. Allied analysis of German radio traffic suggested that U-boats were about to become 'more active and enterprising' and operational reports bore this out.[171] In his report for December the Commander of FAW7 stressed the 'increasingly aggressive tactics' of schnorkel-equipped U-boats 'in the convoy lanes South of Ireland'.[172] Though signals intelligence held that 'every one of the U-boats which have so far reached the South-western Approaches has been disposed of',[173] Coastal Command were worried that 'very little success has been achieved recently in the detection of U boats owing to … the schnorkel and their employment of maximum submerged tactics'.[174]

In the first weeks of December several U-boats were thought to be passing west and south-west of Ireland en-route to the Channel. Mallow Sector reported

166 Ibid., pp 478–9, U-boat Situation. Week ending 30/10/44. 167 Ibid., p. 463, U-boat Trend. Period 26/9/44–4/10/44. 168 MA DRS 1591, 11 Nov. 1944. 169 Ibid. Handwritten note by 'TG'. 170 Syrett, *Signals intelligence*, p. 496, U-boat Trend. Period 20/11/44–29/11/44. 171 Ibid., p. 480, U-boat Trend. Period 23/10/44–1/11/44. 172 NARA RG 38, FAW7, War Diary, 1–31 Dec. 1944. 173 Syrett, *Signals intelligence*, p. 480, U-boat Trend. Period 23/10/44–1/11/44. 174 TNA AIR 2/8436, cypher message,

considerable convoy and destroyer/escort group operations off the south Irish coast at the time. This activity was only just visible to south coast LOPs. On 10 December Ram Head reported 'the masts of 11 ships going in a westerly direction' on the horizon and Sybil Head and Dunmore Head LOPs both saw lights 'flashing at intervals' out to sea eight to thirteen miles west of their posts.[175] The sighting of a periscope twelve miles south-east of Clonakilty on 12 December by a Liberator of 103 Squadron escorting convoy HX323, and a subsequent series of attacks by convoy escorts, showed U-boats operating off the south Irish coast at a time when coastwatchers reported troopships and convoys in the area. Signals intelligence estimated 'with some confidence' that there were three U-boats active off southern Ireland.[176] In mid-December, as this U-boat activity was reported, LOPs in east Cork reported increased destroyer and escort group activity with heavy gunfire, explosions and green, red and white flares regularly heard and sighted at night and in the early hours of the morning. Coastal Command joined in the fray off the south coast with anti-submarine convoy sweeps. U-boats were now thought to be operating in the Irish Sea south of a line from Dublin Bay to Anglesey in Wales and had returned via the Northern Channel into the north Irish Sea. Contemporary U-boat situation reports alerted commanders to a 'favourable position ... in the north-west corner "Anglesea" ... approach possible close along the Irish coast. You can proceed on the surface here at night. Irish coastal traffic moves at a distance of up to 10 sea miles from the coast through the mined area. Navigation good, no patrolling.'[177] To Kapitänleutnant Rolf Thomsen of U-1202, the southern Irish Sea was 'a good operational area with great possibilities of success.'[178] As 1944 ended U-boats moved closer to the east coast of Ireland, the west coast of Britain and the central English Channel. Signals intelligence suggested that 'it is unlikely that there will be any activity in the near future in any area other than the coastal waters of the UK and the Nova Scotia area'.[179] The English Channel and the sea lanes off southern Ireland remained 'very active' with a 'marked increase of boldness ... displayed by U-boat commanders, heartened perhaps by the revival of military effort on the western front' due to the German Ardennes offensive.[180]

MALIN HEAD RADAR STATION

In contrast to the situation off the south coast at the end of 1944, air and marine activity off the north coast declined. High-altitude, high-speed ferry flights

Coastal Command Headquarters to Admiralty, 4 Dec. 1944. **175** MA G2/X/315 Pt III, Mallow Sector AMI, Monthly Report on Coastal Intelligence, Nov. 1944. **176** Syrett, *Signals intelligence*, p. 506, U-boat Situation. Week ending 18/12/44. **177** MA U-260 papers File 7, 'Situation Report Nr. 16 for Type VIIc. Situation Bristol Channel and Irish Sea (Thomsen)'(Translation), undated, October 1944. **178** Ibid. **179** Syrett, *Signals intelligence*, p. 507, U-boat Trend. Period 10/12/44–20/12/44. **180** Ibid., p. 514, U-boat Trend. Period

passed overhead, activity from the Derry bases fell, though routine traffic through the Donegal air corridor remained relatively constant at between 550 and 650 flights each month. Convoy traffic was down, remaining channelled off the south coast. Sightings of corvettes and destroyers fell, with sightings of frigates rising but never regaining their immediate pre-D-Day level. There were sporadic attacks such as the torpedoing of the Captains Class frigate HMS *Whitaker* by U-483 north of Malin Head. *Whitaker* did not sink but was badly damaged; Malin Head LOP sighted a 'Frigate towing what appears to be the stern portion of a Corvette or Frigate seven miles North East going East'.[181] Frigates were later seen patrolling in the area and three of them later moved in one mile west of Malin Head LOP in search of U-483 which was thought to have escaped into Irish waters. The following day, Inishowen Head LOP sighted 'a Tug towing a disabled Frigate into the Foyle' which appears to have been *Whitaker*.[182] The efficiency of schnorkel-equipped boats was seen with the attack on *Whitaker*, Bryan reporting to Archer that the episode was evidence of 'the reported new developments in German Subs about which the British authorities have been enquiring.'[183]

The Allies anticipated a renewed U-boat offensive in the north-western approaches in the winter of 1944–5 'employing new tactics and equipment' such as the schnorkel. Sinkings, such as that of *Jacksonville*, and the attack on HMS *Whitaker* brought the threat home, as did reports that U-boats were active in the Irish Sea.[184] Though coastwatchers had noted a decline in convoys and air and naval escorts off the north coast, the north-western approaches remained 'particularly vital'[185] to Allied convoy traffic. The Admiralty wished to improve navigational aids in the area to prevent escort vessels and aircraft 'hunting and attacking charted wrecks in mistake for bottomed U-boats'.[186] Accordingly, the coverage of the GEE radio navigational system in the area was to be improved. In what follows the British use of the term 'radar' to describe GEE describes a radio navigational aid that enabled ships and aircraft to fix their position by using radio beams sent out by GEE transmitters. The system worked through a network of transmitters, a master and two or more slaves, sending pulsed radio signals which were received and displayed on a screen by the navigator in ships and aircraft. By measurement of the differences between the pulses from the transmitters, the navigator fixed the position of his vessel or aircraft.

The construction of a chain of GEE transmitters for the north-western approaches was planned in the winter of 1944–5. Four sites were chosen: Mull, Saligo Bay and Barra in western Scotland and Downhill in Northern Ireland.

24/12/44–1/1/45. **181** MA LOP 80, 1 Nov. 1944. **182** MA G2/X/315 Pt III, Western Sector AMI, Monthly Report, Nov. 1944. **183** MA G2/X/152, note by Bryan on Power to Bryan, 9 Dec. 1944. **184** TNA ADM 1/16172, Chilver to Under-Secretary of State, Dominions Office, 17 Jan. 1945. **185** Ibid. **186** Ibid., Admiralty to Air Ministry, 11 Nov.

'The damping of signals by the Donegal Mountains' impeded the operation of
the post at Downhill.[187] To 'improve the extent and accuracy of the cover' the
Dominions Office was asked by the Admiralty and the Air Ministry to approach
Dublin 'to site a Radar station on Malin Head or on some other suitable
promontory in the neighbourhood, that is, within the territory of Eire'.[188] When
the Dominions Office investigated, they found from Cecil Liddell at MI5 that
the matter had 'a long past history'.[189] Liddell had already discussed 'informally
with the Eire authorities … the question of setting up somewhat similar though
not identical stations on Eire territory'. Dublin had shown willingness to co-
operate but the condition that Irish personnel operate the station proved too
much for the Air Ministry and negotiations had ended. These events took place
in June 1941 in the aftermath of the German bombing of the North Strand in
Dublin. They centred around the establishment of a series of radar stations on
the Irish east coast to cover a gap in the British radar chain on the Welsh coast
which could only be satisfactorily covered from the Irish side of the Irish Sea. A
handwritten note by N.E. Costar of the Dominions Office explained that this
earlier démarche had a more technically complex scheme in mind. He noted that
the Malin Head radar station now proposed 'may include less secret equipment'.

The activities of schnorkel-equipped U-boats gave the construction of the
Malin Head station a new urgency. The Air Council agreed that the importance
of establishing the station justified an approach to Dublin using the spurious
argument that the 'station could be represented as being to enable civilian
aircraft crossing the Atlantic to determine their position'.[190] The Dominions
Office thought little of this attempt at making the request 'more palatable to the
Eire authorities'.[191] The excuse was 'rather thin'. Nonetheless, the Air Council
wished the Secretary of State for Dominion Affairs 'in whatever manner he
thinks suitable' to make contact with the government in Dublin.[192] There was
a significant rider to the Air Council position. If Dublin agreed to the request,
then it was potentially 'desirable to ask for facilities of a similar nature in
Southern Eire for the benefit of vessels, if the U-boat campaign again assumes
serious importance.'[193] Maffey quietly but firmly disagreed, suggesting raising
only the construction of the Malin Head station in the first instance. Maffey's
plans took shape in a period of improving British-Irish relations where 'the Eire
government has been increasingly helpful during the last few months'.[194] He saw
'no difficulty about furthering' the Malin Head plan to de Valera.[195] The

1944.   187 NAI DFA Secretary's Files A30, Walshe to de Valera, 16 Feb. 1945.   188 TNA
ADM 1/16172, Chilver to Under-Secretary of State, Dominions Office, 17 Jan. 1945.
189 TNA DO 35/2114 WX131/2, minute by Costar, 22 Jan. 1945.   190 TNA ADM
1/16172, Chilver to Under-Secretary of State, Dominions Office, 17 Jan. 1945.   191 TNA
DO 35/2114 WX131/2, minute by Costar, 22 Jan. 1945.   192 TNA ADM 1/16172, Chilver
to Under-Secretary of State, Dominions Office, 17 Jan. 1945.   193 Ibid.   194 Ibid., minute
on file, 20 Jan. 1945.   195 TNA DO 35/2114 WX131/2, minute, Costar to Machtig, 2 Feb.

Dominions Office were optimistic as the scheme had 'no back history' and did 'not carry with it the heavily charged political connotations of a request for ports'.[196]

All the same, the Admiralty, Air Ministry and MI5 remained 'doubtful whether the establishment of a radar station manned by British service personnel' would be acceptable to Dublin. The British considered establishing a mobile station operated by RAF personnel in civilian clothing. Maffey felt that Dublin would probably want the station situated within one of the existing establishments in the Malin Head area and manned by Irish personnel in order to guard against any IRA action and to ensure secrecy. Bryan was not worried about IRA activity amongst the inhabitants of Inishowen but rather that the IRA in Strabane in Northern Ireland might conceivably cross the border to attack Malin Head.

If Irish personnel operated the station and its construction was kept out of the press, then there would be 'a very reasonable chance of our proposal being accepted'. This did not appeal to the Admiralty who enquired 'whether the equipment is of such secrecy that the alternative of manning by I[rish] F[ree] S[tate] personnel cannot be accepted'.[197] The ever-present mistrust of the Irish in the service ministries continued. The excuse given by the Admiralty to keep the station under British operation was that the need for special training for Irish personnel in operating GEE would occasion three months training. This was unacceptable given the exigencies of war. In reality, the reason was that the equipment 'could be misused to give a misleading navigational fix or position [if] operated entirely by Eire personnel'.[198] British suspicions of neutral Ireland ran deep and the Dominions Office suggested to Maffey that a joint British and Irish party totalling fifteen men, with the British component RAF men of Irish nationality, should work at the post. The Air Ministry were prepared to hand over to the Irish as a quid pro quo 'a light warning detection system and instruct them in its use as this might to some extent camouflage the existence of the GEE station'.[199]

Maffey proceeded cautiously. He would seek out de Valera on his own, the United States was not to be informed of the move as 'it might be necessary to make a joint move if [the] first reaction [was] unsatisfactory and if great importance is attached to the project'.[200] Maffey also knew how best to approach the Department of External Affairs. He would 'disclose confidentially' to de Valera and Walshe that 'this help is needed for our counter measures against [the] renewed submarine threat'. He felt that 'this touches an Irish interest, and successful measures obviously reduce risk of Irish neutrality being sabotaged by Germany'. On the afternoon of 14 February Maffey was instructed to approach

1945.   **196** Ibid., minute by Costar, 22 Jan. 1945.   **197** TNA ADM 1/16172, minute on file, 20 Jan. 1945.   **198** Ibid., cipher telegram, Machtig to Maffey, 14 Feb. 1945.   **199** Ibid. **200** Ibid., Maffey to Machtig, 29 Jan. 1945.

de Valera on the siting of the GEE station. He accordingly met Walshe at 1000 16 February about 'a very urgent matter and in regard to which he asked for a decision by this evening'.[201] Maffey's instructions were to tell the Irish the true use of the proposed post. Whatever Maffey told Walshe in private, Walshe later told de Valera that the British had 'earnestly requested us to allow them to establish a mobile and temporary post at Malin Head … to pick up the radio pulsations from planes of the transatlantic airlines crossing the Atlantic to Scotland and to reflect them on to a post at Saligo Bay (Islay)'. It was a quick meeting as Maffey was able to send a cipher telegram to the Dominions Office on the result at 1115 that day. Walshe loved cloak and dagger secrecy and enjoyed being in Maffey's confidence. Walshe was also a great believer in new technologies, having in pre-war years championed Ireland's position as a base for the development of transatlantic aviation.

Walshe gave de Valera only the spurious cover suggested by the Admiralty, but in doing so gave him an incorrect back to front version, indicating that the post was passive and received rather than transmitted information. Walshe continued that

> It appears from what Sir John Maffey told me that it has become vitally important in recent times to know the exact situation of the traffic crossing the Atlantic which may be sending a special kind of information. The radar … location of the plane and the Malin Head mobile post would merely 'reflect' to the Scottish post the directional impulses received.

In fact, the 'exact situation of certain traffic' referred to by Walshe more correctly translated as 'the exact situation of ships and aircraft hunting U-boats'. Walshe's take on the meeting was peculiar, given that he also added in his report that 'the Malin Head wireless station, which is operated for the British by us, had been transmitting signals by telegraph to Scotland giving information about submarine activities'.[202] The following day Maffey wired London that de Valera had accepted the proposal on the grounds that the 'ostensible purpose should be for the guidance of aircraft'.[203] The sub-text was obvious: Dublin knew that the station had another purpose but Irish agreement had been obtained for operation on civilian grounds. The station would be operated by RAF personnel in civilian dress while the war lasted but Irish personnel would be trained 'with the idea of being able to take over at a future date'.[204] It was vague but Maffey considered that 'in practice with tactful handling this clause will involve no difficulty'.[205]

As the Irish had agreed to the construction of the GEE station Squadron Leader R.W. Fraser of No. 60 (Signals) Group RAF, which operated RDF and

---

201 NAI DFA Secretaries Files A30, Walshe to de Valera, 16 Feb. 1945.   202 Ibid., Walshe to de Valera, 16 Feb. 1945.   203 TNA DO 35/2114, Maffey to Machtig, 17 Feb. 1945. 204 Ibid.   205 Ibid.

other radio installations, was charged with picking a suitable site at Malin Head and was to leave London for Dublin on 22 February. Fraser met with officials from the Department of External Affairs and the Irish Post Office. With Wing Commander M.G. Begg, the British Air Attaché in Dublin, and with the Engineer in Charge at the Post Office, Fraser left for Donegal and Malin Head.

By 26 February the Dominions Office had contacted the Air Ministry in connection with 'the recent agreement by the Eire Government to the erection on the Eire coast of a radar station which will be of material and direct assistance to us in the present phase of the anti-U-boat campaign'.[206] Through agreement between the Air Ministry, Admiralty, Dominions Office and Security Service, the editors of the major British newspapers were approached to prevent news of the agreement to construct the installation appearing in the press. The need to prevent any leakage of information to the Germans or the IRA on the existence of the station was paramount. The Admiralty considered that the danger to reference of the station in the press came from the British press as the 'Eire authorities have much wider powers than the Ministry of Information to suppress comment … there is accordingly no risk of leakage from Eire'.[207] From the point of view of the British press 'the essential points seem to be to prevent any reference to the station and, particularly, any statement that the station is being used by our operational aircraft'. Reference to the anti-U-boat campaign was to be avoided at all costs.

The Air Ministry agreed that the 'most technically suitable site' for the GEE station was at or near the Napoleonic War era signal tower on Malin Head, a site adjacent to the Coast Watching Service LOP.[208] The radio antenna array would be mounted on the tower itself. All necessary equipment would be sent by road over the border from Northern Ireland and, subject to the final order to begin construction, No. 60 Group were to proceed with the preparation of the station and the selection and training of the personnel who would operate it. Ultimately it was decided to describe the station as 'merely a form of radio lighthouse (or glorified radio marker beacon) for the guidance of any aircraft in the vicinity'. Maffey added that 'I understand that this is literally true, since all the station does is to send out radio "pulses", like flashes from a lighthouse, which, with similar "pulses" from other stations enable aircraft to fix their positions.[209] These were to an extent side issues as Maffey succinctly informed Machtig that the 'point not to be overlooked is that use of this concession invalidates strict neutrality of Eire territory and provides [a] useful precedent for the future'.[210] The point was important but what were referred to as 'siting and administrative difficulties' had arisen over the location of the station on Malin Head and these

206 TNA ADM 1/16172, Costar to Low, 26 Feb. 1945.   207 Ibid., minute on file, 16 Mar. 1945.   208 TNA DO 35/2114, Notes on meeting held in Room IIA/III, Air Ministry, 28 Feb. 1945.   209 TNA ADM 1/16172, Maffey to Machtig, 6 Mar. 1945.   210 Ibid., Maffey to Machtig, 12 Mar. 1945.

put the actual construction of the station in real doubt. These difficulties included how to billet the station personnel and how to arrange for their 'loan' to the Irish Post Office, how to arrange for spares and equipment for the station to clear Irish customs and the removal of all RAF markings from vehicles to be used and the painting of the vehicles 'with Eire Post Office colours'.[211] The Dominions Office hoped that when balancing these specific difficulties against the precedent created by the Irish decision to agree to construction of the station, it might be that the Irish agreement would 'turn the scale in favour of going on with the project'.[212] However, the Air Ministry felt differently and tests, expected to be completed by early April, were being carried out to see if the Downhill station in Northern Ireland was after all 'reasonably satisfactory'.[213]

The end of the war in Europe in May 1945 occurred before these tests had finished and the GEE network for the north-western approaches was dropped. There is no evidence that Dublin expected the war in Europe to be over before the Malin Head station came into operation. What is puzzling is that de Valera would agree, even as the war ended, to British defence facilities being sited on Irish territory when he so vociferously refused the use of the treaty ports. A single radio navigation station was a very small installation when compared to three defended anchorages but it was on the issue of sovereignty that de Valera based Irish neutrality and allowing British military facilities on Irish territory, no matter what size, still derogated Irish sovereignty and the basis for neutrality. This was where the Dominions Office position had its centre of gravity, very different from the strategic military concerns of the Air Ministry and the Admiralty.

CONCLUSION

As zero hour approached in the summer of 1944 coastwatchers' reports indicated to G2 that the invasion of Europe would soon be underway. Rising convoy traffic with ever larger tonnages of shipping observed, the continuation of delivery flights, sightings of invasion barges in Derry and persistent sweeps by Coastal Command to the west of the likely invasion areas in northern France all pointed towards the imminent launch of Operation OVERLORD.

When Irish and Allied intelligence and security officers met in May 1944 the central role of the coastwatchers in securing the Irish maritime perimeter against information on OVERLORD leaking through Ireland was apparent. Compared to 1939 and 1940 where the British intelligence and security services took a poor view of the abilities of the force, the abilities of the coastwatchers were not called into question in the months leading to D-Day. Co-operation between the Allies

---

211 TNA DO 35/2114, Notes on meeting held in Room IIA/III, Air Ministry, 28 Feb. 1945.
212 TNA ADM 1/16172, Costar to Low, 14 Mar. 1945.   213 Ibid., Low to Costar, 19 Mar. 1945.

and the Irish had developed considerably through the war, not only in intelligence and security matters, but also in the practicalities of war as neutral Ireland prepared to receive shipwrecked invasion forces and provided what turned out to be critically important weather information on which Eisenhower's decision to launch NEPTUNE and OVERLORD ultimately depended.

Further comparisons to 1940 can be seen in the attempt by Dönitz to bring the submarine war to British and Irish coastal waters in the months after D-Day. Despite new technologies, weary and inexperienced U-boat commanders were unable to overcome the strength of Allied air and naval forces ranged against them. Whether the conflict moved north or south of Ireland, escort groups and Coastal Command maintained superiority over the U-boats. That de Valera would agree to the construction of the GEE station on Malin Head to reinforce the abilities of Allied forces to hunt submarines off the north coast of Ireland marks another relocation of the boundaries of Irish neutrality. It was active assistance in the war effort, though Valera made every effort was to interpret the facilities as non-belligerent and non-military. Nonetheless, Dublin and London were well aware that the proposed station would provide assistance to Allied military forces. The episode showed how far de Valera was now prepared to go to support Allied war aims.

CHAPTER TEN

The final months of the Coast Watching Service

MOVES TO WIND DOWN THE COAST WATCHING SERVICE

BY NEW YEAR 1945 THE Coast Watching Service's invasion warning role was long over. Morale slackened somewhat as, perhaps conscious that their wartime vigil was ending, coastwatchers 'carried out their duties with reasonable efficiency'.[1] In anticipation of the end of the European conflict, the number of districts was reduced to sixteen in January 1945. Moves were also underway to close down LOPs which had been established for specific local reasons. Such posts included Parkmore, Kerry, where the LOP covered the entrance to Ventry Harbour and which had been established because of persistent 'reports of alleged submarines using the head of Dingle Bay' for shelter.[2] Where there was duplication in their fields of vision LOPs were also under threat of closure, such as at Kilcreadun and Doon Point where both LOPs covered the mouth of the Shannon with a similar view to the LOP at Loop Head.

Bryan was resolutely opposed to any curtailment in the operations of the Coast Watching Service because, as 1945 began, the war in the Atlantic was still being fought around the Irish coast. He summed up the situation:

> both the North and South coast are important because of convoy, naval and general traffic activities. Ferry and other air traffic across the Atlantic strikes the whole West coast. The East coast ... causes us least worry ... [I]n the Dublin area we should be in a position to know what activity was taking place ... [T]here is still limited contact with Anti-Aircraft defence.[3]

This overview came directly from his analysis of Coast Watching Service reports and showed that even though belligerent activity was definitely down off Ireland as 1944 ended, the watch could not be reduced along the coastline. A British query in December 1944 that a U-boat which had attacked a corvette seventy-five miles off Donegal might be sheltering in Irish waters was shown to have no substance when coastwatchers' logs were interrogated. Archer minuted to Bryan

1 MA General Report on the Army 1 April 1944–31 March 1945.   2 MA G2/X/318, O'Connell to Bryan, 5 Dec. 1944.   3 Ibid., LOPs CW, Bryan to Archer, 18 Dec. 1944.

that 'as long as a query of this nature is likely to arise we can't wipe out the C.W. Service.'[4]

There was still significant belligerent activity close to Ireland. During January seven convoys were sighted moving east along the south coast, while only two were seen to move west. All were well outside territorial waters. Five Europe-bound convoys were reported off the north-west coast; a solitary convoy bound for North America assembling off Malin Head on 13 January. By previous standards this traffic was of 'a limited nature'.[5]

The coastwatchers now showed that in a state without a coastguard they had developed a future peacetime role by alerting lifeboat services to emergencies at sea. On 14 and 17 January 1945 the Ballycotton and Baltimore lifeboats put to sea acting on reports of flares observed by LOPs. Each lifeboat rescued a fishing boat with damaged engines. The operation by the Baltimore lifeboat on 17 January saved the 'exhausted crew of four' whose vessel was 'rapidly drifting to sea before a north-west gale'.[6] Their fate might have been quite different had it not been for the initial actions of the coastwatchers. Coastwatchers and the lifeboat service also continued to pick up survivors from military crashes. On the afternoon of 9 February a British aircraft, believed to be a Halifax bomber, crashed into the sea one mile west of Mullaghmore LOP. The aircraft had circled Donegal Bay and dropped red distress flares before ditching. The Killybegs lifeboat operating with *Robert Hastie* picked up four survivors from a dinghy. Two members of the crew tried to swim to the shore but the *Robert Hastie* and the Killybegs lifeboat left the scene without locating them. Their bodies washed ashore on 11 and 12 February. That of Sergeant John McKaine of the Royal Canadian Airforce at Rossnowlagh Strand, and the body of Flight Lieutenant John Cork, also of the RCAF, at Mountcharles on the northern side of Donegal Bay.

With the war at sea apparently winding down, Bryan anticipated that reporting aerial activity along the west coast of Ireland would be the 'paramount consideration in Coast Watching' through the final months of the war.[7] The usual poor flying conditions dominated in January: 'fog, frost and snow abounded causing a large reduction in all operational activity'.[8] Nevertheless, Western Sector still reported 1,221 sightings of aircraft, mostly flights along the Donegal corridor and off Inishowen. Many Donegal corridor flights infringed Irish territory while 'moving out and returning from Atlantic patrols'.[9] These were routine operations, they were logged and the numbers totted up. Further south, there was considerable activity off the south-west and west coasts. Flights entering Limerick Sector from the ocean flew north-east, indicating that 'they

4 MA G2/X/152 Pt I, minute, 20 Dec. 1944.   5 MA G2/X/315 Pt III, Western Sector, monthly report, Feb. 1945.   6 Ibid., Monthly Report, M&CWS, Southern Command, Jan. 1945.   7 MA G2/X/318, LOPs CW, Bryan to Archer, 18 Dec. 1944.   8 MA G2/X/315 Pt III, Western Sector, monthly report, Jan. 1945.   9 Ibid., Feb. 1945.

were Allied aircraft flying to Northern bases'.[10] These ferry flights continued but in nothing like the quantities of previous years. From January to March 1945 1,100 aircraft were ferried across the Atlantic. Coastwatchers sighted 'small deliveries of American Fortresses and Liberators' on six or seven occasions in January[11] while ninety 'heavy four-engined aircraft' were reported crossing Ireland through February.[12] It was quiet off the North Mayo Corner and a further sign of decreasing military activity was the reduction in training flights from bases in Northern Ireland as January gave way to February. Then, without warning, March saw an increased Coastal Command presence off the west coast as aerial activity in Western Sector suddenly 'almost reached the high level set during the peak period prior to the Allied invasion of Normandy'.[13] A renewed Allied campaign was underway against intensified U-boat activities off the west coast, in the western approaches and eventually in the Irish Sea.

THE U-BOAT WAR OFF IRELAND, JANUARY–MARCH 1945

British intelligence had warned G2 that new developments in German submarine technology suggested that the submarine war would be renewed with vigour in 1945. U-boat activity in the Western Approaches and along the English Channel rose in the first weeks of the New Year. Aware of the capabilities of the schnorkel, as well as of the new classes of German submarines undergoing training in the Baltic, the First Lord of the Admiralty, A.V. Alexander, 'took a singularly gloomy view of the prospects at sea' in January 1945.[14] Signals intelligence suggested three U-boats active in the Irish Sea with further vessels en-route to the area. On 11 January the SS *Roanoke* and the SS *Normandy Coast* were sunk off Holyhead. G2 intercepted reports of the attacks and sinkings but Irish sources added 'nothing definite' except that the Dún Laoghaire to Holyhead mail boat had been 'ordered to sail with extreme precautions and without lights.'[15] Later reports to G2 revealed that a far more acute situation had arisen. The mail boat had been thirty minutes out of Holyhead when it turned back, using the excuse of engine trouble. Passengers saw a fleet of motor torpedo boats leaving Holyhead with depth charges 'being used within sight of the passengers.'[16] When the vessel did eventually leave for Ireland on 12 January 'it zig-zagged violently all the way across'. The mail boat had reason to do so. On 17 January a Coastal Command aircraft sighted a moving oil slick, a sign of submarine activity, in the Irish Sea east of Skerries.[17] The sighting was in 'an area into which [U-boats] had not previously dared to penetrate'. To meet this new threat 15 Group and 19 Group of Coastal Command began intensive night

---

10 Ibid., Intelligence Report Feb. 1945: Limerick Sector.   11 Ibid., Western Sector, monthly report, Jan. 1945.   12 Ibid., Feb. 1945.   13 Ibid.   14 Dan van der Vat, *The Atlantic campaign* (Edinburgh, 1988), p. 526.   15 MA G2/X/152, minute on file, 15 Jan. 1945.   16 Ibid., minute on file, 15 Jan. 1945.   17 At 53°25´N, 05°30´W.

and day air patrols over the Irish Sea.[18] Their deployment was soon seen by coastwatchers, with details being forwarded to G2. The daily reports summary for 17 to 18 January recording 'heavy air activity E[ast] and S[outh]E[ast] coasts during hours of daylight also flashes, flares and gunfire during darkness'.[19] Contemporary reports stopped by the censor in Dublin included reference to 'intense activity by British naval vessels covered by British and American aircraft' off Greenore Point on 21 January.[20] The report continued that 'coastwatchers and many civilians at Rosslare Harbour saw several cruisers, destroyers and corvettes covering zig-zag courses in the area and there were several violent explosions as though depth charges had been dropped.' Bryan was extremely worried by these developments in January. He wrote to Traynor, McKenna, O'Muiris and Walshe that

> the increase in aerial and naval activity off the East coast ... indicates the presence of a German submarine or submarines in the Irish Sea ... [T]hese are the first instances of activity against shipping, known to this Branch, near the Irish coast. If such activities continue they will again direct attention to the question of the Irish Ports.[21]

British forces continued to counter-attack. In the encounter off Skerries sono-buoys were dropped and naval vessels combed the area but with no results. Signals intelligence suggested that up to five U-boats were now in the Irish Sea. They could have a 'most serious' effect on British anti-submarine forces training in the area and 'any success achieved would be hailed as a great victory by the enemy and go far to restore the morale of the U-boat flotilla'.[22] Fearing this, and following a report that Hitler had ordered the intensification of the U-boat war, the Commander in Chief of the Western Approaches, Admiral Sir Max Horton, instructed aircrews to pay particular attention to areas of the Irish Sea where 'U-boats when being hunted seek cover by bottoming in suitable declivities on the Sea Bed'.[23] These areas were to the north of Belfast Lough, around Anglesey, off Howth and Greystones on Ireland's east coast, and off Land's End. South of Anglesey surface vessels sank U-1051 on 20 January and U-1172 on 27 January. U-1014 was sunk off Lough Foyle on 4 February. Signals intelligence pointed to six submarines passing the west coast of Ireland bound for patrols between Ireland and Cornwall.[24] Off the south-east coast an aircraft spotted a suspicious oil slick south of Hook Head on 5 February. Sono-buoys gave indications of a submarine but a surface search yielded no contacts.

18 NARA RG 38, FAW7, War Diary, 1–31 Jan. 1945. 19 MA Daily Reports Summaries, DRS 1647, 18 Jan. 1945. 20 MA G2/X/152 Pt II, minute of deleted section from report by F.G. Braddock, for *Irish Times*, 21 Jan. 1945. 21 Ibid., memo by Bryan, 22 Jan. 1945. 22 TNA AIR 2/586, minute, Horton to Admiralty and Coastal Command, undated, but Nov./Dec. 1944. 23 Ibid., telegram, Horton to ships and authorities in Western Approaches Command, 18 Feb. 1945. 24 Syrett, *Signals intelligence*, p. 531, U-boat Situation. Week

The torpedoing and sinking by U-1276 of Flower Class corvette HMS *Vervain* while she was escorting convoy HX337 south of Tramore[25] on 20 February, and a disappearing radar contact by a Liberator of FAW7 103 Squadron further east soon after, indicated that U-boats remained active off the Irish coast. During a swift counter-attack following the loss of *Vervain* the sloop HMS *Amethyst* sank U-1276 south of Waterford with depth charges.[26] Signals intelligence surmised that in addition to patrols in the English Channel and in the Irish Sea there was now 'a new centre of activity for U-boats south of Ireland where four [U-boats] are patrolling on the convoys in the approaches to Tuskar Rock'.[27] By late February this had become 'the main centre of interest for U-boats' operating in the approaches to the Irish Sea.[28] Their commanders judged attacks on shipping in 'the route south of Ireland more important' than attacking vessels in the English Channel.[29] Oberleutnant Rolf-Werner Wentz, commander of U-963, reported to Dönitz that there was a good coastal route off the southern Irish coast passing the lightships '"Coningbeg", "Tuskar", on both sides'.[30] The commander of an unidentified type IXc U-boat added that 'the enemy has not yet grasped the fact that boats operate preferably in shallow water, hence one is generally safest right up against the coast'.[31] Visual proof of U-boat activity off the south Irish coast came on 23 February when a Liberator of FAW7 103 Squadron 'sighted the possible outline of a submarine beneath the water together with schnorkel smoke and wakes' twenty-five miles south of Crookhaven, Cork.[32] An 'immediate submerged attack was made' and altogether ten explosions 'and other submarine noises' were heard on sono-buoys.[33] On 28 February Liberator 32294 of FAW7 103 Squadron spotted a sinking merchant ship, the Paterson Steamship Company's *Soreldoc*, in the southern Irish Sea halfway between Rosslare and Fishguard.[34] The vessel had been torpedoed by U-775 while en-route from Liverpool to Swansea. In the attack fifteen crew were killed; twenty-one survived to be rescued by the fishing boat *Loyal Star* which was directed to the sinking ship by the patrolling aircraft.

G2 recorded on 6 March that 'since 3rd instant increased air activity has been noted off the East and South East coast. Naval craft have also been reported in these areas. Allied aircraft and naval vessels engaged on training and anti-U-boat patrols would appear to be responsible.'[35] A Reuters report carried in the *Irish Press* and the *Irish Times* on the same day began: 'U-boats are in the Irish Sea –

---

ending 29/1/45. **25** At 51°48′N, 07°13′W; www.uboat.net gives the location of the sinking as 51.47N, 07.06W (www.uboat.net/allies/warships/ship/5490.html, (accessed 13 July 2005)). **26** At 51°48′N, 07°07′W. **27** Syrett, *Signals intelligence*, p. 544, U-boat Situation. Week ending 19/2/45. **28** Ibid., p. 549, U-boat Situation. Week ending 26/2/45. **29** Ibid., p. 544, U-boat Situation. Week ending 19/2/45. **30** MA U-260 papers file 7, 'Situation Report from "Wentz"', undated, but January 1945. **31** Ibid., 'Situation Report Nr. 7 for Type IXc. (Near end of Folder)', undated. **32** At 51°03′N, 09°42W. **33** NARA RG 38, FAW7, War Diary, 1–28 Feb. 1945. **34** At 52°15′N, 05°35′W. **35** MA DRS 1687, 6 Mar. 1945.

the submarine war is on again day and night without a pause.' The Allied counterattack which the coastwatchers were about to observe included the 'largest operational effort ever flown in one day by aircraft of FAW7'. On 8 March twenty sorties, a total of 209 hours flying time, were flown off the Irish coast. These missions took place in full sight of the coastwatchers, who reported considerable American air activity off the south and east coast that day.[36] The first American contact was about twenty-five miles east of Arklow in the Irish Sea when a Liberator of 103 Squadron made radar contact with a submarine and held it for two minutes before the contact disappeared. From U-1058 Oberleutnant Hermann Bruder reported to Dönitz that there was now 'air activity all day' in the middle Irish Sea.[37] Further attacks on submarines suspected of heading for the Irish Sea took place 180 miles west of Loop Head[38] and 120 miles west of Ventry.[39] On the morning of 25 March a Liberator of 110 Squadron made contact with a submarine forty miles north-east of Howth, a position just to the north of the Dún Laoghaire to Holyhead mail boat route.[40] A sono-buoy picked up German voices. However 'no positive indications of a submarine were obtained and no attack was made'.[41] The following morning another Liberator of 110 Squadron 'sighted a V-shaped wake' nine miles south-east of Cahore Point LOP:[42] 'a periscope was later observed but disappeared before an attack could be made'.[43] The aircraft attacked but the sono-buoy picked up no explosions. The same morning, 26 March, LOPs from Greenore Point to Cahore Point reported ongoing air activity along the south east coast, and six unidentified naval vessels moving north. Cahore Point later saw these vessels 'manoeuvring and dropping depth charges and firing guns' in what the LOP misinterpreted as a practice exercise.[44] To FAW7's Commander, Rear Admiral A.C. McFarr, 'the operational effort [in March] was the greatest ever expended in any month by aircraft of this Wing both in number of sorties [539] flown and hours on patrol [5,333]' as 'enemy submarines continued their offensive in coastal waters off the British Isles with considerable success'.[45] March saw four merchant vessels and two escort vessels sunk close to Ireland but two submarines had also been lost in the same area. One was sunk by a FAW7 aircraft, the other, U-260, hit a mine and 'was scuttled by its crew south-east of Ireland; the crew members went ashore on Ireland before they could be intercepted'.[46]

36 NARA RG 38, FAW7, War Diary, 1–31 Mar. 1945 and MA Daily Reports Summaries No. 1690, reports for 24-hour period to 9 Mar. 1945.   37 MA U-260 papers file 7, 'Situation Report from "Bruder"', 10 Mar. 1945.   38 At 52°41′N, 13°34′W.   39 At 52°20′N, 13°03′W. 40 At 53°35′N, 05°09′W.   41 NARA RG 38, FAW7, War Diary, 1–31 Mar. 1945.   42 At 52°31′N, 06°00′W.   43 NARA RG 38, FAW7, War Diary, 1–31 Mar. 1945.   44 MA Daily Reports Summaries, DRS No. 1705, 24-hour period to 0900 27 Mar. 1945.   45 NARA RG 38, FAW7, War Diary, 1–31 Mar. 1945.   46 Ibid.

U-260

On the early morning of 12 March 1945 coastwatchers at Galley Head observed through poor visibility two red distress signals 'about nine miles south of the Post'.[47] They later saw three distress signals nearer to the shore. Naval operations had been ongoing in the area the previous day and LOPs from Ballycotton east along the Cork and Waterford coast to Hook Head had heard heavy explosions offshore. LOPs reported British aircraft in the area acting unusually, as if 'they were searching for something at sea'.[48] Because of the flares seen by the coastwatchers, the Courtmacsherry lifeboat put to sea. It rescued thirty-seven German seamen who were drifting along the Cork coast in rubber dinghies. They were from U-260, a type VIIc boat commanded by 25-year-old Oberleutnant Klaus Becker. U-260 had left Norway on 20 February. On 11 March the submarine hit an underwater mine about twenty miles south of the Fastnet Rock.[49] U-260 was suspected of involvement in a covert operation in the area, lurking near the Fastnet Rock for four British aircraft carriers and their destroyer escort which had left the Clyde on 12 March en-route to Gibraltar.

After the explosion Becker surfaced U-260 hoping to make repairs. He maintained radio contact with headquarters and was ordered to sail for Brest before daylight gave his position away to Coastal Command patrols. When Becker reported that the damage to U-260 was substantial, he was ordered to scuttle.[50] U-260 was now four miles off Union Hall, Cork, close to the limit of Irish territorial waters, and Becker and his crew were told to head for neutral Ireland in their liferafts. A flood tide swept them along the Cork coast. Eleven men made landfall at the cliffs below Galley Head lighthouse beside the local LOP. Just over two hours after first seeing their distress signals, coastwatchers, with the aid of a storm lantern, directed these men to a landing place. As they came ashore Leutnant Gottfried Kuntze informally introduced himself to coastwatcher Volunteer John O'Sullivan: 'I am a Jerry from a U-Boat.'[51] Corporal James O'Sullivan also met Kuntze, who maintained 'that direct enemy action was in no way responsible for their abandoning their ship and that no enemy had struck his ship.'[52] Another member of the crew 'mentioned "mines" several times' and Major J.P. O'Connell of G2 Southern Command concluded that this 'suggested a "mine field" somewhere off the coast in which the submarine became involved.'[53]

47 MA G2/X/315 Pt III, Southern Command (Sub-depot) Report to OC Southern Command, Mar. 1945.   48 MA U-260 papers file 11, Bryan to Traynor, 14 Mar. 1945. 49 At approximately 51°25′N, 09°05′W (see Axel Niestlé, *German U-boat losses during World War II* (Annapolis, 1998), p. 50).   50 U-260 was scuttled at 51°29′N, 09°06′W. Fishermen discovered U-260 in 1974, lying four miles south of High Island on a rocky sea floor. It is regarded as one of the most intact U-boat wrecks located to date.   51 MA U-260 papers File 11, O'Connell to Bryan, 16 Mar. 1945.   52 Ibid.   53 Ibid.

Local Garda Superintendent William Brazil took custody of the eleven German submariners landed at Galley Head. None spoke English but Brazil was able to ascertain their details 'through the medium of French'.[54] Becker, wet through from his ordeal, was among the thirty-seven remaining crew picked up by the Courtmacsherry lifeboat. G2 felt that Becker had 'special reasons for wishing to come through the war unscathed … [H]e was married only a couple of months before leaving on this trip [and] appears to be wealthy.' A mine might have damaged U-260, but it seems to have been in Becker's best interests to scuttle his damaged vessel. Between the actions of the lifeboat and the coastwatchers, all forty-eight of U-260's crew survived. They were taken to Cork under military guard. The ordinary crewmen were, American Military Attaché Hathaway reported to Washington, a 'poor type physically and mentally'.[55] However, Lieutenant Douglas Gageby, the G2 officer who interviewed the officers and NCOs, concluded that these men were

> fit, steady of nerve and convinced of the rightness of their cause. Even when it is obvious that they know the invading armies can't be beaten back, they hope for compromise peace, anti-communist alliance or some other formula. In short, no lack of guts.[56]

G2 reports on Becker's men show that they were not suffering from shock and that there were no injured amongst them; their sole complaint was a handful of cases of exhaustion. They had evidently plenty of time to leave their damaged submarine, many men having personal items with them. David Gray tried to get all the political capital he could out of the landing to discredit de Valera. He told Washington that though 'no evidence exists that any Nazi political officers were included in the ship's company … [O]ur assumption that the Irish coast could be approached by a submarine and passengers landed is supported by the incident.'[57] This was hardly news, having been proved in October 1939 when U-35 appeared in Dingle Bay, but it backed up what Dublin already knew: that, as Walshe put it, 'Gray is recognised even by his best friends as a pathological spy maniac'.[58]

On 13 March, as the crew of U-260 were being taken to the Curragh for interrogation and internment, Marine Service patrol boat *M1* commenced a search operation in the area where the U-boat had gone down. It picked up various personal effects, escape apparatus and dinghies and reported a patch of oil 80 to 100 feet wide on the sea near the area where the Courtmacsherry lifeboat had picked up the submariners. At the same time, a trawler from Union

54 Ibid., Brazil to Murphy, 14 Mar. 1945.   55 NARA RG 319, Box 460, telegram, Hathaway to War Department, 16 Mar. 1945.   56 MA U-260 papers File 10, undated rough notes.
57 NARA RG 319, Box 460, telegram, Gray to Hull, 16 Mar. 1945.   58 NAI DFA Washington Embassy, telegram, Estero to Hibernia, 24 Mar. 1944.

Hall retrieved 'three rubber dinghies and a metal case' from the sea off Glandore; another boat retrieved two 'wallets' from the sea.[59] Intelligence Officers found that they contained Becker's personal log as well as secret papers, sea charts, recognition books and codebooks for the main enigma code (Key M) and its Hydra (domestic and Atlantic waters), Triton (Atlantic) and Niobe (for U-boats stationed in Norway) variants.

The captured documents were given to Dr Richard Hayes of the National Library in Dublin, a code-breaker of repute, for analysis. Cecil Liddell, the head of MI5's Irish Section, then travelled to Ireland to discuss content of the material. The Irish military passed the U-260 material over to the British. Briefing an MI5 meeting, Liddell explained that 'McKenna on his own initiative had decided to transmit the contents of this box' to the British.[60] Though Walshe was among the first to be informed that the crew of U-260 were on Irish soil, the transfer of documents was done without the knowledge of the Department of External Affairs and 'was obviously Unneutral'.[61] The documents were photographed and speedily returned to G2. Admiralty Intelligence felt that 'the Eire authorities and our own over there have played up very well'.[62] It is not clear whether the information on ciphers from U-260 was of the value it would have been earlier in the war as British intelligence were now decoding German naval signals faster than the Germans themselves. However, in addition to the codes, the haul contained details of the latest type of German torpedo which were 'of great interest to the Admiralty' and German charts of British minefields.[63] Admiralty intelligence ultimately thought the material 'very interesting but not vital', yet it was quite a coup for G2. The haul included situation reports of U-Boat operations in the Irish Sea during the winter of 1944 and spring of 1945 which explained to G2 the origins of the rise in activity off the east coast that coastwatchers were now reporting. McKenna denied knowledge of the material from U-260 to the American Military Attaché in Dublin. Costello instead told Hathaway of the episode, thus blowing the British cover of a diving operation on a U-boat sunk off Beachy Head to explain to the United States the origins of the information from U-260.

AIDS TO NAVIGATION: (III) THE 'MOUNTAIN MARKERS'

From early in the Second World War G2 officers analysing reports from the Coast Watching Service noticed the tendency of Allied and Axis pilots entering or leaving Atlantic airspace to favour shortcuts over Irish territory. They cut the coastline between Dingle and Loop Head to the north and between Cork city and Skibbereen to the south, flying overland to reduce distance and reserve fuel.

---

59 MA G2/X315 Pt III, Southern Sector AMI, Monthly Report Coastal Intelligence, Mar. 1945.   60 West, *Liddell diaries, vol. II*, p. 281.   61 Ibid.   62 TNA ADM 223/486, The U-boat Scuttled off Galley Head, 21 Mar. 1945.   63 West, *Liddell diaries, vol. II*, p. 281.

If a flight flew far enough to the north it could expect a relatively safe crossing over neutral Ireland. For those who chose to cross Ireland further south, a combination of bad weather, poor visibility and pilot error could bring a flight perilously close to the 3,000 foot peak of Mount Brandon and a number of aircraft, thinking they were still over water, had crashed into the mountain killing all on board. First Engineer Paddy Watson, an Irishman flying with 461 Squadron of the Royal Australian Air Force, recalled that the quickest way to reach the Atlantic from St George's Channel 'was by way of Cork and Kerry in the neutral Irish Free State [sic], or Eire. This was "officially" forbidden, of course, but in fact was quite common'.[64] 'Most important', Watson informed his captain, was 'to keep well north of Brandon Mountain, near Dingle, Kerry, as it is 3,000 feet high and at least three Allied aircraft have hit it in recent months. I know because my father is in the local Home Guard in Tralee, and he has been called out on each report of a crash'.

On 28 July 1943 at 0430 GMT (0530 IST) BOAC Sunderland flying boat G-AGES en-route from Lisbon to Foynes with eighteen passengers and seven crew crashed at Slieveglass, Mount Brandon, while descending into Foynes through thick cloud.[65] Captain T.W. Allitt and nine of the passengers were killed. The aircraft had arrived at Foynes before dawn and, being unable to land due to cloud, had turned and was flying out to sea to wait for sunrise when visibility was expected to improve. When contact was lost with the flying boat Foynes alerted the police and military, including Coast Watching Service LOPs and air defence observer posts. They instituted a modified emergency procedure as it was 'unwise to broadcast to the enemy that we had an aircraft adrift in case the aircraft was down outside the Shannon and began to transmit from the water when it would be possible for Foch-Wolfs to intervene'.[66] With no results to show, full emergency procedures were put into force and Shannon air radio broadcast to aircraft off the west coast to 'look out for aircraft G-AGES out of communication since 04.08 [GMT] probably in coastal area vicinity S and W coast Ireland'.[67] The Air Corps sent up patrols to search the mouth of the Shannon and, as Corraun Point LOP had observed an aircraft over Clew Bay, they also searched off Achill.[68] Reports soon began to come in via the military in Tralee and ADC officers in Limerick that Dingle Gardaí had received reports of a crash on Mount Brandon. The investigation report on the accident later concluded that the aircraft had crashed due to navigational error on the part of the captain who believed that he was routing over Loop Head while descending in order to break through the cloud base and land at Foynes. The crash was a major disaster in which 'a quantity of highly-confidential matter' was destroyed

64 Franks, *Dark sky*, p. 73.   65 MA G2/X/315 Pt II, Sub-depot, Southern Command, July 1943.   66 TNA AVIA 2/344, Report on the accident to G-AGES, 6 Aug. 1943.   67 Ibid. 68 This aircraft was later identified as a flying boat operating out of Castle Archdale.

and it showed that it was necessary to mark out the peaks of north Kerry in some manner to avoid further crashes.[69]

The interdepartmental Airport Construction Committee, made up of representatives from the Department of Industry and Commerce, the Department of Finance, the Office of Public Works, the Department of Posts and Telegraphs and the Department of Defence, considered various methods of dealing with the geographical obstacle for aircraft created by the Kerry mountains. Initially they turned down a scheme for 'radio mountain markers', but the scheme was reconsidered in August 1944. Shortly afterwards a British flying boat, Shorts Sunderland DD-848, crashed at Slieve Glas, Cloghane, Kerry, killing eight of the eleven crew. The aircraft was from Castle Archdale and was on an anti-U-boat patrol, but at the time was alleged to be 'touring in search of another machine which was supposed to have crashed at sea'.[70] The crew 'thought they were over the sea and crashed into the side of the mountain which was covered with fog'.[71] In the wake of this second crash the construction of a network of six 'low-power radio transmitters at points in the vicinity of the Kerry mountains to give danger warning to aircraft approaching the mountains' was proposed by the Department of Posts and Telegraphs.[72] The construction of six beacons was judged enough to mark the mountains at an adequate height because 'it was not feasible to place the markers on the top of the mountain, in which case a smaller number would have been adequate'.[73] The construction of the radio marker beacons was agreed at a cost of £50 for construction and £900 for annual maintenance. Only four of the beacons were eventually constructed.

In February 1945 the Department of Posts and Telegraphs erected three of the four 'radio marker beacons near the Coast Watching Huts at Brandon Point, Dunmore Head and Lamb's Head, Co. Kerry'.[74] They were joined by a final beacon situated with the direction finding station on Valentia Island. The three were placed near LOPs so the military presence would act 'as a safeguard of risks of interference with the apparatus'.[75] The Radio Warning Transmitters were early forms of aerial radio navigation aids known as a non-directional beacon or NDB in aviation terminology. Normally used to mark an airway or an intersection of airways, in this case they marked a danger zone into which aircraft should not stray. They were aids to air traffic of all nationalities and so not a breach of neutrality. Indeed the Department of Industry and Commerce issued a civil aviation notice on the beacons, stating that they were 'to warn aircraft that they are in the vicinity of mountain peaks exceeding 3,000 ft. in height'.[76]

69 NAI DFA Secretary's Files A8(1), Reports from IO Shannon Airport, Foynes, 12 Aug. 1943.   70 NAI JUS 90/119/298, MacLochalinn to Murphy, 23 Aug. 1944.   71 Ibid. 72 NAI OPW D115/58/1/39, Cussen to Secretary, OPW, 31 Oct. 1944.   73 NAI DFA P34, Airport Construction Committee, minutes of meeting held on 11 Aug. 1944.   74 NAI DF S7/2/40, MacMahon to McElligott, 9 July 1945.   75 NAI OPW D115/58/1/39, Cussen to Secretary, OPW, 31 Oct. 1944.   76 NAI DFA 321/4, Radio marker beacons on south west

However, in an era where Irish and foreign civilian air traffic was limited because of hostilities the move was ultimately designed to facilitate the Allied war effort. Making such facilities available to the Allies was a potentially compromising action on the part of the Irish authorities. The location and frequency of direction finding aids were highly sensitive details; a Royal Air Force training manual from 1941 noting that 'all D/F [Direction Finding] may be subject to a certain amount of enemy interference, and the organisation of D/F facilities must therefore be kept secret'.[77] Even locals knew little of these beacons and it seems that coastwatchers manning the LOPs in the Kerry region kept to themselves the existence of this extra equipment under their command. Ibar Murphy recalled that though he had 'great chats with Kerrymen Coastwatchers I never heard them mention the beacons'.[78] The easiest way of keeping the purpose of the beacons secret was adopted: their existence was fully disclosed as aids to civil rather than military aviation.

LOP logbooks show that the network of beacons came into full operation on the evening of 22 February 1945. The transmitters were 'self-contained and self-operating' and were placed in the open on high ground at a distance from the local LOP.[79] Each of the adjacent LOPs was equipped with a radio receiver to monitor the signal from the local beacon every hour to check that it was transmitting correctly. If the beacon was out of order, the local Post Office linesman was informed. No material has survived on the installation and operation of the beacons. The most complete technical source is the Department of Industry and Commerce civil aviation notice on their introduction into service. It shows that the beacons operated continuously on 3082.5 kilocycles – a shortwave frequency in a standard aviation band.[80] The surviving logbooks from the LOPs monitoring the beacons show that the beacons, bluntly but realistically referred to as 'mountain markers' in the logbooks of the Lamb's Head and Dunmore Head LOPs, sent out a standard steady signal in all directions with the identifying dot call sign superimposed on the signal at regular intervals. They transmitted Morse code dots for three seconds, a signal akin to a slowly transmitted 'S' ($\cdots$) or a fast 'H' ($\cdot\cdot\cdot\cdot$) with eleven seconds of silence following. It is not clear from the civil aviation notice if the transmissions from the four beacons were simultaneous or whether they were staggered, with the silence allowing each beacon to be heard in rotation. Signals from the beacons were picked up by the radio compass or automatic direction finder of passing Allied aircraft, keeping passing aircraft well to the west of the beacons and danger areas of the mountain ranges they marked out. The beacons ceased

coast of Ireland, 17 Feb. 1945. **77** HMSO, *Air navigation* (London, 1941), p. 240. I would like to thank Captain R.N. White for making this publication available to me. **78** MA Owen Quinn papers, Murphy to Quinn, 5 Apr. 1990. **79** NAI OPW D115/58/1/39, Cussen to Secretary, OPW, 31 Oct. 1944. **80** 3805kcs was at this time being used by the RAF as a night time distress frequency.

operation at midnight GMT on 18 September 1945 as a more sophisticated air navigation system, constructed near Shannon airport through 1945 with the help of technicians and equipment from the United States, came into operation.[81]

THE FINAL WEEKS OF THE BATTLE OF THE ATLANTIC

In an overview of the war after D-Day McKenna told Traynor that 'the war has moved so far away from our shores that our territory has ceased to have the same strategic importance for the belligerents'.[82] Though the main theatres of war had moved to Germany and the Pacific, belligerent activity continued in the seas around Ireland in the final weeks of the war in Europe. On 23 March U-1003 was scuttled ten miles north of Inishtrahull.[83] The submarine had already suffered problems with its schnorkel and according to Clay Blair repairs were carried out in 'a remote bay on the west coast of Ireland'.[84] Back in service, U-1003 headed for Lough Foyle and on 20 March was rammed by the Canadian frigate *New Glasgow* and attacked with depth charges by other Canadian vessels in the area. The U-boat was badly damaged and repairs were impossible. Captain Werner Strübing surfaced his submarine and intended 'to run to the coast of Ireland and beach'.[85] Canadian warships again picked the submarine up by radar and on their approach Strübing scuttled his U-boat, thus removing for the Irish authorities the possibility of a tricky incident in wartime relations with the Allies involving the disposal of a beached U-boat.

Two submarines were thought active in the Irish Sea and U-boats remained active in the convoy routes south of Ireland. On 8 April HMS *Fitzroy* and HMS *Byron* sank U-1001 off the Fastnet Rock and on 12 April Escort Group 8 sank U-1024 in the central Irish Sea.[86] The location of submarines in these areas suggested that 'a campaign against convoys outside coastal areas may have been launched'.[87] Only one report of a submarine off the west coast reached Western Sector. On 11 April the captain of the British cargo vessel *Monmouth Coast*, en-route from Liverpool to Sligo, reported a patch of oil on the surface of the water ten miles north-east by north of the Rathlin O'Beirne lighthouse. He also reported the periscope of a submarine a quarter of a mile away from his ship. The periscope submerged and reappeared three times. Suitably alarmed, the captain took evasive action, hugging the coast until he passed Rathlin O'Beirne Island.[88] The vessel was not so lucky on its return voyage, striking a floating mine between Aranmore and Bloody Foreland. Sixteen of the crew of seventeen died. A local fishing boat picked up the sole survivor, Eric Gregg from

81 NAI DFA 321/4, Civil Aviation Notice No. 8 of 1945. Cessation of Radio Marker Beacons on South West Coast of Ireland.   82 MA General report on the Army 1 April 1944–31 March 1945.   83 At 55°25′N, 06°53′W.   84 Blair, *Hunted*, p. 667.   85 Ibid.   86 At 53°39′N, 05°03′W.   87 Syrett, *Signals intelligence*, p. 578, U-boat Trend. Period 8/4/45–18/4/45.   88 MA G2/X/315 Pt III, Western Sector, monthly report, Apr. 1945.

Liverpool. Gregg was taken to Aranmore where he 'received medical aid and stimulants' but he could not tell his interrogators what had struck the vessel.[89]

In March 1945 'the improved defence situation permitted a considerable simplification in the [air observation] reporting system. The two southern reporting centres were closed', their work being transferred to a single centre in Cork.[90] Off the south and south-west coasts there was, Daly reported from Southern Sector, during April 'a marked decrease in the number of flights ... probably as a result of conditions on the battlefronts'.[91] Training over Donegal Bay had by now almost ceased and overland flights in Western Sector were at their lowest total since the beginning of the war. Yet, for the country as a whole, the Army general report for 1944–5 explained that 'there was no material reduction in the total number of flights observed until the termination of hostilities'.[92] Coastal activity in Southern Sector was reduced to 'patrols to and from the Atlantic and occasionally to aircraft accompanying convoys'.[93] Generally these flights stayed outside territorial waters, but forty-four out of 156 flights observed strayed into Irish territory, including eight 'deep infringements' which were 'distributed fairly evenly between daylight and darkness [and] are deliberate rather than accidental'.[94] An insight into Allied intentions came when a Canadian Spitfire spotted flying from Loop Head to Shannon Airport and back west to the coast at Kilkee made a forced landing south of Milltown Malbay. It had passed close to Fort Shannon, the seaplane base at Foynes, and the newly completed airport at Shannon. On inspection, the aircraft was found to have been on a photographic reconnaissance mission.[95]

SURRENDERING GERMAN SUBMARINES

In the final weeks of the war the anti-U-boat campaign continued close to Ireland. On 21 April 1945 U-636 was attacked and sunk 100 miles north-west of Aranmore, Donegal, by the ships of Escort Group 4.[96] Then on 27 April the frigate HMS *Redmill* was torpedoed and badly damaged twenty-five miles north-west of Erris Head by U-1105.[97] *Redmill* remained afloat and was towed to port but, reduced to a total wreck, she was never repaired. As April ended two U-boats remained on patrol in the south-western approaches and two in the Irish Sea.

Following Hitler's suicide on 30 April Dönitz succeeded as Führer. His plenipotentiary, General-Admiral Hans Georg von Friedeburg, surrendered to General Bernard Montgomery on Lüneberg Heath on 4 May and that evening

---

89 Ibid.   90 MA General report on the Army 1 April 1944–31 March 1945.   91 MA G2/X/315 Pt III, Southern Sector, monthly report on coastal intelligence, Apr. 1945. 92 MA General report on the Army 1 April 1944–31 March 1945.   93 MA G2/X/315 Pt III, Southern Sector, monthly report on coastal intelligence, Apr. 1945.   94 Ibid.   95 Ibid. 96 At 55°50′N 10°31′W.   97 At 54°23′N, 10°36′W.

U-boat command broadcast a message en-clair ordering all boats to cease offensive patrols and return to their bases. U-boats were first ordered to scuttle rather than surrender but at 0142 on 5 May commanders were told not to destroy their submarines. On 7 May Germany surrendered unconditionally. At 2140 on 8 May a further German order was broadcast to all U-boats 'directing them to surrender and report their positions'.[98] The Irish military were sent copies of the order and it was relayed from GHQ through reporting centres to LOPs. Crohy Head logbook recorded that a 'General settlement at sea has been announced [and] that German craft and submarines fly a black flag'; if a vessel flying one was spotted by coastwatchers Command headquarters were to be informed immediately.[99] Fighting would stop on all fronts at midnight on 9 May. The first submarine to reply was U-1105, reporting at 0907 on 9 May that it was off north-west Ireland.

One of the last tasks for the coastwatchers was to watch for surrendering German naval vessels and submarines. In November 1944 Walshe had been warned by Maffey that Ireland would be asked to hand over to the Allies 'any merchant ships or planes which the Germans might seek at the last minute to save by rushing them over to Ireland'.[100] Walshe thought such a move unlikely, but told Maffey that Dublin 'would consider very carefully any representations he might make'.[101] Gray backed Maffey up with a similar request made in January 1945 calling Dublin's attention to 'the possibility that before hostilities have ceased German ships and aircraft may endeavor to escape capture by seeking refuge in various neutral countries'.[102] Bearing in mind the need for Germany to pay debts owed to Ireland, Dublin would intern any such vessels or aircraft in accordance with international law until the formal conclusion of a peace. When the war ended at least ten German submarines were thought to be close to Ireland and Britain. At 0125 on 13 May 1945 LOP 59 on Achill Island received orders that

> If German submarines try to come ashore they should be told they are
> disobeying orders and are mutineers and to leave. If they don't leave they
> will be handed over if they cause any trouble. They will be told that they
> are to be handed over and it is best for them to go quietly.[103]

Orders received by Malin Head LOP added that 'if they are in trouble, such as petrol or damage, they are to get outside territorial waters and radio authorities for whom they are acting'.[104] By 1700 on 13 May thirty-one U-boats had

---

98 Syrett, *Signals intelligence*, p. 590, U-boat Trend. Addition to report of 7/5/45, 9 May 1945.   99 MA LOP 74, 8 May 1945.   100 NAI DFA Secretary's Files A2, memorandum by Walshe, War Criminals, 24 Nov. 1944.   101 Though the crew of a German Ju-88 did land their aircraft at Gormanston aerodrome in April 1945.   102 NAI DFA Secretary's Files A75, Gray to de Valera, 20 Jan. 1945.   103 MA LOP 59, 13 May 1945.   104 MA LOP 80, 13 May

'reported or been seen by aircraft travelling on the surface apparently making for the prescribed destinations'.[105] The following day Inishowen Head LOP 'sighted 8 submarines escorted by two destroyers, 1 frigate and 2 Liberators' three miles to the north-east passing down Lough Foyle towards Derry.[106] Further sightings of surrendered submarines followed on 16 May and in the three weeks of May following the surrender of German forces posts along the Western Sector, of which LOP 59 was part, observed a total of thirty-seven surrendered German submarines, 'escorted by 25 Frigates, 4 Destroyers, 1 Freighter, 3 Liberators and 1 Wellington Aircraft'.[107] Among these, Inishowen Head reported U-997 and U-481 passing down Lough Foyle escorted by Captains Class frigate HMS *Keats* (K482) on 25 May.[108] A further twenty submarines were sighted by coastwatchers up to 20 June.[109] Many surrendered submarines were sent to the British and American base at Lisahally, Derry, passing Inishowen Head LOP en-route. Garda reports from mid-June 1945 spoke of forty-eight surrendered U-boats in the Foyle. These included submarines of 'the latest streamlined type ... capable of 28 knots under the surface which is faster than a Corvette can go on the surface [and] constructed as to negative the Radar finding equipment' of pursuing vessels.[110] They were 'being studied by British and American submarine experts' and sailed to America.[111]

THE COAST WATCHING SERVICE DEMOBILIZED

On 28 May the Council of Defence agreed that 'as hostilities in Europe had ended, no useful purpose would be served by retaining any longer the Coast Watching Section of the Marine Service'.[112] Air activity off the Irish coast saw a 'huge decrease' from over 2,000 aircraft observed in May to just under 300 from 1 to 20 June, when Western Sector sent in its final report.[113] There was little now for the Coast Watching Service to watch out for, though Colonel McCorley wrote to McKenna that, with the United States planning to return forces to America by air, a number of more prominent LOPs and the Eire signs should be kept in operation to assist in case aircraft got into difficulties. McCorley felt that any 'offer by our Government to maintain some selected posts would be very much appreciated by the American Government even if it were considered unnecessary to do so'.[114] McKenna did not pursue McCorley's suggestion.

1945. **105** Syrett, *Signals intelligence*, p. 590, U-boat Trend. Period 6/5/45–13/5/45. **106** MA LOP 82, serial 53, 427, 14 May 1945. **107** MA G2/X/315 Pt III, Western Sector, monthly report, May 1945. The figure comes from the logbook of LOP 82. **108** MA LOP 82, serial 35,611. **109** Ibid., Western Sector, Monthly Report, June 1945. **110** NAI DFA Secretary's Files P43/1, O'Coileáin to Murphy, 14 June 1945. **111** Ibid. **112** NAI DF S7/2/40, Memorandum for the Government: Disbandment of the Coast-Watching Section of the Marine Service and disposal of Look-Out Posts, Aug. 1945. **113** MA G2/X/315 Pt III, Western Sector, AMI, Monthly Report, June 1945. **114** MA EDP 20/5, McCorley to

District Officers regularly inspected LOPs through May, with demobilization beginning in the first weeks of June as posts closed and their personnel were withdrawn. The Cork Sub-depot informed Lamb's Head LOP on the afternoon of 12 June 'to have all the equipment of [the] LOP packed and ready for transportation during the week'.[115] Also on 12 June an important step in preserving the history of the Coast Watching Service was taken at Defence Forces GHQ in Dublin. With great foresight, Bryan agreed with Seamus O'Muiris, the Director of the Marine Service, that 'some complete logs from the LOPs should be available in future for specimen study and historical purposes'.[116] It ensured that a detailed account remained of the operations of the Coast Watching Service. Bryan and O'Muiris then wrote to McKenna that the Coast Watching Service 'should not be let go out of existence without some slight formal notice being taken of the occasion.' O'Muiris added that the coastwatchers had 'proved reliable and efficient and consequently deserving of commendation for having done good work ... particularly so since the nature of the work done has been so largely unknown and not visible to the public'.[117] McKenna did not act on this proposal and the Coast Watching Service was demobilized without official notice or commendation.

One by one, the eighty-three LOPs around the coast closed down. On 14 June Corporal Gallagher at LOP 78 at Melmore Head, Donegal was instructed 'to have all men at post at 11.30 tomorrow and to have their ground sheets, oilskin coats and caps and [the] Corporal to have his rubber boots with him and to have all post equipment ready including compass'.[118] There would be one last inspection parade before the men of LOP 78 stood down after six years active service. At 1000 on the morning of 15 June the neighbouring post at Fanad Head rang the reporting centre at Athlone to notify them 'that this was the last call from Fanad Head LOP'. Beside this austere record a coastwatcher has poignantly written simply 'Amen'.[119] This is a heartfelt reminder of the trials of a constant watch kept by the seventeen men who from September 1939 operated this post on the approaches to Lough Swilly. At Malin Head, after logging the passing flight of a Wellington at 1005 on 15 June, the report being number 30,815, there was a last inspection of the LOP and its personnel before District Officer Lieutenant C.J. McGinley called 'Buncrana 40' 'that the LOP was signing off for the last time'.[120] The men on duty at Roonagh in Mayo opened their logbook for the final time and simply entered 'last watch'.[121] On now silent North Mayo Corner Annagh Head LOP and Erris Head LOP both went 'off the air' on the evening of 15 June.[122] On the east coast coastwatchers at LOP 12 at

McKenna, 30 May 1945. **115** MA LOP 33, 12 June 1945 **116** MA G2/X/318, Bryan to O'Muiris, 12 June 1945. **117** MA EDP 20/5, Bryan to McKenna, 11 June 1945, undated minute from Ó Muiris to McKenna referring to Bryan's letter. **118** MA LOP 78, 14 June 1945. **119** MA LOP 79, 15 June 1945. **120** MA LOP 80, 15 June 1945. **121** MA LOP 57, 21 June 1945. **122** MA LOP 61 and LOP 62, 15 June 1945.

Ballyconnigar Hill also prepared for demobilization. On 19 June all men from the post were to travel by lorry 'to Waterford in uniform [and] *every* man should bring his civilian attire with him'.[123] On their last night on duty, along with coastwatchers at LOPs from Howth south to Greenore Point, they had, as if in honour of their last watch 'observed 50 to 300' red, blue and green flares ten to twenty miles east' out to sea from their posts.[124] There was no apparent reason for this pyrotechnic display. In a more sombre mood on Valentia Island, Corporal Dore was to 'collect all stuff in the hut and pack them carefully in soldiers box'.[125] His men would travel to Cork by lorry for demobilization, though they were told that 'any person who wishes to rejoin can do so'. There was no fuss and no official ceremony as the coastwatchers merged back into full civilian life.

Despite the Council of Defence decision, the Defence Forces wanted to retain the network of LOPs 'in the event of a future emergency'.[126] Ireland had been lucky in the Second World War and such circumstances might not arise again. McKenna made the point forcefully to Traynor: 'The fact that this country was not invaded or involved in the recent hostilities when protected by a small force which was inadequately trained and inadequately equipped is no guarantee or assurance of immunity from attack in a future war'.[127] Entering the Second World War with no naval service and having hastily put the Coast Watching Service into operation, the Defence Forces hoped that Ireland's postwar defence plans would include

> a Coast Watching Service similar to that in operation during the present emergency linked up with an air observer and radio location system which would operate throughout the country. The primary purpose of this service would be:—
> (1) to give early warning of the approach of belligerent or hostile sea craft;
> (2) provide continuous information of the approach and movement of belligerent or hostile aircraft;
> so as to enable the government and the Army authorities to take whatever action the situation would demand. In the event of war this service would, in addition, supply operational information to air stations and to intelligence report centres. The bulk of the personnel for the air observer system to be drawn from the LDF.[128]

The government did not agree and recommended the disbandment of the Coast Watching section of the Marine Service.[129] The network of posts was 'not likely

---

123 MA LOP 12, 14 June 1945.   124 MA DRS 1777, 19 June 1945.   125 MA LOP 35, 12 June 1945.   126 NAI DF S7/2/40, Memorandum for the Government: Disbandment of the Coast-Watching Section of the Marine Service and disposal of Look-Out Posts, Aug. 1945. 127 MA General report on the Army 1 April 1945–31 March 1946.   128 MA Memorandum on the Defence Forces, 14 Aug. 1944.   129 G.C. 4/103, 19 Sept. 1945.

to be of use from the military point of view in peace-time'.[130] Initially it was decided that the posts would be entrusted to the custody of the occupiers of the adjoining lands under a caretaker's agreement. Consideration was also given to letting the huts as summerhouses but, though the locations were scenic, this option was considered unremunerative. Other possible usages were as shelter for herds during inclement weather or for ewes during the lambing season. It was unlikely that local caretakers would undertake any repairs to the doors and windows of the huts and 'as there is no knowing when the Huts will again be required it would not be worthwhile to plan for maintenance'.[131]

The Attorney General was worried that as long as the state held the buildings there would be claims for injuries incurred by persons trespassing on the sites. To avoid this possibility the huts and their plots were either leased back to adjoining landowners at a nominal rent or transferred to the OPW, this being confirmed by a Government decision on 1 February 1946.[132] Four huts were transferred to the Coast Life-Saving Service. One, at Cahore Point, raised a specific problem. It was located on the lawn of the community of nuns of the St John of God Order. Representations were made to the Minister for Industry and Commerce, Seán Lemass, on behalf of the Mother General of the Order that the location of hut 'might interfere with the privacy of the nuns' bathing facilities' and that it was 'unsuitable and inappropriate to use it as a coast watching hut since it overlooks the convent's bathing beach'.[133] Lemass was won over and agreed to make alternative arrangements for the Coast Life-Saving Service at Cahore Point.

Where no purchaser came forward the huts remained standing, vacant and unused. The OPW inspected huts in their possession from the late 1940s. Even when boarded up, the windows and doors of the vacant observations posts were decaying. Occasional calls were made to reinstate the Coast Watching service. In May 1948 the Wexford Harbour Commissioners cited the drowning of five fishermen at Ballymoney Strand when the *Issalt* was grounded on 4 December 1947 as a case for the reinstatement of the service. Similarly, between 1951 and 1954 John Barry, a fisherman and Cableship Pilot from Ballinskelligs in Kerry, continually contacted the Minister for Justice and the Minister for Defence to inquire if a Coastguard or Coast Watching Service could be established 'in order to protect our coasts from foreign trawlers and to provide assistance to Irish fishing craft during bad weather'.[134] Coastwatchers had regularly reported illegal fishing in Irish territorial waters through the Second World War. The Western Command IO noted in his report for February 1941 that the large number of British trawlers present off the Donegal and North Mayo coasts was probably

130 NAI DF S7/2/40, MacMahon to McElligott, 31 Oct. 1945.   131 Ibid., minute by E.F.C., 17 Aug. 1945.   132 NAI DT S12014, O Cinnéide to Private Secretary, Minister for Defence, 4 Feb. 1946.   133 NAI DF S7/2/40, minute on file.   134 MA 2/55390, Meehan to Runaí Aire, Department of Defence, 27 Feb. 1951.

accounted for by 'the shortage of fish in England and the approach of Lent'.[135] Barry's request was to no avail. South Kerry TD, P.W. Palmer, wrote to the Department of Defence that 'since I was elected in 1948 I have been asked to get those old Look-out Posts re-established and manned'.[136] He forwarded a petition signed by ten of his constituents for the protection of Irish fishermen from poaching by foreign trawlers and drew attention to a recent 'threatening by French men to our brother fishermen ... who had to leave and make for port'.[137] In was again to no avail.

Vacant and unlikely ever to be returned to their intended use, the LOPs of the Coast Watching Service remained in consideration for possible operational uses over the next forty years. During the 1960s the Defence Forces inspected the sites as possible locations for fallout detection and monitoring stations.[138] Located on the very periphery of Ireland, the positions of the posts would allow the earliest possible reporting of advancing fallout following a nuclear attack on a British or Northern Ireland city. Such remote locations presented opportunities of a different kind to the Defence Forces in the late 1970s and early 1980s. The land around the posts remained Department of Defence property and more isolated LOPs took on a military role as training areas for the Ranger Wing of the Army.[139] Most posts are today in ruins, falling down as their structures give way to the unrelenting elements or to human destruction. Some still have functions relating to communications and aids to direction and navigation. Wicklow Head LOP is in full-time use by Irish marine radio, and Toe Head is available as a local station. Dursey Head and Sheep's Head LOPs form waypoints on local walking trails. The foundations of the LOP in Sorrento Park, Dalkey, are the base for a seat for walkers, but in most other cases the posts are ruined or have simply vanished into the surrounding landscape.

135 MA G2/X/315 Pt II, Western Command Monthly Report, Feb. 1941.   136 MA 2/55390, Palmer to Parliamentary Secretary, undated, but Dec. 1955.   137 Ibid., The manning of our Lookout Posts to prevent loss of life and to help to put down poaching by foreign trawlers.   138 Conversation with Colonel E.D. Doyle, 10 Dec. 2004.   139 Private information.

CHAPTER ELEVEN

'An integral part of the defences of the State'

I N 1940 A DEPARTMENT of Defence memorandum explained that

> at the commencement of the present emergency a Marine Service did not
> form part of our defence forces. In view of the fact that as a neutral state
> we are bound to undertake the surveillance of our territorial waters and
> carry out a number of duties in connection with ports, harbours, etc., it has
> been necessary to build up this service as quickly as possible, and
> consequently much improvisation has been necessary.[1]

In this context the homespun nature of the Coast Watching Service is clear.
Much maligned by civilian and military alike as an unarmed, poor quality,
volunteer force that lived at home and was not subject to the life of the regular
soldier, coastwatchers undertook considerable hardship to fulfil their duties. On
the closing down of the Coast Watching Service the *Irish News* commented that
coastwatchers had 'a grandstand view of thrilling incidents of the air and sea
war.'[2] The reality was often quite different. Coastwatchers from Portacloy LOP
told stories 'of the hardships endured there. Climbing hand over hand along a
rail with howling gales bashing their faces with rain or sleet as well, climbing up
to their post'.[3] Duty could also be extremely monotonous. At 0800 on 24
October 1940 when Volunteers Lavelle and Moloney and Corporal Pat Reilly
took over the watch at Moyteoge Head, Achill, there had been nothing to report
for sixteen hours since 1600 the previous day when a British monoplane had
been sighted to the north-west of the post flying south-west.[4]

By selecting local mariners, fishermen, beachcombers and those with farms
along the coast, the military acquired the services of a specialist group of men
each with a pre-existing 'detailed knowledge of a given section of the coastline'.[5]
This was knowledge of tides, coastlines and underwater obstacles that only a
lifetime's experience with the sea could give and which barrack training could
never provide. After mistakenly identifying a half-submerged rock as a
submarine, District Officer Owen Quinn decided he would leave future
identification to the men of each LOP in his district. He recalled listening to a
volunteer and a corporal at Roskeeragh LOP discussing

---

1 NAI DT S11101, Memorandum on Defence, 3 Oct. 1940.   2 *Irish News*, 22 June 1945.
3 MA Owen Quinn papers, Murphy to Quinn, 5 Apr. 1990.   4 MA LOP 59, 10 Oct. 1945.
5 NAI DF S4/84/38, MacMahon to McElligott, 11 Feb. 1939.

an almost completely submerged bale of some sort out on the water, trying to guess what it was, and I said, 'Will it come in on this tide'? 'Ah no, Sir, nor the next,' he said, 'it will come in about a quarter of a mile down, it will go out maybe half a mile, it will go in and out.' 'By tomorrow evening, round about Ballysadare Bay, that one will land, and we will keep an eye on it.' And right enough he was dead on, to the very tide he was able to predict, and that was about ten miles away.[6]

G2 appreciated the skills of the coastwatchers; they knew that these men combined 'an extensive knowledge of the peculiarities of the coast in the vicinity of their posts with a reasonably good appreciation of the different types of seagoing craft'.[7] The coastwatchers knew what craft normally operated near their posts. The Coast Watching Service ensured that 'under normal conditions of visibility no surface craft can approach our coast unobserved at any intermediate point between LOPs'.[8] By the end of the Second World War the Department of Defence concluded that the Coast Watching service formed 'an integral part of the defences of the State'.[9]

What made the Coast Watching Service work was its very simplicity. It was a local information gathering network where each link in the chain covered a small specific area and had a limited number of tasks to perform. Archer made a point of telling Lawlor that he attached 'the greatest importance to information from this end'.[10] Information in a standard format logged and relayed to G2 and ADC in a routine everyday flow, even of relatively low-grade data, created an elaborate picture of the conflict around and over Ireland. Entries in LOP logbooks, Command level reports submitted to G2, and the analysis of these reports by senior intelligence officers show in detail the Second World War around Ireland's coasts. The Coast Watching Service provided accurate information from which G2 drew generally correct inferences, providing the broad intelligence picture that Archer and Bryan required.

Study of these details exposes a flaw in modern Irish historiography: a tendency to assume Irish exceptionalism to the course of world history, which is magnified in the case of the Second World War as most writers assume that Ireland was oblivious to the conflict. The term 'The Emergency', Seán O Faolain's 'green curtain' and F.S.L. Lyons' 'Plato's Cave' analogies conceal what contemporaries knew and feared: that a global conflict, neutrality notwithstanding, was going on around and over Ireland and that poorly defended Ireland could be drawn in by a move from either side. The records of the Coast

6 Owen Quinn, 'Wartime Coast Watching', lecture to the Irish Maritime Institute, 27 Oct. 1988.   7 MA G2/X/318, Memorandum on Coastal Observation, no date.   8 Ibid.   9 NAI OPW A115/21/1/1939, Industry and Commerce to OPW, 23 Apr. 1956.   10 MA G2/X/318, Archer to Lawlor, 29 Sept. 1939.

Watching Service show just how close that conflict was and how often the Irish Defence Forces were on the edge of involvement by defending, so much as their limited capacities allowed, Ireland's neutrality. Indeed, further than this, the experience of the Coast Watching Service casts considerable light on Irish co-operation with the Allies and shows how the parameters of neutrality were renegotiated during the course of the war.

But what did the coastwatchers achieve? We now know that Hitler's plans to invade Ireland were unfeasible and that the real threat came from the more sophisticated and workable plans drawn up by the British armed forces. Highly developed British-Irish security and intelligence co-operation rendered these plans unnecessary and the coastwatchers were of central importance in this process as information gatherers. Though often considered an inferior service by Britain, Bryan and Archer knew the value of the coastwatchers' eyes and ears along the coast. Constant surveillance provided the raw information that when processed was ultimately to soothe British-Irish tensions when rumours of submarines and spies on the coast of Ireland troubled overworked minds in Whitehall and gave rise to calls for Britain to invade Ireland. Via G2, the Department of External Affairs ultimately used the information provided by the coastwatchers to counteract propaganda from Britain, in particular Churchillian rumours that there were submarines and German agents in bays and inlets along the west coast of Ireland. The coastwatchers could never prevent an actual invasion of Ireland occurring, but they were a crucial Irish weapon in the battle of information, propaganda and counterpropaganda that surrounded the defence of Irish neutrality and the secret British-Irish intelligence relationship. Their reports played a significant part in preventing British-Irish relations overheating in moments of extreme crisis during the early years of the Second World War. Hour-by-hour reports from LOPs allowed G2 to make well-founded risk assessments of the situation along the Irish coastline based on an interpretation of the activities of Axis and Allied forces off the coast. G2 used the coastwatchers' reports to see where future anxieties might arise based on an examination of developing trends. Current threats could be identified and monitored and tactical intelligence reporting of potential problems which could, and in some cases did, become actual problems would flow into the wider strategic picture of maintaining Ireland's non-belligerent and pro-Allied neutrality. The close relationship between Archer and Bryan and Walshe at External Affairs was the essential factor here. It is not surprising that reports and information from the Coast Watching Service survive in considerable quantity in the records of the Department of External Affairs. The work of the Coast Watching Service was an essential component underpinning the execution of Irish foreign and military policies during the Emergency. Processed information from the Coast Watching Service was a crucial weapon not only for the Defence Forces but also for Ireland's wartime government and its senior civil service advisors. Used tactically it was of manifest importance in the formulation of foreign and defence policies at a strategic level. It was in all truth that Bryan could write to McKenna in June 1945 that the Coast Watching Service had 'served the Defence Forces and the state well'.[11]

11 MA EDP 20/5, Bryan to McKenna, 11 June 1945.

Locations of Coast Watching Service LOPs

NAMED SHADED LOCATIONS IN the proposed locations column were not constructed. Shaded blank sections in either location column are included to preserve consistency between locations in each column.

Command	Reporting Centre	District	Proposed locations for LOPs (1939)		LOPs as sited and built (1939–42)	
			Number	Location	Number	Location
EASTERN	Air Defence Command/Waterford Barracks/Eastern Sector/Curragh CIO	1	1	Ballagan Point	1	Ballagan Point
			2	Dunany Point	2	Dunany Point
			3	Clogher Head	3	Clogher Head
			4	Skerries		
					4	Cardys Rock
					5	Rush
			5	Howth Head	6	Howth Head
			6	Dalkey (Sorrento Park)	7	Dalkey (Sorrento Park)
			7	Bray Head	8	Bray Head
			8	Wicklow Head	9	Wicklow Head
CURRAGH		2	9	Kilmichael Point	10	Kilmichael Point
			10	Cahore Point	11	Cahore Point
			11	Ballyconnigar Hill	12	Ballyconnigar Hill
			12	Rosslare Point		
			13	Greenore Point	13	Greenore Point
			14	Carnsore Point	14	Carnsore Point
			15	Forlorn	15	Forlorn
		3	16	Hook Head	16	Hook Head
			17	Brownstown Head	17	Brownstown Head
			18	Dunabrattin Head	18	Dunabrattin Head
SOUTHERN	Cork (later Mallow)	4	19	Helvick Head Ram Head	19	Helvick Head Ram Head
			20	Ardmore	20	Ardmore
			21	Blackball Head		
			22	Knockadoon	21	Knockadoon
			23	Ballycotton	22	Ballycotton
			23	Power Head	23	Power Head

→

Command	Reporting Centre	District	Proposed locations for LOPs (1939)		LOPs as sited and built (1939–42)	
			Number	Location	Number	Location
SOUTHERN	Cork (later Mallow)	5	25	Flat Head	24	Flat Head
			26	Frower Head		
			27	Old Head	25	Old Head
			28	Seven Heads	26	Seven Heads
			29	Galley Head	27	Galley Head
			30	Toe Head	28	Toe Head
			31	Baltimore	29	Baltimore
		6	32	Mizen Head	30	Mizen Head
			33	Sheep's Head	31	Sheep's Head
			34	Blackball Head		
			35	Dursey Head	32	Dursey Head
		7	36	Cod's Head		
			37	Lambs Head	33	Lambs Head
			38	Bolus Head	34	Bolus Head
			39	Bray Head	35	Bray Head
			40	Dolous Head		
	Cork (later Limerick)	8			36	Eask Head
					83	Foileye Head/Feaklecally
					37	Parkmore
			41	Dunmore Head	38	Dunmore Head
					39	Sybil Head
			42	Brandon Point	40	Brandon Point
			43	Fahamore		
			44	Fenit	41	Fenit
			45	Kerry Head	42	Kerry Head
			46	Ballybunion		
			47	Doon Head/ Leck Point	43	Doon Head/ Leck Point
		9	48	Kilcreadun Point	44	Kilcreadun Point
			49	Loop Head	45	Loop Head
			50	Georges Head	46	Georges Head
			51	Carrowmore Point		
			52	Spanish Point		
			53	Hag's Head	47	Hag's Head
			54	Black Head	48	Black Head
WESTERN	Athlone	10	55	Spiddal	49	Spiddal
					50	Kilronan
			56	Golam Head	51	Golam Head
		11	57	Mace Head Slyne Head	52	Mace Head Slyne Head
			58	(Doon Hill)	53	(Doon Hill)

→

Command	Reporting Centre	District	Proposed locations for LOPs (1939)		LOPs as sited and built (1939–42)	
			Number	Location	Number	Location
WESTERN	Athlone		59	Auchrus Point	54	Auchrus Point
			60	Renvyle Point	55	Renvyle Point
					56	Rossroe
		12	61	Carrickvegraly Point (Roonagh)	57	Carrickvegraly Point (Roonagh)
			62	Corraun	58	Corraun
			63	Moyteoge Head, Keem, Achill	59	Moyteoge Head, Keem, Achill
		13	64	Termon Hill, Blacksod Bay	60	Termon Hill, Blacksod Bay
			65	Annagh Head	61	Annagh Head
			66	Erris Head	62	Erris Head
			67	Portacloy	63	Portacloy
			68	Downpatrick Head	64	Downpatrick Head
			69	Kilcummin Head	65	Kilcummin Head
		14	70	Lenadoon Point Rathlee	66	Lenadoon Point Rathlee
			71	Aughris Head	67	Aughris Head
			72	Roskeeragh	68	Roskeeragh
			73	Mullaghmore	69	Mullaghmore
		15	74	St John's Point	70	St John's Point
					71	Carrigan Head
			75	Malin Beg		
			76	Rossan Point	72	Rossan Point
			77	Dawros Head		
					73	Dunmore Head
	Athlone via Filtering Centre at Fort Dunree	16	78	Crohy Head	74	Crohy Head
			79	Burtonport		
					75	Aranmore Point
			80	Gweedore Bay		
			81	Ranaghroe Point	76	Bloody Foreland
		17	82	Horn Head	77	Horn Head
			83	Rinnafaghla Point		
					78	Melmore Head
		18	84	Fanad Head	79	Fanad Head
			85	Dunaff Head		
			86	Malin Head	80	Malin Head
			87	Glengad Head	81	Glengad Head
			88	Inishowen Head	82	Inishowen Head

APPENDIX 2

Members of the Coast Watching Service

THIS APPENDIX IS BASED on material prepared by Commandant Owen Quinn and contained in the typescript 'The Coastwatch' which forms part of Commandant Quinn's papers, held at Military Archives, Cathal Brugha Barracks, Rathmines Dublin. The list has been revised and updated from material held at Military Archives, in particular from Coast Watching Service Logbooks for the names of volunteers and from the 'Emergency Defence Plans' series of files for District Officers and information on Sub-depots. An '?' below indicates that an individual's first name is not identifiable from the records consulted for this section. There is a degree of repetition and overlap in this list as coastwatchers often served at different posts in the same region and were transferred from post to post. For example, the Charles Craney who served at Dalkey LOP and the C. Craney who served at Bray Head LOP is the same person. The use of a two-digit number with a name, for example '51 Walsh at Spiddal LOP, is used (by Quinn) to separate individuals with the same first and last name and is based on Volunteer number. The list should be regarded as incomplete.

(I)   **Sub-depots by Command Area**
       Eastern Command
          Sub-depot Portobello Barracks Dublin:
             OC: Commandant J. McDonald, Commandant Niall Harrington.
             Quartermaster: Lieutenant J.M. Love.

       Curragh Command
          Sub-depot The Prison, Waterford:
             OC: Commandant M. O'Leary.
             Quartermaster: Second Lieutenant J.J. O'Neill.

       Southern Command
          Sub-depot Haulbowline, Cork:
             OC: Lieutenant L. O'Riordan.

       Western Command
          No. 1 Sub-depot Castlebar Barracks:
             OC: Captain Togher.
             Quartermaster: Lieutenant M. Hennelly.

          No. 2 Sub-depot Killybegs Barracks:
             OC: Captain G. Stanton.
             Quartermaster: Lieutenant Gilleran.

(II) District Officers

District number given in brackets where known. See appendix one for details of districts.

Lieutenants:

(Total: 67)

M. O'Sullivan (1), E. Sullivan, M. Love, J. Thornton (1), W. McCabe (1), P.W. Rowe (2), R.G. Kinsella (3), D.G. Kent, D. McDevitt, J. O'Neill, P. MacCarthaigh, F. Busteed, E.J. Furness, Con O'Shea, D. Breen (4), D.M. Barrett (4), W.P. Glavin, J. McLoughlin (5), J. Galvin, P.J. Daly, H. O'Neill (5), J. McCarthy, A.M. Nestor, P. Cahalane, M. Hollingsworth, J. Peterson, T.P. Buttimer, R.P. Keyes, N. Harrington (6), Eamon Coughlan, L. O'Riordan, D. O'Carroll (7), D. Ryan, J. Garvey, D.F. Twohig, W.P. Wren (8), J. Grahan, J.J. Maguire, M. McDonnell, C.F. Irving (9), Owen Buckley, P.J. Coakley, P. Quissick, J. Gibbons, T. Cooke, Patrick Bullistrom (10), Laurence O'Toole, Owen McLean, Eoghan MacGiollaidhe, M. Cottingham (11), Thomas Lyons (12), J.A. 'Fonso' Caulfield (13), Michael Hennelly (14), Owen Quinn (14), J.C. Gatins (15), W.A. Mulligan, P. Sweeney, G. McDonagh, J. Corcoran, T. Teahan, T. McGillicuddy, Owen Gilleran, J. Morgan Dunleavy (16), G. Haire, C. McFadden, O. McLean (17), C.J. McGinley (18).

(III) NCOs and Volunteers by LOP:

Number of known coastwatchers at each LOP given in brackets after post name (Total: 866).

1	**Ballagan Head (10)**
Corporal:	P.M. (initials only available).
Volunteers:	J. Byrne, T. Clarke, P. Connolly, J. Donaghy, J. Gilmore, M. Macken, W.J. Malone, B. O'Rourke, Owen Raftery.

2	**Dunany Point (17)**
Corporals:	Thomas McShane, J.H. (initials only available).
Volunteers:	John Caffrey, Patrick Caffery, J. Dawson, P. Farrell, Patrick Gorman, P. Hodges, Christopher Kirwan, Thomas Lynch, Patrick Matthews, J. Morris, Bernard Mulligan, J. McGuigan, N. McGrath, John McHale, Peter Shields.

3	**Clogher Head (15)**
Corporal:	J. Healy.
Volunteers:	P. Farrell, P. Gorman, P. King, C. Kirwan, P. Kirwan, A. Lynch, J. Lynch, P. Matthews, T. Murray, L. Owens, M. Rafferty, J. Rath, P. Sharkey, P. Smyth.

4	**Cardys Rocks (14)**
Corporals:	S. Carr, D. Duffy.
Volunteers:	John Carr, E. Clarke, K. Connor, George Harpur, L. Howley, S. Hughes, J. Kelly, J. McMahon, R. Robinson, K. Saul, F. Thompson, H Tuite.

5   **Rush (8)**
Corporal: D. Duffy.
Volunteers: P. Barry, J. Creighton, T. Devlin, Sean Hughes, P. Knight, W. Lambe, J. Leonard.

6   **Howth (9)**
Corporal: John Rourke.
Volunteers: Roger Austin, John Gallagher, Thomas MacLoughlin, Tom MacNally, Andy Moore, Paddy Moore, John Redmond, Tom Redmond.

7   **Dalkey (11)**
Corporals: Charles Craney, James Dalton, Henry Mullen.
Volunteers: Vincent Delaney, Alfred Hill, Nicholas Kinsella, John Larkin, John Mooney, Thomas Smiles, James Smith, Samuel V. Williams.

8   **Bray Head (14)**
Corporals: J. McDonnell, P. McNeill.
Volunteers: E. Byrne, J. Cleary, W. Cleary, C. Craney, C. Davies, M. Doyle, J. Garvey, N. Mulvey, J. McDonnell, J. Naylor, J. Nolan, J. Salmon, W. Walsh, E. Wheeler.

9   **Wicklow Head (8)**
Corporal: P. O'Sullivan.
Volunteers: R. Brennan, W. Goodman, J.J. Kavanagh, J. Malone, T. Malone, P. O'Connor, ? Patchell.

10   **Kilmichael Point**
                    (No logbooks have survived from this post so it has not been possible to identify the names of those who served there.)

11   **Cahore Point (9)**
Corporal: J. Cosgrave.
Volunteers: T. Hunter, J. Kavanagh, P. Kenny, E. Kinsella, P. Naughten, B. Redmond, J. Redmond, T. Redmond.

12   **Ballyconnigar Hill (9)**
Corporal: Thomas Goodison.
Volunteers: W. Coady, G. Dempsey, J. Dempsey, G. Murphy, J. Murray, J.R. O'Brien, R. Shiel, M. Walsh.

13   **Greenore Point (9)**
Corporal: Ibar Murphy.
Volunteers: J. Bishop, T. Boyce, P. Brennan, Plunkett Butler, W. Duggan, A. Goodall, P. Green, Peter O'Gorman.

14   **Carnsore Point (9)**
Corporal: Richard Ellard.
Volunteers: James Brown, ? Donohue, Desmond Fenelon, R. Fenelon, ? Newport, ? Pierce, Nicholas Redmond, ? Somers.

15   **Forlorn Point (10)**
Corporals: P. Kelly, J. Power, R. Woodcock.
Volunteers: M. Bates, T. Busher, N. Cloney, J. Conley, J. Connick, W. Doyle, T. Reville.

16   **Hook Head (7)**
Corporal: Matthew O'Murchadha.
Volunteers: T. Banville, J. Colfer, Thomas Colfer, W. Colfer, R. Fortune, P. Murphy.

17   **Brownstown Head (12)**
Corporals: Richard Hanrahan, Thomas Keoghan.
Volunteers: J. Corcoran, P. Dunne, J. Esmond, J. Fitzgerald, J. Keogh, John Keoghan, P. Lennon, J. O'Grady, J. O'Shea, John Power.

18   **Dunabrattin Head (8)**
Corporal: J. O'Sullivan.
Volunteers: P. Bolton, R. Crowley, W. Crowley, '56 M. Power, '60 M. Power, '66 M. Power, R. Power.

19   **Helvick Head (12)**
Corporal: M. O'Curraoin.
Volunteers: E. Bowler, Liam Breathnach, John Cronin, J. Moriarty, R. MacAlsadair, A. McAllister, M. O Cionnfhaolaidh, Sean O Curraoin, Nioclais O Lomain, Deaglan O Reagain, T. O Suileabhain.

20   **Ram Head, Ardmore (9)**
Corporal: Tom Mooney.
Volunteers: Edward Foley, T. Foley, M. Hallahan, Thomas Monsell, J. MacCarthy, Jimmy Troy, P. Troy, W. Whelan.

21   **Knockadoon Head (10)**
Corporals: John Slocum, D. Connolly.
Volunteers: M. Cotter, John Cronin, P. Cronin, D. Fitzgerald, T O'Shea, C. Seward, R. Shanahan, M. Smiddy.

22   **Ballycotton (15)**
Corporals: T. Breen, T O'Driscoll, E.P. Roche.
Volunteers: W. Conaldson, James Johnson, James Keane, Patrick Kelly, J. Moriarty, David O'Brien, T. O'Driscoll, Henry O'Shea, J. O'Shea, ? O'Sullivan, Daniel Scannell, James Walsh.

23   **Power Head (11)**
Corporals: Tobias O'Connell, J. Wall.
Volunteers: J. Bennett, Tom Kelly, James Lynch, L. McCarthy, C. O'Callaghan,
                G. O'Connor, W. O'Shea, H. O'Sullivan, D. Wall.

24   **Flat Head (14)**
Corporal: M. Lynch.
Volunteers: W. Buckley, C. Callaghan, W. Collins, T. de Courcy, D. Delaney,
                D. Desmond, D. Fennell, W. Ferris, M. Finnucane, J. Leahy, J. Moriarty,
                J. Slyne, J. Walker.

25   **Old Head of Kinsale (13)**
Corporal: Denis J. Breen.
Volunteers: F. Bowen, P. Bowen, J. Dennis, J. Dyhan, J. Healy, J. Holland, J. Hunt,
                B. O'Connell, J. O'Connell, W. O'Connell, M. O'Connor, Francis Power.

26   **Seven Heads (11)**
Corporal: C. Finn.
Volunteers: D. Deasy, R. Fleming, M. Foran, C. Madden, D. Moloney, W. Nilan,
                M. O'Brien, Jeremiah O'Sullivan, J. Whelton, J. Whitten.

27   **Galley Head (13)**
Corporals: J. Connolly, John O'Donovan, James O'Sullivan.
Volunteers: ? Deasy, P. Keohane, J.P. Mahony, J. Mullins, P. O'Leary, J. O'Mahony,
                J. O'Regan, John Sullivan, E. Sweeney, J. Twohig.

28   **Toe Head (13)**
Corporal: ? Cronin.
Volunteers: P. Keohane, M. Maguire, J. Minihane, J.P. McMahon, J. O'Mahoney,
                C. O'Neill, D. O'Shea, T. O'Sullivan, P. Pierce, J. Sexton, P. Sexton,
                S. Sullivan.

29   **Baltimore (10)**
Corporals: P. O'Connor, D. O'Neill.
Volunteers: P. Collins, T. Crowley, P. Daly, K. Keane, T. Leonard, J. O'Driscoll,
                M. O'Driscoll, D. Sheehy.

30   **Mizen Head (12)**
Corporals: M. Leahy, John O'Leary.
Volunteers: P. Bell, A. Desmond, M. Finucane, D. Fitzgerald, R. Gorman,
                D. O'Driscoll, C. O'Reilly, J. O'Reilly, Stephen Sullivan, T. Supple.

31   **Sheep's Head (9)**
Corporal: T. O'Donovan.
Volunteers: James Coakley, James Daly, James F. Daly, John F. Daly, Joseph Daly,
                M. Desmond, D. Foley, D. Spillane.

32
Corporal: Michael Harrington.
Volunteers: Patrick Dempsey, P. Holland, P. Morley, Michael Murphy, J. O'Connell, F. O'Leary, D. O'Shea, Peter O'Sullivan, Peadar O hUllachain, J.W. Sullivan.

Dursey Head (11)

33
Corporals: J. O'Connell, J. O'Leary.
Volunteers: D. Beagley, D. Fitzgerald, P. Fenton, J. Mahoney, E. Moriarty, D. O'Connor, M. O'Connor, P. O'Shea, T. O'Sullivan, T. Teahan.

Lamb's Head (12)

34
Corporals: M. Leahy, J. O'Sullivan.
Volunteers: M. Brennan, J. Connor, S. Corcoran, P. Curran, M. Finucane, M. Fitzgerald, P. Fogarty, C. Hanafin, J. Moriarty, P. O'Shea, M. O'Sullivan.

Bolus Head (13)

35
Corporal: John Dore.
Volunteers: M. Curran, P. Erwin, M. Falvey, D. Foley, J. Healy, F. Hickey, J. Moriarty, C. O'Connell, T. O'Connell, J. O'Neill, M. O'Neill, E. Sweeney.

Bray Head (Valentia Island) (13)

83
Corporal: J. Moriarty.
Volunteers: W. King, M. O'Connor, J. O'Shea, M. O'Shea, D. O'Sullivan, M. O'Sullivan.

Foileye/Feaklecally (7)

36
Corporal: J. Rooney.
Volunteers: D. Claney, M. Coffey, S. Corcoran, M. Dowd, M. Finucane, D. Fitzgerald, G. Flaherty, F. Hickey, A. Jeffers, P.T. Landers, J. Moriarty, M. Moriarty, D. Murphy, J. O'Mahoney, E. Sweeney.

Eask (16)

37
Corporals: P. Fenton, P. Landers.
Volunteers: H. Adams, D. Clancy, M. Coffey, T. Corcoran, T. Ferris, J. Flaherty, W. Hoare, A. Jeffers, P.M. Landers, P.T. Landers, J. Long, P. Lynch, S. Mahoney, M. Moriarty, J. Shea, S. Sullivan.

Parkmore (Knockadowney) (18)

38
Corporal: P. Breathnach.
Volunteers: Joseph Boyle, ? Coughlan, ? Fenton, ? Foley, M. Landers, ? Kane, ? Long, ? Lynch, ? Moriarty, J. Russell, ? Sheehy.

Dunmore (Slea) Head (12)

39   **Sybil Head (2)**
                          (No logbooks have survived for this LOP, this record is based on details
                          in G2/X series files.)
Corporal: J. d'Arcy.
Volunteers: G. Gorman.

40   **Brandon Head (12)**
Corporal: F. Goodwin.
Volunteers: Michael Brick, S. Corcoran, P. Fitzgerald, M. Flynn, F. Hickey,
                          J. Hennessy, D. Lynch, M.P. Moore, P. O'Connell, J. Sullivan,
                          E. Sweeney.

41   **Fenit (21)**
Corporal: P. O'Connor.
Volunteers: C. Callaghan, ? Clancy, M. Coffey, P. Coffey, J. Collins, G. Fitzgerald,
                          C. Hanafin, ? Hunt, A. Jeffers, P. Lawlor, ? Lyne, S. Mahony,
                          D. Murphy, L. McCarthy, J. McKenna, ? Neylon, M. O'Connor,
                          E. O'Mahoney, C. O'Shea, R. Savage.

42   **Kerry Head (17)**
Corporals: F. Lawlor, M. O'Shea.
Volunteers: J.J. Cronin, John Drury, J. Hussey, J. Kirby, James Leahy, M. Leen,
                          F. Lucitt, L. McCarthy, ? McElligott, T. Neylon, ? O'Callaghan,
                          R. O'Gorman, P. Pierce, D. Rice, R. Savage.

43   **Doon/Leck Point (14)**
Corporal: W. Purcell.
Volunteers: William Ferris, M. Finucane, Kevin Keane, Liam McCabe,
                          L. McCarthy, J.P. McMahon, J. O'Donnell, Roger O'Gorman, Timothy
                          O'Gorman, T. O'Sullivan, J. Scanlan, P. Twomey, J. Walker.

44   **Kilcreadun (13)**
Corporal: M. Blake.
Volunteers: Patrick Behan, E. Bowler, Cornelius Brennan, C. Brennock, M. Foran,
                          John Lynch, Michael Lynch, M. O'Brien, J. O'Shea, T. O'Sullivan,
                          P. Pierce, E. Sweeney.

45   **Loop Head (13)**
Corporal: P. Crotty.
Volunteers: M. Austin, M. Austin, J. Blake, E. Brennan, T. Crotty, J. Gorman,
                          T. Gorman, M. Griffin, M. Hanrahan, J. Hough, P. Keane, W. Nilan.

46   **George's Head (12)**
Corporal: T. Prendergast,
Volunteers: T. Corcoran, M. Foran, M. Hayes, D. Heaney, C. Hough, J. Hough,
                          T. Keannally, J. Moriarty, E. McGreene, J. McMahon, M. O'Brien.

47   **Hag's Head (8)**
Corporal: M. O'Donnell.
Volunteers: John Considine, Michael Greally, Roger Guthrie, John Logan, Patrick O'Donnell, W. Nilan, S. Queally.

48   **Black Head (11)**
Corporals: Jack Conway, Patrick Linnane.
Volunteers: J. Clancy, M. Clancy, Martin Conway, Patrick Francis, Pat Guthrie, John Irwin, Patrick Irwin, James O'Donohue, John Scanlon.

49   **Spiddal (9)**
Corporal: P. Naughton.
Volunteers: M. Coyne, D. Feeney, M.K. Feeney, M.L. Feeney, S. Keady, J. Naughton, '51 T. Walsh, '71 Walsh.

50   **Kilronan (8)**
Corporal: (Not identifiable from LOP logbooks)
Volunteers: S. Connelly, P. Flaherty, P. Gillan, C. Gill, W. Gorham, A. Kelly, P. Mullen.

51   **Golam Head (8)**
Corporal: Pat McDonagh.
Volunteers: Edward Beatty, John Flaherty, Pat Flaherty, John Mullin, Michael Mullen, Thomas McDonagh, Mark Walsh.

52   **Mace Head (9)**
Corporal: M Casey.
Volunteers: J. Burke, M. Feron, C. Folan, J. Folan, P. Folan, J. King, J. Lydon, M. O'Donnell.

53   **Doon Hill, Slyne Head (8)**
Corporal: (Not identifiable from LOP logbooks)
Volunteers: T. Darcy, F. Flaherty, J. King, P. King, M. O'Malley, P. O'Malley, J. O'Neill.

54   **Aughris Head (8)**
Corporal: J.J. O'Malley.
Volunteers: J. Conroy, K. Conroy, P. Coyne, John Delap, P. Hanley, James King, Thomas King.

55   **Renvyle Point (8)**
Corporal: P. Davin.
Volunteers: P. Connely, M. Coyne, G. Heanue, J. Keane, J. Ribbon, S. Sammon, T. Walsh.

56   **Rosroe (8)**
Corporal: J. King.
Volunteers: John Coyne, Martin Coyne, Charles Flaherty, John Keane, Thomas
               Keane, John McDonnell, Denis Nee.

57   **Carrickvegraly Point (Roonagh) (10)**
Corporal: J.J. Philbin.
Volunteers: D. Gibbons, M. Gill, A. McDonagh, M. McEvilly, D. O'Toole,
               P. O'Toole, R. O'Toole, T. Ryder, J. Sammon.

58   **Corraun (Bollinglanna) (8)**
Corporal: M.G[allagher?] (initials only).
Volunteers: T. Campbell, M. Fallon, M. Gallagher, T. Gallagher, J. Madden,
               T. Madden, M. Moran.

59   **Moyteogue Head, Achill (11)**
Corporals: J. O'Malley, ? Reilly.
Volunteers: P. Cafferty, P. Callaghan, ? Callaghan, J. Farry, M. Gallagher, A. Lavelle,
               ? Moloney, T. O'Malley, T. English.

60   **Termon Hill, Blacksod (8)**
Corporal: Ted Sweeney.
Volunteers   A. Cawley, J.J. Creane, P. Gaughan, T. Meeneghan, W. Meenaghan,
               P. Monaghan, M. Reilly.

61   **Annagh Head (10)**
Corporal: J. Fallon.
Volunteers: T. Carey, M. Cawley, A. Gilboy, P. Kilker, J. Lavelle, M. Lavelle,
               S. MacAndrew, A.J. O'Malley, A. Reilly.

62   **Erris Head (9)**
Corporal: Patrick Reilly.
Volunteers: J. Barrett, Michael Carey, Peter Lavelle, John Lally, ? Lalley, Anthony
               Moloney, P. McAndrew, M.P. Reilly.

63   **Portacloy (Benwee Head) (9)**
Corporal: A. Garvin.
Volunteers: John P. Burns, Thomas Burns, T. Bournes, M.J. Connolly, Charles
               Doherty, Martin Doherty, J.E. Garvin, Redmond Garvin.

64   **Downpatrick Head (9)**
Corporal: Richard Winters.
Volunteers: James Doherty, P. Doherty, P. Farrell, P. Langan, P. Monelly,
               M. Neaton, J. Ormsby, J. Tighe.

65   **Kilcummin (8)**
Corporal: P. Collins.
Volunteers: Joseph Collins, Frank Connor, Martin Langan, Anthony Lynn, Michael Lynn, George Munnelly, John Robinson.

66   **Lenadoon, Rathlee (9)**
Corporal: P. Curley.
Volunteers: P. Callaghan, J. Connolly, M. Connolly, D. Connor, T. Geraghty, E. Gordon, Henry Kilcullen, Daniel J. O'Connor.

67   **Aughris Head (8)**
Corporal: T. Gillen.
Volunteers: J. Boyd, P. Brennan, A. Carney, J. Farry, P.J. Gormley, M. McDonald, J. McKenna.

68   **Roskeeragh (9)**
Corporal: Pat McDermott.
Volunteers: M. Burns, J. Currid, P. Dunleavy, C. Ewing, P. Feeney, James Gilmartin, J. Herity, '91 Herity.

69   **Mullaghmore (8)**
Corporal: Joseph Harrison.
Volunteers: O. Conway, T. Conway, J. Dowdican, M. Gilmartin, D. Herity, J. Moffit, D. McCannon.

70   **St John's Point (15)**
Corporal: J. Craig, P. Tighe.
Volunteers: Patrick Byrne, Daniel Carr, B. Cunningham, D. Cunningham, Norris Davidson, P. Dawson, E. Gallagher, P. Harvey, Pat Ireland, J. Morrow, D. McCloskey, J. McCoy, P. McDyer.

71   **Carrigan Head (12)**
Corporal: M. McNelis.
Volunteers: A. Byrne, D. Cunningham, J.P. Donegan, J. Lyons, B. Maloney, J.G. Mulloy, P. McGill, P.J. McLoughlin, H. McNelis, P. McNelis, P. McShane.

72   **Rossan Point (9)**
Corporal: Colum M. Mockler.
Volunteers: E. Boyle, H. Boyle, F Cunningham, C. Kelly, C. Lyons, J.G. Mulloy, P. O'Donnell, P. O'Gara.

73   **Dunmore Head (9)**
Corporal: T.E. Nicholson.
Volunteers: James Boyle, Joseph Boyle, C. Byrne, J. Craig, D.G. Harkin, B. McCoale, C. McCoale, T. McCoale.

74   Crohy Head (8)
Corporal: H. Divinny.
Volunteers: Con Bonner, P. Gallagher, Patrick Houston, James McCole, James
             O'Donnell, Denis O'Donnell, Patrick O'Donnell.

75   Aranmore Point (7)
Corporal: J.P. Byrne.
Volunteers: J.R. Boyle, C. Byrne, S. O'Donnell, B. Rodgers, J. Rodgers, Frank Ward.

76   Bloody Foreland (11)
Corporals: ? Gillespie, P. McBride.
Volunteers: D. Dowdican, Denis Duggan, P. Duggan, C.S. Gallagher, J. Gallagher,
             J.C. McFadden, F. McGowan, P. O'Brien, P O'Donnell.

77   Horn Head (14)
Corporal: P. Murphy.
Volunteers: C. Durning, James Friel, George Greer, Patrick Greer, John Herrity,
             B. Maloney, C. Mofit, Charles Moore, Martin Murphy, Bernard
             McBride, Owen McFadden, Charles McGinley, J. O'Donnell.

78   Melmore Head (8)
Corporal: J. Gallagher.
Volunteers: ? Arthur, Manus Carr, Owen Carr, M. Gallagher, Michael McBride, Dan
             McClaferty, M. McFadden.

79   Fanad (17)
Corporal: J.J. Doherty, P. Gallagher.
Volunteers: O. Bonner, P.W. Coll, B. Doherty, H. Doherty, J. Doherty, M. Douglas,
             F. Friel, J. Herrighty, C. Kelly, J. Kelly, P. Kelly, J. Lafferty, W. Logue,
             M. McAteer, P. McKinley.

80   Malin Head (9)
Corporal: C. Houston.
Volunteers: E. Doherty, T. Doherty, D.G. Glackin, T. Glackin, H. McLoughlin,
             P. McLoughlin, P. Mc Loughlin, A. O'Connor.

81   Glengad Head (8)
Corporal: J.J. Doherty.
Volunteers: B. Doherty, H. Doherty, J. Doherty, M. Douglas, C.C. Kelly, J. Kelly,
             J. Kelly.

82   Inishowen Head (10)
Corporal: D. McCorkell, John McLoughlin.
Volunteers: Robert Bradley, J. Crumlish, P. Harlin, Thomas Harvey, Thomas
             Hegarty, William Kealey, William McLoughlin, John Peoples, George
             Wilson.

Maps of locations of Coast Watching Service LOPs

1 Ballagan Head
2 Dunany Point
3 Clogher Head
4 Cardys Rocks
5 Rush
6 Nose of Howth
7 Dalkey
8 Bray Head
9 Wicklow Head
10 Kilmichael Point
11 Cahore Point
12 Ballyconnigar Hill
13 Greenore Point
14 Carnsore Point
15 Forlorn Point
16 Hook Head
17 Brownstown Head
18 Dunabrattin Head
19 Helvick Head
20 Ram Head
21 Knockadoon
22 Ballycotton
23 Power Head
24 Flat Head
25 Old Head of Kinsale
26 Seven Heads
27 Galley Head
28 Toe Head
29 Baltimore
30 Mizen Head
31 Sheep's Head
32 Dursey
33 Lamb's Head
34 Bolus Head
35 Bray Head (Valentia)
36 Eask
37 Parkmore
38 Slea Head
39 Sybil Head
40 Brandon Point
41 Fenit

M&CWS LOP
Radio 'Mountain Marker' at LOP
Coastal Artillery
Airport/Aerodrome

Inishtrahull

77 78 79 80 81
Fort
Lenan 82
Downhill
Lough
Foyle
Lough
Swilly
Limavady
nnagry
ungloe
Fort
Dunree
Derry
Derry

gs

Castle Archdale

'Donegal
ner Air Corridor'
ruskmore

o

Belfast

Cootehill

yle

Dundalk 1

wn Longford

2
3

Drogheda 4
Duleek
Skerries 5

Rockabill

Mullingar

Collinstown (Dublin)
Airport

Athlone

Kilcock 6 Dún
Laoghaire

Baldonnell
Aerodrome Dublin

Irish
Sea

8

Portarlington The Curragh
Mountmellick

Greystones

Mountrath

Rathdrum 9

Arklow

annon)
rdnacrusha Johnstown

10

11
12

Clonmel Campile

Wexford
Rosslare
Harbour

13 Tuskar
Rock

Waterford
Tramore
Dungarvan
18 17 16
19

14

15

Saltee
Islands

N

20

21
22
23

Minefield

Coningbeg
Lightship

Celtic Sea

Cobh
(Queenstown)

csherry

0   50 miles

0   80 km

42	Kerry Head
43	Doon/Leck Head
44	Kilcreadun
45	Loop Head
46	George's Head
47	Hag's Head
48	Black Head
49	Spiddal
50	Kilronan
51	Golam Head
52	Mace Head
53	Slyne Head
54	Aughrus Head
55	Renvyle
56	Rossroe
57	Roonagh
58	Corraun
59	Moyteogue Head
60	Blacksod Bay
61	Annagh Head
62	Erris Head
63	Benwee Head
64	Downpatrick Head
65	Kilcummin Head
66	Lenadoon Point
67	Aughris Head
68	Roskeeragh
69	Mullaghmore
70	St John's Point
71	Carrigan Head
72	Rossan Point
73	Dunmore Head
74	Crohy Head
75	Torneady Point
76	Bloody Foreland
77	Horn Head
78	Melmore Head
79	Fanad Head
80	Malin Head
81	Glengad Point
82	Inishowen Head
83	Feaklecally

Bibliography

PRIMARY SOURCES

IRELAND

National Archives
Department of Foreign Affairs:
    Secretary's Files, A, P and S series.
    Number Series Files, especially 200-series files.
    Berlin, Paris, Washington legation series files.
Department of the Taoiseach:
    S Files.
    Government Minutes.
    Cabinet Minutes.
    Rúnaí Aire Files.
Department of Finance:
    S Series.
    F Series.
Department of Justice:
    JUS 8 Series (Crime and Security).
    JUS 90/94 Series (Bodies washed ashore).
    JUS 90/119 Series (Local Security Force).
Office of Public Works:
    A Series files.
    D Series files.
Department of Health:
    A116 Series.

Military Archives
2-bar series Department of Defence files.
Air Defence Command files.
Annual Reports of the Chief of Staff.
Commandant Owen Quinn papers.
Council of Defence Minutes.
Daily Reports Summaries (1939–45).
Emergency Defence Plans.
G2 X series files.
Marine and Coast Watching Service LOP logbooks.
U-260 papers.

Garda Siochána Archives, Dublin Castle
Files relating to the Local Security Force.
Files relating to the Coast Watching Service.

University College Dublin Archives Department
Frank Aiken papers (P104).
Dan Bryan papers (P71).
Eamon de Valera papers (P150).

Papers in private possession
Bob Donaldson papers, Local Defence Force training notes, 1942.
James Sharkey papers (in the possession of Hugo Sharkey), LDF orders March 1941.

NORTHERN IRELAND

Public Record Office of Northern Ireland
CAB 4 Cabinet Minutes.
CAB 9 series.
Sir Basil Brooke Diaries.

BRITAIN

The National Archives, Kew
Admiralty: ADM 1, ADM 2, ADM 116, ADM 199, ADM 223, ADM 234, ADM 326.
Air Ministry: AIR 4, AIR 2, AIR 8, AIR 10, AIR 14, AIR 15, AIR 16, AIR 20, AIR 25, AIR 27, AIR 37, AIR 38, AIR 40.
Ministry of Aviation: AVIA 2.
Board of Trade: BT 166.
Cabinet Office files.
Customs and Excise.
Dominions Office: DO 35, DO 130.
Foreign Office: FO 371, FO 800 Halifax papers.
GCHQ: HW 2.
Security Service: KV 4.
Treasury: T 161.
War Office: WO 193, WO 287.

UNITED STATES OF AMERICA

National Archives and Record Authority, College Park, Maryland
State Department:
    RG 59, Decimal Files, Ireland.
    RG 84, Post Files, Dublin.
    RG 84, Post Files, London.
War Department:
    RG 38 (Office of the Chief of Naval Operations) FAW7 War Diary.
    RG 165 (War Department General Staff).
    RG 319 (Records of the Army Staff).

PRINTED PRIMARY SOURCES

Documents on German foreign policy 1918–1945 series D (1937–1945), vol. vi: The last days of peace: August 9–September 3, 1939 (London, 1956).

Documents on German foreign policy 1918–1945 series D (1937–1945), vol. vii: The war years: September 4, 1939–March 18, 1940 (Washington, 1954).

Documents on German foreign policy 1918–1945 series D (1937–1945), vol. ix: The war years: September March 18–June 22, 1940 (Washington, 1956).

Gilbert, Martin (ed.), *The Churchill war papers, vol. i: At the Admiralty: September 1939–May 1940* (London, 1993).

Gilbert, Martin (ed.), *The Churchill war papers, vol. ii: Never surrender: May 1940–December 1940* (London, 1994).

Gilbert, Martin (ed.), *The Churchill war papers, vol. iii: The ever widening war: 1941* (London, 2000).

Mallmann Showell, Jak P. (ed.), *Fuehrer conferences on naval affairs, 1939–1945* (London, 2005).

Syrett, David (ed.), *The battle of the Atlantic and signals intelligence: U-boat situations and trends, 1941–1945* (Aldershot, 1998).

SECONDARY SOURCES

BOOKS

Allen, Trevor, *The storm passed by: Ireland and the battle of the Atlantic, 1940–41* (Dublin, 1996).

Bardon, Jonathan, *A history of Ulster* (Belfast, 1992).

Beesly, Patrick, *Very special admiral: the life of Admiral J.H. Godfrey, CB* (London, 1980).

——, *Very special intelligence: the story of the Admiralty's operational intelligence centre, 1939–1945* (London, 2006).

Bercuson, Davied J. and Holger H. Herwig, *The destruction of the Bismarck* (New York, 2001).

Blair, Clay, *Hitler's U-boat war: the hunters 1939–1942* (London, 2001).

——, *Hitler's U-boat war: the hunted 1942–1945* (London, 2000).

Blake, John W., *Northern Ireland in the Second World War* (Belfast, 2000).

Browne, Paul, *Eagles over Ireland* (Athenry, 2003).

Bruincairdi, Daire, *The Seahound: the story of an Irish ship* (Cork, 2001).

Carroll, Joseph T., *Ireland in the war years: 1939–1945* (New York, 1975).

Carter, Carolle J., *The shamrock and the swastika* (Palo Alto, 1977).

Christie, Carl A., *Ocean bridge: the history of RAF ferry command* (Toronto 1995).

Danchev, Alex and Todman, Daniel (eds), *War diaries 1939–1945 Field Marshal Lord Alanbrooke* (London, 2001).

Dancey, Peter G, *Coastal command versus the U-boat* (Bromley, Kent, 2002).

Dear, I.C.B. and M.R.D. Foot, *The Oxford companion to World War II* (Oxford, 2005 edition).

Dilks, David (ed.), *The diaries of Sir Alexander Cadogan 1938–1945* (London, 1971).

Dönitz, Karl, *Memoirs: ten years and twenty days* (New York, 1997)

Donaldson, Frank, *The fatal echo: a World War II aircrash off south-west Ireland* (Cork, 1990).

Duggan, John P., *Neutral Ireland and the Third Reich* (Dublin, 1985).
——, *A history of the Irish Army* (Dublin, 1989).
——, *Herr Hempel at the German legation in Dublin* (Dublin, 2003).
Dunmore, Spencer, *In great waters: the epic story of the battle of the Atlantic, 1939–1945* (London, 1999).
Dwyer, T. Ryle, *Strained relations: Ireland at peace and the USA at war 1941–45* (Dublin, 1988).
Feldt, Eric, *The coast watchers* (Melbourne, 1946).
Fell, W.R., *The sea our shield* (London, 1966).
Fisk, Robert, *In time of war: Ireland, Ulster and the price of neutrality: 1939–1945* (London, 1987 edition).
Foot, William, *Beaches, fields, streets and hills … the anti-invasion landscapes of England, 1940* (York, 2006).
Forde, Frank, *The long watch: World War Two and the Irish mercantile marine* (Dublin, 2000).
Franks, Norman, *Conflict over the Bay* (London, 1999).
——, *Dark sky, deep water: first hand experiences of the anti-U-boat war in World War Two* (London, 2004).
Gibbs-Smith, C.H., *The aircraft recognition manual* (London, 1944).
Gillies, Midge, *Waiting for Hitler: voices from Britain on the brink of invasion* (London, 2006).
Girvin, Brian, *The Emergency: neutral Ireland 1939–45* (London, 2006).
Goss, Chris, *Bloody Biscay: the history of V Gruppe/Kampfgeschwader 40* (revised edition, Manchester, 2001).
Grob-Fitzgibbon, Benjamin, *The Irish experience during the Second World War: an oral history* (Dublin, 2004).
Hawkins, Ian, *Destroyer: an anthology of first hand account of the war at sea, 1939–1945* (London, 2005).
Herman, Michael, *Intelligence power in peace and war* (Cambridge, 2005).
Hull, Mark, *Irish secrets: German espionage in wartime Ireland 1939–1945* (Dublin, 2003).
Ireland, Bernard, *Battle of the Atlantic* (Barnsley, 2003).
Irish Defence Forces (Clonan, T.M. (ed.)), *Artillery corps 1923–1998* (Dublin, 1998).
Isby, David C., *The Luftwaffe and the war at sea 1939–45* (London, 2005).
Jane's fighting ships of World War Two (London, 1989).
Kennedy, Ludovic, *Pursuit: the sinking of the Bismarck* (London, 2001).
Leonard, Robert, *The art of maneuver* (New York, 1991).
Lincoln, Siobhán, *Ardmore: memory and story* (Ardmore, Co. Waterford, 2000).
Lord, Walter, *Lonely vigil* (London, 1978).
MacCarron, Donal, *'Step Together!' Ireland's Emergency Army 1939–46: as told by its veterans* (Dublin, 1999).
MacIntyre, Donald, *The battle of the Atlantic* (Barnsley, 2006).
Mackinder, H.J., *Britain and the British seas* (Oxford, 1907).
Maddock, John, *Rosslare harbour past and present* (Dublin and Rosslare, 1988).
Mallmann Showell, Jak P., *Enigma U-boats: breaking the code* (Shepperton, 2000).
McNeill, Ross, *RAF coastal command losses of the second world war, volume I: aircraft and crew losses 1939–1941* (Hinckley, Leics., 2003).

McVicar, Don, *North Atlantic cat* (Shrewsbury, 1983).

Miller, James, *North Atlantic front: Orkney, Shetland, Faroe and Iceland at war* (Edinburgh, 2003).

Milner, Marc, *Battle of the Atlantic* (Ontario, 2003).

Viscount Montgomery of Alamein, *The memoirs of Field-Marshal Montgomery of Alamein* (Barnsley, 2005).

Müllenheim-Rechberg, Burkard, Baron von, *Battleship Bismarck* (Edinburgh, 2001).

Nesbit, Roy Conyers, *Coastal Command in action 1939–1945* (Stroud, 1997).

Niestlé, Axel, *German U-boats losses during world war II: details of destruction* (Annapolis, 1998).

O'Halpin, Eunan, *Defending Ireland* (Oxford, 1999).

—— (ed.), *MI5 and Ireland: the official history* (Dublin, 2002).

O'Higgins, Thomas F., *A double life* (Dublin, 1996).

O'Loughlin, Joe, *Voices of the Donegal Corridor* (Dublin, 2005).

Osborne, Mike, *Defending Britain: twentieth-century military structure in the landscape* (Stroud, 2004).

Powell, Griffith, *Ferryman: from Ferry Command to Silver City* (Shrewsbury, 1982).

Price, Alfred, *Aircraft versus submarine: the evolution of anti-submarine aircraft 1912–1980* (London, 1973).

——, and Darko Pavlovic, *Britain's air defences 1939–45* (Oxford, 2004).

Quinn, John, and Alan Reilly, *Covering the approaches: the war against the U-boats* (Coleraine, 1996).

Robinson, Derek, *Invasion, 1940: the explosive truth about the Battle of Britain* (London, 2006).

Roskill, Stephen W., *The war at sea 1939–1945. Vol. 1: the defensive* (London, 1954).

Shulsky, Abram N. and Gary J. Schmitt, *Silent warfare: understanding the world of intelligence* (Dulles, 2002).

Smith, David J., *Action Stations. 7. Military airfields of Scotland, the North-East and Northern Ireland* (Wellingborough, 1989).

Sims, Philip E., *Adventurous Empires: the story of the Short Empire flying-boats* (Shrewsbury, 2002).

Stephan, Enno, *Spies in Ireland* (London, 1965).

Terraine, John, *Business in great waters* (London, 1989).

Thiele, Harold, *Luftwaffe aerial torpedo aircraft and operations in World War Two* (Crowborough, 2004).

Thomas, David A., *The Atlantic star 1939–45* (London, 1990).

Thompson, H.L., *New Zealanders with the Royal Air Force. Vol. II: European theatre January 1943–May 1945* (Wellington, 1956) (electronic version at www.nzetc.org (accessed, 12 July 2005)).

Van Der Vat, Dan, *The Atlantic campaign* (Edinburgh, 2001).

Vause, Jordan, *U-boat ace: the story of Wolfgang Lüth* (Annapolis, 2001).

Wakefield, Ken, *Pfadfinder: Luftwaffe Pathfinder operations over Britain, 1940–44* (Stroud, 1999).

Watts, Anthony, *The U-boat hunters* (London, 1976).

West, Nigel (ed.), *The Guy Liddell diaries, vol. I: 1939–1942* (Abingdon, 2005).

——, *The Guy Liddell diaries, vol. II: 1942–1945* (Abingdon, 2005).

Whinney, Bob, *The U-boat peril: a fight for survival* (London, 1986).

Wills, Clair, *That neutral island: a cultural history of Ireland during the Second World War* (London, 2007).

Wilson, Kevin, *Bomber boys: the Ruhr, the Dambusters and bloody Berlin* (London, 2006 edition).

Wilson, Theodore A. (ed.), *D-day 1944* (Abilene, 1994).

Wood, John Butler, *Uncharted skies* (Sydney, 1999).

Wood, Derek and Derek Dempster, *The narrow margin* (London, 1961).

Wood, Ian S., *Ireland during the Second World War* (London, 2002).

Woodman, Richard, *The real cruel sea: the merchant navy in the battle of the Atlantic, 1939–1943* (London, 2004).

Wynn, Kenneth, *U-boat operations of the Second World War. Vol. I: career histories U1–U510* (1997).

——, *U-boat operations of the Second World War. Vol. II: career histories U511–UIT25* (1998).

OFFICIAL PUBLICATIONS

Ireland

Department of Defence, *Manual of fieldcraft and battle drill (L.D.F. edition)* (Dublin, 1943).

Department of the Environment, Heritage and Local Government, *An introduction to the architectural heritage of county Waterford*.

Department of the Marine and Natural Resources, *National coastline survey* (CD-Rom, eight volumes) (Dublin, 1999–2005).

Ordnance Survey Ireland, *Discovery series* (maps).

Britain

——, *Air navigation* (London, 1941).

——, *Aircraft identification: friend of foe?* (London, 1940).

Air Ministry, *The rise and fall of the German Air Force (1933 to 1945)* (London, 2001).

Hydrographic Department, Admiralty, *Irish coast pilot* (9th edition, London, 1941).

Ministry of Information, *Roof over Britain: the official story of Britain's anti-aircraft defences 1939–1942* (London, 1943).

Ministry of Home Security, *Silhouettes of British aircraft* (London, 1940).

Ministry of Information, *Coastal Command* (London, 1942).

The Stationery Office, *Fleet Air Arm* (Norwich, 2001).

War Office, *Manual of anti-aircraft defence (army units) Vol. I (Part I – Gunnery)* (London, 1937).

War Office, *Small arms training vol. I, Pamphlet No. 6 Anti-Aircraft* (London, 1939).

War Office, *Manual of anti-aircraft defence (army units) Vol. II War* (London, 1937).

ARTICLES

Bryan, Dan, 'General Dan McKenna', *An Cosantóir*, 35:7 (July 1975), 265–6.

De Cogan, Donard, and Seán Swords, 'Fort Shannon: An example of Irish coastal defence artillery during the second world war', paper presented at the IEE History of Technology Weekend, June 2001 (accessed at www.iee.org/oncomms/sector/management/Articles/Object/9187F9F3–FA12–4CB9–99A850784E94A845).

Joye, Labhras, '"Aiken's Slugs": the Reserve of the Irish Army under Fianna Fáil', in Joost Augusteijn (ed.), *Ireland in the 1930s: new perspectives* (Dublin, 1999), pp 143–62.

Lane, James, 'The "secret" Irish naval bases', *Maritime Journal of Ireland*, 35 (summer 1995), 1–3.

Kinsella, Anthony, 'LOP 6 at Howth Summit', *Dublin Historical Record*, 59:2 (Autumn 2006), 201–5.

Maguire, Brian F., 'Life in an A.A. Outpost 1939–1946', *An Cosantóir*, 24:1 (Jan. 1974), 23–6.

McKenna, Tony, '"Thank God we're surrounded by water"', *An Cosantóir*, 33:4 (April 1973), 103–24.

O'Halloran, C.P., 'The ack-ack', *An Cosantóir*, 33:11 (November 1973), 385–90.

O'Halpin, Eunan, 'The Liddell diaries and British intelligence history', *Intelligence and National Security*, 20:4 (December 2005), 670–86.

Quinn, Owen 'Coast watcher remembers 1940–1946', *An Cosantóir*, April 1983, pp 106–9.

——, 'More coast watching', *An Cosantóir*, September 1983, pp 299–301.

——, 'Coastwatch', *An Cosantóir*, January 1988, pp. 23–7.

Scudds, Colin, 'The North Strand bombing–1941', *Dún Laoghaire Journal*, 11 (2002).

Scutts, Jerry, 'Focke Wulf 200 Condor', *Warpaint Series No. 13* (no date).

Wixley, Ken, 'Incidental combatant: Focke-Wulf's 200 Condor', *Air Enthusiast*, 67 (1997), 68–75.

NEWSPAPERS

Irish Examiner
Irish Times

WEBSITES

http://www.303rdbg.com/index.shtml The 303rd Bombardment Group (H) 'Hell's Angels'.

http://www.457thbombgroup.org The 457th Bombardment Group Association (United States 8th Air Force).

http://aad.archives.gov/aad Records of enlisted men in the United States armed forces 1938–1946 (Electronic Army Serial Number Merged File).

www.archives.tcm.ie/irishexaminer *Irish Examiner* archives.

www.arlingtoncemetry.net Arlington Cemetery Website.

http://www.acseac.co.uk/pages/ RAF Liberator Squadrons.

http://ads.ahds.ac.uk Archaeology Data Servicewww.galwayadvertiser.ie/homepage/fdownloads/06_November_OldGalway.pdf, University of York.

www.blackwatersubacqua.com Blackwater Sub-Aqua Club.

www.cil.ie The Commissioners of Irish Lights.

www.dungarvanmuseum.org Dungarvan Museum.

www.galwayadvertiser.ie *Galway Advertiser* newspaper.
www.historyireland.com *History Ireland* magazine.
www.hms.vengeance.co.uk Royal Navy aircraft carrier HMS Vengeance.
http://home.att.net/~jbaugher/usafserials.html USAAS – USAAC – USAAF – USAF aircraft serial numbers 1908 to present.
www.ibiblio.org/hyperwar/index.html Hypertext history of the Second World War.
www.irishseamensrelativesassociation.org Site for relatives of seafarers who were killed as a result of belligerent action while serving on neutral Irish registered vessels during World War Two.
www.irishwrecksonline.net A divers' guide to shipwrecks around Ireland.
www.met.ie Irish Meteorological Office.
www.military.ie Irish Defence Forces.
www.naval-history.net British naval history site with resources from 1815 to 1982.
www.nzetc.org New Zealand Electronic Text Centre.
www.polebrook.com/history.htm USAAF 351st Bombardment Group.
www.rafcommands.com Royal Air Force.
www.uboat.net Second World War U-boat resources.
www.ubootwaffe.net/ops/ships U-boat and Kreigsmarine resources.
www.usn-dunkeswell.info Dunkeswell Airfield, Devon and FAW7.
www.skylighters.org United States Air Defence.
www.vpnavy.com Fleet Air Wing Seven.
www.warsailors.com Norwegian Merchant Navy.
www.wwiimemorial.com United States National World War Two Memorial.

INTERVIEWS AND CORRESPONDENCE

Bob Donaldson, Dublin, December 2004, February 2005, April 2005.
John Donnelly, Dublin, December 2004.
Colonel Tom Kelly, Fermoy, July 2005.

Illustrations

CREDITS

Unless otherwise stated all images are by the author

10, 12, 13, 21	Military archives, Cathal Brugha Barracks
1, 2, 3, 4, 5, 6, 8, 9	National Archives of Ireland
22	National Library of Ireland
11	Air Corps/Army Press Office

Figures and tables

Index